Becoming the Narcissist's Nightmare

How to Devalue and Discard the Narcissist
While Supplying Yourself

Shahida Arabi

SCW Archer Publishing

New York, NY

SCW Archer Publishing
244 Fifth Avenue, Suite V246
New York, N.Y. 10001
Permissions Requests: scwarcherpublishing@gmail.com

Cover Design by Penoaks Publishing, www.penoaks.com.
Book Layout © 2013 BookDesignTemplates.com.
Illustrations © Katerina Kirilova // shutterstock.com

Becoming the Narcissist's Nightmare/Shahida Arabi. -- 1st Print ed.
ISBN 978-1-52370-246-6

Dedication

Dedicated to all the survivors and warriors out there – healing, thriving and transcending more and more every day.

Your voices, your stories, your contributions are all so important and valuable. Thank you for all you do and all that you are – beautiful, strong, brilliant and finally -- free.

Special thanks to Lilly Hope Lucario, who remained a source of much needed moral support during the writing of this book. Your genuine, loving spirit remained a gentle reminder of a survivor's power to continue working for the greater good.

Paperback Version and Access to Links

Throughout the book, you will find references to links. When possible, I have done my best to provide full hyperlinks. However, for the sake of brevity, some links may be better accessed via the electronic version of the book or per the instructions provided in Chapter 3.

This book is enrolled in the **Kindle Matchbook Program** which enables the reader to gain free access to the e-book version of the book and its hyperlinks via Amazon if they purchased the paperback version of the book on Amazon. Please visit the book's Amazon page for details on how to download your free e-book copy.

PRAISE FOR *BECOMING THE NARCISSIST'S NIGHTMARE*

"Excellent! If there is one person on our side, it's Shahida. Ms. Arabi is our life-saver, cheerleader, saint, healer, best friend, advocate, and go-to expert for victims…when no one else is in your corner; she is there for you in mind and soul to share the truth about this hidden - and for many, life-threatening, devastating experience. This book covers the complete experience of: encountering, surviving, and healing from an emotional terrorist. Ahead of her time, she has forged the way for us - victims and mental health professionals - to start acknowledging this hidden epidemic; and to begin the lonely, painful process of helping ourselves and others survive the reality of personality-disordered relationship trauma." – **Monica M. White, Licensed Clinical Mental Health Counselor**

"Outstanding, comprehensive, thoughtful book for survivors! I will be sending my clients to read this book to help them have a fantastic, thorough understanding of narcissistic abuse recovery. Shahida Arabi skillfully writes from the standpoint of a survivor to a place of thriving…she blends evidence-based research, with survivor stories and integrative healing concepts that are paramount for trauma recovery from the unique aftermath of narcissistic abuse. This book will be a compass and roadmap for many as they reassemble after the rubble and construct anew a life of meaning, purpose, healing and transformation. Shahida Arabi speaks from the heart, from science, and from spirit…she knows how to translate for survivors the path of healing, triumph, and freedom." – **Andrea Schneider, LCSW and Author of *Soul Vampires: Reclaiming Your Lifeblood After Narcissistic Abuse***

"Shahida Arabi has accomplished something that few authors are able to do. She has written a book that is packed with so much wisdom and therapeutically proven tools for daily application, that it leaves the reader healthier than when they started reading. That is an incredible accomplishment for any writer. As a licensed therapist, I am thrilled to see Ms. Arabi's ability to give not only real life practical suggestions of how to find recovery and live it out, but also concrete, go-out-and-implement-them-today ideas. Ms. Arabi provides the reader with the exact tools needed to change their thoughts, which will change their actions and then lead to changed lives." – **Shannon Thomas, LCSW and Lead Therapist at Southlake Christian Counseling**

"I would like to give kudos to Shahida Arabi and her efforts in writing a well-researched book filled with current, accurate and practical information that focuses on the abuse survivors and not the abusers like most books on narcissistic abuse do. Well-written …filled with accurate truth, tons of current information, contributions from legitimate narcissistic abuse recovery experts, hope and inspiration that will facilitate healing and point the readers to effective healers and professional self-help strategies they can tailor to their specific needs." – **Evelyn M. Ryan, Life Coach and Author of *Take Your Power Back: Healing Lessons, Tips and Tools for Abuse Survivors.***

Contents

BY SHANNON THOMAS, LCSW

Foreword

Shahida Arabi has accomplished something few authors have done. She wrote a book packed with so much wisdom and therapeutically proven tools for daily application, that it leaves the reader healthier when they finish reading than when they started. That is an incredible accomplishment for any writer. *Becoming the Narcissist's Nightmare: How to Devalue and Discard the Narcissist While Supplying Yourself* serves as a one-stop shop for survivors who need to know that they are receiving therapeutically sound guidance. Shahida takes a creative play of the words normally used to describe the tactics of abusers and uses them as tools to empower survivors to heal. As a licensed therapist who specializes in recovery from narcissistic abuse, I highly recommend that survivors read this book on their journey to healing.

Becoming the Narcissist's Nightmare is a special book in that Ms. Arabi intertwines survivors' stories, her own experience, current research, the exploration of childhood programming and guided examples of how to emerge from the chaos with wholeness in body, mind and spirit. There are many viewpoints available within the narcissistic abuse recovery community and not all of them are healthy for survivors. Within the pages of this book, you will find not only Ms. Arabi's perspective on narcissistic abuse and recovery, but also the insights of experts she has invited to walk alongside you in the healing process. This unique collection of writers within *Becoming the Narcissist's Nightmare* allows for an engaging reading experience. You are given the chance to learn from several advocates within the psychological abuse recovery community and experience their individual personalities as well as their wisdom.

Within my own private counseling practice, I have had the privilege of working with survivors of narcissistic abuse. As a therapist working with these clients, I look for pervasive, destructive patterns that are present within emotionally and psychologically abusive relationships. There are specific red flags and subtle signs that we must unravel in order for the survivor to recognize the destruction occurring beneath the surface. From that point, we begin the process of the survivor understanding how the abuser has targeted and continued to manipulate them. This often involves looking at messages from the survivor's childhood and inner beliefs about their worthiness. We then move forward into the positive transformation that can take place within post-abuse healing. *Becoming the Narcissist's Nightmare* thoroughly covers the therapeutic work that is done by licensed professionals who "get it" when it comes to narcissist abuse recovery.

There are many distinctive aspects to *Becoming the Narcissist's Nightmare* from other books in the genre. The first one is that Ms. Arabi spends time discussing the subconscious messages from childhood that must be addressed in order for any survivor to truly heal at a deep level. Targets of narcissistic abuse should not blame themselves for the abuse they have endured and this book makes it clear that it is possible to move away from victim-blaming while still protecting oneself. Not all childhoods prepare adults to love themselves enough to ensure their own safety, but this book offers creative methods to rewrite existing narratives. *Becoming the Narcissist's Nightmare* guides the reader through understanding the inner beliefs that need to be rewritten so survivors can become the healthiest version of themselves.

The second distinctive aspect is in the book's ability to offer a variety of methods not only to identify abusive tactics but also to heal from them. As a licensed therapist, I am thrilled to see Ms. Arabi give real life, practical suggestions of how to recover. She discusses a plethora of resources to aid survivors in their journey. This book is packed full of concrete, go-out-and-implement-them-today ideas, providing the reader with the exact tools needed to change their thoughts, which will change their actions and then lead to changed lives. That is precisely the work that counselors are doing when utilizing the specified theoretical model, Cognitive Behavioral Therapy. Ms. Arabi educates the reader on various counseling and life coaching perspectives and this education empowers the reader to decide for themselves which might work best for their individual belief systems. She also offers a number of supplementary healing strategies that can help survivors tackle trauma on the level of the mind, body and spirit.

As a counselor, it is always a joy to read a book that I feel can serve as a comprehensive manual for recovery from narcissistic abuse. *Becoming the Narcissist's Nightmare* absolutely meets that need. I want to thank Ms. Shahida Arabi for her time and dedication to researching this topic, bringing together advocates and writing this book, all with the desire to see survivors set free and empowered to live the beautiful lives that they deserve.

Keep Dreaming Big!
Shannon Thomas, LCSW-S
www.southlakecounseling.org

Preface

A few years ago on a survivor's forum, I asked survivors what made them a narcissist's worst nightmare – the strengths, the talents, the assets, the attitudes and the actions that made them absolutely deplorable "supply" for abusive and toxic people.

Survivors came up with epic lists of traits that annoyed and frustrated their narcissistic partners – this included having an incredible sense of humor and quick wit that could put a narcissist's covert put-down to shame, the psychological resilience they had developed over the course of the relationship, their ability to empathize with others, their ability to intelligently and astutely question the narcissist's false mask, their ability to emotionally connect with others, their thirst for knowledge, their confidence, their sensitivity, their compassion – endless lists of amazing qualities that narcissists feared and abhorred.

What occurred to me was that our strengths – the ones that narcissists often convince us are weaknesses – are the very things that can *save* us from narcissists, which is why narcissists work so very hard to diminish these strengths in the first place. I also realized something even more incredible: that the techniques narcissists use against us can also be merged with those strengths to help us transcend and thrive after narcissistic abuse.

The very same techniques that narcissists use on us are the ones we must use to get over them. Confused? Let me explain. I am not suggesting becoming a narcissist ourselves or being cruel - not at all. These techniques will not be employed in the same way as a narcissist uses them – they will be adapted to detach from the narcissist altogether. Read the following and see if you agree with me here:

You once **idealized** the narcissist, put him or her on a pedestal after he or she did the same to you. You saw them as the love of your life - at least, you saw their false self as the love of your life.

Now, you must ***devalue and discard*** the narcissist - both in your mind and in your physical reality, if you're still maintaining contact with him or her somehow. In this book, these terms will not only be explained in the context of abuse, but be adapted to the survivor's own journey of detaching and healing from a narcissist.

Devaluing the narcissist means reconnecting with the reality of who the narcissist is, not who you wish him/her to be (the false self they once presented to you). In essence, devaluing in this context means dismantling your perception of their false self and replacing it with the reality of their true, abusive self. Chapter 1 and Chapter 2 will give you the information, knowledge and tools to identify the covert manipulation tactics of narcissistic abusers as well as their motives and intentions.

Discarding the narcissist means going No Contact with the narcissist or Low Contact if you share children, have legal matters to sort out with the narcissist or have any other circumstances that prevent you from cutting all ties with this person. This involves giving yourself closure by not giving the narcissist any. In Chapter 5, you'll learn more about the journey to No Contact.

Re-idealizing and supplying yourself refers to using the tips and tools I'll mention Chapter 3 to release the toxic brainwashing from your narcissistic partner and begin to heal some of the biochemical and trauma bonds that have tethered you to your narcissistic abuser. This also involves creating a healthier, positive *reverse discourse* that substitutes self-defeating beliefs with empowering ones about yourself.

Triangulation in this case means welcoming new people into your life that will serve as a support network to you during this time. All this time, the narcissist has triangulated you with others to validate their own sense of superiority. Now you must "triangulate" your narcissist with a new support system to validate your experiences. This is not meant to make the narcissist jealous – it is meant to give you the resources and empowerment you need to heal.

Due to your empathy and ability to emotionally connect, this triangulation has the benefit of adding to your psychological resilience. Having at least one person who has your back and can snap you back to reality, who knows what you've been through, is invaluable. Having a whole community of other survivors who have your back? Well, now you're bound to be invincible. In Chapter 5, we'll learn more about how to connect with these support networks while also getting rid of any defunct or toxic social networks (including the narcissist's own harem) that no longer serve your emotional well-being.

Reverse Gaslighting means that you can use the information you'll learn in the first two chapters about a narcissist's manipulative tactics to resist their distortions of your reality if they try to pull a fast one on you. Applying this knowledge also helps you distance yourself. This means going No Contact or Low Contact in response to their silent treatments, their stonewalling behavior, their petty put-downs and manipulation in order to prevent yourself from being pulled right back into their mind games.

"Reverse Gaslight" the narcissist by saying mentally to their accusations, projections and gaslighting tactics: *I don't believe you. That's not what happened. I know my truth and I own my truth.* Reverse Gaslighting the narcissist is not actually gaslighting - it involves staying grounded in your reality and your own powerful truth while invalidating the lies of a narcissist. This will help to relieve some of the cognitive dissonance you may have been experiencing as a result of being in a relationship with a narcissistic abuser who often manipulates your perception of reality.

Create a false self for the time being that serves as armor if and when you have to interact with the narcissist or even just start

ruminating over them. This self is the strong, logical self that you must wear as you begin to detach and heal from a narcissist. The one you may not feel like during No Contact or Low Contact, but the one you must be, in order to resist their attempts to re-traumatize you and bring you back into the relationship by pressing the reset button. Use this self to interact with the narcissist if you have to interact with them. You'll learn how to do this effectively through the methods we'll discuss in Chapters 3, 4, 5 and 6.

Using this false self enables you to be self-protective, centered and unreactive. Mirror them when you have to, much like they mirrored you during the idealization phase, by withdrawing from them when they withdraw, rather than pleading and begging for them. Strive **not** to mirror them when they attempt to pull you back into the trauma of the relationship. Do not share secrets and do not make them privy to your innermost feelings; in fact, I encourage you not to disclose anything about your personal life once you've realized your partner may be a narcissist. You are permitted to stop giving any information in the case where the narcissist may try to emotionally blackmail or manipulate you. They played mind games all along - now it's their turn to not have the facts at hand.

Finally, think of the narcissist as supply. You do not need them because you have other sources of attention - healthier sources. Think of them as rotten supply. They cannot "work" for you anymore, because they are not functional adults in relationships. They are children in adult bodies, doing real harm to others.

So you see, *it's not about becoming the narcissist*, stooping down to their level or even counter-manipulating them. It's about conquering your own thoughts, beliefs and actions regarding the narcissist and adapting the very same techniques that he or she used to entrap you in the first place. Except, in this case, you use them to set yourself free. Narcissists underestimate a survivor's willpower, you see. A survivor who has been discarded and has nothing left to lose is capable of every success imaginable.

Ultimately, it is not your ability to beat the narcissist at his or her own game that frightens them. Playing games with someone with no remorse or empathy is sure to fail. Rather, it is your ability to seek your own validation and move forward into your success, channeling the experiences that were meant to destroy you into your greatest victories, that is appalling to these predators. How dare their former victims become independent of their bullying and become even greater in spite of it? Oh, but they can, and they will.

From One Survivor to Another

"I grew up with a narcissistic, abusive father, and then spent 12 years of my adult life repeating that dysfunctional pattern when I married a narcissistic abuser. In the context of my 12-year relationship, I never felt safe emotionally, physically, financially or psychologically. I was never "good enough" to please him, even though I gave him the best years of my life and spent my life savings investing in his "dream." I didn't feel safe to ever have children with him… I finally left him and two years later, our divorce has gone nowhere. I am not with him now, but we are still married and he's destroyed the businesses we built and wrecked my finances and credit. I am still struggling to find the courage and strength to end this nightmare. Two years of depression and darkness, living in fear of him and still attempting to support his dreams even though he never loved me or gave me anything in return." —Hallie, Survivor from Kentucky

For those of us who have experienced narcissistic abuse since childhood, many of us are familiar with the trauma bonds that can keep us locked in the vicious cycle of meeting and mating with narcissists. Growing up with a narcissistic parent and witnessing narcissistic abuse was the precursor to the destructive, toxic relationships I had with narcissists - from friends to relationship partners to acquaintances to co-workers. Years later, I can say that the experiences of narcissistic abuse were more of a gift than a curse, because I learned to channel it into some of the greatest victories of my life.

Narcissistic abuse can be a vicious cycle, especially for those of us who experienced it as children, when we were particularly vulnerable. Before I met narcissistic romantic partners, I experienced severe bullying in addition to witnessing domestic violence during my childhood. These experiences essentially primed me for narcissistic abuse. My first ever boyfriend was a grandiose narcissist who would covertly and overtly put me down, wounding me with a sense of unworthiness that I carried forward into early adulthood. Ever since then, I felt "cursed" to meet more narcissists, and I did. Other dating and relationship partners as well as friends followed similar patterns of triangulation (manufacturing love triangles), stonewalling, emotional invalidation and verbal abuse. It was not until I discovered what narcissistic abuse was that I came to realize that this pattern had been ingrained within me ever since I was a young child.

Although I knew I was not to blame for any of the abuse I received, I recognized how these patterns had come to be. Back then, I was not aware that my subconscious wounding was enabling me to stay tethered to these toxic relationships. Our subconscious mind is incredibly powerful; it carries forth the core wounds from childhood and does everything in its power to reinforce those wounds and prove them right. I was unintentionally gravitating towards people who reminded me of my narcissistic parent, of my first boyfriend and of my bullying classmates; they were also gravitating towards me as I had not yet healed my wounds. I had not yet fully embraced myself as a whole, healthy divine being worthy of love, compassion and respect.

It was one of the worst narcissistic abusers I had ever met that finally led me to break the cycle. This relationship had me reeling. I had encountered emotionally abusive people before, but this particular relationship was special in how exaggerated it was, almost like a caricature of the narcissistic abuse cycle – idealization, devaluation and discard on steroids.

Everything about this relationship fit the criteria for narcissistic abuse to a tee – the idealization phase which was heavy with surveillance and an excessive amount of investment early on; the constant triangulation with other individuals (even complete strangers); chronic stonewalling during arguments, and devaluation in the form of degrading, condescending comments that never seemed to end. There were also sleepless nights filled with countless discussions initiated by this partner over seemingly irrelevant things, incredible blameshifting, terrifying narcissistic rage, lies, put-downs and projection as well as verbal abuse.

This devaluation was mixed in with spurts of unexpected idealization and shallow flattery – what I now know to be intermittent reinforcement at its finest. Anyone looking from the outside who understood narcissism could easily identify that it was psychological and emotional abuse. I had tried to deny and minimize this abuse throughout the relationship, but by the end of the horrific discard, I knew I had experienced something that was going to alter the course of my life.

It was difficult, but I knew I had to let the relationship go and never contact this person again. The way this partner had humiliated me and put me down made this a great deal easier. I now had no choice but to move forward with my life. The gift of this particular relationship was that it unraveled new knowledge and new networks. Shortly after going No Contact with my ex-partner, I was lucky enough to find an online community of abuse survivors in the same shoes. Miraculously enough, I remembered the name of the community through a post I had read regarding abuse recovery during my tumultuous relationship. On a hunch, I googled the name of the community, not realizing that this would be the life-changing step that would transform everything I knew to be true.

This same community led me to read a book that would change my life forever, a book called *Psychopath Free* by the community's founder, the brilliant and perceptive Jackson MacKenzie. A survivor himself, he wrote about the manipulative tactics of abusive narcissists in a deeply personal yet eerily accurate way. This book and its accompanying community of survivors opened my eyes to the fact that I was not alone in my experiences; far from it. The accounts of other survivors, their validation and their encouragement, helped me to regain hope in rebuilding a better life, one without abuse and disrespect.

This was when I began to more readily identify the covert manipulation tactics of emotional abusers. One of the most incredible components of my healing journey was the powerful knowledge I gained along the way. I was not necessarily new to narcissism; at the age of 18, while most people my age were reading Cosmopolitan, I was reading Sam Vaknin to understand how manipulative, cruel and callous partners operated. While I had briefly read about the narcissistic personality and had begun to realize that my first boyfriend fit the criteria with his endless, self-absorbed monologues, cruel comparisons, and degrading comments, I did not learn or research the full complexity of narcissistic abuse until this other short-term relationship served as the catalyst in my journey to fully recognize and realize what I had been dealing with.

A few years later, I began to revisit the literature on sociopaths and narcissists in a way that was even more eye-opening, delving into the actual techniques that abusive individuals used. The more books I read, the more I learned about how deliberate these tactics were, and how many abusers were unlikely to change. I read books on narcissistic abusers and antisocial personalities by experts on this topic such as Dr. Robert D. Hare, Dr. George Simon, Dr. Martha Stout, and Lundy Bancroft, many of whom had worked with these personalities as clients.

In addition, I tapped into the infinite wisdom of other survivors, those who had been through the abuse cycle themselves. I regularly visited blogs on emotional abuse, such as the information-rich After Narcissistic Abuse blog and the compassionate Healing from Complex Trauma and PTSD website. I frequently spoke with other survivors as we supported each other on our journey to healing. The fact that we were all transforming ourselves after this heartbreaking experience - or for people like me, a set of heartbreaking experiences - was exhilarating, frightening and emotional. It was also *life-changing*.

Psychology was no stranger to me. As fate would have it, I had studied it extensively through my coursework in school, and had even taken a graduate-level course on psychopathology where I first learned the DSM definition of narcissism. Ironically, however, I had no idea at the time that I was taking this class, I was also in a relationship with a narcissistic abuser. That is because many psychology books do not talk specifically about *narcissistic abuse.*

I also knew licensed mental health counselors who I had spoken with regarding these topics, yet even *they* had not been taught about the intricacies of these types of toxic relationships and how far these manipulative behaviors went. It became a passion of mine to consume psychology articles and books to learn more about this type of abuse. Narcissistic abuse had never been fully explored in my psychology classes and I developed a thirst to uncover the intentions behind the mask that many abusers presented to the world.

It is important to note that knowledge alone, while powerful, cannot heal narcissistic abuse. To heal from narcissistic abuse, I had to employ different healing modalities that targeted the mind, the body and the spirit. Self-exploration and self-improvement was not new to me, but narcissistic abuse led me to a cathartic path of healing that I never would have undertaken otherwise. Due to the anxiety and stress I experienced from witnessing unhealthy family dynamics, as well as being a survivor of other traumas that took place outside of my household such as bullying, abuse and sexual assault, I had spent years experimenting with different forms of mindfulness and self-care. These helped me to reconnect with a sense of wholeness I felt I had lost in the midst of lifelong trauma.

My self-care regimen included everything you could possibly think of: I read hundreds of self-help books, created a daily practice of positive affirmations, cleaned up my diet and learned to do different types of yoga such as Hatha yoga, Vinyasa yoga and Bikram yoga.; I also tried Reiki healing, counseling, meditation, kickboxing, dance classes, art therapy and keeping a gratitude journal. I loved incorporating body and mind in activities geared towards greater healing and self-care. Each part of my regimen helped to build a stronger foundation where I was pulling myself towards self-compassion, self-respect, and self-love. The ending of the toxic relationship, combined with the support of my fellow survivors, was the final push that made me realize that I could also help other survivors with what I was learning.

That is when I took an important step towards my own dreams: I channeled all that I had learned from my previous relationships, everything I learned from my self-care activities, as well as the research I had read about narcissistic abuse into writing a book I had written pieces of but had never had the courage to finish. It was a book about self-care for young women called *The Smart Girl's Guide to Self-Care*. Miraculously, this book would later become an Amazon Best Seller in three categories, its rank right next to one of my favorite authors in the category of Women's Personal Growth.

This is also the book I wrote during No Contact with my narcissistic ex-partner and I wouldn't have had it any other way. Every day of No Contact, I made a commitment: keep writing. Instead of tethering myself to more toxic people, I broke the cycle through my words and rewrote the script of my life. I kept writing and revising my way into rebuilding a better life while also sharing my story to help others find their way to self-care after abuse and trauma.

Life after No Contact was a challenging yet flourishing time for me; it seemed that without a narcissistic partner, I opened up a new space of healing and empowerment where love, community and miracles could enter. One of the biggest miracles I experienced was writing an accompanying blog to my book called Self-Care Haven, which taught people about the warning signs of emotional abuse. To my surprise, my blog went viral due to an entry I had written called "Five Powerful Ways Abusive Narcissists Get Inside Your Head." In this entry, I used all the knowledge and life experiences I had gained on my journey and poured it into an article that survivors and mental health practitioners alike would come to share all over the world. Within a few months, my blog had achieved 1.5 million views.

The letters from abuse survivors around the world began pouring in; both survivors and clinical psychologists began sharing the work through social media. Most importantly, I got comments from survivors who told me that the article had changed their lives and that they were ready to take action to finally end the toxic relationships that had held them back for years. I had always known that the best revenge was moving forward and chasing my dreams, but never had I recognized the value of moving on and sharing my story as deeply as I did then. *The story I had was powerful because it was a story many others had longed to share.* Had I never shared my story, I would have never been able to connect with those who were also looking to transform their lives and share their own stories.

My miraculous connection with a growing community of abuse survivors did not end there. During No Contact, I couldn't sleep at night, so I also began making YouTube videos on how to maintain No Contact with toxic ex-partners. As I spoke about my insights on No Contact and narcissism, survivors began to connect with me about their own No Contact journey and began subscribing to my channel. I was amazed to have gotten even a hundred subscribers at the beginning of my No Contact journey, but by the end of that year, I had achieved more than four thousand.

Deep within my soul, I knew I was on the right path; for the first time in a very long time, things clicked into place and I felt the waves of revolution as I saw the community around me growing exponentially – a community that fully resonated with my work and what I had experienced. A community of survivors and warriors who knew exactly what it felt like to be abused and the courage it took to tackle the numerous hardships after abuse. Life after narcissistic abuse meant the miracle of recognition. I understood that part of my destiny was to help other survivors like me – some of whom had also experienced emotional abuse in childhood that they later re-experienced in adulthood with their narcissistic partners.

I had no idea what I had started and I was astounded at the feedback I was receiving. Survivors from all different backgrounds and experiences were reaching out to me to share their stories of narcissistic abuse; even more powerfully, they were connecting with the other survivors on my blog and supporting each other in loving, compassionate ways that filled me with hope. All I knew was that I was doing my best to channel the experiences life had given me into the greater good and that the people who needed it the most - my fellow survivors, my fellow warriors, were finding healing too along with me.

I grew stronger; by the end of my one year of No Contact with that particular narcissist, I knew I still had a great deal of learning to assimilate, but also, more work to do. I regularly answered the questions of my readers regarding their narcissistic abuse experiences; I invited survivors to share their stories on my blog posts and also rewrite the script of their lives, and it wasn't long before I began a No Contact coaching program for survivors all over the world. I continued to apply what I taught to others to my own personal life. The next few times I encountered narcissistic people, I was able to detach from them more easily and quickly. I recognized the red flags, called them out, and eventually went on my way. I took more initiative in ending these relationships and friendships, going No Contact without further thought for people who were visibly toxic - people who did not support me or my dreams.

I refocused on the people who validated me and wanted me to rise rather than fall. I also made sure to validate myself and realized that while being among the few to recognize a narcissist was an alienating experience, it was also a liberating one. There were many times I saw behind the masks of toxic people, sociopaths or narcissists while others continued to believe in the false self they projected. Instead of attempting to convince others of what I observed, I quietly turned the focus back onto myself and my own self-care. I stopped listening to the dark voices of others and began to reconnect with that divine light inside of me and other survivors. I knew the truth about toxic people and for the first time, my faith in myself was enough to break the spell.

It was by no means easy; sometimes it took longer for me to detach from toxic people than I felt it should have. There were times when I felt I could've done better. Yet I treated myself compassionately and forgave myself for any failures, knowing that any type of "relapse" was simply an inevitable detour on the road to recovery. So I pushed forward and kept moving. I knew that each encounter with another narcissistic abuser, whether friend, foe or relationship partner, was simply a test - a test of how far my core wounds were still tethering me to toxic people.

The journey to healing is not simple; the destination is not some final end point at the end of some torturous maze; it is an exciting journey filled with ups and downs, with new learning experiences and challenges. During life after narcissistic abuse, I tried many different healing modalities to uncover my wounds. I went back far in childhood to better understand how those wounds had been created and how my subconscious had steered me towards self-sabotage.

I am happy to say that today, I have much healthier friendships and relationships precisely because I've learned to set boundaries, recognize my self-worth and adopt a warrior mentality towards my own self-care. No Contact with my toxic ex-partners has helped me incredibly on my healing journey, but I am not afraid to say that I am always in the loving, evolving process of healing and becoming. We all are. The journey to healing is never really over, but that is the exciting thing about life after narcissistic abuse.

You get to heal in so many different ways. Some powerful methods of healing for me were through joining body and mind through meditating, writing, dancing, running, and stretching outwards in a yoga pose. I also stretched myself outwards in other ways – to the larger community of survivors, whose support was vital to my journey. I cannot stress enough the fact that the most important way I healed was to reach out to other survivors through coaching, blogging, making videos and joining support groups. *I discovered that when I helped other people heal, it reconnected me with that divine sense of love and purpose that was crucial for me to rebuild my life.* In this way, the experience of narcissistic abuse and all the lessons it taught me prompted me to make miraculous shifts in my life.

Throughout my journey, I learned that knowledge of narcissistic abuse was not something limited to licensed therapists and researchers - the accounts of real life abuse survivors provided crucial information regarding the patterns of these dysfunctional relationships. Those that offer a cure have often drunk the poison themselves. Experiencing narcissistic abuse yourself is quite different from learning about it from just a clinical perspective.

Some people who have suffered narcissistic abuse may have never met a narcissist previous to that singular experience. But over the last seven years, I have met and encountered many toxic people - through dating, long-term relationships, school and the workplace. I've conducted - unintentionally - an ethnographic experiment of sorts in which I've navigated and confronted different abusive styles, techniques that abusers and otherwise toxic people employ to manipulate their victims, and have observed these tactics in real-life settings. All I would've needed was a tape-recorder and a transcription of all these encounters to have made it a viable sociological experiment.

In addition to these real-life experiences, I've had the privilege of reading hundreds of books on dating, relationships and pathological people from the experts. I've taken undergraduate and graduate-level courses in psychopathology. All of these experiences and my research have given me the insight and knowledge to write this book and hopefully help other survivors of emotional abuse with what I've learned on my journey. From a spiritual perspective, I feel my destiny was tied to learning more about abusive patterns and sharing my stories to strengthen and empower others who have undergone similar experiences.

You may not share the same perspective, and that's perfectly all right. Some of you have undergone such severe suffering and trauma that placing this into a spiritual framework might be challenging. All that matters is that you do what is most empowering for you and beneficial for your unique journey to healing. That is why I've written this book, to offer insights on how to spot emotional predators and ultimately, how to empower and begin to heal yourself after encountering them.

Throughout these encounters with emotional predators, I've revolutionized my understanding of appropriate boundaries, reconnected with my authentic values, and empowered myself to recover from psychological abuse by using reverse discourse, self-care, and the channeling of my experiences into productive outlets.

My journey has not been perfect – it has been filled with adversity and the challenge of confronting and addressing unhealed wounds. Yet I've also written books, pursued my passions, cut toxic people out of my life, graduated from top universities, reached a larger community and have helped others on their own healing journeys. I know firsthand that a better life is possible and that you can always use what you've learned to fuel your success.

I am so grateful for the opportunity to heal and to help others heal. *I am grateful for every miracle that has allowed me to reach so many survivors.* We are all reaching for a greater life and this path can be paved when we begin to channel our pain into our healing, our crisis to our transformation, our crucifixion to our resurrection. I share my story and the stories of other survivors in this book because I want all survivors of abuse and trauma, regardless of what their background is with narcissistic abuse, to know that you should never give up.

That is why at the end of each chapter of this book, you'll not only find articles by experienced therapists, writers, advocates, professionals and researchers on the topic of narcissistic abuse and the effects of trauma, you'll also find a section called "Survivor Insights," collected from hundreds of survey responses I've received from survivors all around the world. These stories shed light on the complexities and intricacies of emotional and psychological abuse in a way that the clinical perspective often doesn't do justice to.

The accompanying articles in this book include works by bestselling authors, licensed therapists and popular bloggers and advocates on the topic. I am honored to include articles by therapist and author Andrea Schneider, LCSW, author and life coach Lisa A. Romano, award-winning blogger and founder of Healing Complex Trauma and PTSD Lilly Hope Lucario, Mental Health News Radio host Kristin Walker, founder of True Love Scam Jennifer Smith, therapist Ingrid Roekke, author and coach Kim Saeed and founder of Ending Abuse Media, Alison Soroka. I've also made sure to include the insights I've gained from the thousands of survivor stories I've received on my platforms in addition to my personal experiences and research. This is meant to help readers bridge the gap between the existing research on this topic and real-life experiences.

In Chapter 1, you'll learn everything you need to know about narcissistic abuse, including more about the narcissistic abuse cycle, the manipulative tactics of abusive predators, the distinctions between narcissistic abuse and mistreatment by a selfish jerk, the origins of narcissism, "translations" of narcissistic behavior, common terms used in the realm of narcissistic abuse and clichés about normal relationships that do not work in the realm of abusive relationships. You'll also learn the victim-blaming myths and stereotypes that usually hold victims back from validating and understanding their own experiences.

Chapter 2 explores the biochemical, psychological and trauma bonds that keep abuse victims tethered to their abusers, long after they've discovered what they're dealing with, as well as the effects of trauma on the brain. This is incredibly important to learn about, because many victims blame themselves for staying in the relationship too long without understanding how the effects of trauma keep us hooked to these toxic partners.

Chapters 3 and 4 are arguably two of the most important chapters in this book, as they delve in-depth on how to combat each one these bonds, as well as the alternative and traditional methods you can use to heal from this type of abuse. They also explore how you can tap into your warrior "superpowers" and strengths in order to detach from abusive people and rebuild an even more amazing life after narcissistic abuse.

Chapter 5 is helpful for those struggling with the journey of No Contact, as it contains resources, tips and methods to begin No Contact and maintain it. In addition, it offers a list of 111 alternatives to breaking No Contact to prevent relapse.

Chapter 6 explores pathological narcissism in our society and culture, giving more insights on how to cope with narcissistic family members, friends, co-workers, and even online narcissists such as cyberbullies. Chapters 7-10 offer closing insights on what it means to be a survivor, how to heal from emotional abuse by owning our power and agency, as well as how to channel our traumatic experiences into victory by rewriting our stories and creating new narratives.

There will be a Frequently Asked Questions at the end of the book that you will not want to miss, as well as an additional resources list that will link to some of the most informative websites, articles and videos on narcissistic abuse.

Throughout the book, you'll also find there are links to "Self-Care Haven" meditations and reflections related to the themes of certain chapters that I normally only offer to my coaching clients, which are now available to e-book readers as well.

As you read through this book, I hope you'll recognize that your own story, when and if you are ready to share it, can help to heal others. This experience, while alienating at first, can be channeled into a greater purpose and can be used to reconnect you with the larger world in ways you might never have thought possible. I know there are moments when it seems hopeless and the pain seems unbearable, especially if you have a pattern of attaching to narcissistic people.

However, there is a whole other world that will open up for you in recovery and healing. Be kind to yourself, even when you feel nobody is kind to you. At the end of the day, you have to save yourself – over and over again, no matter what. You and your story are needed. You are worthy. You are strong. You are extraordinary. You are a fighter. You are a warrior.

I encourage all survivors to take their own self-care journey after narcissistic abuse; you can empower yourself more fully by taking advantage of all the lessons it has to offer. This experience can serve as a portal to healing and a challenge to rise above the ashes and resurrect to your best self.

No matter how much we learn and improve, we can always learn something new along the way. The journey to healing is never really "over" – it's just beginning, and I want to share with you the empowering tools that have helped me towards my destination.

You will find that when you see the blessing in the darkness, many other blessings will also come to light – new support, new dreams to be fulfilled, new ways to connect to your divine inner guidance and God-given worth. In you is something infinitely greater than whatever you are experiencing. This light will always be within you, even during and after the most traumatic moments of your life.

Narcissists assume they can break us down and destroy us, but the truth is, they can never destroy us. Despite the damage they inflict, we are stronger than them, heart, mind, and soul. As broken as you may feel right now, there is something within each and every one of you reading this book that is stronger than their abuse. It is that part of you that knows you want to survive and thrive. It is that part of you that you must connect to before you give up hope for a better life. It is that part of you that will allow you to transcend their destruction and recreate yourself, more victorious than ever.

Your desire for knowledge and healing is just the beginning and it is a calling for something greater. You don't belong in the shadows where you've been forced to hide. You deserve to be in the light with full force. Your destiny is tied to recognizing your worth and how utterly valuable you are to this world. You have so much to give and you no longer have to sacrifice yourself for the needs of another person ever again. You deserve to be seen and heard.

No matter who you are and where you are at this point of your life, you can always use the worst experiences of your life as the key to your best victories. Life after narcissistic abuse is filled with miracles – you just have to be ready to reach out and let them in.

CHAPTER ONE

Recognizing the Narcissist

"We are targeted by narcissists because we have everything that is beautiful and human. We can feel true joy and sadness. They want to live through us, and end up killing us. But we will rise, and we will be stronger and wiser. We need to love ourselves. We are not victims, we are survivors! This is the life lesson." – Dzana, Survivor from Stockholm.

In popular culture, the term "narcissistic" is thrown about quite loosely, usually referring to vanity and self-absorption. This reduces narcissism to a common quality that everyone possesses and downplays the symptoms demonstrated by people with the actual disorder. While narcissism does exist on a spectrum, narcissism as a full-fledged *personality disorder* is quite different.

People who meet the criteria for Narcissistic Personality Disorder or those who have traits of Antisocial Personality Disorder can operate in extremely manipulative ways within the context of intimate relationships due to their deceitfulness, lack of empathy, and their tendency to be interpersonally exploitative. Although I will be focusing on narcissistic abusers in this book, due to the overlap of symptoms in these two disorders, this can potentially apply to interactions with those who have ASPD to an extent.

It's important in any kind of relationship that we learn to identify the red flags when interacting with people who display malignant narcissism and/or antisocial traits, so we can better protect ourselves from exploitation and abuse, set appropriate boundaries with others, and make informed decisions about who we keep in our lives. Understanding the nature of these toxic interactions and how they affect us has an enormous impact on our ability to engage in self-care.

The Diagnostic and Statistical Manual of Mental Disorders (5th ed.; DSM–5; American Psychiatric Association, 2013) defines a narcissistic person as someone who has a pervasive pattern of grandiosity (in fantasy or behavior), an excessive need for admiration, and lack of empathy, beginning by early adulthood and present in a variety of contexts. This is indicated by five (or more) of the following:

- Has a grandiose sense of self-importance (e.g., exaggerates achievements and talents, expects to be recognized as superior without commensurate achievements).
- Is preoccupied with fantasies of unlimited success, power, brilliance, beauty, or ideal love.
- Believes that he or she is "special" and unique and can only be understood by, or should associate with, other special or high-status people (or institutions).
- Requires excessive admiration.
- Has a sense of entitlement (i.e., unreasonable expectations of especially favorable treatment or automatic compliance with his or her expectations).
- Is interpersonally exploitative (i.e., takes advantage of others to achieve his or her own ends).
- Lacks empathy: is unwilling to recognize or identify with the feelings and needs of others.
- Is often envious of others or believes that others are envious of him or her.
- Shows arrogant, haughty behaviors or attitudes.

That's the clinical definition, but the way a narcissist operates in relationships is stealthier and more complex than the visible signs of narcissism depicted on this list. This book will help you gain knowledge about the red flags of narcissism and how it manifests in relationships, how to begin to heal and recover from narcissistic abuse as well as crucial insights drawn from both research and survivors. You'll learn healing strategies and tips to begin to detach from your narcissistic partner if you haven't already, understand the reasons why you may still be addicted to your narcissistic partner, as well as the best ways to channel your experiences into constructive healing.

What is Narcissistic Abuse?

Narcissistic partners engage in chronic manipulation and devaluation of their victims, leaving victims feeling worthless, anxious and even suicidal. This type of continual manipulation, which includes an idealization-devaluation-discard abuse cycle where they "lovebomb" their partners, devalue them, then discard them until the trauma begins again, is known as *narcissistic abuse* – abuse by a partner with NPD is on the far end of the narcissistic spectrum. This type of abuse can leave psychological and emotional scars that can last a lifetime.

In fact, trauma expert Pete Walker (2013) suggests that chronic emotional abuse, especially if experienced in childhood and later re-experienced in adulthood, can cause symptoms of PTSD or Complex PTSD. Psychotherapist Christine Louis de Canonville (2015) also discusses what she calls Narcissistic Victim Syndrome in her book, *The Three Faces of Evil: Unmasking the Full Spectrum of Narcissistic Abuse*. What makes narcissistic abuse so dangerous is that these individuals employ very covert and insidious methods to abuse their partners. Due to the very nature of their abuse, they're able to escape accountability for the abuse because of the false persona they present to the outside world – which is usually a charming mask that hides their cruelty.

What's important to remember is that narcissists don't outright destroy you in the way physically abusive partners may do – they plant the very seeds in your mind that will lead you to your own destruction.

They will cultivate doubts that never existed, manufacture insecurities that were never present, rub salt on the wounds they know you don't want opened – all under the guise of "helping" you or gaslighting you into believing you deserved or provoked the abuse. They also rewrite the abuse they've inflicted, making you look like you're the abuser.

As I'll describe more in-depth in Chapter 2, narcissists will subject you to a dizzying biochemical cocktail of traumatic highs and lows to keep you hooked on the drug that is their abuse. This type of crazymaking is so covert that many victims don't even know they've been abused – some only learn to identify the tactics well after ten years of marriage with a narcissistic abuser, while others are lucky enough to learn about it early on in the relationship.

The toxic behaviors in narcissistic abuse can include but are not limited to:

- Being overly critical and controlling towards their partners, covertly and overtly putting them down though cruel verbal abuse and manipulative behaviors that are employed to isolate and demean them. Narcissists and sociopaths are known for demonstrating contempt for others as a way to demonstrate their power and false sense of superiority. This can include name-calling, harsh insults disguised as jokes, demeaning, contemptuous remarks about the victim's appearance, intelligence, line of work, lifestyle, skill sets, accomplishments, or other support networks the victim has outside of the relationship.

- Being physically and/or sexually abusive. This can include hitting the partner with objects, punching, shoving, slapping, choking or pushing the victim, forcing the victim to have sex without consent, and coercing the victim into sexual situations they are not comfortable with. They may threaten to leave the victim or ruin the victim's life in some way if they do not comply with their wishes.

- Manufacturing hostile or aggressive situations where the victim is led to emotional distress, especially through the abuser's narcissistic rage over seemingly small or irrelevant things. The abuser creates an environment where the victim feels trapped, controlled, and limited in what he or she can say or do.

- Engaging in hot and cold behavior that switches quickly between a loving persona and an abusive one. This is an abuse cycle known as idealization, devaluation and discard. It includes treating the victim cold and callously for no apparent reason, only to return to loving, affectionate behavior through a technique called intermittent reinforcement. This conditions the victim into expecting less each and every time they interact and also programs the victim into associating love with unpredictability, distress and unease. The victim is later discarded in a humiliating, demeaning manner, often followed by a smear campaign so that the narcissist feels they've "won" the break-up.

- Controlling every aspect of their partner's life to the point where they isolate them from family and friends; this includes sabotaging the victim's friendships, familial relationships, important life events or their goals and aspirations.

- Stonewalling their victims into silence should they bring up any concerns about the relationship; subjecting the victim to silent treatments and disappearances throughout the abuse cycle to create a sense of chronic insecurity in the victim, causing the victim to walk on eggshells and increase their efforts to please their abusive partner.

- Triangulating their victims with other love interests including their ex-partners; engaging in pathological lying and deceit while pursuing numerous affairs outside of the relationship; comparing the victim to other people regarding their appearance, personality, success and other attributes to instill in them a sense of worthlessness. This infidelity is not driven by dissatisfaction with the main partner but rather a sadistic need for narcissistic supply. This supply comes in the form of attention from multiple people as well as the victim's emotional distress in response to the triangulation.

- Gaslighting their partners into believing the abuse isn't real by denying, minimizing or rationalizing the abuse. This includes deflecting any conversations about accountability using circular conversations and word salad in order to avoid being held accountable for their actions.

- Subjecting their victim to smear campaigns to slander their character and reputation so that the abuse victim is left with no support network. This includes projecting their own abusive behavior onto the victim so that no one believes their accounts of abuse.

- Blameshifting and projecting their malignant traits onto their partners during conversations while using a false charismatic self to make their victims look like the "crazy" ones. It's almost as if they hand off their own traits and shortcomings to their victims as if to say, "Here, take my pathology. I don't want it."

This is what narcissistic abuse looks like – and unfortunately, the full extent of narcissistic abuse is not taught in any psychology class or diagnostic manual, though these manipulative techniques can be found in numerous books by experts about narcissism, accounts from mental health professionals who have worked with survivors as clients as well as survivor accounts.

It is truly a narcissist's malignant behaviors and how they affect us that are the key to understanding if your partner is a narcissist. Anyone can be a victim of narcissistic abuse, regardless of their gender or background. A narcissistic abuser can lead survivors to feel depressed, suicidal, anxious, constantly on edge and worthless. If your partner displays these types of toxic behaviors, at the very least, they are emotionally, verbally and psychologically abusive. While malignant narcissists are certainly very dangerous, partners who display even some of these behaviors and refuse to change do not need the diagnosis of NPD in order for victims to recognize that they have a toxic relationship partner.

What Causes Narcissism?

The myth of Narcissus is a popular one to depict a narcissist's vanity and self-absorption, but a deeper dialogue about the origins of the full-fledged personality disorder is lacking. It's true that narcissism is rising in our culture, but how exactly does it manifest, especially as a personality disorder? There are many theories about how narcissism arises in the individual – from a "narcissistic wound" in childhood, to a pattern of idealization and devaluation by the parent or even a neurological standpoint that focuses mainly on how a narcissist's brain has structural abnormalities related to compassion (Kernberg, 1975; Kohut, 1971; Lavendar, 2014; Schulze et. al, 2013). Yet there is still no clear answer as to how Narcissistic Personality Disorder arises in an individual.

In "The Cracked Mirror: Features of Narcissistic Personality Disorder in Children," Dr. Karen Bardenstein (2009) notes that there are certain risk factors when it comes to children developing the disorder. The children who become narcissistic are often: the children of narcissistic parents, adopted children who are overindulged by their adoptive parent or face competition with their biological siblings, the children of successful parents, especially if the child lacks the same ability as their parents, overindulged, wealthy children, and the children of divorce, specifically, a divorce in which the child is vied over and is treated as an object to be "won."

Narcissists may have suffered something traumatic when they were a child – emotional neglect or physical neglect, as Kernberg (1975) suggests, by a critical parent. This severe trauma in childhood, what psychologists call a "narcissistic wound," may have led them to shut off the parts of themselves that could empathize with others, as a form of extreme self-protection (Marks, 2012; Lavender, 2014; De Lisle 2015). This may have been caused by a parent who neglected them, abused them and invalidated them, resulting in what Millon (1981) calls "compensatory narcissism," a self-protective false self that enables a child to believe in an illusion of superiority in order to conceal feelings of low self-worth.

On the other end of the spectrum, there are theories that suggest that narcissism can be produced by *overvaluation* of the child, allowing the child to remain like a child forever without any consequences or without any basis in objective reality for their presumed perfection. This pattern of overvaluation rather than devaluation by a parent that may have led a child to arrested emotional development – in other words, a child who is spoiled to the point where they develop an excessive sense of entitlement and disregard for the emotions of others.

A new research study in 2015 by the Proceedings of the National Academy of Sciences discovered that parents who overvalued their children by telling them how special they were produced narcissistic children. In their words, "Narcissism was predicted by parental overvaluation, not by lack of parental warmth. Thus, children seem to acquire narcissism, in part, by internalizing parents' inflated views of them (e.g., 'I am superior to others' and 'I am entitled to privileges')." (Brummelman et. al, 2015).

This new research aligns with what Randi Kreger (2012) calls the distinction between "vulnerable" narcissists and "grandiose narcissists." According to Kreger, *grandiose* narcissists are bred by parents who spoil them into thinking how superior and entitled they are, while *vulnerable* narcissists tend to be the product of neglectful parenting.

As someone who has taught very young children of wealthier backgrounds, I definitely saw this burgeoning sense of entitlement in the parents who enabled their children's misbehavior, allowing their children to trample upon the boundaries of others without so much of an apology. The parents who taught their kids an excessive sense of entitlement had a very indifferent attitude and coddled their children to the extreme even when they overstepped boundaries, while the parents who taught their children healthy boundaries and respect were likely to show empathy, remorse and accountability for their behavior.

We also see narcissism arise when parents treat their children as trophies or live through them vicariously – essentially degrading and objectifying them, teaching them that they are objects – which teaches the narcissistic child to also view others as objects for their disposal, while also overvaluing them as highly important. There can therefore be a dual "overvaluation" and "neglect" taking place in this circumstance that produces narcissism in a child; the parent may overvalue the child as perfect, but may also instill a sense of worthlessness in the child by not providing the child with healthier feedback that validates who they really are as a person.

This is because the narcissistic child is overvalued as "perfect" and this type of feedback is not balanced with realistic feedback. It places pressure on the child to be a trophy, rather than a three-dimensional human being. It also teaches children a high degree of entitlement, instilling in them that they are deserving of things they haven't earned.

Since this parental overvaluation is not balanced with acknowledgment of the child's imperfect humanity, it causes that child to develop a sense of grandiosity that vacillates between feelings of worthlessness and a hyperinflated ego – in other words, narcissism in the place of a healthy self-image (De Lisle, 2015). It can also cause the child to highly emphasize one attribute over others - such as looks, intellectual ability or another talent, in place of healthy self-esteem and self-acceptance.

That being said, parents alone may not be responsible for producing narcissism in their children and there are many parents with narcissistic children who do provide their children a loving, validating home. That's where we have to consider biological predisposition being passed down in families. Twin studies have shown that narcissism is a common, heritable trait (Livesley et. al, 1993). There is also a biological and neurological standpoint that redirects us to consider how the brain of someone with NPD differs from someone who does not have NPD.

Research has discovered there are, in fact, structural abnormalities related to compassion and empathy in the brain of a narcissistic individual, which is interesting to note considering psychopaths can also demonstrate brain abnormalities; psychopaths not only show abnormalities in empathy, they also show abnormalities when it comes to processing of pro-social emotions such as guilt and moral reasoning (Schulze et. al, 2013; Sethi et. al, 2015).

While each theory is compelling and has its own set of evidence, I need to stress that clinicians are still not absolutely certain as to what causes NPD. The answer is likely more complex than any individual theory. In my opinion, psychopathology is often caused by an interaction between biological predisposition and environment. There are also multicultural components that can make certain disorders more likely than others in specific countries or manifest differently across various contexts.

We have to consider that there are protective factors or risk factors that determine whether narcissism actually manifests in a full-fledged personality disorder or not as well as how it manifests in the individual. It's usually not nature versus nurture but rather a combination of nature and nurture. These factors include strong support network, access to therapy/medication, upbringing, religious beliefs, culture, media, as well as other experiences outside of the family unit like bullying, sexual assault, witnessing violence, or other traumas can all weaken or strengthen that predisposition towards pathology.

To put it simply, narcissists can probably be produced through a number of different ways and can come from a variety of backgrounds.

I personally have met narcissists from both types of backgrounds: traumatic ones as well as overvalued ones where their parents taught them an excessive sense of entitlement.

So while survivors can't be 100 percent certain what caused their partner's NPD, what survivors can be certain of is that being with a partner with NPD can be extremely dangerous and devastating due to their lack of empathy and tendency to be exploitive. I find that the questions of "why?" and "how?" can often cause confusion in accountability that shames the victim rather than the abuser. Just because someone has a disorder does not mean their abuse is not hurtful. Having a disorder does not make them less responsible for their abusive behavior, or make the abuse less impactful on the victim.

Quite the contrary. Someone who has a disorder and does not get professional support in changing the behavior that harms others, and instead uses that disorder as an excuse to continue to abuse others, can still be accountable for their actions. Yes, we can be compassionate towards the fact that our abuser may have been traumatized, but we cannot let that compassion blind us to the fact that if they are unwilling to change or receive treatment, as many narcissists aren't, we need to make our own self-compassion and self-care a priority in order to detach from them.

In this type of one-sided relationship, you will ultimately be used as an object to supply admiration, praise, attention, and whatever they may need at the moment; this is what Otto Fenichel (1945) calls a source of "narcissistic supply." If you enter a relationship with a narcissist, be careful: the false self is often so charming and so different from the true self that you may fall prey to a vicious cycle of narcissistic abuse that can be very difficult to extricate yourself from. The cognitive dissonance that results in being in love with an emotional predator is enhanced by the false mask that the narcissist presents to the world.

A relationship with a narcissist often contains some degree of psychological, emotional and in some cases, physical and sexual violence depending on where the narcissistic person falls on the spectrum.

Who is the Narcissist?

You may be wondering if your partner is a narcissist, a sociopath or a psychopath. There are distinctions among narcissists, sociopaths and psychopaths, but this book will be focusing on the overlapping symptoms, namely a lack of empathy and interpersonally exploitative behavior. According to Dr. Scott Bonn (2015), a professor of criminology and sociology, sociopaths and psychopaths both fall under the larger category of Antisocial Personality Disorder. Both sociopaths and psychopaths share a heinous disregard for laws, social mores, the rights of others and have a tendency to demonstrate violent behavior. According to the Psychopathy Checklist created by Robert Hare (1993), psychopaths tend to demonstrate callousness and lack of empathy, glib and superficial charm, a parasitic lifestyle, failure to accept responsibility for their actions, shallow affect, and sexual promiscuity. These are all traits that narcissists can share as well.

However, psychopaths often have juvenile delinquency in their history and criminal versatility. Narcissists tend to commit more emotional and psychological "crimes" in the way they devalue, slander and sabotage the lives of their victims; they are theoretically capable of remorse and guilt unlike sociopaths and psychopaths, though more often than not, their self-absorption and lack of empathy prevents them from showing remorse for their behavior and being willing to change. Both narcissists and psychopaths have been shown to have brain abnormalities – with narcissists, brain scans reveal abnormalities in structures of the brain related to compassion, while for psychopaths, brain scans revealed abnormalities in the areas of the brain related to moral reasoning and guilt (Schulze et. al, 2013; Sethi et. al, 2015).

While narcissists crave and need external validation, sociopaths and psychopaths often don't; sociopaths tend to exploit others for fun while narcissists tend to exploit others as a way to eliminate threat (Holbrook, 2013). That being said, these individuals tend to be similar in the callous ways they exploit others and I have witnessed firsthand that both narcissists and sociopaths tend to get a sadistic pleasure in harming others. This is because narcissistic abusers thrive on power and control. Due to their internal emptiness and inability to experience the full range of human emotions, they get their daily nourishment from inflicting trauma on their victims. The lines can be blurred among these categories, so the "label" matters less than the fact that these individuals pose considerable harm to their victims, whether emotional, psychological, financial and/or physical.

The first thing you must know about a narcissist is that you will truly never know anything about the narcissist. This is because a narcissist is someone who constructs what Sam Vaknin, a self-professed narcissist, calls a "false self" to hide away from their true selves. Their false self is the self they present to everyone else: the narcissist often presents the image of behind charming, well-loved, intelligent, successful, generous, and kind. However, in private, and often to the most intimate partner the narcissist has (whether it is a spouse or boyfriend or girlfriend), they are selfish, cruel, exploitative, rageful, abusive, demonstrate an irrational sense of entitlement, are lacking in empathy, and are prone to being unfaithful. They also manufacture situations where jealousy and insecurity is secretly provoked while outwardly disparaged to make the victim appear "crazy" and "needy."

I have dated and befriended narcissists from a wide variety of fields. The sociopathic social worker, the grandiose famous blogger, the disturbed award-winning director, the successful, contemptuous corporate attorney, the entitled programmer, the superficial banker - you name it, I've encountered it. These experiences were secret blessings, as they led me to research narcissistic personality disorder extensively both inside and outside of the classroom, as well as connect with the survivor community in life-changing ways. Due to the breadth of my real-life experiences with these predators, I've noticed the commonalities among them as well as the quiet nuances that someone who has only read about this disorder but has never encountered it in the flesh, may miss.

One thing I would like to note is that while the image of the self-assured, successful, powerful narcissist is popular in the corporate world, not *all* narcissists have reached their full potential in life. One misconception people have of narcissists is that they're all very successful people in power. However, that's not *always* true.

Narcissists come in all varieties and backgrounds. They could be powerful CEO's of companies who dominate the little people or they could be waiters at restaurants who create a harem through all the people they serve; they could live in mansions or at home with their parents. Some of them actually aren't very successful and have not achieved many of their goals – these are likely to be "vulnerable narcissists," though they can still put on an air of grandiosity to hide their feelings of failure (Kreger, 2012). Narcissists can lie anywhere on the spectrum of incredible success or incredible poverty.

Narcissists can also inhabit positions that are seemingly charitable and philanthropic. They can be in both helping professions (social workers or pastors at the church for example) as well as professions that are ideal for the narcissist to execute his or her power. Now, there *are* wonderful, validating and helpful counselors out there, but there are also counselors who abuse their power, just like in any other profession where power is granted. There are mental health professionals who have NPD and masquerade as caring, empathic people to gain supply from their clients. Unfortunately, abuse by a therapist is not uncommon, and it is likely that these professionals themselves suffer from NPD or ASPD. They misuse their power and abuse what is meant to be a validating, therapeutic alliance to provoke, taunt and manipulate the victim according to their agenda.

Regardless of their professional background, prestige or status, the majority of narcissists share a devastating lack of empathy, a grandiose sense of entitlement and an unwillingness to change their destructive behavior regardless of their station in life. This is what ultimately makes a relationship with them so damaging.

The Narcissist's False Self and True Self

The narcissist does not feel empathy for others; he or she makes connections with other people for one purpose and one purpose only: narcissistic supply. Narcissistic supply is the attention and admiration of the people the narcissist collects as trophies. It is anything that gives the narcissist a "hit" of praise, or even an emotional reaction to their ploys. They need these sources of supply because they suffer from perpetual boredom, emotional shallowness and the inability to authentically and emotionally connect to others who do have empathy.

A narcissist is prone to seeing you as an extension of himself or herself – a handbag or a piece of furniture rather than a complex individual with needs, wants and desires. While genuine, non-narcissistic people wish to connect to others on a deep emotional level, narcissists fear and are disgusted by intimacy because intimacy would expose their true self rather than the false self they project.

Narcissists, you see, lack empathy. They are unable to identify with the needs and feelings of others. They can "fake" emotions quite well, and are charming chameleons that adapt to what they perceive others want and need for them. They do so in order to get what they need and want – a harem, an audience, narcissistic supply in the form of attention, praise and superficial relationships which fulfill their need to be extolled while evading real intimacy.

This false self is a patchwork of different personas, qualities and traits they put together after years of learning to imitate other people as well as information from any media they observe. Narcissists have what we call "cold empathy" – they are able to intellectually understand why someone may feel what they do, but they do not truly feel the same remorse or shame that others do for harming others (Vaknin, 2012). They may appear remorseful or cry crocodile tears, but often it is when there is no other course of action to take to escape accountability for their actions.

However, narcissists do lure their victims with a *false* sense of intimacy and security early on in the relationship with this false mask. The majority of narcissists tend to be charming, charismatic and grandiose; they often have a magnetic pull that combines faux innocence with the seductive pull of "kindness" and edginess. Many of my coaching clients and readers note that it was the narcissist's devil-may-care attitude that first attracted them to the narcissist; many narcissists appear unfazed by emotions and many are bold in the way they interact with others while others may seem "off" or emotionally disconnected.

It is no surprise, then, that a recent study noted that females with more romantic experience and a desire for marriage actually preferred narcissistic personalities due to their charming personality, social status and resource provision (Haslam and Montrose 2015). These women had presumably encountered narcissists before and yet still wanted them as long-term partners! Despite their long-term destructive nature in relationships, narcissists can still appear to be desirable romantic partners and have a talent for projecting a sense of confidence and uniqueness that make them alluring to potential mates.

To the outside world, narcissists can appear incredibly generous, even spiritually minded, and humane. It is usually only to their closest and dearest, their victims, that their full-frontal cruelty is displayed. Much like sociopaths and psychopaths, narcissists hide behind this sweet, alluring, charming demeanor to hook their victims and escape accountability should they ever be threatened to be exposed – after all, who would believe the victim, if the perpetrator hides himself or herself in plain sight?

That is exactly how narcissists keep up the façade - the mean and sweet/hot and cold cycle of abuse wouldn't be as nearly traumatic without the incessant doubt about the narcissist's character - a doubt that is constantly reinforced every time we see their "nice" side and begin to wonder if we are the ones imagining things. The truth is, we're simply witnessing the narcissist's mask during the sweet periods and their true self during the dark ones.

Narcissists can fool anyone and everyone with their false mask – including highly educated, successful, confident and attractive individuals. Many intelligent people can be duped by narcissistic people, simply because they can't imagine someone deliberately manipulating and hurting others in the way that narcissistic or antisocial personalities are prone to doing. Let's get real: nobody wants to believe the person they care about is out to harm them - they'd prefer believing in the false mask because the alternative is too horrifying to consider.

It can take a great deal of time and effort before we can resolve the cognitive dissonance that this type of relationship evokes in us, as we are likely to develop conflicting beliefs, feelings and thoughts about an abusive partner who can switch masks so rapidly (Carver, 2004). Resolving our cognitive dissonance involves grounding ourselves in the reality of the abuse rather than engaging in the denial, minimization or rationalization of the abuse, which is inevitable in trauma bonding with our abusers.

The first truth that survivors must accept is that narcissists do not feel authentic empathy for their victims' emotions. The closest narcissists get to feeling anything is a "narcissistic injury," which is the rage and despair they feel when a person "critiques" them or poses a real or even false threat to their excessive sense of superiority and entitlement. This makes them scramble to protect their false selves even more... so to attempt to make them remorseful is a lost cause. They will always be protecting their true selves and this is why you can never win with the narcissist– they will always be defending the fortress of their false self.

How do narcissists get away with such shapeshifting? The truth is that narcissists can embody *multiple false selves* across various contexts and with different people in order to gain supply (praise, attention, money, sex, etc) from their audiences. They are also proficient at gaslighting and projection, techniques they use to convince society that their victims are the crazy ones and to convince their victims that their perception of reality is inaccurate.

Narcissists gaslight you so you begin to gaslight yourself into thinking what you are feeling, hearing, seeing and experiencing isn't true. A narcissistic partner can manipulate you into thinking that perhaps that hurtful comment really was just a joke and that their infidelity was just a one-time thing. Many of these partners engage in pathological lying and rewrite reality on a daily basis to suit their needs and to conceal their manipulative agenda.

It is no wonder, then, that victims of narcissistic abuse often feel very isolated and invalidated in their experiences. It is easy for narcissists to convince the outside world that they are the sane, rational ones: pathological narcissists enjoy calling anyone who challenges their self-perception "crazy." It's the word they'll use to describe any valid emotional reaction victims have to their shady and inconsistent behavior. It is gaslighting (invalidation of one's perception of reality) at its simplest form but over time becomes a complex type of psychological torture in which the victim starts to mistrust his or her perceptions of the covert abuse and feels unable to trust his or own reality.

Who Does the Narcissist Target?

Narcissists can target anyone and everyone for supply – so long as they have empathy. It does not matter how beautiful, brilliant, successful, likeable, funny, and strong you are – you can, in fact, still be duped by a narcissist, a sociopath or a psychopath because these people are wired differently and use manipulative tactics that are beyond our wildest imagination. Mental health professionals, especially couples' therapists who don't know much about narcissistic abuse, are fooled every day. Individuals with high levels of empathy tend to be targeted because the narcissist is able to appeal to their sympathy and good-hearted nature to continue engaging in the toxic relationship cycle.

In "Why Do Smart Women Date Abusive Men," survivor and writer Hayley Rose Horzepa notes that anyone who understands the dynamics of an abusive relationship knows that being with and staying with an abusive partner has little to do with intelligence. She notes that what makes victims susceptible to staying in an abusive relationship has more to do with their *vulnerability*, rather than intelligence – a vulnerability that can be exacerbated by past traumas and losses.

Counter to the typical stereotypes about abuse victims, research indicates that women who are employed are twice as likely to be victims of domestic violence than those who don't; in fact, women who get involved with disordered personalities can also be very independent and lead active lives (Franklin and Menaker, 2012; Brown, 2010). This is proven by countless public figures who have been domestic violence victims – women who were smart, talented and successful. Although the normative discourse is that these individuals had low self-esteem, the truth is that an abuser can also bring down someone from a place of high self-esteem and security – we'll discuss how later in this chapter.

This is not to dismiss or minimize anyone who has been with a narcissist and who feels dependent as a result, or feels they are, in fact, codependent, but it does reveal that our stereotypes of abuse survivors lack nuance, are outdated and need to be dismantled to include a wider variety of people who come from different backgrounds and have different personality traits than might be normally assumed or expected.

Narcissists do not choose us because we are like them; they choose us because we are the light to their darkness; regardless of any of our vulnerabilities, we exhibit the gorgeous traits of empathy, compassion, emotional intelligence and authentic confidence that their fragile egotism and false mask could never achieve.

While abuse survivors who have been traumatized before by child abuse are undoubtedly more susceptible to being re-traumatized, it's important to acknowledge that there are also survivors who were not traumatized in childhood that encountered narcissists, sociopaths and psychopaths, got hooked, and then were subsequently abused by them. I receive messages from abuse survivors all around the world who come from a variety of trauma histories.

Abuse survivors can come of *any type of background* and many of them are strong, intelligent, talented and successful. What puts them at risk is their empathy and their vulnerability – any cumulative trauma that has led them to have malleable boundaries and difficulties with self-esteem can certainly make individuals extra susceptible, but it has little to do with intelligence or strength and everything to do with the nature of the trauma they've endured – both within the abusive relationship and outside of it.

The Abuse Cycle: Idealize, Devalue, Discard, Destroy, Hoover

The abuse cycle with a narcissistic abuser includes an early idealization phase or honeymoon period, followed by an abusive incident or a series of abusive incidents before the cycle of idealization starts again, this time through the method of intermittent reinforcement which includes both devaluation of the victim as well as elements of excessive attention and adoration.

Narcissistic abusers first idealize their partners, flattering them excessively, giving them all sorts of attention in the form of constant texts and gifts. They share secrets and stories with you to create a special bond; this technique also enables you to feel as if you can share your deepest insecurities and desires with them. Later, they will use your disclosure as ammunition and pick at your weak spots to regain a sense of psychological control.

Yet it is during the honeymoon phase that these toxic partners reel you in and make you dependent upon them, hook, line and sinker. In a narcissist's idealization phase, you've never felt better: you feel beautiful, loved, cherished, and you feel like you've met your soulmate – this is a technique known widely in the survivor community as "love-bombing." In the love-bombing or idealization phase, narcissists mirror their victim's deepest values and interests to make them feel like they've met the "one."

The devaluation that follows, combined with periodic love-bombing, conditions the victim to walk on eggshells during a period of tension, hoping that the honeymoon period will last, only to inevitably experience yet another abusive incident that adds onto the cycle of trauma. Narcissistic abusers rely on the victim's need for validation and approval, as well as the sense of worthlessness they've instilled in them throughout the abuse cycle, to remain dependent on their abusers.

These abusers will give you just the minimum amount of attention to keep you by their side, wishing you could go back to the idealization phase. As the abuse gets incrementally worse, the abuse victim gets more and more conditioned to the abuse and invested in the abusive relationship due to the biochemical and trauma bonds I'll discuss in Chapter 2.

While there is no time limit as to how long the cycle can continue, victims are likely to be discarded at some point, especially if they become aware of the narcissist's schemes or if they leave the narcissist themselves, although they are sometimes manipulated back into the relationship or quickly replaced with another source of supply.

Much like other survivors of narcissistic abuse, the pattern in my relationship with a narcissistic abuser went something like this: a period of sweet, excessive idealization which served as the honeymoon phase, where I was properly "groomed," complimented, flattered, placed on a pedestal, followed by incidents of devaluation littered throughout the idealization phase. I say littered because many covert narcissists are incredibly strategic about how they choose to devalue – they may leave essential clues and red flags throughout even the idealization phase, because they know you won't catch on; you'll mistake their rudeness as awkward openness or constructive criticism; you'll be tempted to exorcise the abuser inside of them and rescue them from their misconceptions of you.

Narcissists are covert, underhanded and incredibly manipulative in the way they devalue their victims. They target both your insecurities as well as what you're most proud of. It's a mix of both; if you tell them what you're most insecure about, they'll make sure to sneak in a cutting remark at some point about it. If you tell them what you're most proud of accomplishing, they'll find ways to diminish your pride and make you feel as if you're not special – because, of course, only they are allowed to be special and unique.

This devaluation could be disguised as harsh "jokes," or "brutal honesty," when they in fact involved verbal abuse, name-calling, condescending sarcasm, a sudden withdrawal of affection, overt or covert put-downs or unhealthy comparisons to others to instill a sense of worthlessness. The devaluation can also be overt and heinous. In my own experiences, during more overt, full-fledged devaluing explosions, there was often a verbally and emotionally abusive argument that would last for hours, followed by false remorse and a glimpse of the narcissist's sweet false self to pull me back in.

The cycle repeated over again until the temporary "discard," where the narcissistic abuser would abandon me through narcissistic rage and stonewalling if confronted, only to reappear again through "hoovering," a tactic in which the abuser attempts to regain control over the victim by pretending he or she has changed. The final discard, of course, gave me the opportunity to go full No Contact with the abuser and end the cycle.

The narcissistic abuse cycle is difficult for survivors to extricate themselves from due to the immense amount of gaslighting, projection and psychological manipulation involved. Abusers are able to convince their victims that the abuse they are suffering isn't real, leading them to deny or minimize the abuse. They may even convince their victim that the abuse is their fault by projecting their own flaws onto their victims or making the strengths of the victim appear to be weaknesses.

Victims are then mislead into thinking that the abusive incidents are just "misunderstandings," and that the hot and cold behavior is due to something the victim did. Unfortunately, for narcissists and their conscience-lacking cousins, those with antisocial personalities, the intent and pathology behind these actions are much more malicious, much more harmful and goes deeper than we'll ever realize.

Survivors spend a lifetime waiting - waiting for their abusers to change, waiting for their kindness to turn into cruelty, waiting for the next blow or hit in an attempt to avoid it or escape it, waiting for the right time to end the relationship. It is only when they stop waiting and start walking away that they begin to process what they've escaped and begin a journey back to wholeness. It is challenging to walk away, even more difficult to heal, but more than possible with the right resources and support.

Devaluation and Discard

It won't take long before the narcissist begins to devalue you in the abuse cycle; they will put you down in subtle as well as blatant ways to instill a pervasive sense of worthlessness in you, throwing you off the pedestal without so much as a second glance. Psychologists speculate that narcissists engage in devaluation of their partners because while they rely on their partner's ability to enhance their own self-esteem and bolster their sense of false superiority in the beginning, the partner inevitably becomes "real" and "imperfect" to them throughout the course of the relationship because they are less likely to see the narcissist as perfect (Campbell, 1999).

A victim's plea for the abuser to acknowledge his or her emotional needs is presumably one that the narcissist perceives as a narcissistic injury, and indeed, this causes what Kohut (1972) calls "narcissistic rage," a reaction to the perceived challenge to the perfect image the narcissist cultivated of themselves in the idealization phase.

Remember that the narcissist may fake compassion, use pity ploys, demonstrate support and understanding in order to get on your good side and convince you he/she is your match in life. While the narcissist is idealizing you, in essence, you are idealizing them. When they revert back to their true colors, or when their mask slips, and you begin to question their behaviors, they will demean you in an effort to salvage the illusion of their false self.

During the hot and cold phases, there may be "hot" periods of support with many "cold" periods of stonewalling, ridiculing and belittling. Here is a classic example from a reader of how devaluation can happen in small, covert ways:

"I fell in love with a narcissist, and it has been the hardest thing I've ever had to go through. He fell in love with me too. I thought he was the man I was going to marry. I do believe he was actually in love with me, but I guess narcissists can only love someone else for so long until their need for newness, attention, and admiration kicks in...but only from other people (being a male nurse in a predominately female atmosphere does not help.) We haven't been together for 4 months now, but I still miss him and get that feeling of dread. I don't want to miss him, but I do. I don't want to love him, but I do. We also work at the same hospital together and I just found out he's dating someone. I don't know why it kills me, but it does.

Your article, "Five Powerful Ways Abusive Narcissists Get Inside Your Head," was scarily accurate.

I guess now I'm struggling with my confidence because he made it seem like it was ME/MY faults when in reality it was HIM. I know this in my head but it still gets to me. It was so intensely passionate in the beginning, but then the whole withdrawing thing happened. He would back away and act like I was being "needy." He made me feel unwanted and wanted at the same time...and after we actually broke up 1 1/2 years into the actual relationship, it became 1 1/2 years of the back and forth game. He'd disappear for a couple weeks and then come running back for me...but, silly me, I'd finally get to trust him again, and then he'd pull right back. It was ridiculous. I guess I don't understand how someone can literally have no remorse, emotion, etc. towards others.

He would tell me things like, "you're not really that outgoing," "you don't really talk that much," "I'm just bored," "I hope one day my wife is like this _____ (fill in the blank)," "I need someone who challenges me," "I just don't know what I want," and my favorite, "I just don't want to settle" like he would be settling for me if he stayed with me. Little comments that, when repeated, can start making the other person believe they are true. When I confronted him about these comments and how rude they were, he would tell me how overly sensitive I was. But then he'd do a 180 and tell me how much he missed me and how much he thought about me and wanted to be with me.

Now that he's dating someone I'm left with these horrible thoughts in my head thinking that I'm not "good enough." Like I said, I know he is the problem, but I'm having a really hard time controlling my thoughts. I'm left with the emotional baggage feeling depressed, angry, frustrated...It is so irritating to me when people comment on how sweet, handsome, honest, and funny he is. He can be, but that's his game. He puts a front on so no one sees who he really is on the inside, and it really irks me.

I'm not the first girl he has done this to, and I know I won't be the last. Hell, he even is like this with his friends...he just does not care.

It still doesn't make me feel any better. I guess what I'm trying to ask is how can I stop obsessing over him? Do you have certain methods/techniques to help me control the negative thoughts in my head? I do catch myself asking if I'm "outgoing" enough, "challenging" enough, "pretty" enough, "spiritual" enough, etc... It honestly just sucks. I know I'm great the way I am, but the emotional abuse lingers on. Thanks for listening."

As you can see from this example, narcissists can conduct this devaluation in a chronic, covert way, in a way that can escape your notice. They will plant seeds in your mind in the hopes that they will become fully germinated ideas about your lack of self-worth. They will tell harsh "jokes" that are actually cruel insults they can say without consequences. They will call you names and criticize your every move. They will flirt behind your back and in front of your face. They will disappear and subject you to silent treatments, both randomly and at opportune moments where you're seeking to hold them accountable for their inconsistent, shady behavior. They will engage in a technique known as "triangulation," where they use the presence of another person as a way to make you jealous and make themselves seem more desirable.

These people can be anyone – from waitresses or waiters at restaurants to close friends of the opposite sex, even people from your own family or even their own family – that's how sick narcissists can get, because they have no boundaries. Whoever it is, they will make sure that they've charmed them and they will make sure you see it or hear about it. They love to play games and make you feel like you're in competition for their affection and attention.

When you complain or bring up any behavior that makes you feel uncomfortable, narcissists will call you "crazy" or "sensitive." They will stonewall you and abruptly end arguments, subjecting you to the silent treatment for hours, even days and in some extreme cases, months. They will invalidate your emotions and gaslight you to the point where you really do feel like you're crazy. You will doubt yourself and apologize even when you have nothing to apologize for. You will find yourself trying to teach a grown man or woman the basic rules of respect.

It is important to recognize that the narcissist constructs a false, dark alternate reality in which he hands over his pathology to you. You will be labeled the crazy, oversensitive person throughout the relationship even while enduring mind-blowing verbal and emotional attacks from your abuser. The abuser enjoys employing gaslighting and projection techniques to essentially rewrite the history of abuse in the relationship and misplace all blame onto you. Since you are prone to cognitive dissonance, you will often start to blame yourself for the abuse and seek to deny or minimize the severity of the trauma you're experiencing in an effort to survive and cope with the fact that the person you love and care for is a pathological abuser.

After the devaluation phase, you will be discarded, often in the worst manner possible. Discarded is the term we use for when the narcissistic gets tired of his current supply and often moves onto his next one. During the discard, the narcissist is done with you, so there will be no emotional support, much less any form of closure or attempt at making you feel better about the discard.

Narcissists want you to feel so small that they will perform the discard in the worst way to make you feel less than human and less than worthy. It is often during the devaluation and discard phases that victims of narcissistic abuse are most humiliated and degraded. This is a way for the narcissist to prove to himself or herself that you are no longer necessary in their life, because in their perspective, you have not "met" their needs as a source of supply who can endlessly cater to their false image despite subjecting you to emotional and possibly even physical beatings.

Believe it or not, a horrific discard by a narcissistic partner is in fact a traumatic event because it challenges everything we know to be normal. Much like when we experience physical pain, the brain releases pain-killing opioids when we experience rejection (Hsu et. al, 2013). Rejection literally hurts! Imagine how much it hurts, then, to have someone who once seemingly adored you, devalue and discard you and, even worse, abuse you horrifically before they throw you away like nothing ever happened. A discard in itself is a traumatic event, but the numerous microaggressions, rejections and abuses throughout the relationship created a chain of traumatic events, and it is that chain of trauma that makes it so very difficult to recover from being involved with a narcissist.

Hoovering

Many victims, but not all victims, experience an additional phase of the abuse cycle after the discard known as "hoovering." This is when the narcissist, like a Hoover vacuum, attempts to suck you back into the traumatic vortex of the relationship. Usually this occurs when the narcissist loses control of the victim and wants to regain control at the very moment the victim attempts to move forward with his or her life. They begin to "re-idealize" their former partner and the relationship, while devaluing any current relationship they have.

Hoovering has no time limit or boundaries; narcissists have been known to hoover old victims when they are newly married, have children, or years later, unexpectedly. It gives them a thrill to know that their old sources of supply are ready and waiting in case they decide to swoop in for a temporary rendezvous and re-traumatization before exiting their lives yet again.

The "hoover" may come in a phone call, an e-mail, a text, or even showing up at the victim's house. It can also take place through the messenger work of a third party. Hoovering on a smaller scale is integrated throughout the abuse cycle after devaluation, as well, but usually that is when the victim is still within the relationship as opposed to out of it. After the discard phase, hoovering confuses victims into thinking the narcissist misses them, when in reality, the narcissist employs hoovering as a way to regain power and control, especially if the victim "discarded" the narcissist first. This method enables the abuse cycle to continue, especially if the victim is susceptible to their hoovering attempts.

Victim-Blaming and Stereotypes About Narcissistic Abuse

Society is just beginning to understand what narcissistic abuse is and how it differs from a normal relationship. Thankfully, mental health professionals like psychotherapist Christine Louis de Canonville, Ross Rosenberg, LCPC, Michelle Mallon, LSW, Shannon Thomas, LCSW and Andrea Schneider, LCSW are now exploring what it means to be narcissistically abused and how it affects survivors of abuse through Narcissistic Victim Syndrome. Many of these professionals are training other clinicians about this pandemic.

Survivors are also sharing their stories, writing books, creating YouTube channels, and starting support groups of their own. Survivors and mental health practitioners are both participating in the revolution to shed light on emotional and psychological abuse and its damaging effects, but this is just the beginning. Victim-blaming stereotypes still abound. Not every mental health professional knows about this form of abuse, and some victims themselves are prone to blaming themselves for the abuse. We need more education, knowledge and dialogue on this topic in order to dissolve the barriers that are hindering victims from getting the support they need.

To outsiders who have never experienced this form of abuse, narcissistic abuse appears to be an elusive phenomenon to grasp. Let's be clear about this: narcissistic abuse is not about an oversensitivity to the normal ups and downs of relationships, nor is it a complaint about incompatibility or mere emotional unavailability in relationships. All narcissists, sociopaths and psychopaths are emotionally unavailable, but not all emotionally unavailable people are narcissists, sociopaths and psychopaths. The difference lies in their intention to harm, their inability to change and their sadistic nature.

The abuse described here in this book is not a matter of everyday envy, anger or healthy conflict that eventually leads to resolution and growth in a relationship. Rather, it is a matter of a person with a real-life personality disorder subjecting a victim to extreme, chronic devaluation, control, sabotage and disrespect. It is also not a matter that can be "worked" out, as narcissists are not willing to change because their manipulative behavior rewards them.

If you have experienced the deliberate cruelty of a narcissistic abuser (as in, they fed off your pain and would make sure to provoke you where it hurt) through the techniques I've described combined with a lack of empathy, it is likely that your partner is on the narcissistic spectrum. If on the other hand, if you feel this partner had the ability to empathize but simply did not want a close relationship, it could be emotional unavailability. These people can be downright scary and dangerous. If forced to choose between the two, many survivors would prefer to encounter a regular emotionally unavailable person over a full-fledged narcissist any day. The former is undoubtedly painful, but the latter is inevitably harmful.

Whether this partner had the full-fledged personality disorder is difficult to say without learning the partner's full spectrum of behavior, which is often observed throughout the course of a very intimate, long-term relationship, although it can surface sooner. Many outsiders do not know who a narcissistic partner is behind the mask because they never get close enough to them for them to uncover the mask through devaluation and discard.

What you may have experienced can be just a brief portrait of this person, which means there can be something much deeper beneath the surface - the ways in which narcissists act in long-term, romantic relationships can be different from short-term ones, as the long-term relationship partner is often subject to a horrific cycle of abuse, while the short-term one can also have horrific abuse but the cycle is cut thankfully short before the victim can live through the full, prolonged nightmare.

A common victim-shaming stereotype is that "now everyone thinks their partner is a narcissist." It's true that the term is entering the public discourse and I am sure there are some people who have been applying the term liberally – that is true of *any word* in society and culture. We certainly don't want to depict everyone with the label of malignant narcissist. However, the idea that everyone who claims to be a victim of narcissistic abuse is merely hiding behind the label of "narcissistic abuse" to blame their partners or escape accountability can be very damaging to real victims who are finally beginning to speak out.

Real victims of emotional and psychological abuse usually do not shirk responsibility – they are often the ones asking, "Is it me? Is this my fault?" when they are coming out of the situation. Many of them don't even share their stories with their loved ones because they fear looking "crazy." I know this not only from speaking with survivors but also from coaching clients who have been through some of the most horrific abuse you can imagine. Their lives have been ruined by their abusers and their self-esteem has taken a severe hit. They have been financially exhausted, spiritually shaken, emotionally bankrupt and physically depleted by the long-lasting effects of this form of abuse. Since their predators tend to be charming and covert, they usually find themselves feeling further alienated and isolated by their communities.

They are confused, ashamed, hurt, and broken by the abuse they've experienced, and for victim-shaming people to dismiss them and tell them that they are imagining the verbal, emotional, at times even physical abuse they're experiencing, is a dual traumatization. Not only are they being gaslighted by their abuser, they are being gaslighted by society. There is a clear difference between your average jerk and a malignant narcissist, but victims of narcissistic abuse *know* and have experienced that distinction firsthand.

To any survivor who may be doubting whether what they've experienced is truly abuse, remember that emotional, verbal and psychological abuse will never be, and should never be, considered part of the messy equation of a normal relationship. As both mental health professionals and survivors can attest to, the traumatic highs and lows of being with a narcissist, a sociopath or a psychopath are not the normal highs and lows of regular relationships. That suggestion is quite damaging to society and to survivors all around the world.

Are Narcissists Victims?

Some people wonder, "Well, aren't narcissists just as much victims as the victims of their abuse?" The answer is a loud, resounding *no*. The victims of narcissistic abuse do not go out of their way to smear a narcissist's name, devalue them or harm them for a thrill. The narcissist does and often succeeds in destroying many facets of a victim's life without any empathy and very little remorse. Survivors collectively suffer a great deal more from the projections of the narcissist than the narcissist ever has in his or her original "narcissistic wound," if such a wound exists. While some narcissists may be children of trauma, others are notorious for lying about childhood abuse, trauma and illnesses, so that many times, we cannot take them at face value.

Additionally, as discussed previously about the origins of NPD, while there are clinical theories about why NPD arises in an individual, there is actually still no definitive answer for the cause of this disorder - whether it be trauma, or overvaluation by a parent of the child. I have personally seen both: incidents where a narcissistic predator did seem to come from a traumatic background, and other incidents where a narcissist was severely spoiled by their family members.

We still do not know for certain what causes this disorder, so we cannot assume that *every* narcissist is a child of trauma. There may be narcissists who are taught a sense of entitlement by having everything handed to them in childhood, which is another plausible theory. Many personality disorders arise from complex interactions between biological predisposition and environment.

If narcissists are victims of any form of childhood abuse, they should be actively seeking professional help, which a large majority of them do not because their behavior rewards their sense of entitlement and superiority. Victims of narcissistic abuse do not use their traumatic experiences as excuses to abuse others; many of them are the ones who end up getting professional help precisely because they wish to heal their wounds and not take out these wounds on others. It bears repeating that full-fledged narcissists, on the other hand, tend to the manipulate their therapist, drop out of therapy due to narcissistic injury and refuse to acknowledge areas of self-improvement.

Does Mental Illness or Addiction Excuse Their Abuse?

Since NPD is a personality disorder, others may wonder why we are holding these types of abusers accountable for their abuse. After all, why should someone be held accountable for their illness? I believe it is counterproductive to compare NPD to mental illnesses like schizophrenia, as many self-professed narcissists such as Sam Vaknin and sociopaths like M.E. Thomas do admit to enjoying the damage they do to others and feeling a sense of control/power when they do inflict that damage. These are two different conditions that should not be compared.

Narcissists and sociopaths are aware of their actions and the impact of their actions – we know this not only from the voices of narcissists and sociopaths themselves but also in the way they smear their victims and the various methods they use to escape accountability such as gaslighting and projection. *You cannot plot to blame someone else for your actions if you are not aware of your own blame and are attempting to escape exposure.* You also cannot switch your mask rapidly from the true self to the false self when there is a witness if your behavior is not under your conscious control.

In addition, even if a narcissist does not feel remorse for their actions, remember that their victims often plead with them to behave more kindly. Rather than at least take in this feedback, which they are perfectly capable of doing, they continue these behaviors even more maliciously. They could easily spend that same energy owning up to their actions and seeking to change positively - but they do not have any sense of empathy towards their victims and therefore, do not care.

Narcissistic abuse is calculating, deliberate and designed to harm victims. An excellent book I recommend for all survivors is Dr. Simon's *In Sheep's Clothing* (2010) which dismantles this harmful stereotype that we should feel sympathy for our abusers to the point where we allow them to manipulate us - it is that sympathy that they take advantage of to harm us further. In addition, a victim who recognizes and identifies the abusive tactics is calling out the abuse as they should. Abuse is not a nuanced issue, it is abuse, and there are no excuses for emotional or physical abuse, including addiction or NPD.

I believe there is also a difference between an addict who has become dependent on his or her addiction and a *narcissistic abuser who uses alcohol and/or other substances as a means to abuse and escape accountability* - this means that their substance use is comorbid and co-exists with their narcissism. Many survivors meet narcissistic partners who used alcohol or drugs as an excuse to engage in verbal and psychological abuse. Narcissists can abuse drugs in order to fill the void and perpetual boredom and numbness they feel. The difference lies in whether the abuser carries out their manipulative behavior and self-centeredness outside of his/her addiction, and narcissists most certainly do.

I want to stress that there *are* people with legitimate addictions to alcohol and they need help, support and compassion. What's important to remember is that *there are many people who abuse alcohol or other drugs but do not abuse others when they do.* Those who abuse alcohol and abuse others are often the ones who are using their addiction as an excuse to hurt others without having to be held accountable for the abuse they dish out while under the influence.

The truth of the matter is, curing a narcissist of his or her addiction will not cure his or her lack of empathy. Lundy Bancroft, author of *Why Does He Do That?: Inside the Minds of Angry and Controlling Men* (2013) confirms this from his own professional experience. Bancroft worked with many abusive partners who still made conscious decisions while abusing substances. Their abusive behavior also continued outside of their substance abuse, even if it was in more covert and subtle ways.

It is not a distinction that's discussed often enough, but the overlap between substance abuse and narcissism must be discussed because victims may stay in relationships with narcissists if they are addicted to something, believing that if they help the narcissist cure his or her addiction, they will help to resolve the abuse. Nothing could be farther from the truth. So be very careful if you're dating someone with signs of both narcissism and substance abuse – especially if they're not willing to get treatment.

I applaud anyone who has NPD and who seeks help and treatment (often these are people on the lower end of the NPD spectrum), but many full-fledged narcissists do not, and continue to hurt others to gain supply. Their lack of willingness to seek treatment is intrinsic to their disorder. Due to this, victims should be on the lookout for these types of abusive behaviors because more often than not, the abuser is unlikely to change.

To read more about the distinctions between mental illness and abuse, addiction and abuse, as well as the myth of "mutual abuse," see the following articles by the National Domestic Violence Hotline.

The National DV Hotline Links

The Myth of Mutual Abuse by Jessica R.
http://www.thehotline.org/2016/01/myth-of-mutual-abuse/

Why We Don't Recommend Couples' Counseling for Abusive Relationships by B. Rollings
http://www.thehotline.org/2014/08/why-we-dont-recommend-couples-counseling-for-abusive-relationships/

Drugs, Alcohol and Abuse by B. Rollings
http://www.thehotline.org/2015/03/drugs-alcohol-and-abuse/

Blame-shifting and Minimizing: There's No Excuse for Abuse by Kathryn Robinson
http://www.thehotline.org/2014/01/blame-shifting-and-minimizing-theres-no-excuse-for-abuse/

Abuse and Mental Illness: Is there a Connection?
http://www.thehotline.org/2015/05/abuse-and-mental-illness-is-there-a-connection/

Should We Feel Compassion for the Narcissist?

Survivors are often asked to coddle abusers and police how they speak about the abuse they experienced, as well as how they talk about their abuser. We are taught that we should not blame the abuser because "their childhood trauma" made them do it, their "addiction" made them do it, their "brain is just wired differently." I am not attempting to invalidate anyone's experience of trauma or the effects of trauma as I know from personal experience how much of an impact trauma, particularly chronic trauma, has on a person.

However, I can tell you, from speaking with thousands of survivors throughout my lifetime, that many of these trauma survivors were afraid to become abusers themselves and were extremely careful about their behavior. They would often reach out to me, scared that their abusers had rubbed off on them, when in reality, they were coming to terms with the legitimate anger they felt at the injustice of their abusers and consciously made efforts to be self-aware of any maladaptive behaviors. They were kind, compassionate, incredible individuals who wanted to make sure they didn't take out their wounds on others and were introspective to a fault – I often had to guide them gently away from self-blame.

So what I *am* invalidating is this idea that any of these reasons somehow makes the abuse okay or that abusers should be let off the hook. They are still responsible for their behavior and they are still responsible not only for acknowledging the damage that their behavior had on their victims but also to make committed actions to change. We forget that abusers have free will and can at the very least, intellectually process right from wrong, see the victim's pain at the various behaviors they engage in and get support to change those behaviors – regardless of whether or not they have any disorder or a past history of trauma.

The more we justify any form of abuse, rationalize it, minimize it, or attribute it to anything other than the abuser, we fail to support the victims who actually need our compassion and empathy. We cannot expect change in any society where an abuser is not held accountable for his or her actions.

The cycle of misplaced shame goes like this: 1) A victim is abused, and tries to speak about the abuse. 2) Society attempts to silence, blame and shame him/her for the abuse and speaking out. 3) The victim is left feeling further alienated and unsupported, while the abuser is free to continue to abuse without any accountability. Throughout this book, you'll find that I don't engage in frills or justifications, even if I do contextualize abusive behavior or discuss the nuances among different disorders. I won't feed into this blameshifting, minimization or denial of the impact of abuse. Abusers and victim-blamers have been getting away with this discourse for way too long. I am here to support survivors and place the shame where it really belongs - on their abusers.

We are empathic beings, which means that some survivors may feel pity or compassion for their narcissistic abuser. This is an individual decision and not one that other survivors or non-survivors should police. If you wish to feel compassion for your abuser, please be sure that you are putting your own self-compassion first and not using your compassion to release your abuser from accountability or using that compassion as an excuse to prolong the relationship. If you do not understand this predatory personality and seek to sympathize with them more than you are detaching from them, rest assured that there will be harm done. This type of manipulation is cruel and the trauma can last a lifetime.

In society, there are victim-blaming individuals who will try to shame abuse survivors into feeling compassion for their abuser. If you want to feel compassion towards your abuser or forgive your abuser, that is your choice. However, please do not force other survivors to feel a certain way towards their abuser because this is re-traumatizing. Survivors have been taught their entire lives to feel, think and act in a certain way due to the controlling behavior of their abusers – the last thing they need is other people in society, survivors and non-survivors, to compel them to feel a certain way.

I also do not subscribe to the idea that an abuser and victim are equally at fault for abuse, nor will I ever subscribe to that idea. This idea of "co-creating" abuse, while empowering for some, to me personally feels dangerous and verges on victim-blaming. I understand that when writers speak about "co-creating," they often encourage us to address our own wounding and perform inner work to address unhealthy relationship patterns if we have a pattern of tethering ourselves to toxic people. I fully agree with this assessment, but I think there is another way "co-creating" can be used in a spiritual or victim-blaming perspective and that is the perspective I do not agree with.

Survivors can certainly look within to ensure they are maintaining a healthy relationship with themselves. However, regardless of past wounding, we cannot truly and fully "co-create" anything in a relationship that has a dysfunctional power imbalance. Especially one in which the narcissist controls, brainwashes and abuses the survivor. As I will discuss in Chapter 8, there is a distinction between victim-blaming and owning our agency.

I hear survivors blame themselves for not knowing better, but the truth is how could you have known with a convincing false mask? And what decent human being would suspect such malice? Once we have woken up to the fact that there are people who may lack empathy or a conscience, only then do we stop projecting our own capacity for compassion onto them. Remember that a victim does not get involved with an abuser because she or he knows that person is a narcissist - he or she falls for the false mask, which is only uncovered once the victim has developed an emotional and psychological investment in the relationship.

This creates trauma and biochemical bonds which I'll discuss in Chapter 2, that keep the victim tethered to the abuser. What society still fails to understand is that an abusive relationship like this literally reshapes and rewires the brain, making it difficult to heal from the narcissistic abuse cycle. A survivor of this type of trauma needs a great deal of support, validation, knowledge and resources to move forward. An abuser is in fact fully responsible for his or her actions and should be held fully accountable.

As to the question whether the victim can become abusive, we have to be careful about distinguishing between reactions to abuse and abusive behavior. A survivor who goes No Contact with his or her abuser, for example, is not engaging in stonewalling. They are engaging in self-care. Reactions caused by chronic abuse are not the same thing as "mutual abuse" – they are maladaptive coping mechanisms to survive in an abusive environment. In some cases, they are also self-defense.

Victims *should* own their agency by arming themselves with the knowledge of these abusive tactics, professional support and the appropriate self-care to heal from the abuse, but they are not responsible for the pathology of another person.

Simultaneous Wounding and Complex PTSD: How Our Past Wounds Can Make Us Susceptible to Toxic Narcissists

Spiritual communities may convince us that the wounds the narcissist brings up are only our wounds, that there is something within in us that needs to be healed, lest we attract more narcissists into our lives. Victim-blamers take it one step further by dismissing the abuse and holding only the victim accountable for falling for the narcissist, dismissing the fact that victims do not fall for the narcissist, they fall for the narcissist's false mask. If you've been a victim of chronic abuse, please know it is not your fault that you are traumatized, nor are you in any way less deserving of love and respect. It is not your fault that you were traumatized and it is certainly not your fault if you are retraumatized. We can own our agency and power in healing ourselves while still remaining compassionate towards ourselves and not blaming ourselves for the pathology of others.

The oversimplification that toxic partners only bring up what already exists for us internally ignores a great deal of the complexity involved in how toxic partners can weave a manipulative web that connects both past and present experiences. The idea that narcissists only bring up our own wounds falls short of explaining how they also manufacture new ones. This is what I've dubbed "simultaneous wounding" – a term that encompasses the complex nature of how narcissists can bring up past wounds, reinforce them and also manufacture new wounds simultaneously by projecting onto us *their* own wounds.

Narcissists and sociopaths not only bring up past wounds – they compound them and add onto them, creating a chronic chain of stressors that can even result in Complex PTSD, the symptoms of which can include the regular symptoms of PTSD as well as toxic shame, emotional flashbacks, and a never-ending inner critic that diminishes us and demeans us (Walker, 2013). I talk more about this relationship between narcissistic abuse and Complex PTSD in the second chapter.

On my YouTube channel and blog, I discuss how our childhood experiences of not feeling heard, seen, loved and validated can condition us to accept less – while also asking for more. Although anyone can be a victim of love-bombing, the excessive attention a narcissist uses to manipulate us in the idealization phase of a relationship can hook survivors even more strongly when they are being re-traumatized by their need for unconditional positive regard and validation, something they may have never had in childhood. This enables the trauma repetition cycle to become strengthened, so that we are encountering what I call "trauma upon trauma," making it difficult for survivors of chronic abuse to break the cycle. There are also biochemical and trauma bonds involved that feed the addictive cycle we have to disrupt in order to regain our sense of agency, power and control which I will discuss more in-depth in the second chapter.

Due to past experiences of trauma, we can be extra susceptible to the love-bombing and idealization of a narcissist because we have more reason to seek that validation we did not gain in our past experiences. When a toxic person love-bombs us and later devalues us, it results in the reinforcing of those wounds as well as new emotional injuries that maim us. This makes the injury all the more entrenched and painful for survivors to detach from.

In addition to the severe pain survivors experience as a result, toxic shame and self-blame are symptoms of the trauma we've experienced. Victims have been led to blame themselves for the abuse and the current victim-blaming stance in society does not help that. The fact of the matter is, while narcissists prey on the wounds of individuals, they are also very attracted to the strengths of those individuals. They enjoy surrounding themselves with people who are unique and special (in fact, that is part of their diagnostic criteria!) As I mentioned earlier, survivors are not necessarily the meek, codependent personalities society assumes they must be – rather, they can be incredibly driven, independent, and have high compassion and empathy which enables them to stay within these toxic relationships far past the expiration date.

Regardless of what our vulnerabilities and wounds are, we do not deserve to be abused or mistreated. Being a trauma survivor does not mean we deserve extra wounding or that we ask for it – quite the contrary. It makes the person who is attempting to wound us by using our past wounds all the more sick for doing so. Blaming an abuse survivor would be similar to blaming a rape victim for being raped – and due to the nature of the biochemical and trauma bonds that form in an abusive relationship, there are actual changes in the brain and in the body that tether victims to their abusers (we will discuss how in Chapter 3). We do not fall for the narcissist – we fall for the person they pretend to be. There are many survivors who are able to run quickly in the other direction when they interact with overt narcissists, but the problem is that there are many covert narcissists, sociopaths and psychopaths who manipulate and deceive individuals very well, deceiving even the most intelligent and competent mental health professionals.

Another common victim-blaming assertion in the survivor community is the idea that victims must be like narcissists in some way in order to have these toxic people in their lives. What many people forget is that a narcissist could never be with someone like them – they would eventually find it just as despicable and frustrating as we find them. They do not wish to be with someone who displays no emotion or has no empathy like them – that would be no fun for them. They need someone with empathy, with compassion, with insight (so they can manipulate the insight to cater to them – ex. convincing a very introspective individual that the abuse is their fault) They need someone with the willingness to see good in others – they are attracted to talent, to strength, to "special and unique." Simultaneously, they are pathologically envious of our amazing qualities – because these are the very qualities they will attempt to destroy throughout the course of an intimate relationship. You cannot seek to destroy what was never there and narcissists seek to destroy these qualities because they do, in fact, exist.

While I do believe childhood abuse can make us extra susceptible to gravitating towards abusive partners in adulthood, that does not mean victims deserve this abuse or are in any way asking for it. Truly, *anyone* with empathy can be a victim of narcissistic abuse, especially if they have something special in them which narcissists tend to target. Do not let any ignorant person convince you that you are at fault for abuse. It is the abuser's fault alone. Even if you have been traumatized in the past and find yourself gravitating towards that type of individual, that does NOT make it okay for you to be abused. Instead of focusing on the victim, it's time to focus on the perpetrator who would actually prey on these types of traumatic wounding to manipulate victims who are already hurting. These are the people who are truly sick, not the person who is seeking to form a loving relationship.

No one deserves to be abused, bullied or mistreated. We can own our agency in changing our lives and perform inner work, set better boundaries and rework our relationship patterns without blaming ourselves for the abuse. Healing from narcissistic abuse or a lifetime of trauma requires that we unravel and heal both types of wounds layered upon one another – both past and present.

The Narcissist's False Mask Gaslights the Public, Enabling the Abuse to Continue

Now, if you've been discarded by the narcissist, count yourselves lucky. There are people out there still married to their narcissists and have to raise children with them. There are people out there who still don't know who the narcissist truly is...but they will during the devaluation and discard phase. Those who serve as the narcissist's supply often do not know who the real person is behind the mask the narcissist creates.

Remember: you didn't either. In fact, if you've ever been discarded after being in a relationship with a narcissist, you'll probably realize that your partner's friends and family are on his or her side no matter what. Some of your own friends and family members may even be gaslighted successfully. This is because the narcissist has convincingly portrayed his or her false self to them and has made you out to be the crazy one.

The truth is, narcissists don't just gaslight us – they gaslight the public too. Their charming exterior convinces the public to shame and silence victims who speak out against them. In society and culture, pathological narcissists and sociopaths like serial rapists can get away with their crimes because society bashes and bullies victims who dare to speak out against them, especially if they are well-loved figures such as Bill Cosby.

Many narcissists cry crocodile tears, fake remorse for their misdeeds, and can be easily forgiven by society. Any slipping of their masks, any risk of their exposure, is often swept under the rug while the stories of their victims continue to be silenced and degraded. It can take years and multiple victim accounts to attain justice. Meanwhile, their victims are often alienated, shamed and blamed for speaking out in the first place.

Narcissists and sociopaths can also hide themselves in helping professions to extract narcissistic supply, so be wary of anyone who attempts to overstep your boundaries or exhibits the red flags discussed in this book. Just because someone is a licensed professional or has a certain status or prestige does not make them exempt from having a personality disorder or from having narcissistic traits themselves. In fact, there are many narcissists and sociopaths who pretend to help victims in the Narcissistic Abuse Survivor community while extracting supply: be selective about the support you surround yourself with and be wary of any individual who exhibits narcissistic rage or engages in cyberbullying and/or plagiarism.

This book is not about promoting passivity with a narcissist. You are certainly encouraged to press charges against anyone who has assaulted you and has committed a crime against you. This includes getting an order of protection if your narcissistic abuser is stalking and harassing you, and you feel this is a safe action to take in your particular circumstances.

While I don't recommend seeking revenge or starting a smear campaign against a narcissist, you *can* speak out against injustice in productive ways that don't violate your values and are aligned with the law. Just be very careful because narcissists can fool the courts easily. Here is a list of attorneys in the USA that are familiar with narcissistic personality disorder: https://onemomsbattle.com/resources-attorneys/.

The most challenging part of the smear campaign from a narcissist and the narcissist's ability to depict the victim as the abuser, is that we cannot control the extent to which people believe it. We gain the most power when we seek our own validation, as difficult as it may be. Attempting to expose the narcissist can worsen the situation, as the narcissist will use any means to ensure that your reputation is ruined.

That being said, in terms of legal matters, it may be appropriate for you to document the abuse if, in the future, you should ever need this documentation in court. Narcissists, sociopaths and psychopaths are notorious for manufacturing reactions in their victims via text message, in-person or phone call and rewriting history as it suits their agenda, in order to make victims appear unstable in court. That's why having documentation of abusive incidents is not only important, it's often necessary to counter the evidence a narcissist may already have manufactured against you.

Here are some articles that may be helpful to you for documenting the abuse:

DomesticShelters.org - Why You Should Document Abuse
http://www.domesticshelters.org/domestic-violence-articles-information/why-you-should-document-abuse

Love is Respect - Documenting Abuse
http://www.loveisrespect.org/legal-help/documenting-abuse/

The Hotline - Building Your Case to Document Abuse
http://www.thehotline.org/2014/05/building-your-case-how-to-document-abuse/

Due to how difficult it often is to convince those closest to us that our partners were narcissists, what I want to stress is that our biggest priority after moving on from a narcissist should not be to convince society – it is to gain internal validation and a supportive community that does understand what we've been through, such as a community of other survivors.

I know that many survivors get temporary satisfaction from one-upping the narcissist in some way. However, this satisfaction is often short-lived because who wants to compete emotionally with someone who lacks empathy and remorse for a lifetime? In the long-term, we shouldn't strive to get direct revenge on our pathological partners through physical or emotional retaliation because any attention, even negative attention, will stimulate the narcissist's ego and ignite their narcissistic rage, causing them to up the ante on their manipulative, controlling and abusive antics. It also theoretically builds the case against you in any court case in which your narcissist is involved.

Your job is to validate yourself, seek a supportive community of people who've been there, stay as calm and centered as much as possible during a high-conflict divorce or court case with a narcissist, educate yourself about narcissistic abuse, surround yourself with lawyers and counselors who understand this type of abuse and empower yourself to rebuild an even better life due to this experience. Indifference and exposure are two of the narcissist's biggest fears; so is a victim who leaves them and achieves even more despite their attempts to destroy them.

Self-care, self-love and success are in fact the best revenge. Take it from someone who's been there: true revenge, the type that enables you to move forward and use your experiences as fuel to achieve your big dreams, is one of the most satisfying things you can experience in your life. A narcissist's true nightmare is a survivor who is able to transcend the abuse and use it to empower himself or herself. *That* is the type of revenge that lasts a lifetime.

The Narcissist's Next Victim

It is a blessing to escape a lifelong commitment with a narcissistic partner who is unwilling to seek treatment, *regardless of how happy they appear with their next victim because it is a mask much like the rest of their false self.* Survivors have to take into account that it is usually when people are the most miserable that they tend to overcompensate by showing off their relationship.

From the perspective of the outside world, the "happy relationship" others tend to see between narcissists and their next victims is when the new target is still being idealized just like their former victim once was. Eventually the narcissistic partner will get bored, devalue/discard this target and seek new supply (even if they end up marrying this target instead of discarding them fully) because the majority of them are not able to be fully committed to anyone or anything but their own egos.

Truly happy couples are too busy being, well, happy, to care about what society thinks of their lives. Victims of narcissistic abuse, because they are subjected to cognitive dissonance, gaslighting and projection, may attempt to reconcile the reality of the horrific abuse with the narcissist's false charming self to the world by presenting their relationship as a happy one to the outside world. This is an attempt to cope and convince themselves that it's not as bad as they think - and because other people around them see their narcissistic partner as kind and generous, they may feel compelled to protect their partner's image and the image of the relationship due to the fear of being labeled crazy or a liar.

Behind the closed doors of an abusive relationship, it can be a different story altogether – this is part of the reason why many survivors of narcissistic abuse take so long to exit the relationship. Also, due to the complex biological and psychological that develops between abuser and abused, the victim may even seek to protect the abuser due to trauma bonding which we'll discuss in-depth in Chapter 2.

The only way you can win against a narcissistic partner is by establishing No Contact, which is a prolonged period of detachment from your abuser which includes no contact via phone, social media, the mail or in-person interactions. Ideally, No Contact should last forever. No Contact or Low Contact (if you are forced to have contact) allows you to no longer be the narcissist's source of supply.

There may be a time when a narcissist still wants to use you for supply, but doesn't want to fully commit to you, so he or she may ask for your friendship. This is a tactic known as **hoovering** in which a toxic partner attempts to reinstate contact with you for the sole purpose of feeling in control and toying with your emotions.

Remember that anyone who has abused you in an intimate relationship does not deserve to be your friend. At the very least, you should maintain No Contact for at least **90 days** before making the decision to reengage with anyone who has abused you. According to TIME senior science writer Michael Lemonick (2007), there is a 90-day rule that appears most effective regarding addictions to drugs. Thus it should be applied to the addictive biochemical cocktail that is produced in a relationship with a narcissist. Their behavior will most likely not change – but yours can.

So long as you can leave the relationship once and for all, you have already taken your first step to recovery from the addiction the narcissist created when he groomed and lovebombed you into feeling love, compassion and awe for him or her. You have already become victorious from the first day of No Contact.

The day you became a survivor who went No Contact with her abuser, you essentially gave yourself a gift: a life without being numbed by the narcotic of narcissistic abuse. The potential for a peaceful life, even a happy and healthy relationship, await you. Most importantly, the path to self-love and healing has now been secured.

As Jackson Mackenzie, bestselling author of *Psychopath Free* once said, from the moment you left, or were left, by the narcissist, you were given the first true compliment by the narcissist. You are now the narcissist's nightmare, the type of person he no longer wants and will want to avoid at all costs. And that is exactly who you will remain and strive to be, because rejection never felt so good.

Let's summarize what we've learned so far about narcissistic partners.

Five Powerful Ways Abusive Narcissists Get Inside Your Head

I've revised and incorporated more detailed information into one of my most popular articles to help capture the narcissistic abuse experience. Watch out for the following covert manipulation tactics when you're dating someone or in any other kind of relationship.

1. The Idealization-Devaluation-Discard Phase

Narcissists and those with antisocial traits tend to subject romantic partners to three phases within a relationship known as "idealization, devaluation and discard." The idealization phase (which often happens most strongly during the early stages of dating or a relationship) consists of putting you on a pedestal, making you the center of his/her world, being in contact with you frequently, and showering you with flattery and praise. You are convinced that the narcissist can't live without you and that you've met your soulmate. Narcissists mirror and mimic their potential supply's feelings, values, hobbies and interests to manufacture this "soulmate" effect.

Be wary of: constant texting, shallow flattery and wanting to be around you at all times. This is a technique known as "love-bombing" and it is how most victims get sucked in: they are flattered by the constant attention they get from the narcissist. You may be fooled into thinking that this means a narcissist is truly interested in you, when in fact, he or she is interested in making you *dependent* on their constant praise and attention.

The devaluation phase is subsequent to this idealization phase, and this is when you're left wondering why you were so abruptly thrust off the pedestal. The narcissist will suddenly start to blow hot and cold, criticizing you, covertly and overtly putting you down, comparing you to others, stonewalling you, emotionally withdrawing from you and giving you the silent treatment when you've failed to meet their extreme "standards."

Remember that when you don't cater to a narcissist's sense of entitlement and threaten their sense of superiority– their false belief that they have a right to treat people like objects, playing with them and putting them down whenever they please, it results in what we call **narcissistic rage**. Narcissists can't comprehend that there may be anyone independent of them, with boundaries, values and beliefs that don't align with the narcissist's unreasonable demands. When the victim begins to question the narcissist's abusive and cold, withholding behavior, they often stonewall their victims, gaslight them and invalidate them further so they feel guilty about reacting in the first place.

The first time a narcissist throws you off the pedestal is actually the best moment to leave and it is usually the moment most survivors wish they had left, had they known what they were dealing with. It is at this time when the investment in the relationship isn't as heavy as it might be and the pain is fresh, shocking and traumatizing.

They can throw you off the pedestal in many ways – there may be a negative outburst followed by a great deal of gaslighting and blameshifting; there may be a hideously insulting remark or incident of name-calling disguised as a joke, following by stonewalling because "you're too sensitive"; there could even be an hour-long conversation which consists of primarily bashing every strength and accomplishment of yours that the narcissist pretended to love in the early stages of the relationship,

Remember, narcissists don't truly "admire" anyone – if they do praise you on your strengths and accomplishments in the beginning, more often than not, they are planning ways to set you up to fail and sabotage you in those same areas. They suffer from pathological envy – which means anything you're better at will eventually be a subject of denigration rather than praise during the devaluation phase. In the devaluation phase, all bets are off – the true abuser starts unmasking himself or herself.

What drags most survivors back in after this first incident is the makeup period. The narcissist will convince you that this incident and future incidents have a reasonable explanation behind them – it was really your fault that they called you a terrible name, or they just become abusive when they're drinking, or sometimes they just have "bad days." You, the willing, compassionate, empathic partner, will be prone to agree – perhaps you did do something to provoke it and nobody's perfect.

Then comes the narcissist's most insidious trick: they turn you into someone who's more like an addictive gambler at a slot machine waiting for the big bucks rather than your normal, stable self. Since the "hot" aspect of this phase relies on intermittent reinforcement in which the narcissist gives you inconsistent spurts of the idealization phase throughout, you become convinced that perhaps you are at fault and you can "control" the narcissist's reactions.

This intermittent schedule of rewards is the same way many gamblers get hooked on slot machines – although they know a reward is random, unpredictable and rare, they will still continue to play in the hopes of getting a reward, because an unpredictable schedule of rewards is more effective than a predictable one – in fact, an unpredictable schedule of rewards allows more dopamine to flow readily to the brain, strengthening the very reward circuits that compel us to engage with our source of pleasure over and over again.

In the economics world, this is called the Law of Diminishing Returns, where everything else stays constant while the output decreases over time. The narcissist gets away with giving you less while getting more of your time, energy and effort. That's why the narcissist sneaks in tender moments of love, kindness, generosity and great sex periodically throughout the abuse cycle, so that each and every time an abusive incident happens, you feel as if you can win the lottery again – if only you could be "perfect" and everything the narcissist demands you to be.

You are mislead into thinking that if you just learn not to be so "needy" or "clingy," the narcissist will reward you with the loving behavior he or she demonstrated in the beginning. These are words that narcissists often use to demean victims when abuse victims mourn the loss of the idealization phase or react normally to being provoked. It's a way to maintain control over your legitimate emotional reactions to their stonewalling, emotional withdrawal and inconsistency.

Unfortunately, it is during the devaluation phase that a narcissist's true self shows itself. You have to understand that the man or woman in the beginning of the relationship never truly existed. The true colors are only now beginning to show, so it will be a struggle as you attempt to reconcile the image that the narcissist presented to you with his or her current behavior.

Even though the narcissist can be quite possessive and jealous over you, since he or she views you as an object and a source of narcissistic supply, the narcissist is prone to projecting this behavior onto you. The narcissist makes you seem like the needy one as you react to his or her withdrawal and withholding patterns even though the expectations of frequent contact were established early on in the relationship by the narcissist himself.

During the discard phase, the narcissist abandons his or her victim in the most horrific, demeaning way possible to convince the victim that he or she is worthless. This could range from: leaving the victim for another lover, humiliating the victim in public, blatantly ignoring the partner for a long period of time without any closure on the break-up, being physically aggressive and a whole range of other demeaning behaviors to communicate to the victim that he or she is no longer important.

Although "normal" relationships can end in a similar manner, as well, the difference is that the narcissist often makes it clear he or she intends to hurt you by giving you the silent treatment, spreading rumors about you, moving on very quickly with a new victim, insulting you and disrespecting you during the discard phase.

Unlike "normal" partners, they ensure that you never have closure, and if you decide to leave *them*, they might decide to stalk you to show that they still have control. The narcissist may still reach out to you after the discard or attempt to provoke you in other ways to hoover you back into the trauma of the relationship, keeping tabs on you even after the discard.

It's all about control for the narcissist, especially the horrific discard – so if they see you thriving and moving on with your life, they'll attempt to reel you back in just to subject you to an even more humiliating discard than before. They want to demonstrate you are worthless and that you are their property - often simultaneously. It makes no sense to us as empathic human beings who would often wish the best for our partners after a break-up but then again, rational behavior has never been their forte.

2. Gaslighting.

While healthy relationships have room for respectful disagreement and consideration of one's feelings, with the narcissist, gaslighting and constant emotional invalidation become the norm. Gaslighting is a technique abusers use to convince you that your perception of the abuse is inaccurate. During the devaluation and discard phases, the narcissist will often invalidate and criticize your emotions, and displace any blame of his or her abuse as your fault.

They will suddenly develop abuse amnesia, where they'll forget horrific incidents of abuse or deny saying or doing something that they actually did. This allows them to escape accountability, but it's also a type of crazymaking that enables the abuser to rewrite reality for you and control your world. In an abusive relationship with a narcissist, you are no longer the owner of your perception – you are a slave to the narcissist's projections and reshaping of your own perception.

Frequent use of phrases such as "You provoked me," "You're too sensitive," "I never said that," or "You're taking things too seriously" after the narcissists' abusive outbursts are common and are used to gaslight you into thinking that the abuse is indeed your fault or that it never even took place.

Narcissists are masters of making you doubt yourself and the abuse. This is why victims so often suffer even *after* the ending of a relationship with a narcissist, because the emotional invalidation they received from the narcissist made them feel powerless in their agency and intuition. This self-doubt enables them to stay within the abusive relationship even when it's clear that the relationship is a toxic one, because they are led to mistrust their own instincts and interpretations of events. More often than not, narcissists target sensitive souls like empaths – so they are able to lock us into the fear that we're *too* sensitive quite easily. The truth is, *anyone* would be "sensitive" to verbal abuse and psychological manipulation.

3. Smear campaigns.

Narcissists keep harems because they love to have their egos stroked and they need constant validation from the outside world to confirm their grandiose sense of self-importance and fulfill their need for excessive admiration. A harem is a group of people the narcissist has gathered around himself to validate his opinions, cater to their constant need for attention, and stroke their ego. This is why they are clever chameleons who are also people-pleasers, morphing into whatever personality suits them in situations with different types of people to get what they want – supply. Think of the story of the emperor's new clothes – the victim will often be the only one telling the narcissist he is a naked fool, which will cause a narcissistic injury, rage and denial. The harem wouldn't dare because these members are too loyal to the narcissist's false self.

Beware of people who seem to shape-shift suddenly before your eyes into different personas — this is a red flag that they are not authentic in their interactions with you and others. It is no surprise, then, that the narcissist will probably begin a smear campaign against you not too long after the discard phase, in order to paint you as the unstable one, and that this is usually successful with the narcissist's support network which also tends to consist of other narcissists, people-pleasers, empaths, as well as people who are easily charmed.

This smear campaign is used to accomplish three things: 1) it depicts *you* as the abuser or unstable person and deflects your accusations of abuse; 2) it provokes you into responding, thus proving your instability to others when trying to argue his or her depiction of you; and 3) serves as a hoovering technique in which the narcissist seeks to pull you back into the trauma of the relationship as you struggle to reconcile the rumors about you with who you actually are by speaking out against the accusations.

The only way to not get pulled into this tactic is by going full No Contact with both the narcissist and his or her harem.

4. Triangulation.

Healthy relationships thrive on security; unhealthy ones are filled with provocation, uncertainty and infidelity. Narcissists like to manufacture love triangles and bring in the opinions of others to validate their point of view. They do this to an excessive extent in order to play puppeteer to your emotions. In the book *Psychopath Free* by Jackson MacKenzie, the method of triangulation is discussed as a popular way the narcissist maintains control over your emotions. Triangulation consists of bringing the presence of another person into the dynamic of the relationship, whether it be an ex-lover, a current mistress, a relative, or a complete stranger.

Remember that saying about never trusting anyone who's rude to the waiter on a date? Well, this same saying also applies in the opposite direction as well: never trust anyone who's overly friendly to the waitress – especially if it's each and every time. It's a sign that your potential partner needs constant attention and energy from other people – even if they are complete strangers!

This triangulation can take place over social media, in person, or even through the narcissist's own verbal accounts of the other woman or man. The narcissist relies on jealousy as a powerful emotion that can cause you to compete for his or her affections, so provocative statements like "I wish you'd be more like her," or "He wants me back into his life, I don't know what to do" are designed to trigger the abuse victim into competing and feeling insecure about his or her position in the narcissist's life.

The last example is especially potent because the only time a narcissist's victim is not made to feel jealous about their partner's ex is during the idealization phase, when the narcissist often devalues or her ex as "crazy" to make you feel special and unique. It is only when you begin to reconnect with the reality of the abuser that you realize that the narcissist's ex-partner was not the crazy one, but rather a victim of abuse just like you – and that perhaps you two should get together to exchange notes!

Unlike healthy relationships where jealousy is communicated and dealt with in a productive manner, the narcissist will belittle your feelings and continue inappropriate flirtations and affairs without a second thought. Triangulation is the way the narcissist maintains control and keeps you in check — you're so busy competing for his or her attention that you're less likely to be focusing on the red flags within the relationship or looking for ways to get out of the relationship.

5. The false self and the true self.

The narcissist hides behind the armor of a "false self," a construct of qualities and traits that he or she usually presents to the outside world to gain admiration and attention. Due to this armor, you are unlikely to comprehend the full extent of a narcissist's inhumanity and lack of empathy until you are in the discard phase. This can make it difficult to pinpoint who the narcissistic abuser truly is – the sweet, charming and seemingly remorseful person that appears shortly after the abuse, or the abusive partner who ridicules, invalidates and belittles you on a daily basis?

You suffer a great deal of cognitive dissonance trying to reconcile the illusion the narcissist first presented to you with the tormenting behaviors he or she subjects you to. In order to cope with this cognitive dissonance, you might blame yourself for his or her abusive behavior and attempt to "improve" yourself when you have done nothing wrong, just to uphold your belief in the narcissist's false self during the devaluation phase.

During the discard phase, the narcissist reveals the true self and you get a glimpse of the abuser that was lurking within all along. You bear witness to his or her cold, callous indifference as you are discarded. This is as close you will ever get to seeing the narcissist's true self.

The manipulative, conniving charm that existed in the beginning is no more — instead, it is replaced by the genuine contempt that the narcissist felt for you all along. See, narcissists don't truly feel empathy for others – so during the discard phase, they often feel absolutely nothing for you except the excitement of having exhausted another source of supply. You were just another source of narcissistic supply, so do not fool yourself into thinking that the magical connection that existed in the beginning was in any way real. It was an illusion, much like the identity of the narcissist was an illusion.

It is time to pick up the pieces, go No Contact, heal, and move forward. You were not only a victim of narcissistic abuse, but a survivor. Owning this dual status as both victim and survivor permits you to own your agency after the abuse and to live the life you were meant to lead — one filled with self-care, self-love, respect, and compassion. In this fairytale, the happy ending lies not in Prince Charming but rather the awakening that he never existed at all.

Learning the Language of Narcissists: How Abusers Use Anything and Everything Against Their Victims

Narcissistic abuse can leave psychological and emotional scars that can last a lifetime. Yet what makes narcissistic abuse so dangerous is that it is often not recognized as abuse. Mental health professionals are only now beginning to research and understand what psychotherapist Christine Louis de Canonville calls "Narcissistic Victim Syndrome" is, as well as the connection between chronic abuse and complex PTSD, although survivors have been speaking about it through their stories for years. Narcissistic abuse is primarily psychological and emotional (though victims can suffer physical abuse as well), and since these abusers employ very covert and insidious methods to abuse their partners, they're able to escape accountability for the abuse because of the false persona they present to the outside world – which is usually a charming mask that hides their cruelty.

Survivors often blame themselves for narcissistic abuse, not being able to put into words what they've experienced. Once they learn the vocabulary of narcissistic abuse, they are armed with the tools, the insights, and the resources to heal. Learning the "language" and techniques of these predators means that we are better prepared to identify the red flags, detach from and cut ties with toxic people, engage in better self-care and set boundaries with those who frequently cross them.

These pathological individuals walk among us every day in their false masks, often unseen and unnoticed because of how eerily normal they are. They can be of any gender, background, and socioeconomic status. Often times, they are charming, charismatic, the life of the party, able to hook their victims in and dupe the public effortlessly. It's very possible you've dated, worked with, had a family member or friend with Narcissistic Personality Disorder or Antisocial Personality Disorder in your lifetime - even if you didn't know it then.

Learning their emotional language means acknowledging that their cruelty is not only explicit but implicit, deeply ingrained in nuances in their facial expressions, gestures, tones, and most importantly, the contradictory mismatch between their words and actions. Most importantly, their cruelty is deliberate and designed to control and ultimately destroy their victims.

Their manipulation is psychological and emotionally devastating – and very dangerous, especially considering the brain circuitry for emotional and physical pain are one and the same (Kross, 2011). What a victim feels when they are punched in the stomach can be similar to the pain a victim feels when they are verbally and emotionally abused, and the effects of narcissistic abuse can be crippling and long-lasting, even resulting in symptoms of PTSD or Complex PTSD.

These types of abusers are fluent in manipulation, well-versed in sadism, in control and in rage - their deliberate cutting down of you, which can be best described as "death by a thousand cuts," can be just as slow and insidious as it is swift and vicious. It is akin to psychological and emotional rape - a sordid violation of boundaries and of the trust the victim has given his or her abuser.

Narcissistic abusers lure their victims into a false sense of security so that they can attack at any given moment, using their choice weapons of sarcasm, condescending remarks, name-calling, and blameshifting whenever they perceive you as a threat or whenever they need entertainment in the form of an emotional reaction.

They can also use their nonverbal language in the form of a sadistic smirk, the cold deadness in their eyes while professing to love you, their bored, sulky looks or their cruel laughter to bully you into believing you are inferior to them. Survivors note that these predators often have intense eye contact upon first meeting you, demonstrate a flat affect with their "dead eyes," during the devaluation and discard phases, the narcissistic "smirk" when they've duped you, and the mocking, contemptuous laugh when they are sarcastically putting you down.

There are **three key pieces of information** that narcissists frequently collect in the idealization phase of the relationship that they later wield against you in the devaluation and discard phases using their language of cruelty:

1) The flaws, shortcomings, insecurities and secrets you've confided in the narcissist about. The narcissistic abuser rejoices when you share your wounds, your struggles, and your triggers early on. It is then that much easier for them to get underneath your skin and inside of your mind. During love-bombing, you are likely to feel so trusting and open with a narcissist that you share everything with them: your past, your heartbreaks, what you perceive to be your flaws.

You may see this as a way of establishing rapport, a connection with your partner, a way of being vulnerable and intimate. A narcissistic abuser sees it as dinner laying itself on the table. They will pretend to support you and empathize with you when you reveal these to them initially, but will later use these to provoke you, belittle you and demean you during the devaluation phase.

While some narcissists are overt in their put-downs, covert narcissists employ a faux "innocence" or "concern" when insulting you. They covertly question your competence, your skill set, and your ideas by attempting to innocently ponder to what extent they exist. To them, evidence is arbitrary in the matter. They will use the smallest piece of irrelevant information they can find from what you've told them or what they've observed in an effort to sabotage and undermine you. They cannot stand you having the upper hand in something or succeeding. In their world, only they are entitled to win.

Remember: the narcissist has no limits as to what he or she will use. If you tell your narcissist you're insecure about your weight, be prepared for covert and overt put-downs about your body in the devaluation phase. If you reveal to a narcissist that you've been through a past trauma, such as being sexually assaulted, it won't be long before they are using degrading lingo in the bedroom to make you feel like a used object. They thrive on the fact that you are being re-traumatized. Their ability to make you regress right back into the original trauma with just one turn of phrase makes them feel powerful. And they live for that power, because it is the only power they have in their pathetic, empty lives.

To a narcissist, *any* open wound is an invitation to cut deeper and the narcissist can and always will cut a wound that goes even deeper than the first.

2) Your strengths and accomplishments, especially the ones they are pathologically envious of. Initially when you were on the pedestal, the narcissist couldn't get enough of your strengths and accomplishments. They couldn't stop raving about you to family and friends, showing you off, treating you like a trophy, an essential part of them. Their association with you inevitably made them feel superior and important. It bolstered their false image of being a normal human being who could get a "prize" like you.

In the devaluation phase, a narcissist will literally **translate** your strengths into perceived flaws. Once you were "confident and sexy," – but now you're "cocky and vain" (a clear projection of themselves, of course). Before, you were "intelligent and driven," and now you're just a "know-it-all" or a "smartass."

Narcissists gaslight you into believing that your value and worth is not real, all while projecting their own sense of inferiority onto you. They will degrade, minimize, and ignore what you accomplish, now acting as if it means nothing to them and as if it is of little importance or value to the world. They will feed you falsehoods about your lack of competence and ability. They will claim to be better at it than you, all the while stealing your ideas. They will taunt you into believing that you're not capable of the smallest of tasks, even if you are out of their league professionally and personally. They will threaten to ruin your reputation and they will often sabotage major events as well as support networks you may have, attempting to turn everyone against you. They will trample upon your dreams, your aspirations, your beliefs, your personality, your goals, your profession, your talents, your appearance, your lifestyle – all the while extolling their own.

Their sudden turn of language takes a toll; it is traumatizing, shocking and unexpectedly vicious. Everything they once praised will inevitably be turned and twisted into a weakness. This is because they cannot stand you "winning" and being better than them at something. To them, everything is a competition and a game they must win at all costs. They seek to destroy you in every way possible so that you, in turn, destroy and sabotage yourself – all the while they sit back, relax and watch the unraveling of everything you've worked hard for.

3) Your need to please them and their need to be perpetually dissatisfied. The narcissist cultivated your need for his or her validation and approval early on in the idealization phase. By making you dependent on his or her praise, they conditioned you to seek the excessive admiration that only *they* could dole out. Now, as they devalue you, they use your need for validation to their advantage by withdrawing frequently, appearing sullen at every opportunity, and converting every generous thing you do for them as a failure on your part that falls short of their ludicrous expectations. Nothing can meet their high standards and everything wrong will be pointed out. In fact, even the things *they* do wrong shall be pinned on you.

Their blameshifting language, passive-aggressive sulky behavior and narcissistic rage at the slightest injury becomes all-consuming for the victim, as the victim attempts to strengthen his or her efforts to meet the standards of the narcissist – standards which inevitably set the victim up for failure. For this, the victim is met with verbal assault, accusations and unfair comparisons which instill in him or her a pervasive sense of worthlessness and never being "enough."

These are diversion tactics that narcissistic abusers use to divert accountability for their actions and belittle you covertly. Abusers are constantly "moving the goal posts" to ensure that you can never meet their impossible standards and expectations; they are perpetually misrepresenting your viewpoints to make them seem ludicrous and absurd; they are continually demeaning and emotionally invalidating your experiences, your perspectives and your goals.

20 Diversion Tactics Highly Manipulative Narcissists, Sociopaths and Psychopaths Use to Silence You

What's important to remember that while human beings in general can engage in toxic behaviors from time to time, abusers use these manipulation tactics as a dominant mode of communication. Toxic people such as malignant narcissists, psychopaths and those with antisocial traits engage in maladaptive behaviors in relationships that ultimately exploit, demean and hurt their intimate partners, family members and friends. They use a plethora of diversionary tactics that distort the reality of their victims and deflect responsibility. You can find a list of the 20 diversion tactics they use in my article located here: thoughtcatalog.com/shahida-arabi.

Although those who are not narcissistic can employ these tactics as well, abusive narcissists use these to an excessive extent in an effort to escape accountability for their actions.

The more power they have over your emotions, the less likely you'll trust your own reality and the truth about the abuse you're enduring. Knowing the manipulative tactics and how they work to erode your sense of self can arm you with the knowledge of what you're facing and at the very least, develop a plan to regain control over your own life and away from toxic people.

If the victim ever attempts to make the narcissistic abuser accountable for being a decent human being, they will lash out in rage, blaming them for the abuse and stonewalling the victim into silence. They love to have the last word, especially for the language they've created.

Taking back our control and power from a narcissistic abuser means going to war with the language they use against us. This means seeking validating, professional help for the abuse we've suffered, detaching from these people in our lives, learning more about the techniques of abusers, finding support networks, sharing our story to raise awareness and finding the appropriate healing modalities that can enable us to transcend and thrive after their abuse.

We can channel this experience of abuse for our highest good and for the greater good. We just have to be willing create in its place what I call a "reverse discourse"—a new language and a rewriting of the narrative that instead lifts us, motivates us, inspires us and revives us by replacing the narcissist's cutting words with our own powerful truth.

*To learn about the *20 Diversion Tactics of Highly Abusive Narcissists, Sociopaths and Psychopaths* be sure to visit my author page at www.thoughtcatalog.com/shahida-arabi. You may also want to check out my full essay collection in my new book, *POWER: Surviving and Thriving After Narcissistic Abuse* at tinyurl.com/PowerSurviving.

Dating Emotional Predators

What about those who are not full-fledged narcissists but belong somewhere on the spectrum? Dating an emotional predator, a narcissist, a sociopath or anyone else who has the potential to be an abusive or toxic influence in your life is a devastating emotional roller coaster of highs and lows. I chose to make this section of the chapter inclusive of all types of abusers because in dating, you are likely to come across a variety of people, both with and without NPD. Some of these tactics can also be used by people who don't have NPD, though that doesn't make the impact of these actions any less toxic.

For example, emotionally unavailable people or smooth-talking players (who don't quite meet the criteria of NPD) can blow hot and cold, be superficially charming, disappear without a word, use intermittent reinforcement (both intentionally and unintentionally due to the many other people they're pursuing simultaneously), have a harem, all without meeting the full criteria for this disorder. Unlike narcissists, these predators may still feel empathy towards others while remaining manipulative and unable to enter healthy relationships until they choose consciously to change their behavior.

On the other hand, we must remember that these abusers could very well be narcissists who fake remorse. That's when it can become difficult to tell them apart. Normally what would distinguish them is how they act during and after the ending of a relationship – do they stage a vicious smear campaign? Do they pursue a new partner immediately, with a level of indifference that seems inappropriate for the length and investment of the relationship you've been in? Are they verbally and emotionally abusive, responding to any perceived threat with excessive rage? Did they subject you to an excessively hot grooming phase, only to subject you to cold, callous mistreatment? Is this a cycle that often repeats itself, despite your proclamations that this is hurting you?

Do they attempt to still contact you even while with a new partner? Do they seem to be able to callously or cruelly discard you multiple times, all the while claiming they love you? Does it seem they deliberately stage personal attacks against you throughout the relationship, engage in stonewalling, chronic emotional invalidation and gaslighting? Do they frequently triangulate you with others to the point where it seems they get sadistic pleasure out of it? Do they stalk you if you leave them as a result of narcissistic injury? Do they follow the idealization, devaluation and discard phase to a tee? These are signs that something deeper than emotional unavailability may be going on.

Although some tactics are frequently used by narcissists moreso than others – triangulation for example – emotional predators of any kind (with other disorders such as Antisocial Personality Disorder or no disorder) can still be capable of being toxic. They may have a host of other problems such as anger issues, addictions, control issues and jealousy issues which don't necessarily stem from that particular disorder or may be co-morbid with an existing disorder. That's why even if they are not full-fledged narcissists, they are not worth pursuing in the long run and can still be harmful to your mental health.

Abusers tend to unfold and reveal their true selves long after they've already reeled their victims in. However, there are some key signs to look out for when dating someone that can foreshadow their future behavior.

The great thing about dating is that you are not committing to a relationship, so you can use this process as a way to find out more about a potential partner, and if necessary, cut ties should he or she turn out to have abusive traits *without* investing further in the relationship.

Whoever it may be – a narcissist, sociopath, psychopath, or an emotionally unavailable toxic individual with abusive traits, let's explore more in-depth about how these types of abusers use their language combined with their manipulative tactics to further reinforce their power over their victims. There are three main ways they demonstrate their pathology:

1) A need for control.

Abusers want to control and manipulate their victims, so they will find covert ways to maintain control over you psychologically. They can maintain this control in a diverse number of ways:

Excessive contact.

Although many people don't realize this, excessive flattery and attention from a charming manipulator is actually a form of control because it keeps you dependent on their praise. If you find yourself being bombarded with text messages, voicemails, calls and e-mails on an hourly basis in the early stages of dating, keep a lookout for other signs.

It might seem incredible that someone is so besotted with you after just one date, but it's actually a red flag for dubious behavior and unwarranted attachment. It's not normal to be in contact with someone 24/7 especially if you've only gone on a couple of dates with them. No one has the time to "check in" constantly with someone they're "just" dating.

This form of contact is perfect for abusers to "check in" with you to see what you are up to, to make sure that you are suitably "hooked" to their attention, and is a form of "idealization" which will place you on a pedestal that at first, seems irresistible. Of course, if you're familiar with the vicious abuse cycle of narcissists which include idealization, devaluation and discard, you'll know that you'll soon be thrust off the pedestal.

An unhealthy response to rejection or boundaries.

Unlike dating partners who are simply excited to see you again and express their interest with polite enthusiasm, toxic partners will get considerably upset if you choose not to respond to them right away or if you resist their idealization by giving yourself necessary space. They won't wait for your response, either: they will continue to persist and pursue you with an unhealthy level of attention without knowing much about you. This level of attentiveness is not actually "flattering" even though it may appear so initially - it's downright *creepy* and dangerous. It reveals a sense of entitlement to your time and presence without regard for your personal preferences, desires or needs.

When you place boundaries with a potentially toxic partner, they will be sure to step over them. If you say no to coming home with them on a first date, for example, they may still continue pestering you despite knowing your reluctance. When your "no" always seems like a negotiation to someone you're dating, beware. This means you're in the presence of someone who does not respect your right to make your own choices and maintain your boundaries or values.

Physical aggression.

As perpetual boundary-breakers, abusers can also overstep the *physical space* of their victims. This type of behavior may not come out until months into a relationship, but sometimes abusers can be physically aggressive with you just a few dates in. Grabbing you too harshly, pushing you during an argument or conflict, violating your personal boundaries in any way, pressuring you for sex, touching you inappropriately without consent is a red flag that must be heeded. It's a sign that things will only get worse in the future.

This physical aggression may happen under the influence of alcohol or other drugs, so you're not quite sure what to make of it except that you feel threatened and unsafe. Don't attempt to justify this if it happens with or without the involvement of alcohol - alcohol may lower inhibitions, but it doesn't cause personality transplants. It's very likely that the abuser is revealing his or her true behavior even while claiming that the "drink" made him or her do it.

Mistreatment of others.

Even if the abuser idealizes you quite convincingly in the early stages of dating, you may witness his or her behavior towards others as a red flag of future behavior. For example, is he or she rude to the waiter or waitress on your date? Does he or she get excessively angry if another person flirts with you, talks to you or hits on you in front of them? How about the way they talk about others? If they call their ex a "crazy psychopath" and include a whole range of expletives about their annoying coworker, recognize that these are toxic temper issues which you will eventually be on the receiving end of.

Demonstration of unwarranted anger

...is an incredibly important tactic that abusers use to 1) preserve their self-image and their ego, 2) project blame onto others, 3) take back control by recreating a "version of events" that makes them look superior and saintly and 4) evoke fear and intimidate others into doing what they want.

2) Addicted to provoking you.

Covert manipulators are quite gifted at provocation. As they learn more about you, they are investigating your weak spots and catering their comments towards what they know will hurt you the most. Knowing you're triggered by their comments gives them a sadistic sense of satisfaction that alleviates their secret sense of inferiority and strokes their delusions of grandeur, control and aptitude. Having control over your emotions also gives them the power to effectively manipulate you and convince you that you don't deserve any better.

Debasing comments

...about your personality, your looks, your line of work, what you should wear, who you should hang out with, are all inappropriate, especially when just getting to know someone. If you find yourself frequently confronted with these so-called "helpful" comments in the first few dates, be wary. Nobody should be trying to "change" you immediately when they're just getting to know you, and if they are, this is a recipe for chaos.

These provocative comments might be disguised as constructive criticism or "just jokes," but you can distinguish them because they are often comments laced with condescension rather than compassion and consideration. Harsh teasing that serves no other purpose but to ignite your anger or annoyance, put you down and insult you *is different* from playful teasing which is used to flirt and build rapport with a partner.

Disparaging, chronic sarcasm.

Beware of the tactics of the covert sarcastic put-down. Sarcasm is one of the mighty weapons in an abuser's arsenal. Emotional predators enjoy invalidating your thoughts, opinions and emotions by making frequent sarcastic remarks that shame you into never questioning them again. Since sarcasm isn't often considered "abusive" by society, abusers use it as a way to escape accountability for their harsh, condescending tone and belittling behavior. They become more and more condescending in their approach to sarcasm over the course of the relationship – what was once a "playful" sarcastic comment now becomes frequent emotional terrorism that questions your right to have an opinion that challenges theirs.

Efforts at making you jealous.

Triangulation is a popular way narcissists maintain control. Narcissists in romantic relationships manufacture love triangles, often by giving others what you most want and rubbing it in your face. Narcissistic friends use gossip to triangulate and maintain control in their peer group. Narcissistic parents can pit siblings against each other to play puppeteer in family dynamics. If your date consistently brings up past romantic partners, looks at other women frequently on your dates (while furtively checking to see if you're observing them while doing so), and talks about having a romantic "type" that is quite far from your description, **run.**

A healthy partner will strive to make you feel secure and cherished, not insecure and doubtful. This could be a form of toxic triangulation in which an abusive partner attempts to create an image of desirability while demeaning your merits so that you are encouraged to compete for his or her attention.

The silent treatment and stonewalling.

Narcissists emotionally invalidate and manage your emotional reactions to their abusive behavior through a technique known as stonewalling, which involves ending a discussion before it's even begun through phrases such as, "I am done!" "Goodbye!" or "I can't deal with you anymore." Abusers may retreat into silence if you question their authority or bring up their mistreatment. This may provoke you into pursuing them even more, in order to try to coerce them into "validating" your emotions and admit that they are in the wrong. Unfortunately, you're only giving them more power by doing this. They will eventually come around, but only after you've vented at them and eventually apologized for being too "harsh" even when you have doing nothing wrong but express yourself.

3) Inconsistent character and behavior.

The most skilled abusers will save the "hot and cold" tactics for when they enter long-term relationships, but other abusers may give you a sample of this even within the first month of dating. They do so by the following:

Superficial charm.

I cannot count the endless number of toxic people I have met who begin their ploys with superficial charm accompanied by self-absorption and an actual lack of empathy or substance. You can begin to spot how superficial their demeanors are once you've had some practice in identifying nonverbal gestures, nuances in facial expressions and tone of voice. Skilled predators are quite charming and you can easily learn to see through this by observing the way they exaggerate how they feel about you and their glib ways of showing you that they "care" when *they really don't.*

For example, hearing "I've never felt this way about anyone else," on a first or second date is not only premature, it's most likely a *lie* to impress you. When this charm is paired with actions that don't align with the individual's words, like the fact that this person never actually asks you about your interests or passions despite being so "enamored" with you, you'll soon realize these are just shallow ways of getting into your head (and most likely your bed).

Projection and gaslighting.

Narcissists and other types of toxic relationship partners project their own fragile ego on anyone who calls them out on their reprehensible behavior and challenges the status quo of the relationship in which they play the powerful puppeteer. When their victims calmly explain to them that their behavior is unacceptable and why, they claim their victims have temper issues, are overreacting to a pattern of abuse and are acting childish - all because their victims attempt to hold them accountable and/or provide a different perspective.

This is gaslighting and projection at its finest. Meanwhile, they engage in narcissistic rage and tend to be immature, close-minded and unable to see anyone else's perspective. Insults, put-downs, name-calling and derogatory language soon follow to regain a sense of control. The narcissistic bully does not disagree respectfully; rather, he or she must make the victim feel as small as possible if the victim dares to challenge the status quo and the false self.

In addition, it will appear that the person you are dating often accuses you of the same characteristics, traits or actions that they themselves seem guilty of committing. For example, I had a few narcissistic partners who would often be very possessive of me, track where I went and who I was with, seemed to check up on me 24/7 and call me out if I ever dared to show signs of flirtation or interacting with another man – even before our second date!

Yet the moment I ever called out discrepancies in their stories or lies that didn't add up, they unleashed their narcissistic rage and gaslighted me into thinking I was the jealous, possessive one, telling me I was getting too heavily invested in the relationship too soon. Mind you, this was coming from the same dating partners who prematurely treated me as if I was already their girlfriend when I clearly wasn't and subjected me to a creepily excessive amount of attention and surveillance of my whereabouts within the first few dates.

It was eerie how all their possessive and fast-forwarding actions seemed to be minimized as "just teasing" or "not serious" while my otherwise rational confusion at their nonsensical stories or actions were painted as attempts to stifle them. After listening to and reading thousands of other survivors' stories throughout my lifetime, I realized I was not the only one who had been met with this form of crazymaking projection and gaslighting.

Narcissists and other toxic partners will also depict you with words that are best left describing them; they may refer to you as a hypocrite, a cheater or a liar, when in fact, it is they who frequently engage in shady behavior that contradicts their words. The projection and gaslighting of narcissists is so adept, so sneaky, so conniving, and so utterly convincing, that you are often led to apologize for being alive at all.

Pathological Envy.

Narcissistic and otherwise toxic partners are pathologically envious of people. This comes out in covert ways, even in the early stages of dating. The starry-eyed admiration followed by anger and envy is a classic case in friendships and relationships with toxic people, especially narcissists. Narcissists suffer from pathological envy so whatever happiness they seem to feel for us is merely a facade for the deep contempt they feel for anyone they feel threatened by. What many people don't realize is that narcissists don't just gravitate towards us because of our vulnerabilities; they are also attracted to our assets - because it stirs envy within them. This strengthens their desire to destroy us and our success in every way possible.

Signs of a Toxic Person's Pathological Envy

- Praises you highly for your accomplishments initially; uses your accomplishments as a way to associate themselves with you and look good. Likes feeling as if they have the "successful girlfriend" or boyfriend – while simultaneously resenting you for it.
- Competes with you often; if you bring up what you achieved, they have to bring up something bigger or downgrade what you've achieved to make you feel small. Nothing you do is truly special – or, it's really, really special until the narcissist

gets tired of praising you and wants to cut you down a thousand pegs or so.

- Highly competitive; even in petty games, will be a sore loser and resort to immature actions to "win" or insult your ability.

- Behind closed doors, devalues and minimizes the things they once praised, making them seem unimportant and lacking because they know they would've never been able to accomplish those things themselves. They will emphasize the idea that people are against you (projecting the fact that it's them that is against you), that your contribution isn't valuable or degrade/ignore accomplishments that are in fact a big deal, all with an innocent or smug look on their face.

- Sabotages important events in your life such as big interviews, projects, deadlines using methods like put-downs, crazymaking arguments that lead to sleep deprivation, pressuring you to drink or spend time with them right beforehand, insulting you, covertly casting doubt onto your abilities and talents, one-upping you and making themselves seem more important, accomplished and talented to stroke their sense of superiority.

- Treats your goals, dreams and interests with contempt or a condescending attitude, while bringing the conversation back to them. Once, on a date with a narcissistic partner, I expressed my interest in getting a Ph.D. The narcissistic partner, without even blinking said condescendingly and haughtily, "That's great. It's good to have *goals*. That's how I achieved mine."

Pathological lying.

Do you catch the person in frequent lies or stories that simply don't add up? Do they "drip-feed" you information so that the full story eventually unravels over time? A girl he hung out with was once just a "female friend," and now suddenly he mentions that he used to date her. A man she sees for Sunday brunch is "just" a colleague, but then you find out that it's an ex-husband. It's true that everyone reserves some crucial information on the first few dates for later and everyone makes mistakes or tells "white lies" to preserve their self-image occasionally. However, if these lies seem to be chronically common, it's not a healthy pattern to start off a relationship with. Disclosure, honesty and open communication are foreign words to the abuser, who lives in a world of falsehoods.

Frequent disappearances.

In the beginning, the person you were dating was constantly on top of you, bombarding you with calls and texts. Suddenly, they disappear for days, only to come back again as if nothing ever happened. These disappearances, which are often staged without convincing explanations, are a way of managing your expectations and making you "pine" for contact.

Attitude changes towards you.

Abusers may engage in "splitting," emotional polarization in the ways they view you. This is particularly true of those with Borderline Personality Disorder, yet you are likely to experience splitting in the idealization and devaluation cycles with a narcissistic or emotionally unavailable partner as well. You're either "the one" when you're meeting their needs or you're suddenly the villain if you disappoint them in any way or threaten their fragile sense of superiority. Beware of this "hot and cold" behavior, because it's another tactic to manage your expectations and keep you on your toes. Even if you don't even like the person, if you tend to be the people-pleasing type, you might fall into the trap of attempting to avoid rejection and win their favor. It's "reverse psychology" at its finest.

Intermittent reinforcement.

Intermittent reinforcement is a term coined by B.F. Skinner (1957) which we'll talk more about in-depth in Chapter 2 in the context of narcissistic abuse. It is another term for variable ratio reinforcement in which the abuser gives his or her victim "rewards" at random points of the relationship cycle. The victim then continues the relationship in hopes that he or she will get a reward (for example, affection or attention) at some point despite the abuse. Much like a gambler continues on the slot machines despite knowing the rewards are inconsistent, variable ratio reinforcement has a high response rate in which the victim keeps going forth with the relationship regardless of the amount of pain involved.

This is a psychological tactic that provokes victims into pleasing their abusers, even if the abuser is mistreating them. If you are the victim of an emotional predator, the abuser gets to have you on your "best behavior" without changing his or her own behavior. Abusers love giving "crumbs" after they've already seduced their victims with the idea of the whole loaf of bread. You might find yourself on the receiving end of praise, flattery, attention one day, only to be given cold silence the day after. Occasionally you will get the same idealization that you received on the first few dates, but more likely, you will get a mixture of hot and cold, leaving you uncertain about the fate of the relationship.

Furthermore, the reactions of emotional predators to your vulnerabilities are telling signs of their pathology. Survivors from my survey, for example, noted that their narcissistic abuser was callous or indifferent when they were ill, facing an emergency or upset in general. This is because any distress you are going through takes the attention off the narcissist and the narcissist needs to draw the attention back to them. It's all about power and control. You can also tell if you're dating a toxic person in the following ways:

1) Their reaction to your accomplishments (as noted before, their pathological envy).

2) Their reaction to you asking them to take accountability (gaslighting, stonewalling, verbal abuse).

3) Their reaction to the neediness they have manufactured in you (gaslighting, contempt, emotional invalidation, increased triangulation, projection).

4) Their reaction to your healthy expression of emotions, needs and boundaries (emotional invalidation, put-downs, verbal abuse, stonewalling, gaslighting, projection).

Tips for Dating Emotional Predators:

If you notice any of these red flags after the first few dates or within the first few months of dating, **do not proceed.** Since within the first few dates you are usually presented with a person's best behavior, you can be sure that things *will not get any better.* You cannot fix this person and you run the risk of emotionally investing in someone who is out to deliberately harm you.

Be careful: if you choose to reject an abuser outright, it may infuriate them or he or she may use "pity ploys" or angry harassment to convince you should go out with them again. Going No Contact if someone is bothering you, harassing you or making you feel uncomfortable in any way is a better tactic. Block their number and any other means they might use to communicate with you. If they've been disrespectful, they don't deserve a polite response.

Should they continue to harass you, document the evidence and tell them you will take legal action if necessary. If you're trying online dating, make sure you block the predator from the site you are using after you document their messages by using screenshots.

Tread lightly when you're dating someone new. Don't give out personal information like your address, home telephone number or other means of reaching you besides a cell phone number. If possible, use an alternative like a Google Voice number or other text messaging app while still getting to know someone. I personally benefited from this, especially with predators who attempted to harass me after I clearly expressed my disinterest. You **must** put your safety and privacy first.

Resist projection and gaslighting. Stick to what you know to be true. Do not allow your toxic dating partner to minimize or deny things he or she may have said or done. When a dating partner attempts to gaslight you or project qualities onto you, know that this is a clear red flag of emotional infancy that will not be suitable for a long-term relationship.

It is helpful to keep a journal during your dating process to note any inconsistencies, red flags, emotions and/or gut feelings that may arise.

You will want to refer to this journal often in order to keep grounded in your own perceptions and inner sense of truth.

Keep your eyes open. Be willing and open to recognizing both the bad and the good. While we all want to see the best in people, it's important not to also gaslight ourselves into denying or minimizing the signs that someone is not compatible with us. The signs will always be there, and even if they don't present themselves quite as visibly, your gut instinct will tell you when something is not quite right.

References

American Psychiatric Association. (2013). Diagnostic and statistical manual of mental disorders (5th ed.). Arlington, VA: American Psychiatric Publishing.

Bancroft, L. (2002). Why does he do that?: Inside the minds of angry and controlling men. New York: Putnam's Sons.

Bardenstein, K. K., Ph.D. (2009). The Cracked Mirror: Features of Narcissistic Personality Disorder in Children. *Psychiatric Annals, 39*(3). doi:10.4135/9781412950510.n565

Bonn, S. A. (2014, January 22). How to Tell a Sociopath from a Psychopath. https://www.psychologytoday.com/blog/wicked-deeds/201401/how-tell-sociopath-psychopath

Brummelman, E., Thomaes, S., Nelemans, S. A., Castro, B. O., Overbeek, G., & Bushman, B. J. (2015). Origins of narcissism in children. *Proceedings of the National Academy of Sciences Proc Natl Acad Sci USA, 201420870.* doi:10.1073/pnas.1420870112

Louis De Canonville, Christine (2015). *The Three Faces of Evil: Unmasking the Full Spectrum of Narcissistic Abuse,* Black Card Books.

Eisenberger, N. I., & Lieberman, M. D. (2004). Why rejection hurts: A common neural alarm system for physical and social pain. *Trends in Cognitive Sciences, 8*(7), 294-300. doi:10.1016/j.tics.2004.05.010

Fenichel, O. (1945). *The psychoanalytic theory of neurosis.* New York: W.W. Norton & Co.

Hare, R. D. (1999). Without conscience: The disturbing world of the psychopaths among us. New York: Guilford Press.

Haslam, C., & Montrose, V. T. (2015). Should have known better: The impact of mating experience and the desire for marriage upon attraction to the narcissistic personality. *Personality and Individual Differences, 82,* 188-192. doi:10.1016/j.paid.2015.03.032

Holbrook, C. (2013, May 13). Sociopath Signs: Is Your Ex a Sociopath or a Narcissist? http://www.huffingtonpost.com/2013/05/13/sociopath-signs-is-your-e_n_3181512.html

Hsu, D. T., Sanford, B. J., Meyers, K. K., Love, T. M., & Hazlet, K. E. (2013). Response of the [mu]-opioid system to social rejection and acceptance. *Molecular Psychiatry, 18,* 1211-1217. doi:10.1038/mp.2013.96

Jacoby, M., & Kohut, H. (1990). Individuation and narcissism: The psychology of the self in Jung and Kohut. London: Routledge.

Kreger, R. (2012, April 4). Why they can't feel joy: Narcissistic shallow emotions. Retrieved from https://www.psychologytoday.com/blog/stop-walking-eggshells/201204/why-they-cant-feel-joy-narcissistic-shallow-emotions.

Lavender, N. J. (2014, January 10). The Narcissistic Wound. Retrieved from https://www.psychologytoday.com/blog/impossible-please/201401/the-narcissistic-wound

MacKenzie, J. (2015). Psychopath free: Recovering from emotionally abusive relationships with narcissists, sociopaths, and other toxic people. Penguin Group.

Stout, M. (2005). The sociopath next door: The ruthless versus the rest of us. New York: Broadway Books.

Vaknin, S., & Rangelovska, L. (2007). *Malignant self love: Narcissism revisited.* Prague: Narcissus Publications.

Vaknin, S. (2012, April 25). Psychopathic Narcissists: The Uncanny Valley of Cold Empathy. Retrieved April 11, 2016, from https://samvaknin.wordpress.com/2012/04/25/psychopathic-narcissists-the-uncanny-valley-of-cold-empathy/

Clichés That Fail Within Narcissistically Abusive Relationships

There are certain clichés and adages that are entrenched in society's philosophy of relationships that can be incredibly harmful to survivors of this type of abuse. I've listed them below because I think it's time for society to understand that many of these do not apply when it comes to relationships with these predators. It would be downright dangerous, in fact, to subscribe to them when it comes to abusive situations. I've listed them below so that survivors can find solace in the fact that they do not need to subscribe to outdated norms that harm their healing process.

Cliché #1: Forgive and forget.

With the narcissist, forgiving and forgetting the abusive incidents is one of the most dangerous things you can do and it is one that caters to the narcissist's malicious agenda. Abuse amnesia sucks you back into the toxicity and before you know it, you're forgiving and forgetting your way into a fifty-year marriage with an abuser. By that time, you feel as if you can't forgive yourself for investing so much time and energy. Many of us suffer abuse amnesia because our brain creates defensive mechanisms in the form of disassociation to protect ourselves from the abuse we're suffering – but to heal from trauma, we have to at some point address it. To stop going back to an abuser, we have to stay connected with our anger while we're still detaching, so that we don't fall into the trap of romanticizing that abuser.

Cliché #2: To be happy, you must let things go.

"Let it go," was one of the most abusive phrases I ever heard on my healing journey – and yet it wasn't just said by abusers. Whether it's invalidating friends, family members, a spiritual community, a therapist who's unaware of narcissistic abuse - victims can be easily re-traumatized by those who do not believe in the severity of their trauma.

Society is sadly misinformed about the severity of emotional and psychological violence. We are trained to pay attention to physical scars, not emotional wounds. The thing about narcissistic abuse and the covert manipulation, brainwashing, love-bombing, devaluation, verbal attacks and emotional violence involved is – you can't just *let it go* – or the smaller events that remind you of the trauma, because it triggers an entire chain of reactions connected to the original trauma. Any type of abuse and bullying can be a traumatic event and trauma literally rewires our brain.

Our brain literally needs to think about what has happened to us in order to process the trauma. We may to go through every event, every trauma and understand it in the new framework and vocabulary that we're beginning to develop about narcissistic abuse, with the support of professional help. Telling an abuse victim, especially a victim who has complex PTSD and a history of abuse, to "let it go," is quite frankly, one of the most selfish and ignorant things you can do.

Remember, any event that is traumatic – even if it seems small to you – may have triggered a lifetime's worth of memories for this person. Saying, "I am here for you," or "I may not know what you're going through, but I see and hear your pain and want to help" are much healthier alternatives. As survivors, we have the distinct disadvantage of being alienated and misunderstood. However, we do have an advantage in connecting with and empowering other survivors who do understand what we've been through.

Cliché #3: Never stoop down to anyone's level.

We have this myth that abusers can abuse us on all levels but if we finally react to a long pattern of abuse in a way uncharacteristic of our usual morals and values, we should be ashamed. The truth is, we're all human, and when we're being traumatized we might act in maladaptive ways that enable us to survive even during the worst circumstances. If you've had an adverse reaction to someone's chronic abuse of you – as in, they provoked you into crying madly, feeling suicidal, plotting revenge fantasies – know that you're not alone. You have survived a great deal and no one has the right to judge you for a journey they know nothing about.

Abuse survivors are placed in a war zone the moment they form a bond with their abusers – so unless you really are going to act on your feelings in a way that harms someone else, no one has the right to judge the way you defend yourself or for acting normally to abnormal behavior. Sometimes, you may find yourself stooping down to someone's level in an effort to survive and cope in a controlling, abusive environment. That *doesn't* mean you'll remain there or that you are as terrible as them. It simply means you're human and you're reacting to a toxic situation.

Cliché #4: Beautiful and smart people never get abused or traumatized. Only vulnerable ones do.

I once read a strange comment on my YouTube channel that said, "You're too cute to be a codependent." Ha! *Let's be clear: nobody* is too "cute," too "smart," too "wise," too strong, too *anything* to be a victim of abuse. Beautiful, strong, intelligent, successful, confident and wonderful people from all backgrounds can be subjected to abuse and no one is immune to the effects of trauma. I always hear from ignorant people who say, "Oh, if I had an abusive partner, I would do this or that" – yet these are the same people who've never been in a toxic relationship in their lives! You can never be sure how you will react to abuse until you've actually been there, and even for people without past childhood abuse in their backgrounds, it can be very difficult to leave an abusive situation.

I've heard from clients and readers who were on top of their game, attractive, highly educated individuals who felt as if they had lost themselves in an abusive relationship because they thought they had met the love of their lives, only to discover further down the line that their soulmate became their daily tormenter, breaking down their confidence and feeling of self-worth.

Abuse is never about the victim; it is always about the abuser's own pathology. Nobody ever deserves to be abused and everyone is worthy of love, care and respect. Yet a lot of the comments by narcissists - who tend to be fixated especially on our appearance throughout the idealization and devaluation phases (initially lots of compliments, then covert put-downs) - train victims to believe that their worth lies in their outer beauty alone. Nothing could be farther from the truth - it is in embracing the divine spirit that lies in each and every one of us, that we are able to recognize our real worth is derived from within, and this knowledge allows us to embrace all the forms of beauty we possess, both inside and out.

Cliché #5: It is better to have loved and have lost than never to have loved at all.

Nope. It's better to have loved in a normal relationship and then have lost than it is ever to be in a relationship with a narcissistic abuser. Many survivors of abuse after having gone through this experience would now take being lonely over this type of abuse any day.

Cliché #6: You have to learn to trust someone until they've given you reason to do otherwise.

No, you have to learn that trust has to be earned. Unfortunately, everyone is a potential predator and you will never know who someone truly is until you've already invested in a relationship with them. In the United States alone, 1 in 25 people is a sociopath according to Dr. Stout (2005). Sometimes only time can tell.

Cliché #7: You have to risk it all for real love.

In truth, real love doesn't require as much risk as you might assume. Real love is compassionate, authentic, natural. It flows much more smoothly and doesn't need to be forced or fought for. In fact, you'll be amazed how much real love flows without as much "work" needed. The riskiest relationships are the abusive, toxic ones that require attempting to "fix" someone pathological while ultimately resulting in harm to the victim.

The Essential Dictionary to Understanding Narcissistic Abuse

These are terms to familiarize yourself with as you come to terms with the abuse you've suffered – many of them have been mentioned in the first chapter, but I find it helpful to look at this list as a quick reference whenever you need a reminder. Abusers use language to manipulate and control us, rewrite reality to suit their agenda, and devalue our strengths. It's time to build a vocabulary and language to empower survivors to identify and dismantle the methods they use as well as the effects these methods have on the victim.

Since we still require more education in the mental health community about this type of abuse, being well-versed in the tactics and techniques will enable you to identify the abuse you're suffering more readily rather than being susceptible to minimizing or denying it. For any counselors or mental health professionals and coaches who are reading this book, I am sure you are already familiar with these and hope you will keep these terms in mind if you ever have a client who has gone through this type of abuse.

Ambient abuse – The atmosphere of fear, anxiety and self-doubt created due to the covert abuse taking place. Sam Vaknin writes that ambient abuse creates an environment of fear and intimidation with no indication of what he calls "traceable explicit abuse."

Link: Vaknin has an excellent and in-depth look into how this atmosphere is created through five categories of ambient abuse here: http://samvak.tripod.com

Abuse amnesia – The victim's tendency to suppress abusive memories after they have been chronically abused. The victim may even demonstrate a positive outlook on the abuser, repressing the trauma they've experienced due to their investment in their relationship as well as trauma bonding created by intense, shared experiences with the abuser.

Cognitive Dissonance – A distressing mental state where an individual finds themselves holding two conflicting beliefs at once. In order to resolve this internal conflict, the individual has to look for reasons that one belief over the other is true. When an abuse victim meets his or her abuser, they often see the charming, loving façade in the early stages of the relationship. When abusers eventually unmask themselves and reveal their true ugliness, abuse victims struggle to reconcile the horrific abuse with the sweet, tender and seemingly compassionate person they first encountered at the beginning of the relationship. This may lead them to deny or minimize the abuse as a way to survive the reality they're experiencing and resolve their cognitive dissonance.

Conditioning – Conditioning occurs when a neutral stimulus is paired with a stimulus that already evokes a response to create a conditioned response. In Pavlov's experiment, dogs were conditioned to associate the ringing of a bell with the arrival of food, causing them to salivate whether or not food was present or being offered. In the context of abusive relationships, conditioning is used to reward or punish behaviors that the narcissist wishes to ignite or extinguish.

The abuser doesn't want you to succeed? They will begin to pair abusive incidents with moments incidents of your success, by treating you to a big helping of neglect, verbal assault or an emotionally abusive rage attack when they see that you're accomplishing things. The abuser doesn't want you hanging out with other friends? They will begin a big argument right before you go out or before a big event. Soon, you begin to stop seeing friends to prevent the abuse or downplay your accomplishments as a way to avoid their envy.

Narcissists also condition us throughout the abuse cycle to associate abusive incidents with loving, tender moments – so we expect those moments of tenderness even after we've been abused, hoping that we will eventually be loved and cherished again. Over time, this becomes so normalized that before we know it, we're in the middle of one big Pavlovian experiment, associating pain with pleasure.

Devaluation – After love-bombing, the abuser has sufficiently hooked you into the idea of the fantasy relationship. This is when he or she feels permitted to unmask himself or herself a bit more by degrading you emotionally and at times, even physically. The devaluation phase will begin with a "test period" where the abuser will see what types of critical comments and denigrating actions he or she can get away with. Then, over time, the abusive incidents become incrementally worse as the narcissist tests and pushes your boundaries, seeing how far he or she can take the abuse.

Discard – This is a final act of "leaving" the victim or appearing to leave him/her, often staged in the most horrific, demeaning and humiliating way possible to instill in the victim a pervasive sense of worthlessness and a sense that there is no closure to be had. Although cruelty becomes normalized throughout the abusive relationship, this is the narcissist's opportunity to package the greatest amount of cruelty possible into the shortest amount of time, so that you will never forget them and will find it difficult to recover from them.

The narcissist may disappear without a word, he or she may cheat, may subject the victim to an angry or violent outburst, and/or move on happily to their next victim while devaluing their former one. There are many ways to "discard" the victim like trash while discounting everything the victim has done for the narcissist. The discard is what often leaves victims so traumatized so that they feel unable to move forward and they become susceptible to a narcissist's hoovering later on (see Hoovering below).

Gaslighting – A technique abusers use to deny or minimize abusive incidents. These include denying things they said or did. There is no "time limit" on gaslighting – abusers can even deny saying something they said five minutes ago or five years ago. They may also manipulate your perception of reality in other ways, such as misplacing, hiding or stealing your property and/or pretending something was in a certain location when it wasn't. For more information on gaslighting, see Christine Louis de Canonville's excellent article on gaslighting called "The Effects of Gaslighting in Narcissistic Victim Syndrome" on her website, narcissisticbehavior.net.

Harem – A narcissist often gathers a group of people around him or her to support them and feed them narcissistic supply. This is what we call a narcissist's harem – his or her audience who only sees the narcissist's false, public mask and often dismisses, denies, and minimizes any accounts of abuse. The harem serves as a narcissist's portal of normalcy and a source of support when the narcissist decides to start devaluing the victim and staging a smear campaign against the victim.

Since the harem usually only sees the false mask of the narcissistic abuser, it is easy to convince that harem that the victim is in fact the pathological one, while the abuser is able to escape accountability for his or her actions. The harem may be filled with both supporters as well as other sources of romantic supply that the narcissist can use to triangulate the victim with. When the victim tries to open up about the abuse, the harem members often alienate the victim and ridicules him or her for speaking out, because they live in the false reality that the narcissist has constructed and manufactured for them, not the true reality of the victim.

Hoovering – A narcissist is likely to reach out to a former victim, especially if the victim left them first or if the victim has moved forward with his or her life, in order to draw them back into the trauma of the relationship. This is what we call "Hoovering," named after the Hoover vacuum, to describe how a predator like this can "suck you" back into the abusive cycle all over again, often subjecting you to a discard even more horrific than the first. It's important for victims to understand that hoovering is not about missing the victim, loving the victim or even showing remorse. Hoovering is all about the power dynamic between an abuser and his or her victim. This reinforces in the narcissist a sadistic sense of control and power. The narcissist feels satisfied in knowing that they can still go back to their old "supply" whenever they need them for something, while pursuing new supply. To learn more about hoovering, you can watch my video on it here.

Intermittent Reinforcement – This is part of the conditioning that abusers subject their victims to which involves merging abusive incidents with elements of love-bombing. Intermittent reinforcement permits abusers to get away with more and more abuse while giving "scraps" of attention and tenderness to their victims to keep them hooked. This technique will be explored in-depth in Chapter 2.

Love-bombing/Grooming/Idealization – In the early stages of the relationship, abusers can "groom" and "love-bomb" their victims, causing their victims to trust them and bond with them on a deep level emotionally, physically, and psychologically. Abusers often use immense flattery, gifts, excessive attention, amazing sex, and time-consuming activities such as 24/7 texting or spending time together to draw us into an intense relationship very early on.

Narcissistic Injury/Rage – Narcissists are very sensitive to any slight or criticism that threatens their sense of perceived superiority. This results in what we call a **narcissistic injury** and **narcissistic rage**, in which the narcissist lashes out in what is a perceived attack on that superiority and sense of entitlement. Mind you, anything that the narcissist perceives to be an attack can make you the object of narcissistic rage, even an innocuous, well-meaning comment.

Narcissistic Supply – Supply is any form of praise, admiration, emotional attention, or physical resource the narcissist gets from the individuals they form relationships with or have interactions with. Sam Vaknin distinguishes between two types of supply (primary supply) and secondary supply (the secure source of supply the narcissist has for their everyday needs). You can read more in his article on narcissistic supply here.

Projection – When an abuser manipulates you into thinking you possess the very qualities, traits, and motivations as him or her. Rather than being held accountable for their negative characteristics, abusers prefer to hand over their pathology to you, calling you jealous, possessive, needy, hypocritical, abusive or narcissistic when, in fact, it is them that fits this criteria.

Flying monkeys – Allies that the narcissist recruits to spread misinformation about you, slander your character and retrieve information on you. These are members of the narcissist's harem but can also include former members of your own support network the narcissist has charmed into believing him or her.

Smear Campaign – Related to the help of the flying monkeys, narcissists will often begin speaking behind a victim's back when they begin the devaluing stage. They will slander their victim's character, reputation, sabotage their relationships with others and often spread misinformation about the victim, projecting their own abusive behavior onto the victim. They may or may not explicitly threaten to smear the victim, so be careful – even if the narcissist has never threatened to do this, he or she may still do it in order to hinder your chances of having a support network after the abuse.

The smear campaign can work on both the narcissist's own harem as well as your own support network. This way, the victim is set up to fail and look like the pathological one should the victim ever choose to speak up about the abuse after the discard. The narcissist often feigns concern for the victim or acts like the victim while employing the smear campaign, and the smear campaign is at its height after the discard, so that the narcissist can reinforce the false belief that the victim was not "worthy" enough to be in a relationship with the narcissist.

Stonewalling – An abusive tactic in which an abuser shuts down a conversation even before its begun, subjecting his or her victim to the silent treatment. The abuser withdraws emotionally and physically. The most drastic scenario of stonewalling I've seen was of a survivor whose abuser kept calling the police whenever she brought up an issue in their relationship. The most common one is when an abuser subjects you to the silent treatment as soon as you bring an issue up or displays narcissistic rage to make you fearful of ever expressing your feelings.

Most abusive people do realize when they are stonewalling. They are conscious of when they need to defend themselves from what they perceive to be an attack on their sense of entitlement and false sense of superiority; they feel the need to punish their victims for the perceived attack – even if it's a simple request to talk about the victim's emotions. They gain satisfaction and regain a sense of control when they are able to shut a conversation down and escape accountability for their actions while also making their victims feel guilty for questioning them in the first place.

An important distinction to note is when the victim goes No Contact on an abuser or avoids them after an incident of abuse: this is not the same as stonewalling. Rather, avoiding an abuser is a form of **self-protection and self-care**. Stonewalling has the deliberate intent of making someone feel unimportant and invalidated so that the abuser can escape accountability. From the survivor perspective, the emotional response of avoidance is triggered by being the victim of abuse rather than a perpetrator of it. Everyone has different coping mechanisms around people who are abusive, triggering and/or otherwise hypercritical. I repeat: No Contact is not stonewalling. It is self-care.

The Narcissist Translator

Although survivor forums can be filled with stories of narcissists wreaking havoc on our lives, there are many ways in which connecting with other survivors is cathartic and *fun*! One of the most incredible exercises I did in a survivor's forum was participating in a group discussion that challenged us to "translate" commonly used phrases by narcissists into what they really meant. Laughter is medicine and so is knowledge. I hope you enjoy the combination of both below, inspired by my own personal experiences as well as the accounts of survivors from all over the world.

"You're my soulmate."

TRANSLATION: You're my new supply and love-bombing you is the first step to getting you hooked.

"She/he is just a friend."

TRANSLATION: You're my main supply, but I keep this other person around for sex/money/shelter/praise/whatever else I may need. I also love to triangulate you with this "friend" of mine. It makes me feel powerful to have two people desire me at once.

"My ex never reacted that way."

TRANSLATION: My ex did in fact react that way, that is why he/she is now my ex. I love gaslighting you into feeling as if you're the abnormal one for reacting normally to my abuse and the way all my other victims have before. It helps me get away with my despicable behavior and has the added benefit of triangulating you so that you feel unworthy and undesirable.

"You're so dramatic/sensitive/overreacting."

TRANSLATION: I need to gaslight you into thinking your reactions are abnormal so I get away with more crap. The truth is, I am the one who is dramatic and love provoking chaos in every conversation.

I am also very sensitive to criticism and overreact to any threat to my perceived superiority. I am also very talented at projecting – how did you guess?

"You're so much better than my ex. He/she was crazy."

TRANSLATION: The truth is, I am the pathological one, but I'd hate for you to think the break-up was my fault. Soon, you'll be labeled as the crazy one too.

"Let's take a break."

TRANSLATION: I need time to gather new supply, sleep around, and make you feel undesirable, longing for more of my attention. Besides, I need to save my energy for a bit. Pretending to have empathy is really draining me.

"I am done!"

TRANSLATION: I'll never really be done as I'll hoover and stalk you for years after, but I am done with the conversation that's trying to shed light on my cruelty and make me accountable for my actions. I simply don't have the time or empathy to take responsibility. I'd rather stonewall you instead, minimize your feelings and make you feel as if you don't matter.

"We're just so different."

TRANSLATION: I have no empathy and you do. We really are different, but I'd like to minimize it and act as if it's a problem with our compatibility rather than my pathology. The truth is, an abuser such as myself is not compatible with anyone who is healthy. In fact, I don't get along with anyone.

"You have no sense of humor/you take my jokes too seriously/it was just a joke!"

TRANSLATION: I actually have a warped sense of humor as I only use jokes as a vehicle for being cruel without being held accountable. If you don't "get the joke," it's probably because you recognize it for what it is: a covert put-down.

"Let's have sex."

TRANSLATION: I've recently just subjected you to a horrific abusive incident…quick! Let's have sex to bond so that your love for me is driven by a crazy, biochemical cocktail that associates pleasure with pain. That way, you'll always come back for more.

"I don't even care about having sex/I don't want to have sex."

TRANSLATION: Sexually withdrawing from you and triangulating you with others helps me to manipulate you into thinking that you're undesirable. I love the feeling of power that I get when you feel insecure. It gives me a rush that makes me feel superior.

"We don't have enough sex/you don't do x, y, z sexually/all my other exes (or the porn stars I watch) did [insert heinous sexual act or behavior you've told the narcissist you don't wish to do] here."

TRANSLATION: Actually, most of my exes never let me overstep their sexual boundaries or were just as outraged as you, but let me convince you otherwise so you feel guilty and less than. Plus, there's a chance you'll actually do it despite not wanting to. Coercing people is so fun and makes me feel super powerful.

"I am sorry/I am sorry you feel that way."

TRANSLATION: I am tired of arguing, so I'll fake remorse to end the conversation quickly and move onto more important things...like how you're going to serve my needs. Plus, the problem isn't my abusive behavior. It's the fact that you are a normal human being feeling actual emotions and having reactions to my abuse. How dare you!

"I'll never do it again."

TRANSLATION: I will definitely do it again, but perhaps I'll try it in a different style, tone or word choice to keep things interesting and leave you doubting about my intentions. I like keeping my abuse versatile. Plus, this fake promise will keep you off my back for a bit and maintain the relationship.

"I am such a nice guy/girl."

TRANSLATION: If I was such a nice person, would I have to convince you of it frequently with my words rather than actions? Probably not.

"Let's be friends."

TRANSLATION: (1) Despite our heavy romantic investment, let me manage down your expectations so I can use you until other supply comes along. **(2)** You've broken up with me or I've discarded you, but I'd still like to have you around to triangulate you with my new supply and put you through an even more horrific discard than the last. Interested?

"Ugh, you're too much."

TRANSLATION: Ugh, you're so human with real emotions and empathy...I can't even deal.

"Stop being a smartass."

TRANSLATION: I know you're intellectually superior and right, so I am going to pretend you're just obnoxious instead to protect my fragile sense of superiority.

"You really think you're hot shit."

TRANSLATION: I know you're hot shit, but you being confident in that fact makes me insecure. I'd rather you feel terrible about yourself so you won't go out and look for something better. Plus, I love projecting my own arrogance onto you.

"Nobody cares about you/what you do/what you've accomplished."

TRANSLATION: Too many people care about you and that's a problem. I need to isolate you from your support networks and anyone who would convince you that you're a worthy, valuable human being. Plus, your accomplishments evoke my sense of pathological envy and I am not going to let you surpass me in any way.

"You're the narcissist/you're abusive/damaged and deserve the abuse."

TRANSLATION: I am really the narcissist, but I want to make you feel as toxic as I feel. Convincing you that you're the pathological one helps to gaslight you into believing my abuse isn't real and allows me to project my malignant traits onto you. Here, take my pathology. I don't want it. Also, you're damaged because people have hurt you – forget the fact that I am severely sick and damaged because I purposely hurt others to make myself feel better.

How to Break Up with a Narcissist, Sociopath or Toxic Partner Safely and Securely

So we've got a lot of the information down on these individuals and we know that a long-term relationship with them would probably end not only in heartache but also years off of our lives, dreams shattered, and potentially even our reputations ruined. So what do we do about it? Anyone who's ever been in a relationship with a toxic abuser knows ending a relationship with an emotional predator is one of the most difficult things to do.

In the past, I have also struggled to end these relationships due to my own compassion, empathy and willingness to see the good in people, and I've spent my entire life trying to "retrain" myself in this area when it comes to toxic people like this. It has taken me a long time to learn how to cut ties in both friendships and relationships sooner than later. Many survivors come to the healing journey not because they themselves ended the relationship, but because their partner discarded them first, after subjecting them to a horrific cycle of abuse that would leave the most attractive, talented or successful person feeling worthless.

If you don't believe me, look at super successful figures like Madonna, Halle Barry, Rihanna, Whitney Houston, – just to name a few – who've been the victim of abuse by their partners. The effects of abuse are indiscriminate; as powerful and as confident as you may feel, as successful or wealthy you may be, *anyone* can be broken down and made to feel like a mere speck of the bright, shining light they used to be. Personally, the survivors I've spoken to are highly intelligent, articulate and driven people from a variety of different backgrounds, professions and trauma histories. Many of them are changing the world as I write this.

An unfortunate fact regarding a break up with a toxic, disordered person is that it will probably look very little like a normal break up with a person you were simply not compatible with. In a normal break-up, you probably won't be biting your nails and walking on eggshells in anticipation of a smear campaign or suffering from the stress of one that's already been launched; you won't be struggling with the biochemical and trauma bonds that I'll discuss in Chapter 2; you won't be traumatized to see your partner move swiftly onto the next source of supply without any remorse or shame whatsoever, nor will you be "hoovered" back in multiple times, just to face an even worse discard than the last, just so that the narcissist saves face.

Here is what an ideal standard for a break-up with a narcissist looks like: you should always be the one instigating the break-up, do it immediately as soon as you figure out this partner is a narcissist, and go full No Contact (the specifics of which we'll discuss in Chapter 5) with your ex-partner, enabling you to move forward forever and never repeat the same mistake again.

Boy, that sounds wonderful, doesn't it? Unfortunately, while I encourage this standard for anyone who thinks they are capable of committing to it fully, I know from coaching clients on No Contact as well as my own personal experiences that this cookie-cutter ideal doesn't cut it for some people. By all means, if you are able to go No Contact without a second thought right at this very moment, please do so because that is the ideal outcome for all abuse survivors. Chances, are, however, not everyone can go full No Contact immediately with their abusers. They will likely struggle with obstacles when attempting to break up with them.

Real break-ups with abusers like this take time, effort, strength, resources, support, empowerment – they take everything you've got and more. Does that mean you shouldn't shoot for the ideal? Of course not, we should always shoot for more than what we think we're capable of and acknowledge our strength, power and agency. At the same time, we have to practice self-compassion and practicality when it comes to break-ups like these because these situations call for extra caution.

There are five major ways we can break-up with our narcissistic partner – some better than others. Each has its advantages and disadvantages, but I offer these different methods here because while abusers are eerily similar across the board in their tactics, every situation will be different due to its unique circumstances and the resources that the victim has.

Some victims may live with their abusers, work with their abusers, share children or a business with their partners; others may be the caretakers of an elderly narcissistic parent or relative while other survivors may face an unsafe physically violent situation. It's important to keep in mind that there will be different circumstances for each situation. The goal, of course, is eventual No Contact or Low Contact, but the ways to get there can be numerous and varied.

Cold turkey.

You don't wait for the right time to break-up, you just do it. You do it firmly, even if your voice is shaking, your heart is breaking and your body is quaking (see what I did there?), because you'll deal with the emotional heartbreak later. Right now, you just need to deal with keeping yourself safe and sound.

This method is highly recommended for abusive relationships that have an element of physical violence or aggression or even just very high, toxic levels of emotional and psychological abuse. Check out Kelly Jo Holly's Domestic Violence Safety plan on verbalabusejournals.com for survivors who live with their partners as well as The National Domestic Hotline's tips on Physical and Emotional Safety Planning on thehotline.org.

Remember that a victim is more likely to be assaulted violently when she is preparing to leave than at any other point in an abusive relationship, so please be cautious about this. Create a safety plan, collect your basic necessities if you live together, grab your children if you have any, tell a friend and/or family member about your whereabouts and if your partner is violent, avoid any face-to-face confrontation if possible.

2) Weaning off the drug.

This method is for circumstances that are particularly complex, especially if it's a long-term marriage with children involved or if you and your partner share a business together or have legal matters to sort out. Sometimes, victims are so trauma-bonded to their abuser that going No Contact cold turkey feels virtually impossible to them. Weaning off the drug means taking the space for extreme self-care, reflection and minimizing contact with your ex-partner as you develop a plan to leave. If you are currently married, this is an ideal time to secure your finances, seek out professional support, get a lawyer who is informed about narcissistic personality disorder or high-conflict divorces, and build a support network that will help you in the aftermath.

Link: Check out this list of attorneys who are well-versed in Narcissistic Personality Disorder:
https://onemomsbattle.com/resources-attorneys/

Be aware that the disadvantage of this method is that the narcissistic partner may notice you are backing off and may attempt to hoover you with sweet actions, so you may fall prey into wanting to stay. In order to implement this method successfully, there has to be no threat of physical violence in the relationship, you have to be willing to ground yourself back into the reality of the abuse even in the face of re-idealization and love-bombing, and you have to act as if nothing has changed so that the narcissist doesn't know what you're up to. Pretend to be overwhelmed by work or another situation if you have to get the suspicious narcissist off your back for a bit. This method should not be used to proactively prolong an abusive relationship – it should always be seen as a framework for getting out and towards the goal of leaving and going Cold Turkey.

3) Last-Straw Method.

This is more of a pre-meditated breakup. It means getting to what I like to call the *The Pain Threshold*. Getting to that pain threshold is not something you should do intentionally. It will probably happen naturally as you continue to re-experience trauma. However, if you're set on keeping yourself in check with the harsh reality of the situation, I recommend keeping a light Abuse Journal. Keep a record of any and all abusive incidents. You don't want to stress yourself out by detailing all of them if it's too traumatic for you, but if it's helpful, find a way to write down each incident in a way that keeps you in touch with what is happening. Keep documentation if abuse takes place over social media, voicemail or texts, in order to refer to after you implement No Contact.

For this method, you promise yourself that the next time your partner disrespects you, big or small, you will leave. This is best for people who feel they are already at their breaking point but just need that extra push to get them to the finish line, to that "Screw this, enough!" moment. No excuses, no justifications, no rationalization is permitted when you get there. Again, in order for this method to be effective, you have to begin creating a detachment to your partner by reconnecting with your anger at the way they have treated you – write down any and all abusive incidents so you have a reference that you read daily. This will build up your motivation and incentive to leave, and stay strong in spite of any last-minute hoovering attempts to get you to stay. You may also want to confide in someone you trust, who is in no way affiliated with your partner, that you plan to do this, so you have some social accountability in the matter.

In addition to this, you may wish to include this as part of a dual method that includes the **One Solid Step Method - The Unbreakable Contract**. What helped me finally leave two of my narcissistic partners was the unbreakable contract I made by taking "one solid step." This is a step that is virtually irreversible and would be embarrassing to take back. The consequences of reversal far surpassed any compulsive need to go back to the relationship. It could be as simple as texting them a paragraph about how you respect yourself too much to stay in this relationship - something that, once you send, would be potentially humiliating to backtrack on. It could be deleting all photos of you two together, changing your Facebook relationship status for the world to see and blocking them from all social media platforms so that it would be difficult to reach them through this medium again or explaining to your friends what just happened.

It could be finally admitting to your friends or a trusted friend that you're in an abusive relationship and you need help to get out (choose a trusted friend who is likely to be validating and supportive if you choose to do to his). Use this friend as an unbreakable contract - ask them to hold you to it if you haven't broken up yet with the narcissist. While my examples don't sound that extreme, feel free to be creative. What is one thing that would be so humiliating or painful for you to backtrack on that you would be less likely to ever go back? This should be customized to your particular priorities because not every example I've mentioned will work for everyone.

4) Grey Rock and Discard Method.

Developed by LoveFraud member, Skylar (2012), the Grey Rock Method suggests that victims should become "boring" to the emotional predator by giving little to no reaction to their manipulative ploys. Since these abusers are motivated by high stimulation, they will eventually get bored of you and look for new supply. This method is usually only suggested for circumstances where the person is forced to interact with the predator.

Used in the context of a break-up, it's more likely that the predator will eventually leave you alone and pursue other supply, which gives you more time and space to reflect, plan and eventually leave. This can be a tough one to execute with a malignant narcissist, sociopath or psychopath, because sometimes, they may react by upping the ante on their tactics to get a response. I would only recommend this method if you're comfortable with the idea of being discarded first and are hoping they'll do it because you feel unable to.

When No Contact simply isn't an option, there are still resources to empower you and enable you to remain in your power.

Links: Check out Shrink4Men's article on Emotional Detachment with No Contact is Not an Option and therapist Ross Rosenberg's Observe, Don't Absorb technique on his YouTube Channel.

5) Take No Shit Method.

Although predators thrive on high stimulation, many of them can't stand a victim that sticks so firmly to their boundaries. A victim that no one can ever take advantage or get a reaction from. This method can best be described as a "STOP IT!" method and it is ideal for children of narcissists who are forced to interact with their parents, mutual friendships or even a workplace bully in certain cases. *Do not use this method if you are in a situation where there is a possibility of physical violence. Only to be used in situations where you feel safe.

The Take No Shit method is for people who don't have any moral qualms about getting in a narcissist's face (respectfully and firmly) or treating them to a sound dose of their own medicine. This can be done via the "silent treatment," a discard, or complete, callous indifference, and what we may call "stonewalling" up the wazoo should the narcissist even dare try to gaslight you or put you down for calling them out on their B.S. each and every time. It can also be used when the narcissist attempts to continue the conversation with their usual justifications. Again, this is not really the silent treatment or stonewalling – it is actually self-care to step away from an abuser who has been abusing you. Silence is an abuse survivor's best friend, and it is perfect for reinforcing a boundary you've set.

The Take No Shit Method should also be used in conjunction **with boundary-setting** and **limit-setting** early on in the relationship. This is all about telling the narcissist what you won't tolerate and how you won't be having any of it if you're forced to interact with them. Most importantly, you actually do leave the interaction whenever the narcissist trespasses that boundary.

Be careful with this method, as some malignant narcissists do not react well to self-defense and are likely to respond in rage and narcissistic injury. However, I have heard accounts from some survivors that demonstrate that this method has worked in getting a narcissist to back off, especially if you do it in the early stages of manipulation when they are less sure whether you are a vulnerable target or not.

Link: To learn more about how to set clear boundaries and engage in behaviors that abide by those boundaries, check out Dr. Craig Malkin's article on *One Simple Way to Protect Yourself from Narcissists* on Psychology Today.

For some narcissists, this will be their kryptonite and they won't be able to sustain a relationship with someone like that. They will search for easier prey and "better" supply that will continue to believe in their lies and falsehoods. The Take No Shit method is ideal for the early stages of dating – not so much after you've already invested a great deal in the relationship, because the narcissist will have already investigated your weak spots.

For others, it may cause their narcissistic partner to suddenly become more enamored because now you're an exciting challenge to them to win over again, destroy and discard in a more horrific fashion than ever. This is not what you want. So if it turns out this is happening in your particular situation in response to the Take No Shit method, try another method effective immediately. The last thing you need is a seemingly loving narcissist attempting to hoover you back to the trauma house of smoke, gaslighting and mirrors.

Although I don't recommend this method as highly as the others because counter-manipulation only works short-term and not as a long-term solution, I do want to present it as an option because many narcissists will end up discarding you if they feel you are way too educated about their schemes. By that time, you'll have spent so much time practicing being indifferent and cutting off abusive incidents even before they've begun that you'll walk away a bit stronger, with your head held up high.

A note about financial abuse: Abusers think their money is theirs and that your money is theirs too. Narcissistic abusers not only micromanage their victims' lives, emotions, thoughts, careers, and belief systems, they also manage their money. Be wary. Never give a "loan" to someone you're just dating or even in a relationship with unless they've shown they have character and integrity in the long term. If you can, have a separate bank account if you're married to a narcissist.

If you're divorcing a narcissist, hire a divorce financial planner and ensure that you have good credit in your name as well as records of your financial paperwork together. Stay as independent as possible and as safe as possible. Keep good records of your financial paperwork in a safe place. Narcissistic abusers have no empathy regarding your needs and they will do everything in their power to deplete you of every type of resource so that they can come out on top. An excellent book I would recommend reading if you're feeling stuck is *Divorce: Think Financially, Not Emotionally* by Jeffrey A. Landers, CDFA which will give you the tips, tools and resources you need to get through a financially tumultuous divorce.

Regardless of what method you choose to end a relationship with a narcissist, remember that your goal is still to get out of the relationship, **not to cope with it, actively prolong it, or romanticize it again.** You may even want to place a "break-up date" on the calendar just so you feel that it's in the future for you, even if it's not an action you feel able to take right in this present moment.

It will happen, it can happen, and you're looking forward to it, damnit! So here is a method I've lived by in preparation for the discard, however it may come. I call this the APP method.

Discarding the Narcissist: In preparation for the final battle

Creating a Life Outside (Activities, People, Purpose) or APP Method.

The narcissist becomes our whole life during the idealization phase - we want to spend most of our time with him or her, exchanging cute texts, loving phone calls and going on adventurous dates. As you'll learn in Chapter 2, we build important biochemical bonds with them that attach us to them and become addicted to the oxytocin, dopamine and adrenaline that bond us to our abusers and make us feel like we're in love. In our skewed perceptions, we can't live without this person's attentiveness, support and flattery.

During this time, you may have put the other important activities in your life on the back burner - such as hanging out with friends, your weekly yoga sessions, schoolwork or even real work, just to accommodate the narcissist's persistent desire to see you, talk to you, and be with you – all motivated by their need to manipulate rather than a genuine interest in you. Once you hit the devaluation phase, however, you realize that the narcissist is no longer putting forth the same energy or effort. It is exactly at this time which is prime for regaining your life. Tackle this time with a simple method I call **APP (Activities, People and Purpose)**. This means incorporating the following:

Physical Activities to counteract the effects of cortisol as well as to feed our inner "adrenaline junkie" with outlets aside from the narcissist. Yoga. Running. Pilates. Dancing. These all release endorphins that are a much better use of our body chemicals than being addicted to the narcissist.

Social and Creative Activities. Make a list of five activities you engaged with in the past, before the narcissist, that you would like to re-engage in. Underneath, write down five activities you want to try out for the first time. Engage in one new and old activity from this list each week. For example, go back to that yoga class while also trying out rock-climbing with a validating, supportive friend. Get back to writing poetry while joining a dance cardio class, alone or with a friend. These new and old activities will activate dopamine centers in the brain and provide you an adrenaline rush so you don't feel the need to continue to rely on the narcissist and your biochemical addiction to them, an addiction we'll discuss further in Chapter 2. You can also find extended recommendations for battling each biochemical bond you develop with your narcissistic abuser in Chapter 3.

These activities will also enable you to spend time forming new relationships with others as well as give you the necessary space/time to reconnect with yourself. Note: during each and every activity, I challenge you to make sure you keep your phone off so that you do not have any contact with the narcissist whatsoever during these activities. This time is for YOU, not to be disturbed by his or her predatory actions.

The more time you spend on these activities, the less time you spend engaging with and ruminating over your abuser, and the more you detach from your abuser.

People - Meet new people - as friends. I don't recommend seriously dating anyone else at this time, as that will only create more problems and you certainly don't want to introduce a new romantic interest into the dynamic of an abusive relationship you're attempting to end. While in the midst of experiencing trauma, we're more likely to be hypervigilant and overwhelmed by emotions to have clear judgment of romantic partners at this time. Attend the events you are invited to such as networking, school-related or work-related events. Visit new shops and restaurants to make new connections. Join websites like Meetup.com that connect you to people with similar interests, goals and hobbies.

Purpose – Reconnect with your higher purpose. What is that specific dream, goal or talent you've been putting off as you engaged in your relationship with the narcissist? Is it to become a professional dancer? Take dance lessons. Is it to write the next bestselling novel? Start writing it. Is it to go back to school in order to become a teacher? Do it.

If you're already living your dream, keep at it. If you're not, set aside time from your current job to work on this dream. It will make a world of difference in how you see yourself and will enable to find joy, light and life in something other than the toxic individual who has ensnared you. If you're not sure where to start, I always recommend volunteering for a greater social cause or multiple causes. This will help you focus in on how your skills, talents and natural gifts can help serve the world and what causes you are most passionate about contributing to.

Other tips. We'll be discussing a variety of alternative and traditional healing modalities in Chapter 3, so stay tuned. Here are a few of these tips below as they can help get you in the right mindset with the **APP method.**

Self-Compassion and Loving Kindness Meditations. Compassion for ourselves is paramount at this time. Take at least five minutes each day to listen to a meditation or do a breathing meditation that incorporates a sense of self-compassion and self-love. Include mantras like, "I forgive myself," "I love myself," "I accept myself fully." The focus should be on forgiving yourself, not forgiving your abuser, though certainly if you want to also use meditation to "release" the toxicity of the abuse, it can also be a helpful tool for doing so.

Link: Loving Kindness Meditation can also be helped to increase compassion for yourself as well as others. Check it out at contemplativemind.org.

Laughter - Laughter helps with cortisol levels and has proven health benefits. Get into a routine of doing things that make you laugh. Read satire. View movies and television shows that are light, carefree and humorous. Watch a comedy show, go to a live stand-up, get together with your funniest friends, or reflect on the funniest moments of your life. You can even try laughter yoga to get that extra benefit of aligning your laughter with physical movement.

Music – You can find a whole library of suggested music for different moods in Chapter 3. Music gives us emotional power because we can select what we want to listen to. So long as you're not listening to music that is personally triggering for you, music can be cathartic and healing, and listening to upbeat music with the intention of feeling more positive has been shown to lift our mood (Ferguson and Sheldon, 2013). When you're tempted to rage and engage with your abuser, tune them out and tune into your favorite power song instead. This is especially helpful when you're living with a narcissist and are developing a plan to get out – ignore them with the power of music. Not only will it help as an outlet for releasing emotions, it will redirect your brain to whatever mood you're seeking to achieve. It's a win-win!

*Some people with PTSD or complex PTSD may be more sensitive to music than others, so please adjust these suggestions accordingly to your particular situation and always consult a mental health professional if you are suffering from severe triggers of any kind.

Selfish with a Side of Disordered by Kristin Sunanta Walker

Are They Just a Selfish Jerk or Are They a Disordered Obnoxious, Selfish Jerk?

Are they a narcissist or just a selfish jerk? This is a question that has confounded both survivors and outsiders, but Kristin Walker, host of the popular radio show Mental Health News Radio and author of the upcoming book, *Emotional Impotence*, is here to set the record straight.

I've met both. All genders, races and sexual preferences.

I've definitely had my own selfish moments. And I've acted like a jerk.

Anyone who has experienced narcissistic abuse knows there is a significant difference between the selfish jerk and the disordered-obnoxious-selfish jerk. One doesn't trauma-bond with a mere selfish jerk. You don't obsess, have panic attacks, develop an eating disorder, dive into mental illness, and have your soul ravaged over *just* a selfish jerk. You don't question every relationship as well as your ability to differentiate what is real and what is Memorex with *just* a selfish jerk.

Selfish jerks make promises they never deliver. They rarely apologize. They are obtuse. They are passive aggressive and, yes, they are weak. They leave people hanging. They don't share their feelings even when someone is being extremely giving to them. They disappear over ridiculous slights without offering the ability to confront anything. Some rant and rage and wallow in the hood: The Victimhood.

Selfish jerks can have temporary missives with their behavior. They say they don't want to hurt anyone. If cornered, some will even apologize and evolve. They were triggered. Sometimes they were triggered out of an abuse they've suffered. Afraid of rejection, they may run with their tail between their legs while espousing their "word as their bond."

Selfishly-disordered jerks (psychopaths and sociopaths) do all of the above but they do it with sadistic enjoyment of other people's pain. They plot, strategize, and plan soul-crushing emotional time bombs and then smile like Damien's child when they see the carnage they've created.

I watched a man decimate his wife regularly and publicly while smiling as the blood drained from her face and pooled in her neck. It was frightening and sickening to witness his black, vacant eyes and the smirk on his face as he left her emotionally bereft by an unauthorized, sneak attack or a full frontal assault.

I witnessed another as he sat back in his office chair, smiling widely while stretching out his arms and lacing his fingers behind his head. He had just figured out that he had complete control of one of his employees who was in desperate trouble with her child and her finances. "Who would hire her after what she's done to her kid? She's got medical expenses for the rest of its life. She'll take whatever I dish out and beg for more."

This was bone-chilling to witness. She still works for him but he is probably right–she'll never quit. He will pass her over, use her to triangulate with his wife, her coworkers, her husband and friends for two reasons–the eternal boredom of his emotionless life, and, because he can. This is better salvo than an orgasm. For predators like this it is a calculated traumagasm they've been perfecting all their lives.

I always wondered why he chose to show me what he looked like under his mask of sanity and "Aw, shucks" persona. It didn't scare me but I certainly was disgusted. I was also and already trauma-bonded with him and it took a full year after the latest round of pain infliction on everyone around him before I got out for good.

Was he a selfish jerk? Absolutely, but he wasn't obtuse. A selfish-disordered jerk doesn't have occurrences of insight about their behavior in order to change their ways. Selfish-disordered jerks know exactly what they are doing and feel they are entitled to do whatever they want. They *know* it–not feel it–and are just entitled to know it. Disdain is the favored resting place when they have ravaged another source of adoration to the point of exhaustion. Or they simply do it out of boredom. Or because something shinier came along.

Selfish jerks also use social media to attack because they cannot deal with face-to-face confrontation. They hide behind self-righteousness and the flavors of a weak constitution. They don't mean to inflict pain, they are acting out of their pain. On the other hand, the psychopathically disordered are far removed from their pain. *They hunt to hurt.*

While we know the difference through our own experience and by educating ourselves about the ravages of narcissistic abuse, let's try to behave responsibly. Not everyone is a sociopath or a psychopath or even a high-spectrum narcissist. Some people are just plain selfish: temporarily or permanently. Watering down the significance of narcissistic abuse by labeling anyone who's *just* a selfish jerk as a member of the satanic club of psychopathy is not good for the cause.

Confront and move on from *just* selfish jerks. Always and forever go NO CONTACT with disordered-selfish jerks. They'll beat you with your own goodness, enjoy your beheading, and convince you to come back for more.

Don't fret.

Life always comes back to serve them up with a wonderful thing called **age**. Selfish-disordered jerks don't age well. The older one gets, the uglier it is to behave like a spoiled, demonic child, unwilling to share the toys in their shrinking sandbox of life.

About the Author

Kristin Sunanta Walker is the host of Mental Health News Radio and Mental Health After Dark. She is also the CEO of everythingEHR, a company dedicated to working within the Behavioral Health technology space helping vendors and mental health organizations create and utilize incredible tools for excellent patient care. Her radio shows cover all aspects of Behavioral Health, however the shows on the topic of Narcissistic Personality Disorder are downloaded in over 170 countries, clearly showing the epidemic has reached global levels. It is her mission to make Narcissistic Victim Syndrome an officially recognized yet treatable disorder. Her book *Emotional Impotence* will be released in early 2017.

Social Media Platforms

Mental Health News Radio: www.mentalhealthnewsradio.com

EverythingHR: www.everythingehr.com

Twitter: www.twitter.com/everythingehr

Facebook: www.facebook.com/everythingehr

LinkedIn: https://www.linkedin.com/company/everythingehr

Blog: www.emotionalimpotence.com

While a sociopath exists on the far end of the narcissistic spectrum, both narcissists and sociopaths can subject us to horrific abuse while also shifting the blame of their tactics onto us. It's important that we do not blame ourselves for the abuse or engage in the magical thinking that they would have changed had we stayed. For those targeted by sociopaths, the scam goes beyond just emotional and psychological – in many cases, it's downright criminal. Jennifer Smith, Founder of truelovescam.com, explains why a sociopath's scam isn't personal – it's inevitable in this type of toxic partnership.

The Sociopath's Scam – It Isn't Personal by Jennifer Smith

We all wonder what just ripped through our lives – our heads spinning, we have to keep our feet on the ground to resolve the damage and destruction. But running around in circles through our minds making recovery a longer harder road is: *Why? What did I do wrong?*

Sociopaths are all alike in method and madness; as inexplicable as it all seems – sociopaths are limited in thinking, identical in tactics and are predictable - and most importantly: none of the wreckage they bring is personal. Sociopaths have no attachment or positive bonding feelings.

They're born with a brain that biologically is incapable of registering love, like, care or compassion. Therefore, they have no conscience. They're left with only an animalistic survival instinct. An instinct for their own survival - not even for a family group or fellow sociopaths - only for themselves as an individual entity. They do things we couldn't conceive of in order to obtain that survival. They leave wreckage in their wake. We can disarm their influence in the aftermath.

The victim wonders:

How can someone do this?! If I stayed maybe we could work it out – he's nice too, and sweet sometimes – maybe he can change and not do horrible things and stop blaming me – he acts like he's faultless – he's always telling me I'm bad... maybe I am. I feel hopeless.

Maybe this will help:

Sociopaths know *they're bad.* They love, love, love being bad. They are "faultless" – from their myopic view because the concept of "fault" - as in: "It's your fault and *you* lied *to me*" - is not an emotion their bodies can feel. To a sociopath, it's no big deal to hurt someone.

They can't relate to the concept of feelings. Nope. Not one bit. They have no feelings aside from burning "want." It helps if we look at the hijacking – the time we spent with a sociopath - from the point of view of their malfunctioning brain. Sociopaths operate essentially from a primal reptilian brain. A reptile's entire DNA is wired to focus on individual self-preservation. They have no concern or connection to other reptiles - they only want to survive, eating anyone else to do so, including their own offspring. Voila - the sociopath.

Sociopaths pretend we're at "fault" and make every appearance of blaming us to keep us under their control so they can keep taking from us. They actually *feel* none of it. They don't really care. They just want our stuff - which they perceive as their stuff - even if they have to smash our head against a wall to get it.

We feel so deeply betrayed because we believe it's a real relationship – it isn't. We don't understand that it wasn't personal. We could have been anyone to the sociopath. These are not relationships. They are crimes. Emotional, spiritual, physical, mental, financial theft; defrauding, misrepresentation, deception and larceny.

It's important to understand the mind of a sociopath and realize: what they do has nothing to do with us - they target great people of loyalty and commitment who believe in love, invest in relationships and have empathy for others to defraud and steal for their livelihood. We could have been anyone - anyone with a heart, a bed, a bank account, some food, an extra toothbrush, and some skills to hijack, which the sociopath enlists to propel their miserable sham of a life forward. We're amazing people – after all - no one robs an empty house.

The victim thinks:

It looks like he really loves this new woman. He tells everyone he never loved me. Maybe he treats her better than he treated me and they'll be happy.

Maybe this will help:

Such a gracious outlook is a trait of a perfect target for a sociopath. They choose magnificent, loving people to borrow and to do the work of upholding their false world.

No one gets treated "better" by a sociopath than anyone else. The sociopath makes it look this way because they want to appear to be wonderful people. He – or she – will take from the new victim just as they have from every victim – they only ruin lives. Sociopaths are unable to love. Some targets are treated worse than others, but no one is treated well; some are utterly destroyed financially, physically, mentally, emotionally; in extreme cases some are killed.

All sociopaths use the very same sociopathic skills of perception and manipulation in assessing a target, winning trust, then taking things, then ruining us behind our backs. Then we break up - or they leave suddenly and unexpectedly and coldly - and then they smear us.

This is all a sociopath is capable of. They also always have anywhere from 5 - 20 people they're scamming in cycles of overlapping beginnings and endings in constant rotation. There is no "He was with me, then he dumped me for her." They have many women or men all at the same time Always. It only looks like a succession of "relationships" because that's what they show us. None of these is a real relationship – they're crimes. They love no one aside from themselves.

And we might still wonder:

Why, why, why did he marry her and not me?! I know I shouldn't care – but I do and it looks like he really loves her. Was I not good enough?

Maybe this will help:

We're more than good enough. It's the sociopath who is total garbage.

We're in love. We discover it's a scam; we kick them out or they take off. We pick up pieces, start from scratch, and - still we can harbor lingering pain. It's the tiny-giant things inside the true love scam that haunt us; a disharmony between our heart and our mind. The sociopath is gone, but the cognitive dissonance goes on. A hideous cycle of opposing doubt and certainty: the bitter pain and humiliation in wondering why he found us "less than" another woman - colliding with knowing he's horrible and admonishing ourselves for caring what he thinks.

And on it goes, keeping us up at night, gnawing at us through the day, eating our hearts out. We know what a sociopath thinks of us is completely unimportant beyond belief. And even still, in lingering doubt and pain we wonder – *why?*

Here's the thing – it's important to grasp what a sociopath is. It isn't personal. No woman is any better than any other woman. She's no better, we're no better. It isn't even a matter of consideration - sociopaths don't love anyone. Sociopaths don't like anyone. They don't prefer anyone over anyone else. They have no feelings. We could be absolutely anyone to them. Their victims are interchangeable and replaceable. They run several hidden as well as visible "relationships" constantly. This is always the way it is. Always. It's a *faux*lationship.

None of us matter in the least except for one reason and one reason only: each target supplies something the sociopath wants or needs:

Money.
A car.
A laptop.
A new wardrobe.
A bed.
A nice house.
A Green Card.
A place to hide.
A new trick-of-the-trade.
Respectability.
Food.
A place to put it. (Uhghm.)
A shower.
An internet connection.
Laundry service.

Here's how personal it is - imagine this:

A sociopath walks into a bar. He scans the room, narrowing in on 3 or 4 possible targets. He gets 7 phone numbers before the club closes. That night and early in the morning and through the next day he sends text messages to them every hour until 2 of them make a date with him. A week later he moves in with one of them, bringing only one suitcase and carrying his laptop. She can't believe she has found such great love!

That lucky lady is Target A.

She doesn't know he lives in another neighborhood with a woman he's "done" with because that woman is discovering his real monster-self. And to him - it's getting boring - he already took most of her money. Her head is spinning.

She is Target B.

After about 8 weeks of bliss, mingled with a few odd moments that Target A chalks up to getting to know one another, she can't for the life of her make sense of why she finds him locked in the bathroom at 3:00 in the morning with his cell phone. A lot.

She doesn't know he's busy texting and talking with (among others) his "fiancé" in another state who knows nothing about Target B, or A. None of the women know about her. The "fiancé" is 5 months pregnant with his child. She thinks she's the only one.

She is Target C.

And in a not-to-distant neighborhood he has a wife and a 3-year old child. She owns a beautiful house. Now he does too. He travels so much for business it's getting really hard on her. She has pictures of them as a family on her Facebook page. He has pictures of the child on his Facebook page. And pictures of himself. Lots of those. This woman believes she's the only one.

She is Target D.

He has an ex-wife in another state. They have no children. He comes from Sweden via who knows where; she was his ticket to a Family Green Card to the USA. This woman knows he's a scammer – he drained her bank account. He tells people she only wanted him for his money and she's crazy.

She is Target E.

And in another state he has another woman who's waiting for him with their 4-year old kid and her child from an earlier marriage. He put off marrying her, though he always promised he would. This woman knows now about the new wife, Target D, but not his ex-wife, Target E. She's heartbroken. He tells people she won't let him see his child and is on drugs.

She is Target F.

He has another woman who he's been with for years - they have two kids - 9 and 6 years old; they wait for him in another state entirely. She thinks he's doing business and travels a lot. She doesn't look at Facebook ever. He blocked her from his FB page long ago and she knows not to question him. She's madly in love with him and wildly in pain and just waiting until the day they get married.

She's Target G.

And, there's a woman, a married woman, married to someone else, who had an affair with him and had his baby who's only 2 months old. She thought he was going to marry her. He's never seen the baby and never will. - Her husband left her because of it. Now she's a single mom.

She's Target H.

And there's a woman back in Sweden who thinks he's wonderful and sends him money every month.

She's Target I.

He has a harem of rotating and overlapping "girlfriends", code for: potential deep targets. Some are told he's divorced; some that he's never been married; some are told he has a baby with a woman who won't let him see his child – and - she's on drugs. (Target F).

These "girlfriends" are Targets J, K, L and M.

He's working on N, O, P and Q as K and J don't put out money for him and as Target D begins to get more and more suspicious, and a lot more miserable - even though she's the current public woman.

So A or C or M, or L, or another new woman will become the public woman if B and D keep up their suspicions; if they see through a crack and things fall apart. Which of course they will. Lucky A, C, M or L.

They all were told: He had a true love who broke his heart by sleeping with his best friend. Now he doesn't trust easily anymore. He doesn't trust his woman to meet his male friends. He's really hurt and reluctant to commit because of being betrayed. This draws out our empathy and created a valid reason for their reluctance to get really close - allowing them to do all kinds of horrid things while we forgive them over and over.

And when any of these women questions him about being locked in the bathroom at 3:00 a,m, with his cell phone he says: He's soooooo stressed out with business - these people who are trying to screw him over. And he has to travel a lot. Sometimes last minute. That's just the way it is and wouldn't we rather have him work hard than lay around and be a nobody? And by the way - do we have some money or a credit card he can use for a business lunch? His next "Big Deal" - he'll make millions from this lunch! He can't look cheap - he has to pay for the lunch and maybe a dinner and he's broke because he lost on a deal last week and… If we don't stop questioning him he just really can't take it! And his blood pressure is going to kill him – he's going to have a heart attack if we don't just… stop! And he's feeling "physical" and he warns us we don't want to see that – so just - STEP BACK! Don't we trust him?! Everything he's *doing is for US!!!*

All these words. So many words. The same words over and over. All lies - twisted bits of whispers of a shadow of one fact woven into an absurd labyrinth of lies. The "meetings" are dates. The money is for a lunch with one woman. A dinner a night out with another woman. A movie with a 3rd. To give to his wife for groceries – remember Target D? That's as personal as it gets.

We're targeted because we're amazing. Because we have resources, skills, ethics. Because we love, care, support and are loyal. Because we invest in relationships. Because we believe in love. Because we're human.

Sociopaths have no concept of love. Not one tiny bit of an idea of what love feels like. Imagine trying to explain the taste of a strawberry to someone with no experience of a strawberry so they can comprehend "strawberry". As impossible as that is to convey - a million times harder than that — that's how much sociopaths have no idea what love is.

Prey are given the role the sociopath deems necessary within the schematics of their ploy. This is based on what the sociopath thinks they can get from that target, what they need or want at that moment, and the timing in conjunction with other targets already in their control, and other circumstances of the sociopath's ruse of a life. Maybe they're on the run. Maybe they need to lay low. Maybe they're on a high from a huge score - and broke away relatively clean - and want a nice little "family" to publicly show the world they are Super Duper Great. That's as personal as it gets. It's all about him.

Harboring self-doubts, wondering "why" - leaves the sociopath winning. Harbor no doubts about how awesome we are. Harbor no doubts about how malevolent and deliberate the sociopath is. They aren't an enigma — they're just pure evil. These are crimes not relationships. There's nothing we could have done differently. We were in love; not clairvoyant. And we'll be more than okay because we are human beings who can love. Embrace our own life. It's time to thrive.

Here's to REAL true love and happiness!

Jennifer Smith
www.truelovescam.com

About the Author

Jennifer Smith is a real person who got played by a parasitic sociopath of a con man. Jennifer manages a True Love Scam Meet-Up recovery group in Los Angeles. Most of Jennifer's time is spent supporting those going through escape and recovery from a sociopath. She's got an upcoming book adapted and expanded from the blog posts, and a creative-nonfiction novelization of her nightmare with a sociopath. These aren't relationships - they're crimes; it's time to thrive!

Social Media Platforms

Personal True Love Scam chats in support of recovery can be scheduled here: http://www.truelovescam.com/true-love-scam-chat/

True Love Scam on Facebook:
https://www.facebook.com/recognizesurviveasociopath/

True Love Scam blog: http://www.truelovescam.com

On Tumblr: http://truelovescamrecovery.tumblr.com/

On Twitter: https://twitter.com/truelovescam

On Pinterest: https://www.pinterest.com/truelovescam/

On Hub Pages: http://hubpages.com/relationships/Sociopaths-Lie-Always-With-one-Exception

Survivor Insights

Question: How has narcissistic abuse affected you? What types of trauma did you experience in this type of abuse?

"I have experienced major setbacks in my life on all levels of my life. The same types of abuse that I experienced caused setbacks in those areas. The physical abuse caused emotional and spiritual pain. I am struggling to recover financially, working full time and freelancing other part time jobs to try to dig myself out of debt. I had PTSD from prior abuse and that was triggered in a big way from the physical and sexual abuse. My spirit was damaged from the whole experience and I struggle daily to be able to stay productive and professional. I struggle with fatigue and low energy because of the enormous amount of stress related to the lack of validation from former friends who align themselves with my abuser, and the huge debt that I was left with. My abuser committed spousal rape in what I think was an attempt to break me down when he sensed he was losing control of me, and that is not something that I am proud of or find it easy to talk about with friends. Most of them have no concept of what I have been through and I can't talk about it with them because they would just think I was crazy. I have definitely been greatly harmed, in all ways, and I have no recourse except to suck it up and keep going." - Anne, Indiana

"My husband presented himself to me initially with the typical blazing attention of the narcissist and then systematically isolated me from my friends and family, withdrew his affection and began belittling me. He was totally indifferent to my health, which declined radically, and my mental health which also eventually declined to the point that I was hospitalized and lost my job. He was indifferent to my innumerable efforts to make our lives together tolerable and insured anything I tried to do failed. "By the time I left I was exhausted and a shadow of my former self, and unable to see my own self-worth or trust my own decisions.

He controlled all of our finances to support his many hobbies and insisted on extravagant trips which left us in debt while we had cheap used furniture in our home. Both the debt and the cheapness in our home shamed me. He never said anything positive to me yet demanded sex and made me feel guilty for withholding. Sex became a chore that reminded me of the 1950's "lie back and think of something else." There was no connection at all. This situation was ironic because I was raised in a culture of sexual liberation. Cut off from real friendships, I became enmeshed in a band of health professionals who were unable to really help since the stress in my home was so extreme, but nobody saw that for 10 years. I became fearful of identifying and stating what I wanted. I hid everything important to me. He ridiculed my spiritual practices so I stopped them... leaving another glaring hole." – Sandra, Washington

"I have experienced physical, emotional, verbal, sexual, spiritual. It has been both an undercurrent and overt in the form of PTSD, which I did not realize until age 62. It has prevented me from having a healthy relationship with a partner; i.e., I had 3 unhealthy partners followed by 30 years of being divorced from the last one. My lifetime has been about recovery and growth as I gradually awoke and dealt with both memories and the results of trauma." – Penelope, Location Undisclosed

"I lost myself, my inner strength, my confidence, my voice, my opinion. I lowered the threshold every week of what was acceptable to me until he only spoke to me in disrespectful, insulting, minimizing ways. What I said was ignored or criticized and I had no voice. Sex was amazing then near the end withheld as he used the triangulation affairs over me. He destroyed me slowly over 18 months until I finally lost my job and then found the courage to leave him." – Karen, NJ

"I went from a confident, self-assured young woman who wanted so much to be loved for who I was to being a woman who second-guessed herself constantly and wondered why women in other relationships didn't seem to have the same struggles. I realized how messed up the relationship was when I convinced a friend to ask my then husband if I could go with her to get my nails done the next weekend. I knew that if I brought it up solo it would be either refused or granted with conditions. By having my friend ask him, he was forced to say yes in order to keep people from seeing how controlling he really was. The grumpy attitude still happened, but I was saved the confrontation and insinuations that I was lazy and selfish for wanting some time away with a friend." – Amy, Pacific Northwest

"Old wounds were made new, as new ones were inflicted. He somehow always brought any pain in my past to the present as he twisted and warped my world, until it was all I could do to put one foot in front of the other. Since he dumped me on the roadside of life, leaving me disabled, depressed, penniless and without the means to support myself, I have dealt with PTSD on a daily basis. Every day is a challenge. He used mental, emotional and financial abuse. He threatened physical abuse every day, but never actually used it. He loved to threaten harm to my son too." – Laura, Oregon

"Oh wow. How it has affected me? In every way possible. My view of the world was tainted, my view of myself was tainted. The world became a scary place filled with people who were untrustworthy. The person in the mirror didn't look like me anymore. I didn't know what I liked. I didn't know who I was. I experienced physical, emotional, verbal abuse from a narcissistic parent." – Eva, Location Undisclosed

"I now have PTSD. I have trust issues and most likely will never get to the point of trusting another man. I experienced physical abuse as I was strangled while trying to leave him, emotional abuse with constant cut downs and gas lighting, sexual abuse by being raped and sodomized when I said no, took my house, all my savings and tried to destroy my car and then left me homeless in the street. All the while professing the Bible was untrue and I was an idiot and weak to believe in those things. I was very open to him about my strong Christianity and work for my church." – Stacy, Nebraska

"So many ways, first he stripped away any doubts I had with lies disguised as future dreams, talk of how I was the one; different from all others, alluring, sexy, wanted, smart and interesting. He knew I was at an emotional turning point in my life and marriage and took full advantage of my turmoil to be the calming, beautiful sea of life I thought I needed. He lied about everything, I mean everything and I gladly ate it all up. His lies have affected me deeply. I don't trust my own judgment at all anymore. I don't trust strangers, friends, mostly myself. I find myself investigating everyone now. I take nothing at face-value anymore. I am in my 50's and he has taken the last bit of magic I could find in this world and stomped it out. I no longer believe in the "goodness" of most people. I know now that the ugliest people come in the prettiest packages and say the most lovely things until you upset them. I believe that most people wear masks now and am always waiting for the mask to fall off so I can see what's really underneath." -Claudia, California

"It caused me to be depressed and isolated. I've had low self-esteem, trust issues, weight gain, difficulty focusing, insomnia, anxiety, guilt, self-loathing, intrusive thoughts, a feeling of emptiness, problems with self-care, and being unable to enjoy what I like. I experienced a little physical

and verbal abuse. Most of the abuse was emotional (passive-aggressive)."
– Lisa, Ohio

"I have experienced psychological and emotional and verbal and physical and sexual and financial abuse from narcissists. I suspect that I'm suffering from CPTSD as a consequence of lifelong narcissistic abuse. The abuse (from my father and boyfriends) has left me with extremely low self-worth and constant anxiety and depression and recurrent anger (at them and also at myself for being fooled by them and allowing them to treat me so badly). Because my self-confidence has been smashed so low and because I'm scared of being hurt again, I self-isolate. I only see my mum and one friend and find it difficult to leave my apartment because of agoraphobia and social phobia and fear of bumping into one of my narcissistic ex partners.

My most recent relationship (with a covert narcissist) has also left me feeling deeply disturbed and in shock because of the stunning contrast because the illusory dream man he initially pretended to be (in order to ensnare me) and the hate-filled rage-filled insane monster he really is. I still love and miss and long for the wonderful person he pretended to be. It's weird and heartbreaking to try to accept that he never existed. I'm experiencing a terrible feeling of loss, as if someone has died. My ex demanded that I focus all of my time and energy on him so, now that the relationship is over, my life feels empty and pointless and bleak. During the year that we were together he isolated me from my friends and family and messaged me almost constantly so, now that I've severed contact with him, I also feel desperately lonely." – Aurla, Brighton, England

"My heart broke in to pieces when he left me. It's the thought of WHY he left. He never explained any reason for leaving. That was the hardest part of the breakup for me. Not knowing the reasons behind it. I thought I was doing everything he expected from me, but obviously not! I felt so much anger inside of me than anything else. Disappointment came a little later. Though he did not physically abuse me in any way, he emotionally, verbally, financial, spiritual brought me down. Sexually, he was never making love with me, he was always fantasizing of the woman he really wanted in his life. Someone older, wiser & richer. He often talked about it to me and because I loved him, I accepted it (even though I hated the thought of it)." – Nyree, New Zealand

"Too many to write without creating a book of my own. Physical abuse a few times. Emotional abuse almost daily. Verbal abuse during the devalue stage. Not abusive sexually but rough at times, cheated a lot. Financial devastation. Spiritually he kept me on my knees and distracted from doing what I knew best." – Donna, Chattanooga, TN

"Most of the abuse I suffered was the emotional, verbal and sexual kind. It greatly damaged my self-esteem and my whole sense of self-worth, for a long time. In looking back at it, I don't even know who that person was. It is only now, more than a year after getting out of it, that I feel like my true self again." – ProudSurvivor, California

"It has made me insecure. I had to move out of my city because he painted a negative image of me to the people in my community." – Gloria, Mexico

"I lived with a narcissist for 38 years. The original "love bombing" got me first . Early in the relationship the violence came all with the abuse it was my fault. So yes I stayed the triangle was there almost all of our courting days . Marriage came but so did the affairs. I lost my mother when our first child was born. Do I guess from not long after I experienced every type of abuse and after many years I eventually found the courage to leave. But after suicide threats and again being love-bombed I allowed him back after making him go for help about his anger. So 15 years later he walked again for good new love! Yes I was a victim and I have survived." – Michele, Melbourne, Australia.

"Narcissistic abuse has affected my ability to feel independent or self-reliant. I feel like a lot of my emotional and spiritual well-being has been suppressed especially my ability to speak up to the abusers because of fear that I will make the situation worse. The abuse has come from people I assumed to be friends, workplace abuse, and ex-husband and a few boyfriends. It was always where I was in some vulnerable position."
- Ms. L, Idaho

"I went from feeling like a strong independent woman to thinking that I needed to check with him about everything. I no longer felt strong. I felt like things that went wrong were because I didn't give enough. I wanted someone to share my life with but ended up with someone who eventually stopped trying to please me and became to demand more and never was satisfied.

He no longer wanted to be at my house because I had a child, mother and animals. He wanted me to go to see him at his place always and then he no longer interacted with anyone in my life. I was with him for 9 years and he constantly wanted me to call be over there, run to the door "act enthusiastically" when I saw him. Sexually, he knew I had been raped in my past and had gone through counseling. I told him I didn't like it if he was touching me sexually while sleeping and explained why. I would feel him at 3 am trying to get put my hand on his privates trying to get off. I was in a dead sleep. I didn't know how to react since I was so shocked that he would do this after what I shared. When I said this was like a rape since I didn't give consent he blew up and me. By then, I found myself apologizing to him. At another date, he did it again. This really messed with my head." – Kathy, Florida

"So far I have discovered the reality of Cluster B personality disorders and have educated myself. This has been validating! I have also discovered blogs and youtube authors who teach about this; again very helpful. So far I have implemented no contact and am just beginning to work on my own issues. I'm just beginning my journey out of the "fog" (fear, obligation, guilt.)" – Laurel from San Francisco

Question: What is the most powerful way a narcissist has manipulated/degraded you? How did you react and what did you wish you could have done?

"Love-bombing with spectacular sex soon followed by withholding of all compliments, affection and sex. I reacted by blaming myself, assuming I was not attractive enough and making an enormous effort to improve my appearance. This only made the narcissists lose even more respect for me and reject me (physically) even more so it was a vicious circle. I should have ended the relationships as soon as the narcissists started withholding affection and sex.

With my last boyfriend I eventually realized that he was deliberately withholding affection and sex to punish me (for not seeing him literally every day) and that it was a power trip for him which was designed to undermine my self-esteem and manipulate me (for instance, if I would stay overnight he would reward me with sex). I then tried an experiment: I stopped being affectionate towards him (stopped stroking and cuddling him etc. while we watched movies & stopped kissing him etc.) and, almost immediately, he became affectionate and aroused again! This narcissist also degraded me by (one month into our relationship) suddenly bombarding me with unprovoked abusive viciously cruel text messages for seven hours straight, calling me things like "loser" and "fucking foul scumbag" etc. I should have never spoken to him again but he claimed he was drunk and did not mean any of it. Another way this narcissist degraded me was by using OkCupid online dating site (listing himself as "single") the whole time we were together. I stayed with him even after I found out he was on OkCupid & he then demoted me from "girlfriend" status to "playmate" which further eroded my self-esteem." – Aurla, Brighton, England

"Verbally and repetitively negating whatever I said. Making me feel unheard, disrespected and whatever I had to say had no impact or bearing on anything. I shut down, disconnected from my family/friends, felt suicidal. I wish I would have left sooner and realized it was a unhealthy family to begin with and yes I was different but in a good way not negative." – Megan W., Minneapolis, Minnesota

"She used my abusive relationship with my ex-husband to continue verbally abusing me and belittle me. I would just leave the room and shut the door. She would follow and continue. I wish I would have never bought the house and left her early in the relationship." -Good2befree, NJ

"He stonewalled me…completely ignored me unless it was dinner time. Never came to bed. Told me he was no longer attracted to me and wanted others. Told me what I felt was wrong. Told me I didn't make enough money, though I considered myself successful. I didn't respond negatively in front of the kids (i.e. dinner) I cried myself to sleep most nights, alone, while he viewed porn on the computer…and cried all my way to work the next day. Over and over again. I wish I could have moved out sooner." – Lonna, Colorado

"Verbally and emotionally, he used gaslighting and love bombing. I felt consumed in every aspect of my being, there was no me left, just him and his needs. The more vile things he said, the more I tried to prove my love and worth. He did the silent treatment like a star and I would try to jolly him out of black moods, taking responsibility for everything and apologizing just to stop the fights. In so many ways I wish I'd never met him. But would I have learnt this much about myself and my childhood? I wish I still had the money. I'm still struggling with depression and now I'm broke at 41." – Lilly, Auckland, New Zealand

"Taking my childhood trauma and turning it into everything that happened was all my fault." – ShaBaBee, WI

"He used to insist that he had checked with other people and that they agreed that my behavior was not ok. His use of implied support from people I knew (most likely not at all true, I know that now) was the strongest tool he had to get me to question whether I had the right to feel the way I did. I wish I would have trusted myself more and confronted him by asking for names and making HIM own the burden of proof." - Amy, Pacific Northwest

"Everything you described in your blog with the business partner. I often knew something was up but it was like being on a railroad that I couldn't get off until things totally blew up and I was a mess. Then I went to a therapist." -Jane, Massachusetts

"He used my capacity for forgiveness against me. He told me that one of the reasons he liked me so much was that I forgive easily. He took advantage of my forgiving nature to carry out the idealize-devalue-discard cycle many times, until it almost destroyed me and I literally got so sick of it all that I left him behind for good, with no chance of reconciliation or rekindling our relationship even as friends or whatsoever. I wish that the first time he had discarded me I would've just severed all ties with him and never look back instead of trying to work it out, because the problem really was him and not me." -Diyanah, Kuala Lumpur

"The most effective way was their friendliness, charming charisma, grandiose successes in life as far as it goes with romance. With friendships it was the warm acceptance and that ability to relate in a personable way. The most degrading in all situations was how they would publicly put me down in front of others in ways that I was taken off guard or set up to look like the bad person. My reaction was to not lower myself or feed the more negativity into the events, but inside I wanted to have revenge.

One of my most unforgettable moments was when someone I thought was a good friend betrayed me by openly pursuing my boyfriend. After my relationship was over with both they both paraded around in the social circle I was in. She took pride in the ability to destroy my relationship while appearing to advance herself above me. She made a point to make this drama public and to put me down in front of the social circle. At the time it was so emotionally depressing that it was causing me physical illness like hyper tension, loss of appetite, a lot of crying and confusion. I don't think there was anything I could have done, because it was an early learning experience on just how cruel a person could be to someone who was a respected friend." – Ms. L, Idaho

"By turning the tables on me when he cheated on me in marriage and made me feel like it was my fault because I wasn't perfect. I started condemning myself on the inside for having weaknesses. I wish I could have detached right away, but it was hard cuz all through our marriage I was a stay at home mom and very dependent on him emotionally." -Jean, Minnesota

"He uses any weakness or flaw that I have and condemns me for it. Uses it like a weapon. He also wedged himself between me and any other person or place or situation that gave me security. My family, my friends, my church, my job…" - Tricia, California

"Because I don't have the financial knowledge I should have, he got away with a lot in the divorce agreement. He makes the most money and "offered" to pay for so many things regarding our daughter (insurance, copays, private schooling). I didn't realize it at the time but this is giving him a stronghold on keeping her in the 50/50 custody arrangement we currently have. Being naive about finances was the worst thing for me because it lead to him having more control over me after the divorce. I stayed in his house (he moved in with his parents) and let him have financial reign over so many things because it seemed to ease the burden on me. I've since moved out of his house. He's still coming after me for what he thinks I owe him from this. I've gotten an attorney involved with a letter to cease and desist. However, I know it won't be over." - Shannon, Central Ohio

"By pretending to be my soul mate. I truly believed we were best friends for 16 years until we moved in together and I got pregnant and the mask came off. I just wish I was aware of what to look for in a healthy person. I would have been able to see past the act and recognize that the little "weird" things about him were signs of narcissism." -Lynn, Houston, Texas

"The manipulation I endured was full-blown brainwashing. I was gaslighted to believe that I was the crazy one. Then he convinced me that my family was the problem in our marriage, and if I went no-contact with them then we would be ok. My heart always felt heavy, but I grew used to it after a few years. When I finally left, I felt a freedom I had not experienced in a long time: the freedom from the bondage of sin. I was in bondage to his sin; I had to hide it because of how it would look if people found out I was staying with an abusive spouse. He had me so entangled in his sin that I became party to it. Now that I'm out, I feel so free. I can repent of my own sin. I can read my Bible with a clear conscience, and not be afraid to act on my convictions." -Elle, Virginia

"He used every trick in the handbook...Flattery, admiration, coercion, name-calling and threats of bodily harm. Also sexual degrading acts of which I participated in because I was curious, then afraid. At first I was wary. Then I was astonished at his words and actions. He said I was special then sent me pics of him with other women. Then I became like a detective and wanted to figure him out. Finally I became very sad and then angry. I wish the first time he showed me disrespect and lack of boundaries I would have gotten up and left never to talk to him again." - Angelina M., Ohio

"He played the 'poor me' attitude and induced lots of guilt. I did lots of things out of being guilt tripped into feeling sorry for him. Then I constantly tried to live up to his demands and please him to maintain my position of being made to feel special and his 'perfect woman'. When in fact he had several. He made me doubt my own mind when I asked questions. He turned things around to look like my fault. I was so confused and unhappy in the end he told me I was an object of pity and he was glad to get shot of me. He never apologized or owned up to any of his lies. I realized it was impossible for me to relate to him - I wasted so much emotional effort to get him to see the light I now realize that was pointless. I wish now I had just walked away after first big red flag - without even bothering to explain. Just go and don't turn back. There's no 'good ending' with these people." - Gemma, United Kingdom

CHAPTER TWO

Your Brain on Love, Sex and the Narcissist

Why Your Bond to Your Abuser is Difficult to Break

Before we get to the effects of our brain on narcissistic abuse, let's talk about...

Your Brain On Trauma

The impact of trauma is hugely underestimated in the public discourse about domestic violence and emotional abuse. I can't tell you the number of times I've heard an ignorant person talk about how if they had been in an abusive relationship, *they* would've left right away – in a condescending tone that often judges an abuse survivor for not doing so. Mind you, these are the same people who have never been in abusive relationships and probably have never read a book about trauma. This adds onto the toxic shame survivors already feel, as many survivors "most [survivors] suffer from agonizing shame about the actions they took to survive and maintain a connection with the person who abused them" (Van der Kolk, p.13, 2015).

This compounds the two-fold experience that trauma survivors experience: emotional numbing through dissociation and forced emotional numbing due to the social norm that we have to "let it go," and "move forward" somehow. These are all very damaging and re-traumatizing things for a trauma survivor to hear, as trauma can live in our bodies as well as our minds for a lifetime. No one should be allowed to "compare" your trauma to another person's trauma. Everyone reacts to trauma differently and each reaction is valid based on the trauma and its impact on that person. Society must unlearn this idea that we should "get over" trauma as this only adds to the effects of emotional numbing and repression that causes so much damage to our hearts, minds and bodies.

While victim-blaming and victim-shaming individuals judge survivors as weak-minded, their own small-mindedness prevents them from being compassionate towards individuals who need it the most. According to Bessel van der Kolk, MD (2015), the changes produced by trauma explain why those who are traumatized experience a form of hypervigilance as well as paralysis or what Maeir and Seligman (1967) call "learned helplessness," that disrupts their lives. According to Maier and Seligman's studies of dogs who received inescapable electric shocks, a form of learned helplessness developed in dogs whose attempts to get out of a traumatizing, seemingly inescapable environment were continually thwarted. Eventually, these dogs gave up trying to escape, even when they were eventually offered a way out. This was compared with dogs that received the shocks but could take action to get out of their environment; the dogs whose attempts were not continuously thwarted did take action to escape when presented with the opportunity to do so.

The results are clear: being in a traumatizing environment where the outcome becomes independent of any actions on the subject's part can lead to the subject giving up altogether and succumbing to their situation. Peterson and Seligman (2010) later clarified that this form of learned helplessness could also apply to victims of other forms of inescapable situations.

Learned helplessness works hand in hand with that paralysis we may feel when we're in an abusive relationship as well as the changes in our brain that are occurring due to trauma. If we are not able to engage in "fight" or "flight" to get out of the abusive situation, the stress tends to be stored in our bodies. Emotional pain keeps us stuck and exhausted unable to escape the ever-firing stress hormone system that generates signals long after the threat is over (Walker, 2013, Van der Kolk, 2015).

That is why survivors of psychological and emotional abuse, especially narcissistic abuse, tend to feel as if they cannot get out of their situation – their sense of perceived agency becomes misaligned with their actual agency after numerous attempts of attempting to plead with the abuser to change, of being thrust into dangerous situations with their abuser and subjected to multiple emotional and psychological "shocks" of abusive incidents.

Traumatized individuals who are in constant "flight" mode become hyper-reactive to their environment, can demonstrate social anxiety as well as constant avoidance of anything that resembles their trauma. This research also helps to shed light on why traumatized people tend to go through a trauma repetition cycle, often repeating destructive behaviors and relationship patterns with seemingly no sense of being able to escape, resulting in a diminished sense of agency.

According to Dr. Bessel van der Kolk's book *The Body Keeps the Score*, "We now know that their behaviors are not the result of moral failings or signs of lack of willpower or bad character – they are caused by actual changes in the brain" (Van der Kolk, 2015, p. 2).

You don't have to endure inescapable electrical shocks in order to feel a sense of helplessness – nor do you have to be held in captivity or subject to the most extreme cases of physical violence.

There is an underestimation of the effects of verbal aggression and psychological attacks against an individual which makes up a large component of narcissistic abuse. As I've mentioned before, what people fail to understand is that the same brain circuitry activated when we experience physical pain can be activated when we suffer emotional pain. Verbal aggression and social rejection of *any kind* can hurt, much like physical abuse.

Survivors who have experienced both know that either can have long-lasting effects, though undoubtedly many abusive relationships have components of both. According to research conducted by Naomi L. Eisenberger (2004), the same circuitry associated with physical pain can be activated through emotional pain such as that of social exclusion. In another study by Ethan Kross (2011), pain tests revealed that thinking about a painful breakup can reactivate the same parts of the brain as when an individual feels the physical discomfort of heat applied to their bodies. Heartbreak causes a surge of adrenaline, causing us to respond to **an emotional threat as if it were a physical one**, raising blood pressure, speeding up breathing, and causing a host of physical symptoms caused by the increase in stress hormones.

The effects of trauma are certainly not limited to adulthood; in fact, it is most impactful on the brain when we are children. For those who have been abused as children by narcissistic parents, trauma literally changes the structure of a child's developing brain which is extremely malleable during that time. Dr. Martin Teicher (2006) pointed out the growing evidence that verbal abuse in childhood can change the way a brain is wired, increasing the risk for anxiety and suicidal ideation in adulthood. There has been corresponding research that confirms that **parental verbal aggression** can in fact lead to changes in the brain (Choi, et. al 2009; Teicher, 2006).

Being raised by a narcissistic parent can literally change our brain, potentially making us a completely different person than we would have been pre-trauma. Brain areas affected by trauma can include the hippocampus, the amygdala, the corpus callosum and the frontal cortex. In addition, trauma results in alterations in the key neural systems involved in stress responses, such as the HPA axis – this chronic activation wears out parts of the body, resulting in hippocampal/limbic abnormalities in children (Perry, 2000) The hippocampus and amygdala are key areas of the brain involved in memory, emotion, and arousal, the frontal cortex is the "planning," cognitive center of our brain and the corpus callosum helps the integration of the two halves of the brain.

It is no wonder that when we have been abused in any way, we have difficulties with planning, memory, and emotion regulation. Our brain has literally been impaired by the stress of the trauma and the connection between the "rational" aspects of our brain and the emotive aspects has been broken. Have you ever engaged in what is seemingly irrational behavior as a result of the trauma, but which seemed rational in the context of the emotions and bodily sensations you experienced? Now you know why – the changes that take place are enough to make anyone have an interruption in their decision-making process.

Victim-blaming individuals fail to recognize that someone going back to the trauma of an abusive relationship is not reacting to the trauma through the rational part of their brain, but rather their limbic and reptilian systems – the parts of their brains where emotions are stored and processed. These are the parts of the brain that dominate during trauma as well as recollections of the trauma, and is hypervigilant to anything that resembles the trauma that has been experienced.

That is why we tend to have visceral and bodily reactions to trauma or recollections of trauma. For example, when I am having an emotional flashback to something an abuser has said, my stomach tenses up and I feel an uncomfortable tightness in my chest. I feel "physically" hurt by their words. I tend to stop what I am doing at the moment, as it interrupts whatever task I am doing, and constantly have to redirect myself by interrupting these thought methods with "reverse discourse," a method I'll describe in Chapter 3.

FACTS ABOUT YOUR BRAIN ON TRAUMA: Here are some facts about trauma you may or may not know that are helpful to understanding why victims go back to abusive relationships and why they cannot simply let an experience like narcissistic abuse or any other form of trauma "go" easily.

- We have three "brains." The neocortex is the rational part of the brain and is also the newest. The reptilian brain is the oldest and bottom part of the brain. The limbic system is the center of the brain and it is the part of our brain where our deepest emotions are seated. Our responses to abuse and trauma are driven by the limbic and reptilian parts of our brain, *not* the neocortex (Van der Kolk, 2015).

- It is our limbic system that takes in the trauma immediately and sets off the brain's alarm system. Our amygdala, which processes our emotions, tends to become hyperactive when we are traumatized, while our medial prefrontal cortex and hippocampus, which deal with learning, memory and decision-making tend to be dampened in the face of trauma (Nutt and Malizia, 2004; Shin, Rauch and Pitman, 2006).

- Trauma tends to stay "frozen" in our brain. According to Theresa Burke, Ph.D (2008), traumatic memories tend to stay stuck in the brain's nonverbal, subcortical regions like the amygdala, thalamus, hippocampus, hypothalamus and the brain stem, which are not accessible to the frontal lobes. In fact, trauma "shuts down" executive functioning associated with the frontal lobes of the brain. These frontal lobes that are negatively affected due to trauma are the reasoning, logical aspects of our brain which help us to pay attention, manage time, switch focus, plan and organize, remember details, and perform tasks based on experience.

So this means that survivors of any form of trauma often face interruptions in their ability to focus and perform tasks in the way they are accustomed to. Someone who has been traumatized may suffer lapses in memory as well as judgment in planning and organizing because much of the trauma may still be "frozen" in the parts of the brain that process memory and emotion.

- So for those who think abuse survivors can simply "logically" process their situation and get out of and over the situation easily, think again. The parts of our brain that deal with planning, cognition, learning and decision-making become disconnected with the emotional parts of our brain – they can cease to talk to each other when an individual becomes traumatized. It usually takes a great deal of effort, resources, strength, validation, addressing wounding on all levels of body and mind, for a survivor to become fully empowered to begin to heal from this form of trauma.

- When trauma survivors encounter stimuli that remind them of their trauma, regardless of how many years have passed, the amygdala (part of our limbic system) reacts as if they are re-experiencing the same event (Walker, 2013). Stress hormones are released and the body goes into "fight or flight" mode. The danger of the trauma can be reactivated even by a seemingly innocuous event – resulting in overwhelming physical sensations as well as impulsive and aggressive actions in response to the distress the individual re-experiences.

- These traumatic flashbacks can turn off Broca's area of the brain, the center for speech, which renders us unable to express the trauma in words (Van der Kolk, 2015). It also diminishes frontal cortex ability, making it difficult for trauma victims to distinguish a false threat from a real threat.

- When recalling a traumatic memory, the left frontal cortex shuts down and the areas of the right hemisphere, especially the areas of the amygdala, light up. Since the left hemisphere is associated with thinking and rational planning, and the right side of the brain collects sensory information, such as visual memories and the emotions associated with them, cutting off the "left" side while activating the right can disconnect the two (Burke, 2008). This results in an incoherent narrative that the victim still attempts to make sense of.

- The logical, thinking brain is no longer in conversation or in dialogue with the tangible memories of the trauma, so it's no wonder that both our bodies and our brains are freaking out over emotional and visual flashbacks – we're not able to integrate these two parts of ourselves when it comes to trauma.

That is why experimenting with diverse healing modalities, such as art therapy as we'll discuss in Chapter 3, can be so helpful to patients suffering from PTSD, because it enables them to express and channel the trauma nonverbally. That is also why meditation and mindfulness activities can also be helpful to a survivor of trauma, because it allows them to become mindful of their physiological reactions, slow down, take a breath and assess whether or not the threat they are currently facing is a real or a false one. To the brain, it may be a real one because we do "regress" back into the state of the original trauma, but mindfulness enables us to react proactively rather than impulsively.

- This lack of integration feeds into the larger phenomenon known as *dissociation,* a clever defense mechanism of the brain that protects us from the trauma (Bremner, 1996; Kalshed, 2013). Mild dissociation can take place even without a traumatic event, when we lose track of time doing a task we always do or are daydreaming. However, in a major trauma, the brain can "split" the information from the trauma to make it easier to digest.

- Dissociation leaves us disconnected from our memories, our identities and our emotions. It breaks the trauma into digestible components, so that different aspects of the trauma get stored in different compartments in our brain. What happens as a result is that the information from the trauma becomes disorganized and we are not able to integrate these pieces into a coherent narrative and process trauma fully until, hopefully with the help of a validating, trauma-informed counselor who guides us to the appropriate therapies best suited to our needs, we confront the trauma and triggers in a safe space.

Understanding the effects of trauma and PTSD, as well as the learned helplessness model, is essential to dismantling victim-blaming and victim-shaming regarding why abuse survivors enter or stay in abusive relationships. The reasons are far more complex than we think and are related moreso to the effects of trauma rather than the strength, intelligence or character of the survivor. In fact, as you'll learn in the next section, the way our brain interacts with trauma plays a large role in why abuse survivors get traumatically and even biochemically bonded to their abusers.

Your Brain in the Abusive Relationship: The Biochemical Bonds That Get Us "Hooked" On Narcissists

Many survivors of narcissistic abuse are confounded by the addiction they feel to the narcissist, long after the abusive relationship took a toll on their physical, mental, and emotional well-being. Make no mistake: recovery from an abusive relationship can be very similar to withdrawal from drug addiction due to the biochemical bonds we may develop with our toxic ex-partners.

As a survivor myself who has studied psychology and has also coached other survivors on No Contact from their abusive partners, I knew that the answer to that question was more complex than what appeared, on the surface, to be irrational behavior. Abuse creates complex bonds between survivor and perpetrator that are difficult to break; it also causes a great deal of cognitive dissonance as the survivor attempts to reconcile the brutal reality of the abuse with the person he or she once saw as their greatest confidante and lover in the early stages of the relationship. This cognitive dissonance is a defense mechanism that is often resolved not by seeing the abuser for who he or she really is, but rather by denying, minimizing or rationalizing the abuse that is occurring as a way to survive and cope with the trauma being experienced (Carver, 2004; Louis de Canonville, 2015).

This form of abuse amnesia is compounded by the nature of the abuse cycle. Abuse is often slow and insidious, building up over time from tiny infractions to major meltdowns. What was once a glimpse of an abuser's false mask occasionally slipping in the beginning becomes a horrific cycle of idealization, devaluation, and eventually, discard that the survivor has not only grown accustomed to, but also inadvertently becomes addicted to due to the strength of the "trauma bond" that forms between abuser and victim.

Motivated to understand why survivors such as myself felt a sense of paralysis that made it difficult to leave an abusive relationship, I set out to compile the research that I wish I had possessed as a survivor myself when I began looking for information. Stigmatizing labels of abuse survivors as meek and irrational didn't ring true to me, as the survivors that often reached out to me in my coaching practice were incredibly intelligent, accomplished and introspective—there was something, I knew, about the nature of the abusive relationship that created a complex, psychological, even physiological reaction in the victim, regardless of who the abuse victim was personally or professionally.

Discussion of the biochemical bonding that occurs between an abuse survivor and perpetrator has been scarce. My research into the chemicals and hormones at work—applied to the knowledge I had about the traumatic highs and lows of these turbulent relationships—has been eye-opening. What I uncovered though was that when it comes to leaving toxic partners such as narcissists, sociopaths or psychopaths, our brain's biochemistry is not on our side.

Due to these biochemical bonds, survivors struggle with No Contact and may suffer many relapses on the road to recovery from the psychological trauma of the relationship. In this chapter, I'd like to explore how our own brain chemistry can lock us into this addiction to the narcissist or sociopathic partner. Some of these same biochemical bonds also make it difficult for us to detach from non-narcissistic partners, as well.

Oxytocin.

This hormone, known famously as the "cuddle" or "love hormone," is released during touching, orgasm and sexual intercourse; it promotes attachment and trust (Watson, 2014). It is the same hormone released by the hypothalamus that enables bonding between mother and child. During "lovebombing" and mirroring in the idealization phases with our abusive partners, it's likely that our bond to them is quite strong as a result of this hormone.

Intermittent reinforcement of positive behaviors dispersed throughout the abuse cycle (e.g. gifts, flowers, compliments, sex) ensures that we still release oxytocin even after experiencing incidents of abuse. Intermittent reinforcement is a concept coined by B.F. Skinner (Ferster and Skinner, 1957) which describes a schedule where a subject's desired behavior is only rewarded occasionally, rather than every time. His studies showed that rats pressed a lever to get food in an even steadier, more persistent fashion when rewards were given out sporadically than when there was a consistent schedule of rewards. The most common metaphor used in real life is a gambler at a slot machine who continues playing, even though he will only win something a fraction of the time and the loss may be large in comparison to the actual gain.

It may not be that the narcissist is always skilled in bed, but rather *messing skillfully with our heads*. I find that it's often a combination of physical, psychological and emotional reasons working together to create this addiction to our toxic partner. Sex is just another way for them to regain control and push our buttons, but it's certainly not the only way. It's a feedback loop: our psychological trauma with the narcissist shapes our sexual experiences with them and our sexual experiences with them further strengthen this bond, which in turn compels us to continue to invest in a relationship that is inevitably traumatic.

Anytime we are emotionally or psychologically smitten with someone, this tends to heighten our sexual attraction and chemistry to them as well - so during the idealization phase, the narcissist becomes good in bed because of the level of emotional security, trust, attachment and intimacy a victim feels given all the attention, praise and flattery he or she receives from the narcissist.

During the devaluation phase, the victim becomes hooked by the traumatic highs and lows of the relationship which condition him or her to the adrenaline rush of unpredictability, fear and the hope for another scrap of the idealization phase. Susan Anderson, LCSW (2010) notes that intermittent reinforcement in abusive relationships contains a push-pull dynamic that secure relationships lack, causing victims to become addicted to the drama and the chaos of the relationship. Paradoxically, individuals in toxic relationships actually feel more attached and trauma bonded to unhealthy relationship partners rather than healthy ones who give them a sense of security.

We tend to feast on every incident of makeup sex or small scrap of tenderness due to the emotional hunger we experience during the devaluation phase of the relationship. Sex with the narcissist or sociopathic partner acts as an emotional reset button as well as grooming tactic that makes us crave the early idealization phase and continue to invest in our partner in the hopes that the outcome will be a positive one, despite evidence to the contrary.

Dr. Harriet Braiker, author of *Who's Pulling Your Strings?: How to Break the Cycle of Manipulation and Regain Control of Your Life* (2004) explains how intermittent reinforcement is a key manipulative tactic of emotional manipulators. In the context of narcissistic abuse, this looks like the following: an abuser creates conflict in the relationship and often mistreats the victim but also at times "rewards" the victim with occasional tenderness, to solidify the victim's persistent efforts to restore the relationship back to its original lovebombing stage.

Therapist Christine Louis de Canonville describes these complex dynamics of how intermittent reinforcement and cognitive dissonance in the realm of narcissistic abuse can perpetuate the abuse cycle quite eloquently in her discussion of Narcissistic Victim Syndrome:

> "Victims living in a household where there is narcissistic abuse are living in a torturous war zone, where all forms of power and control are used against them (intimidation; emotional, physical and mental abuse; isolation, economic abuse, sexual abuse, coercion etc.). The threat of abuse is always present, and it usually gets more violent and frequent as time goes on. The controlling narcissistic environment puts the victim in a dependency situation, where they experience an extreme form of helplessness which throws them into panic and chaos. The narcissist creates a perverse form of relationship wherein the victim has no idea what will happen next (alternating between acts of kindness or aggressive raging).

> This prolonged torturous situation is likely to trigger old negative scripts of the victim's childhood internal object relations (attachment, separation and individuation). To survive the internal conflict, the victim will have to call on all their internal resources and defense strategies in order to manage their most primitive anxieties of persecution and annihilation. In order to survive, the victim has to find ways of reducing their cognitive dissonance, the strategies they employ may include; justifying things by lying to themselves if need be, regressing into infantile patterns, and bonding with their narcissistic captor. Most defense mechanisms are fairly unconscious, so the victim is unaware of using them in the moment; all they are intent on is surviving the madness they find themselves in." ***Christine***

Louis de Canonville, "The Place of Cognitive Dissonance in Narcissistic Victim Syndrome."

Like a gambler at a slot machine, victims become hopelessly addicted to any perceived gain, no matter how small that gain may be; they do everything they can to survive and cope with an environment that is ultimately rigged against them and in doing so, become traumatically bonded to their abusers. In essence, the abuser conditions the victim to receiving less while he or she gets more effort from the victim.

I've heard from many survivors who reminisce about the great sexual relationship they had with the narcissist, that it contained an electrifying sexual chemistry they feel unable to achieve with future partners. This is because charming emotional predators such as narcissists are able to mirror our deepest sexual and emotional desires, which leads to a strong sexual bond, which then, of course, releases oxytocin, and promotes even more trust and attachment. Meanwhile, the narcissist, who is usually devoid of empathy and does not form these types of close attachments, is able to move onto his or her next source of supply without much thought or remorse.

On the dark side, sex with a narcissist can also be devaluing, manipulative, and abusive in itself, especially if the narcissist in question engages in highly risky sexual behaviors or attempts to coerce victims into engaging in sexual acts that they don't feel comfortable with. They may also sexually withdraw from their partners and sexually triangulate their partners frequently with comparisons or infidelity in an attempt to make them feel undesirable during the devaluation phase. This can also bond victim to abuser because it conditions the victim to associate fear with sex and betrayal with love – creating a trauma bond that will be discussed later in this article.

The addictive nature of oxytocin is also gendered according to Susan Kuchinskas, author of the book, *The Chemistry of Connection: How the Oxytocin Response Can Help You Find Trust, Intimacy and Love* (2009). The unfortunate fact is that estrogen promotes the effects of oxytocin bonding whereas testosterone discourages it. It has been suggested that vasopressin is actually the bonding molecule for men. This means in any type of relationship, it is more difficult for females, than for men, to detach from the bond created by oxytocin.

Dopamine.

The same neurotransmitter that is responsible for cocaine addiction is the same one responsible for addiction to dangerous romantic partners – dopamine. Our cravings for a partner we are in love with who has rejected us causes activity in the reward system of the brain similar to cravings for a drug like cocaine (Fisher, 1992).

Survivors who are often rejected and devalued in the devaluation and discard phases of the relationship undoubtedly suffer the consequences of a narcissist mixing bonding with betrayal to get them hooked on the drug that is their abuse. This craving is exacerbated by the fact that we tend to ruminate over memories with our past partners. According to Harvard Health, both drugs and intense, pleasurable memories trigger dopamine and create reward circuits in the brain, essentially telling the brain to "do it again."

Do you remember constantly ruminating over the pleasurable, beautiful first moments with your narcissistic partner? The romantic dates, the sweet compliments and praise, the incredible sex – even long after you two had broken up? Yeah - it's releasing the dopamine in your brain that's telling you to "do it again."

Dopamine is not just about pleasure. It's also about survival. The salience theory of dopamine suggests that our brain releases dopamine not just for pleasurable events but to important ones that are linked to survival (McGowan, 2004). As Samantha Smithstein, Psy.d, (2010) puts it, "Dopamine is not just a messenger that dictates what feels good; *it also tells the brain what is important and what to pay attention to in order to survive*. And the more powerful the experience is, the stronger the message is to the brain to repeat the activity for survival."

Abuse survivors are unfortunately hijacked by dopamine. According to Susan Carnell, Ph.D (2012), abusive tactics like intermittent reinforcement work well with our dopamine system, because studies show that dopamine flows more readily when the rewards are given out on unpredictable schedule rather than predictably, following conditioned cues. Helen Fisher (2016) notes that this "frustration-attraction" experience which we encounter when we have obstacles in the face of love, actually heightens these feelings of romantic love rather than deterring them. The very nature of the trauma within an abusive relationship actually serves our unhealthy addiction to these partners.

So the random sweet nothings whispered to us after an incident of emotional abuse, the apologies, the pity ploys, the rare displays of tenderness during the devaluation phase, right before another incident of abuse - actually help cement this type of reward circuit rather than deter it.

What helps these dopamine cravings is a powerful form of cognitive dissonance that arises when we hold conflicting beliefs regarding our abuser that are undoubtedly affected by our physiological bonds with them as well as their false mask and intermittent moments of kindness. Dr. Joseph M. Carver (2004) speaks about the power of cognitive dissonance in his article "Love and Stockholm Syndrome," where he refers to cognitive dissonance arising with an antisocial personality disordered partner as a survival mechanism in an "abusive, controlling environment."

We are able to rationalize, minimize and even deny abuse due to cognitive dissonance, attempting to uphold our original beliefs about the abuser being a kind, loving, and affectionate person while recalling and romanticizing the early stages of the relationship.

Combine this with powerful experiences of abuse which alert our brain to "pay attention" as well as pleasurable memories we recollect over and over again - and we've got ourselves a biochemical bond from hell.

Cortisol, Adrenaline and Norepinephrine.

Cortisol is a stress hormone, and boy, does it get released during the traumatic highs and lows of an abusive relationship. It is released by the adrenal glands in response to fear as part of the "fight or flight" mechanism. Since we are unlikely to have a physical outlet of release when cortisol is triggered during cycles of emotional abuse, this often traps the stress within our bodies instead, especially if we are experiencing symptoms of PTSD or complex PTSD from the abuse (van der Kolk, 1991; Walker, 2013).

New research confirms that cortisol strengthens the impact of memories associated with fear and that oxytocin and cortisol actually work together to consolidate fear-based memories (Drexler et. al, 2015). Cortisol is released both in the creation of new traumatic memories as well as the recollection of them. During a flashback, "cortisol levels spike…as the memory reconsolidates and is encoded into specific neurons" (Bergland, 2015). The inevitable flashbacks and secretion of cortisol to fear-based events further consolidates and embeds the memory more deeply into our neural networks, ensuring that the memories from the trauma are more intense, more vivid and ultimately more difficult to recover from.

As we ruminate over incidents of abuse, increased levels of cortisol lead to more and more health problems. Christopher Bergland's excellent article, "Cortisol: Why The Stress Hormone is Public Enemy No. 1" (2013) suggests numerous ways to counteract the effects of this hormone, which include physical activity, mindfulness, meditation, laughter, music and social connectivity.

Adrenaline and norepinephrine also prepare our body for the flight or fight response, and are culprits in biochemical reactions to our abusers (Klein 2013). When we see the person we love, adrenaline is released, causing our hearts to race and our palms to sweat. Yet this same hormone is tied to fear – research has confirmed that when we share an intense, scary experience with our partner, we become more attached and drawn to them because fear also releases dopamine, which caters to the reward system in our brain (Georgia Health Sciences University, 2011).

That is why partners who have ridden a roller coaster together tend to be fonder of each other afterwards, or why two people who have experienced a horrifying experience become more bonded – the fear creates a biochemical bond between them. This means that when we fear retaliation from our narcissistic partner in the form of a smear campaign, when we become scared of their narcissistic rage or outbursts — we actually become more bonded to them in a way we wouldn't expect — addicted to the pain, the fear, and the anxiety embedded within the abuse cycle.

According to Bergland (2012), adrenaline also promotes an antidepressant effect, triggering fear and anxiety which then releases dopamine - this can cause us to become "adrenaline junkies," addicted to recklessly seeking the rush evoked from vacillating between tender bonding and betrayal. During No Contact, withdrawal from that "rush" can be incredibly painful. This is why so many partners of narcissists tend to relapse and go back to their abusers. This is also why it can be difficult to maintain No Contact.

Serotonin.

Serotonin is a hormone that regulates mood. When we fall in love, the serotonin levels in our body fall in a way that mimics the way they are lowered in individuals with Obsessive Compulsive Disorder (Marazziti, 1999). This may come as no surprise to individuals who have been groomed early on in a toxic relationship to expect excessive praise and flattery from a charming emotional predator. Individuals with low levels of serotonin are also more likely to engage in sexual behavior, which then again releases dopamine and oxytocin to bond victim to abuser. As you can see, these chemicals and hormones involved interact with each other to contribute to this vicious cycle.

This is why narcissistic abusers dominate our brains in the early idealization phases of the relationship with their love-bombing, the excessive adoration we receive in the beginning. Imagine how this effect is compounded in the devaluation and discard phase, when we are made to think about our narcissistic partner 24/7 due to their covert put-downs, their silent treatments, their stonewalling, their infidelity, and their sudden disappearances. We become obsessed with them not just through love, but again, through fear, through anxiety and rumination.

Trauma bonding.

All of these jolts of fear and anxiety in the face of danger can reenact past traumas and create what Patrick Carnes (2013) calls "trauma bonding" or the "betrayal bond." Trauma bonding occurs after intense, emotional experiences with our abusers. It tethers us to them by creating subconscious patterns of attachment that are very difficult to detach from. It is part of the phenomenon known as Stockholm Syndrome, in which hostage victims become attached to their perpetrators and even defend their captors. Trauma bonding is prevalent in abusive relationships as well as kidnapping, hostage situations and addiction. According to Carnes (2013), "Little acts of degradation, manipulation, secrecy and shame on a daily basis take their toll. Trauma by accumulation sneaks up on its victims."

These daily acts of degradation - of stonewalling, projection, gaslighting, verbal abuse, triangulation and manipulation are the exact ingredients that cumulatively create the insidious and covert abuse inflicted upon us by narcissistic abusers. Narcissistic abuse creates an environment of fear, shame and control in which victims are left constantly walking on eggshells, waiting for the other shoe to drop. They are betrayed emotionally, spiritually, and physically by their partners every day by their condescending remarks, infidelity, pathological lies, put-downs and name-calling.

Although survivors of narcissistic abuse come from many different backgrounds and anyone can be a victim of narcissistic abuse, trauma bonding is even more significant for those who grow up in violent or emotionally abusive homes, and/or have had a narcissistic parent in addition to their most recent experiences with trauma and abuse.

Survivors of multiple incidents of abuse by various narcissistic individuals can further reinforce subconscious wounds they experienced in childhood in the trauma bond with their current abusers. If there has been victimization in the past, such as the experience of having to survive in an abusive household, this can lead to **trauma repetition or reenactment**, the root of which Gary Reece, Ph.D in his excellent article, "The Trauma Bond," calls "relational trauma."

For more information on trauma bonding, please see *The Betrayal Bond: Breaking Free of Exploitative Relationships* (2013) by Patrick Carnes.

Complex PTSD and Narcissistic Abuse

It was Harvard medical professor Judith Herman (1992) who first described the distinction between PTSD and Complex PTSD in her book, *Trauma and Recovery*. The mental health community has been slow to recognize and acknowledge C-PTSD, which has led to misdiagnoses of long-standing traumatized individuals with anxiety and depressive disorders, and borderline or dependent personality disorders (Walker, 2013). While Complex PTSD has been discussed in the framework of physical and/or sexual abuse in childhood, it can also be caused by emotional and/or verbal abuse, long-term domestic violence as well as long-term childhood emotional neglect.

Complex PTSD is PTSD that develops from *chronic* trauma – a trauma that is long-term and often inescapable. In addition to the regular symptoms of PTSD which the majority of C-PTSD victims also meet the diagnostic criteria for, survivors with Complex PTSD find that their ability to adapt to stress, interact with others and regulate their emotions are severely affected.

When it comes to complex PTSD, no trauma is too small. Every trauma is valid in its own right. Chronic trauma can cause painful events that are seemingly minor to seem life-threatening. This is why the phrase "let it go," can be so damaging to victims of long-standing abuse and trauma.

Survivors who have endured long-lasting emotional abuse from their partner, who have been bullied, who've been with multiple narcissists and/or have been raised by a narcissistic parent or caregiver may find that they suffer from the following symptoms:

- **Emotional Flashbacks** – Reliving the abusive events with a strong emotional component that includes feelings of abandonment, shame, and fear. Seemingly minor events can trigger a flashback and cause major emotional and psychological distress.

- **Nightmares** – Vivid dreams regarding traumatic events, with a high emotional component – survivors often feel shame, humiliation, and powerlessness.

- **Heighted Inner Critic** – A high degree of excessive negative self-talk and judgment that permeates every day thoughts and emotions.

- **Avoidance** – Avoiding thoughts, people, places and activities for fear of being triggered.

- **Numbing** – Victims may feel emotionally numb or shell-shocked, unable to connect with the full emotional depth of the experience.

- **Social Anxiety**– Isolating oneself from social situations, feeling ashamed and defective. Avoiding situations involving interacting with others, for fear that they will be exposed as "different."

- **Increased Anxiety, Hypervigilance and Arousal** – Heightened distrust of others, panic attacks, emotional outbursts, overwhelming emotions.

- **Difficulty concentrating** – A lack of focus and interrupted concentration due to emotional distress.

- **Toxic Shame and Self-Abandonment** – Survivors feel defective, worthless, and shameful. They "abandon" themselves because of the way they have been abandoned by others, not feeling worthy of care, protection, love, respect or compassion.

- **Disassociation** – Survivors may forget traumatic events or feel detached from their bodies or mental processes. The most extreme version of disassociation is Dissociative Identity Disorder, a rare disorder which often results from sexual abuse in childhood. Individuals with DID split into multiple "alters," different identities that "speak" to the different aspects of the victim while the victim is unaware or fairly unconscious about the actions of these alters.

- **All-or-none/black and white thinking** – In this cognitive distortion, everything is categorized as all good or all bad; survivors are prone to seeing themselves in black and white thinking as well, judging themselves as worthless and useless.

- **Distorted perceptions of the perpetrator** – Victims may be preoccupied with revenge, assigning total power to the perpetrator or excessive preoccupation with the perpetrator.

- **Self-harm** – In order to cope with overwhelming emotions, survivors may engage in self-harm, including but not limited to cutting, excessive drinking, placing themselves in dangerous situations, self-sabotaging or self-mutilating behaviors.

- **Suicidal ideation** – Survivors may struggle with suicidal thoughts and feel as if they can no longer cope with the pain. Due to their sense of helplessness and paralysis, they feel as if they no longer want to live and have to give up in order to escape the pain.

Therapist Pete Walker (2013) discusses how children who suffer abuse at a young age are at risk for complex PTSD, in his book *Complex PTSD: From Surviving to Thriving.* For those who continue to "reenact" their old childhood trauma through abusive relationships, this type of PTSD is more likely.

Due to complex PTSD, we may be prone to nightmares, hypervigilance, intense flashbacks, emotional numbing and avoidance of situations that remind us of the abuse. Due to chronic abuse, individuals may also develop into what Walker calls one of the four "F" types, which consist of "Freeze, Flight, Fight and Fawn" types or a hybrid of two of the types. "Freeze" individuals are paralyzed by their own trauma; they socially isolate themselves from others and avoid situations that might re-traumatize them.

"Fight" individuals (those who tend to be on the narcissistic spectrum) tend to fight back against the trauma by reacting aggressively towards anyone who threatens to make them vulnerable. "Flight" individuals exit situations that make them vulnerable to an excessive extent even when the threat posed by their environment is seemingly minimal. Finally, the "Fawn" type tends to become overly compliant to the toxic people who are draining them, in order to avoid conflict – these tend to be the people-pleasers in the 4 F group.

If you are a childhood narcissistic abuse survivor who has also experienced narcissistic abuse in adulthood, you may find yourself fitting into one of these 4 F types or perhaps even a hybrid of two or more types. Finding professional support from a trauma-informed counselor who specializes in Complex PTSD and its effects is important to the recovery process. Chapter 3 will offer tips on not only how to combat the bonds and psychological reasons that keep you hooked to your abuser, but offer a variety of healing modalities that target the mind, body and spirit that is often overwhelmed by the toxicity of these relationships.

Reflection Time ♥ Link: Check out *Why Do Abuse Survivors Stay So Long in Abusive Relationships?* on youtube.com/user/selfcarehaven.

Emotional and Psychological Reasons Why Victims Stay

What about the emotional and psychological reasons victims stay in abusive relationships? To the outside world, abuse survivors appear to face an easy decision: leave, or stay in the abusive relationship as soon as they endure an emotionally or physically abusive incident. However, as mentioned earlier, victims of abuse can be struggling internally with cognitive dissonance, damaging conditioning from intermittent reinforcement, PTSD-like symptoms, trauma bonds, previous trauma from past abusive relationships or abuse in their childhood, Stockholm syndrome, feelings of worthlessness and what psychologist Seligman (1983) calls a state of "learned helplessness" – *just to name a few.*

Although it may seem counterintuitive, leaving a long-term abusive relationship can actually be even harder than leaving a nourishing, supportive and positive one. This is because narcissistic or antisocial abusers are masters at playing mind games and covert manipulation, are able to deny the abuse through gaslighting while presenting a false image to the world which supports their denial. Survivors are then subjected to a battle within their own minds about whether the reality they experience is truly abuse – a type of cognitive dissonance that society seems to encourage by engaging in victim-blaming.

Remember that abusers present a false, charming self to the world and their true self is exposed primarily to their victims. In the initial stages of dating or relationship, abusers are likely to present their best image. It is only after they've "hooked" the victim with their covert manipulation tactics such as mirroring and lovebombing, that they begin devaluing, demeaning and hurting the victim. The victim then has to find ways to psychologically process the trauma of this sudden "turn" in personality – a process that can take months to years depending on the duration of the relationship, the availability of the victim's own coping resources, as well as the severity and nature of the abuse.

I am a passionate advocate of ending abusive relationships, going No Contact and owning our agency after abuse. However, at the same time, I want to encourage survivors to empower themselves after the abuse, I also want people to understand that the act of leaving such a relationship is rarely as easy as it seems. Not leaving sooner is not an indication or a measure of a victim's strength or intelligence. It has more to do with the severity of trauma they have experienced.

This false narrative of how easy it is to end an abusive relationship is actually holding us back from creating safer spaces for survivors to feel validated, supported, and able to speak out about their experiences – this support is essential to any victim in an abusive relationship. This is why I want to dismantle the harmful stereotypes of why abuse survivors stay, by offering some insights on why they really do. If you're not an abuse survivor, the reasons might surprise you.

The reasons survivors stay are complex and tied to the effects of trauma, the ways in which abuse survivors start to see themselves after the abuse, and the ways in which society makes it more difficult for them to speak out about their abuse:

1. In a nourishing, positive relationship, we can love the person enough to let go with a sense of closure. In an abusive one, ending the relationship is a decision filled with fear of retaliation and anxiety. In healthy relationships, there is mutual respect and compassion, something that has existed throughout the course of the relationship despite any obstacles. Even if it is difficult, we trust that the person we are letting go will respect us enough to take time to heal before jumping into another relationship the day after the breakup. We trust they will not threaten or stalk us because we left them (in a narcissist's mind, only *they* are allowed to discard). And we trust that they will not violently assault us or stage a smear campaign against us because we discarded them first.

Partners who are not narcissists or sociopaths will most likely leave us alone after a breakup and not bother to "hoover" simply because they need supply. They are understanding about boundaries and the need for space after the ending of a relationship.

Abuse victims of narcissists suffer potential infidelity, manipulation, put-downs, gaslighting and deception throughout their relationship. Therefore, cognitive dissonance about who the abuser is, as well as incessant doubt, means survivors may lack a sense of closure and certainty about ending an abusive relationship. Understandably, many abuse victims don't wish to let their abusers move onto the next victim after terrorizing them, because they fear the next person might be treated better, thereby confirming their own sense of worthlessness that was instilled by the abuser in the first place. They may also have an unending sense of needing a real "apology" or seeing karma at work before they feel they can truly let go.

Of course, abuse survivors eventually learn they can only gain closure from within – *after* they've ended the relationship and begun the work of healing and recovery. They also realize the next victim will most likely be subjected to the same abuse, even if it appears otherwise when their abuser treats the next victim to the idealization phase. Apologies from the abuser won't suffice, as they are recognized for what they truly are: pity ploys or hoovering tactics designed to pull us back into the toxic dynamic rather than signs of genuine remorse. Self-forgiveness, instead, becomes paramount.

2. Abuse survivors start to view themselves through the eyes of their abuser. The belittling, condescending remarks and the physical violence abusers subject their victims to leads to a sense of learned helplessness and self-doubt which make survivors fearful that they really aren't as worthy as they think they are. Abuse survivors could be the most confident, successful and beautiful people to the outside world, but they are subjected to an internal world of fear, self-doubt and a shaky self-esteem as a result of the traumatic conditioning their abusers have put them through. They have been taught to live on a diet of crumbs (the occasional compliment, some shallow show of attention, perhaps even a showering of gifts and flattery before the abuse cycle begins again) which serves to remind them that they must "work" for a love that will never be unconditional, a love that will never contain real respect or compassion.

As a result, they may compare themselves to people in happier relationships or even to the seemingly idealized way their abusers treated their exes (as narcissists are likely to either place their exes on a pedestal or demean them as crazy) and wonder, *why not me? What's wrong with me?* Of course, the problem is not them – it is the abusive relationship which is the source of toxicity in their lives.

The abuser is likely to subject the victim to many comparisons to drive the point home that it is somehow the victim's fault that he or she is being abused (also known as triangulation). Due to this, survivors have a difficult time accepting the fact that even if they were the most confident, successful, beautiful and charismatic people on earth, they would still be abused by the abuser because that is what abusers *do* in intimate relationships. They abuse victims because they enjoy the feelings of power and control, not because victims themselves lack merits. In fact, narcissistic abusers feel particular joy at bringing down anyone whose accomplishments and traits they envy. Doing so reinforces their false sense of superiority.

Due to the skewed belief system which develops after the abuse, survivors feel that ending it would paradoxically confirm the narcissist's view of them. They associate the ending of the relationship to a failure on their own part, the inability to win the affections of someone who has made themselves look like a prize by constantly idealizing them then subsequently withdrawing from them.

Narcissistic abusers blow hot and cold throughout the course of an intimate relationship to make it seem like *you're* the problem and not them. Survivors struggle to win the game of gaining an abuser's affection, especially if they're prone to people-pleasing habits and fears of rejection as well as abandonment. The terrible things the abuser has done to us somehow don't compare to the pain of also being abandoned after being abused: it's almost as if the abandonment would prove our so-called "unworthiness" which has been manufactured by the abuser to make us feel unable to leave.

On the healing journey, survivors rediscover their authentic selves and learn how to depart from toxic people-pleasing habits instilled in them by their abuser as well as in childhood. They begin to reclaim their worth, separate from their social interactions and romantic relationships. It is one of the most freeing, empowering experiences to finally leave an abuser and stick with No Contact. Rebuilding your life after abuse is not easy, but it is an unbelievably transformative experience.

3. Ending the relationship would mean that the survivor has to face the reality of all the traumas they've experienced, on their own.

Although this is not always a conscious choice, abuse survivors may feel more comfortable rationalizing the abuse and avoiding the pain of the harsh reality they're experiencing, which can be quite easy given that they tend to experience abuse amnesia during the good times. They may also experience the defense mechanism of dissociation which enables them to survive during moments of horrific abuse. Staying in the abusive relationship allows survivors to still engage with the good parts of the relationship while psychologically protecting themselves from having to face the trauma of it.

As narcissists and sociopaths tend to be excellent masters of gaslighting, flattery and even sex, creating certain pleasurable bonds that appear to surpass the pain we experience during the abuse, abuse amnesia becomes a tempting form of psychological protection from their own demons. Abuse amnesia is aided by the abuser's performances of being apologetic, kind, caring and compassionate during the positive highs of the abuse cycle. Dissociation, on the other hand, is often not intentional on the survivor's part – the mechanism of dissociation occurs quite naturally in response to traumatic events. Of course, the reality is that those bonds we have with our abusers are trauma-based bonds that have little to do with actual fulfillment, love or respect, and everything to do with the illusion of who we believe narcissists are.

Ending the relationship is made even more difficult if trauma from previous relationships or childhood exists, as this can affect the child's attachment style (The National Child Traumatic Stress Network). According to UNICEF, children who grow up witnessing domestic violence within their own families have been reported to more likely be victims of abusive relationships themselves (2006). A part of our addiction to our abusers, aside from biochemical and trauma bonding discussed earlier in the book, may be due to what Dr. Halpern (2004) calls, in his book, *How to Break Your Addiction to a Person,* "attachment hunger." As he describes it, our "addictive compulsion" to a romantic person is driven by our desire to gain what we lacked from our caregivers, in the hope that we can finally feel what it means "to be safe, to be happy" (p. 21).

Abuse may almost seem normalized because of the behaviors we've been unconsciously modelling from our childhood. We might identify with the victimized parent, or may even have promised ourselves we would never be like them, only to have unconsciously chosen a partner that has enabled us to attempt to "fix" our past by attempting to fix our abusive partner. Knowing what we know about the effects of trauma on early adolescent brain development, the idea that someone who grew up witnessing such violence and abuse would not be psychologically affected is dubious. Thinking someone would not be affected by the same type of trauma in adulthood (especially if they've already experienced it in childhood) is even more unlikely.

After the ending of an abusive relationship, survivors have the challenge of uncovering their past traumas and the trauma they've just experienced and begin to work through them. The ending of this relationship is actually a golden opportunity to heal from the wounds that were never healed in the first place. The fear of being left alone with the pain now has to be overcome – the survivor now has the space and time to independently act, think and feel outside of the toxic dynamics of the previous relationship.

4. Society shames abuse survivors into thinking it's their fault and this can create barriers to a strong, validating support network. As a result of the stigmas associated with being and staying in an abusive relationship past the first signs of blatant disrespect, many people who have not undergone abusive relationships themselves are prone to pass judgment upon survivors. *How could he/she stay?* they ask. *Why didn't you leave the first time they hurt you? Are you sure it's really "abuse"?* The victim-blaming, shaming and doubting leaves abuse survivors feeling incredibly isolated in their situation and alienated from their own support networks. This question of "why didn't you leave?" can further persuade survivors to seek the false comfort of the abusive relationship because they would rather stay than speak out and risk being shamed, stigmatized, judged and questioned by the very people who are supposed to care about them – friends, family, and even the criminal justice system.

Here's a thought: if society stopped viewing abuse survivors in such a negative, judgmental light, they might actually be more likely to report domestic violence. If friends of abuse survivors adopted a mindset of compassion and understanding rather than ignorant judgment, they may actually get the support they need to feel like they wouldn't be alone after the end of the relationship.

The fact of the matter is, if you haven't been in an abusive relationship, you don't really know what the experience is like. Furthermore, it's quite hard to predict what you would do in the same situation. I find that the people most vocal about what they would've done in the same situation often have no clue what they are talking about – they have never been in the same situation themselves.

By invalidating the survivor's experience, these people are defending an image of themselves that they identify with strength, not realizing that abuse survivors are often the strongest individuals out there. They've been belittled, criticized, demeaned, devalued, and yet they've still survived. The judgmental ones often have little to no life experience regarding these situations, yet they feel quite comfortable silencing the voices of people who've actually been there.

While being a survivor can sometimes alienate us from society, it can also give us an intense connection with other survivors, in interactions filled with understanding and compassion. We have the ability to offer empathy and insight to others on a level other individuals aren't capable of. Survivors on the healing journey learn how to use their voices, connect with alternative communities and reach out to those who have been there.

5. They aren't psychologically ready to leave. Tony Robbins makes an astute observation in his book, *Awaken the Giant Within*: we only stop a bad habit or behavior when the pain of it far surpasses any pleasure or reward. While this theory might be a bit too simplistic to apply to the complex dynamics of abusive relationships, it often plays true for the moment the survivors finally leave. There are many psychological factors that may be holding abuse survivors back as well as hindering their readiness to leave, such as learned helplessness and Stockholm Syndrome as well as external barriers such as financial dependence, having children with the abuser, the threat of physical violence or a combination of these reasons.

We may plan when to leave and how to leave and fantasize about that moment, but there are usually a couple of factors that postpone the time of escape. None of the best advice in the world can convince us until we feel that inner transformation, until we reach that turning point where we say to ourselves, "*I've had enough. I am enough. And so much better than this.*" That moment often comes after an experience of extreme pain – a turning point when we've reached our pain threshold, whatever that threshold may be. Unfortunately, until we've made this decision from our own internal compass, there is not much others can do to intervene apart from offering their support. The decision must come from the survivor – and because he or she has been in the abusive relationship for so long, robbed of his or her choices, it may be the first powerful choice they make in years.

Once the decision has been made and actions have been taken to maintain No Contact, leaving becomes the ultimate victory. The turning point, whatever it was, has made them psychologically ready. Survivors truly own their agency and power when they can leave an abuser and never look back. They learned all they can from being in the relationship and are ready to begin their healing.

It is important to understand the various types of biochemical and psychological bonds that often create attachments between abusers and their victims. Better understanding these bonds enables us to move past victim-blaming and move forward into greater understanding, compassion and support for survivors who struggle with leaving abusive relationships. We must not judge, but continue to empower ourselves and others with this newfound knowledge.

References

American Psychiatric Association. (2013). Diagnostic and statistical manual of mental disorders
(5th ed.). Arlington, VA: American Psychiatric Publishing.

Anderson, S. (2010, November 08). Can't let go of a bad relationship? Retrieved April 11, 2016,
from https://susanandersonlcsw.wordpress.com/2010/11/08/cant-let-go-of-a-bad-relationship/

Bergland, C. (2015, July 10). Cortisol and Oxytocin Hardwire Fear-Based Memories. Retrieved April 8, 2016, from https://www.psychologytoday.com/blog/the-athletes-way/201507/cortisol-and-oxytocin-hardwire-fear-based-memories

Bergland, C. (2013, January 22). Cortisol: Why "The Stress Hormone" Is Public Enemy No. 1. Retrieved from https://www.psychologytoday.com/blog/the-athletes-way/201301/cortisol-why-the-stress-hormone-is-public-enemy-no-1

Bergland, C. (2012, November 29). The Neurochemicals of Happiness. Retrieved from https://www.psychologytoday.com/blog/the-athletes-way/201211/the-neurochemicals-happiness

Bremner, J. D., Krystal, J. H., Charney, D.S., & Southwick, S. M. (1996). Neural mechanisms in dissociative amnesia for childhood abuse: Relevance to the current controversy surrounding the "false memory syndrome." American Journal of Psychiatry, 153 (7), 71-82.

Bremner JD (2006). Traumatic stress: effects on the brain. *Dialogues in clinical neuroscience, 8* (4), 445-61.

Burke, T., Ph.D. (2008). *How trauma impacts the brain.* Speech presented in Rachel's Vineyard Ministries. Retrieved from http://www.rachelsvineyard.org/Downloads/Canada%20Conference%202008/TextOfBrainPP.pdf

Braiker, H. B. (2004). *Who's pulling your strings?: How to break the cycle of manipulation and regain control of your life.* New York: McGraw-Hill.

Brummelman, E., Thomaes, S., Nelemans, S. A., Castro, B. O., Overbeek, G., & Bushman, B. J. (2015). Origins of narcissism in children. *Proceedings of the National Academy of Sciences Proc Natl Acad Sci USA,* 201420870. doi:10.1073/pnas.1420870112

Carnell, S. (2014, May 14). Bad Boys, Bad Brains. Retrieved from https://www.psychologytoday.com/blog/bad-appetite/201205/bad-boys-bad-brains

Carnes, P. (2013). *The Betrayal Bond: Breaking Free of Exploitive Relationships.* Health Communications Incorporated.

Carver, J. M. (2004). Stockholm Syndrome: The Psychological Mystery of Loving an Abuser, Page 3. Retrieved 2016, from http://counsellingresource.com/therapy/self-help/stockholm/

Drexler, S. M., Merz, C. J., Hamacher-Dang, T. C., Tegenthoff, M., & Wolf, O. T. (2015). Effects of Cortisol on Reconsolidation of Reactivated Fear Memories. *Neuropsychopharmacology,* *40*(13), 3036-3043. doi:10.1038/npp.2015.160

Eisenberger, N. I., & Lieberman, M. D. (2004). Why rejection hurts: A common neural alarm system for physical and social pain. *Trends in Cognitive Sciences, 8*(7), 294-300. doi:10.1016/j.tics.2004.05.010

Ferster, C. B., & Skinner, B. F. (1957). Schedules of reinforcement. *Appleton-Century Crofts.* doi:10.1037/10627-000

Fisher, H. E. (1994). *Anatomy of love: The mysteries of mating, marriage, and why we stray.* New York: Fawcett Columbine.

Fisher, H. E. (2016). Love Is Like Cocaine - Issue 33: Attraction - Nautilus. Retrieved from http://nautil.us/issue/33/attraction/love-is-like-cocaine

Georgia Health Sciences University. (2011, February 28). Brain's Reward Center Also Responds to Bad Experiences. Retrieved from https://www.sciencedaily.com/releases/2011/02/110222121913.htm

Harvard Health. (2007). Drug addiction and the brain: Effects of dopamine on addiction - Harvard Health. Retrieved from http://www.health.harvard.edu/press_releases/drug-addiction-brain

Herman, J. L. (1992). *Trauma and recovery.* New York, NY: Basic Books.

Hsu, D. T., Sanford, B. J., Meyers, K. K., Love, T. M., & Hazlet, K. E. (2013). Response of the [mu]-opioid system to social rejection and acceptance. *Molecular Psychiatry, 18,* 1211-1217. doi:10.1038/mp.2013.96

Halpern, H. M. (2004). *How to break your addiction to a person.* New York: Bantam Books.

Jacoby, M., & Kohut, H. (1990). *Individuation and narcissism: The psychology of the self in Jung and Kohut.* London: Routledge.

Kernberg, O.F. (1975). Treatment of narcissistic personalities. *Int. J. Psychoanal.,* 56:245-248.

Kross, Ethan, Marc G. Berman et al. "Social rejection shares somatosensory representations with physical pain" (2011) *PNAS,* vol, 108, no.5, 6270-6275.

Kalsched, D. (2013). *Trauma and the soul: A psycho-spiritual approach to human development and its interruption.* London: Routledge.

Klein, S. (2013). Adrenaline, Cortisol, Norepinephrine: The Three Major Stress Hormones, Explained. Retrieved from http://www.huffingtonpost.com/2013/04/19/adrenaline-cortisol-stress-hormones_n_3112800.html

Lavender, N. J. (2014, January 10). The Narcissistic Wound. Retrieved from https://www.psychologytoday.com/blog/impossible-please/201401/the-narcissistic-wound

Livesley WJ, Jang KL, Jackson DN, Vernon PA (December 1993). "Genetic and environmental contributions to dimensions of personality disorder."

Am J Psychiatry **150** (12): 1826–31.doi:10.1176/ajp.150.12.1826. PMID 8238637.

Louis De Canonville, Christine (2015). *The Three Faces of Evil: Unmasking the Full Spectrum of Narcissistic Abuse*, Black Card Books.

Marazziti, D., Akiskal, H. S., Rossi, A., & Cassano, G. B. (1999). Alteration of the platelet serotonin transporter in romantic love. *Psychological Medicine Psychol. Med., 29*(3), 741-745. doi:10.1017/s0033291798007946

McGowan, K. (2004, November 1). Addiction: Pay Attention. Retrieved from https://www.psychologytoday.com/articles/200411/addiction-pay-attention

Mental Health Daily. (n.d.). How To Overcome Adrenaline Addiction: Tips From A Former Addict. Retrieved March 4, 2016, from http://mentalhealthdaily.com/2013/03/02/how-to-overcome-adrenaline-addiction-tips-from-a-former-addict/

Millon, Theodore (1981). *Disorders of Personality: DSM-III Axis II*. New York: John Wiley & Sons.

Nutt DJ, & Malizia AL (2004). Structural and functional brain changes in posttraumatic stress disorder.*The Journal of clinical psychiatry, 65 Suppl 1*, 11-7 PMID: 14728092

Pavlov, I. P. (1928). *Lectures on conditioned reflexes*. (Translated by W.H. Gantt) London: Allen and Unwin.

Peterson, C., & Seligman, M. E. (1983). Learned Helplessness and Victimization. *Journal of Social Issues, 39*(2), 103-116. doi:10.1111/j.1540-4560.1983.tb00143.x

Reece, G. (2013, February 25). The Trauma Bond/Abusive Relationships. Retrieved from http://garyreece.blogspot.com/2013/02/the-trauma-bondabusive-relationships.html

Seligman, M. E., & Maier, S. F. (1967). Failure To Escape Traumatic Shock. *Journal of Experimental Psychology, 74*(1), 1-9. doi:10.1037/h0024514

Sethi, A., Gregory, S., Dell'acqua, F., Thomas, E. P., Simmons, A., Murphy, D. G., . . . Craig, M. C. (2015). Emotional detachment in psychopathy: Involvement of dorsal default-mode connections. *Cortex, 62*, 11-19. doi:10.1016/j.cortex.2014.07.018

Smithstein, S. (2010, April 19). Dopamine: Why It's So Hard to "Just Say No" Retrieved from https://www.psychologytoday.com/blog/what-the-wild-things-are/201008/dopamine-why-its-so-hard-just-say-no

Shin LM, Rauch SL, & Pitman RK (2006). Amygdala, medial prefrontal cortex, and hippocampal function in PTSD. *Annals of the New York Academy of Sciences, 1071*, 67-79

Teicher, M. (2006). Sticks, Stones, and Hurtful Words: Relative Effects of Various Forms of Childhood Maltreatment. *American Journal of Psychiatry Am J Psychiatry, 163*(6), 993. doi:10.1176/appi.ajp.163.6.993

The National Child Traumatic Stress Network. (2016). Effects of Complex Trauma. Retrieved from http://www.nctsn.org/trauma-types/complex-trauma/effects-of-complex-trauma#q4

UNICEF. (2006). *Behind closed doors: The impact of domestic violence on children*. The Body Shop International. http://www.unicef.org/protection/files/BehindClosedDoors.pdf

Van der Kolk, Bessel (2015). *The body keeps the score: Brain, mind, and body in the healing of trauma*. New York: Penguin Books.

Walker, P. (2013). *Complex PTSD: From surviving to thriving: A guide and map for recovering from childhood trauma*. Azure Coyote Publishing.

Watson, R. (2014, October 14). Oxytocin: The Love and Trust Hormone Can Be Deceptive. Retrieved from https://www.psychologytoday.com/blog/love-and-gratitude/201310/oxytocin-the-love-and-trust-hormone-can-be-deceptive

Narcissistic Abuse Can Cause Complex PTSD by Lilly Hope Lucario

Let's hear from a survivor, advocate and writer with Complex PTSD. Her name is Lilly Hope Lucario, and her name is fitting, as she is bringing hope to hundreds of thousands of people around the world with her story. Her award-winning blog, Healing from Complex Trauma and PTSD/CPTSD, is one of the most comprehensive and informative websites on Complex PTSD. Her work is endorsed by esteemed mental health professionals such as trauma expert Pete Walker, as well as survivors all over the world. She is also someone I am proud to call a dear friend and who has brought so much light to this world with her honesty, courage and strength.

What is Complex PTSD and how does it feel?

Complex Post Traumatic Stress Disorder, is caused by severe, prolonged, ongoing, inescapable complex trauma. It can also be caused by enduring multiple types of trauma. Complex trauma occurs within a captivity situation where the child or adult doesn't perceive a viable escape.

Types of complex trauma that cause Complex PTSD can be: prolonged severe child abuse (due to age and immaturity of brain development), prolonged physical and emotional abuse, prolonged severe domestic violence, kidnapping, hostages, sex trafficking, and being a prisoner of war.

Complex PTSD is life-changing, severe and often has life-threatening symptoms. It creates a negative self-concept, severely affects emotion regulation, often causes a fragmented sense of self, dissociative symptoms and disorders. It is a very isolating disorder and causes a deep fear of trust and an agonizing fear of abandonment.

It is no surprise then, that being in a relationship with a narcissist, having multiple relationships with narcissists or being raised by a narcissistic parent may cause Complex PTSD.

How can a narcissist's behavior cause Complex PTSD?

In order to understand how a narcissist's behavior, especially if it is ongoing and chronic, can lead to complex PTSD, it's important to remember how a narcissist behaves, thinks and feels. Narcissists thrive only for themselves. They are completely self-motivated, feel entitled to everything they want to do, have no compassion and no remorse. They lack empathy completely.

Narcissists and sociopaths operate in similar ways. They use you as prey.

They get close to you, build up your trust, mimic your emotions, take full advantage of your vulnerability and compassion, get you on your own, build a relationship where you begin to need them and depend on them.

They groom you and are highly clever at doing so. They are emotional vampires, and are dangerous, abusive people. Once they are done with you, or you figure them out, or leave them, it all changes. The narcissist's worst nightmare is being exposed.

They will resist this at all costs. They will lie, deceive, deny and manipulate those around them, they will act outraged at what you are doing to *them* and if all else fails, will manipulate those around them into believing *they* are the victim.

Not once in all of this, do they actually care about their "supply," the people they use to fulfill their selfish agenda. All the fake emotions they showed, all the words they used to reel you in, all the times they said "I love you" and "I care deeply about you" and "I want to help you" were all fake. They didn't mean a word of it.

Once exposed, you see their real motives and their real feelings about you. Then, they are hot on the pursuit of ensuring that no one believes their supply and will set out - with the help of their supporters - to make you seem crazy, like a liar, or evil.

All along, they have no concept of the fact that they ripped your heart out, stomped all over it and left you in pain.

They have no empathy for the hurt they caused, just a complete sense of entitlement, a complete lack of insight, and complete lack of courage to face what they have done.

Interacting with a narcissistic person, especially if raised in childhood with a complete lack of love, care, compassion or empathy means a great deal of invalidation. This degree of invalidation, combined with a sense of toxic shame and worthlessness instilled in us by the abuser, can lead us to complex PTSD.

Healing Complex PTSD from Narcissistic Abuse

It takes a long time to recover from narcissistic abuse and it's so hard for many victims to just watch them carry on and enjoy their lives, whilst the victim grieves, is confused, is hurt and cannot understand how their abuser can do this, after all they had said and done.

Often, complex trauma survivors struggle with self-compassion, especially if the trauma was caused throughout childhood, by parents. I think childhood complex trauma survivors, often have an inner voice that says "If your own parents didn't love you, then you must be unlovable and defective."

It's important to remember that traumatized people tend to go to what feels safe, even if it isn't safe. We tend to go to what we know, and what we know is what we were raised in. It takes a long time for this message to change and for a healthier message to develop.

It's so hard for victims to understand how they were not loved at all, just used and abused, chewed up and then spat back out, left to deal with all the hurt and pain and deal with others who now believe a whole pack of lies too, due to the smear campaign of their abusers.

Recovery is slow and painful, particularly so when it involves multiple narcissistic or sociopathic abusers and especially when the abuse is still raw.

Complex PTSD from this type of abuse requires very specialized, empathic, sensitive and insightful therapy and healing modalities that address subconscious wounding and the formation of trusting, healthy relationships in order to begin to heal significant wounds.

What's important to remember is that recovery includes grieving *twice:*

(1) Grieving the person you thought they were – the person whom you loved and believed loved you too.

(2) Grieving the real person they are, the narcissist, who never cared and used you as supply, with no remorse.

I will never forget this verse as it captures this type of abuse perfectly: *Matt 7:6 Do not give what is holy to dogs, and do not throw your pearls before swine, or they will trample them under their feet, and turn and tear you to pieces.*

Lilly's Healing Journey

I am a survivor of multiple severe complex trauma, from interpersonal abuse. I have been diagnosed with both Post Traumatic Stress Disorder and Complex Post Traumatic Stress Disorder. I have survived ongoing severe abuse throughout my childhood, including sexual, emotional, psychological, physical abuse from my mother, step-father and their circle of pedophile and sex offender friends. I have also survived domestic violence and other ongoing trauma, as an adult.

At 40 years old, my healing journey began when I commenced counselling. I started writing a blog, to express my journey. My blog and my website became very popular and I have received awards for them. I am very thankful they are recommended, supported and shared, by many mental health professionals in the trauma field.

It is my passion, to reach out to others, with a level of understanding, validation, empathy, honesty and insight, that have been described as rare, but are vital to help complex trauma survivors. I am in the process of writing my first book, which I hope will further reach and assist people, in their healing journeys. Complex trauma is still a relatively new field in psychology and I am thankful to be able to contribute towards assisting others, raising awareness and education, about the painful and life impacting wounds, caused by complex trauma.

My journey towards healing has made me become a caring, empathic person with integrity, honesty and a conscience. Overcoming every single abusive person, every single abusive action I suffered. Overcoming decades of severe abuse, to be someone so very different to every abusive person who tried to destroy me. No matter how much they projected their own self-hatred and darkness, onto someone they knew was vulnerable, no matter how much they wanted to make me suffer -- I did suffer, and yet I survived and overcame it and became the opposite of their dark souls.

I've suffered and survived what was meant to kill me. Overcome what was meant to cause deep suffering. Overcome multiple, highly abusive people. Who I am is defined not by what they did, but defined by all I have overcome.

About the Author

Lilly Hope Lucario is an award-winning blogger, author and advocate for survivors of complex trauma. She is the founder of HealingFromComplexTraumaandPTSD.com, an incredible website endorsed by numerous mental health professionals including trauma expert Pete Walker and visited by hundreds of thousands of people all over the globe. Lilly is currently working on her first book on healing complex trauma. You can donate to her gofundme page to support the publication of this book.

Social Media Platforms

> **Website:** http://www.healingfromcomplextraumaandptsd.com
> **Blog:** https://healingfromcomplextraumaandptsd.wordpress.com
> **Twitter:** https://www.twitter.com/HealingCPTSD
> **Donate to support Lilly's book on Complex PTSD through GoFundMe:** https://www.gofundme.com/chp1jc

CHAPTER 3

How to Heal from Narcissistic Abuse

As we've started exploring in the book, recovery from narcissistic abuse is complex and multifaceted. Every journey is also unique. However, I find there are eleven universal steps survivors usually take on their healing journey. We will explore them throughout the book.

Recovery from narcissistic abuse usually involves the following 11 steps.

11 Steps for Healing from Narcissistic Abuse

1. Identifying narcissistic traits and behaviors that are pathological and abusive.

2. Breaking the habit of projecting your own morality and ability to empathize onto the abuser.

3. Validating your reality as opposed to the one the abuser has created and distorted for you through gaslighting and projection.

4. Creating a solid support network of validating people who will hold you accountable for detaching from and leaving the relationship.

5. Maintaining No Contact or Low Contact, depending on whether you share children with your abuser or have other legal matters that require communication.

6. Extreme self-care to begin to heal from the effects of abuse, encompassing physical, emotional and spiritual methods.

7. Creating a "reverse discourse" to rewrite the scripts the abuser has written for you, which is especially helpful for victims who suffered from severe verbal abuse.

8. Reconnecting with the "lost" pre-trauma identity or a spiritual identity that transcends trauma if there is no pre-trauma identity, while permitting post-traumatic growth.

9. Healing subconscious programming and addictive or self-sabotaging behaviors during the period of recovery through alternative and traditional methods.

10. Constructively reframing the experience to benefit your personal development and the larger society around you. This can include sharing your story with other survivors and channeling the experience into the greater good.

11. Realigning yourself with your purpose, goals, hobbies, interests and passions to rebuild an incredible life while using your adversity as fuel for your success.

How to Combat Biochemical and Trauma Bonds

To combat the biochemical bonds we discussed in Chapter 2, we have to understand that we will inevitably go through withdrawal when we cut contact with the narcissist. This means that we have to address withdrawal from high levels of oxytocin, dopamine, adrenaline and even the spikes in cortisol our body has become habituated to. There are ways to fulfill these needs in a healthier manner that do not involve the narcissist. Here are some of the ways to naturally boost your feel-good chemicals and substitute your addiction to the narcissist with productive activities.

Boost Oxytocin

No Contact or Low Contact is essential to start to wean off of the effects of the oxytocin bond, although of course it will come with cravings to reconnect with the narcissistic partner. Rather than giving into this temptation to reconnect, supplant that craving with healthier connections. Here are some examples:

Increase physical contact.

You can produce oxytocin by cuddling a cute animal or a loving friend or family member; research shows that cuddling with a dog actually increases the oxytocin levels of both the dog and its owner (Odendaal and Meintjes, 2003). If you can, adopt an animal or snuggle with a pet you already have or volunteer to dog sit for a friend.

You can even give yourself a hug whenever you need it– yes, it will still release oxytocin. Make it a regular habit to give hugs to the people you care about. If you feel comfortable doing so and have ended the relationship with your narcissistic partner, and if you are able to distinguish between physical contact and emotional connection, you may want to spend time with someone you're attracted to - this is only if you're able to see them as a casual partner - during this time, attempting to forge a long-term relationship is discouraged unless you feel you've healed considerably.

Keep it simple – interact with, talk to, or go on a casual date with someone with no strings attached, but only if you can keep your expectations and investment very low. Be mindful that engaging in sexual activity can potentially bond you to this person, so act accordingly depending on what you feel you can handle since this can be triggering and re-traumatizing. We're not trying to create another bond with a potentially toxic partner here – we're just opening up the opportunity for flirtation and social bonding.

This technique won't work for everyone because not everyone is able to separate physical affection from something more serious. But for others, going on a simple date or flirting with someone else can provide a pleasurable distraction and help get the survivor back on the path of feeling like a loveable, desirable human being. It will also remind you that you have other options for close contact and intimacy with other people besides the narcissist. I would warn you against serial dating, as this can lead to complications and feelings of rejection and further abandonment if for whatever reason you become attached to a casual partner or multiple partners.

Enhance social bonding.

According to the latest research, oxytocin can increase compassion and pro-social behavior in those suffering from the symptoms of PTSD (Palgi et. al, 2016). Intimacy is at the root of oxytocin bonding and while oxytocin has been spoken about in the framework of romantic relationships, there's nothing to suggest that this form of bonding doesn't work in other types of interactions. Hang out with friends that really care about you to increase affection and intimacy in your life as well as social bonds. If you don't have any supportive friends, join a new gym or support group that challenges you to interact with people. Given the connection between oxytocin and compassion, it can help to support a friend, donate to a cause or lend a listening ear to someone. Not only will you help someone, it'll make you feel better as well. It's a win-win situation that benefits everyone.

It's also important to show self-compassion, as research indicates that this too can heighten oxytocin levels. Loving kindness meditations can help increase compassion towards yourself and others. For more information about the connection between self-compassion and oxytocin, see Dr. Kristin Neff's article on the Huffington Post, "The Chemicals of Care: How Self-Compassion Manifests in Our Bodies."

Boosting Dopamine and Adrenaline

I am putting these two bad boys together because I think we can combat both with the same activities. Seeking that adrenaline rush? Take up an activity that makes you tremble with both fear and anticipation. Whether it's rock climbing, skydiving, bungee jumping or boldly going on a job interview, do things that give you that rush that the narcissist used to give you. I promise it will have a better result than seeking your rush from a toxic relationship. Looking to feed your reward system? Create new reward circuits that have little to do with the narcissist by taking up a new hobby to be absorbed in, a new volunteer venture or a new project. For example:

Go after your passions and explore job opportunities that excite you. On my own journey of No Contact, I created a YouTube channel, wrote a book, got a new job, and attended Meetups to meet new friends. This gave back to my reward system in a way that was productive, not destructive. It also made me hopeful that I was rebuilding a better life with a new support system – this hope is so essential in moving forward from the devastation of a relationship with a toxic partner. What are at least three activities, goals and/or hobbies you could be pursuing right now to replace the time and energy you spent on the narcissist?

Write an exciting bucket list and instead of letting it collect dust, actually start doing the activities on that list. Make sure this list has items that challenge and excite you – add an element of "fear" (healthy fear this time around!) to make your anticipated schedule as unpredictable as your narcissist's hot and cold behavior was. For example, I went on a number of adventures on my journey that made life more interesting and exciting – from the super weird and silly to rewarding and challenging. Everything from riding a mechanical bull for the first time to taking a pole dancing class (for the sole purpose of fitness, of course) to going on my first ever roller coaster. I also attended an art therapy group, tried my first ever yoga class in a scalding hot room and joined a brand new gym. Try things you've never done and do things you have done in a new way – whether it's just for laughs or a productive activity, as long as it's brand new, your brain, your body and your mind will thank you.

The sky's the limit! Life can be exciting, and yes, even more pleasurable without the narcissist. It's time to "love-bomb" yourself with all the attention, excitement, luxury and self-care you deserve. Make sure you also do these things spontaneously and try new things on a whim. I used to look up different events on a daily basis to see what new adventure I could go on every day. This unpredictable, "intermittent schedule" of rewards will allow dopamine in your brain to flow more readily. Yes, I really just wrote that sentence. I think I just reached hardcore nerd level.

Go out with friends that make you feel your best. These friends must be people who you can honestly say make you feel good because they have positive and supportive attitudes. The friends who make you laugh, the friends you always have a good time with, who love you dearly, can get that dopamine flowin' like no other.

Alternatively, plan solo dates with yourself that give you that "me" time while also providing pleasure. This can include buying your favorite food, going to the spa, soaking in a bubble bath with scented oils and candles, getting a massage, buying yourself a new outfit, buying a ticket to a country you've always wanted to explore - whatever makes you happiest, engage in it at this time more frequently on your own. This will help you become more independent and less people-pleasing, because you will remember the positive experiences you had alone and will therefore be less likely to fall prey to attaching to toxic people just for the sake of having someone with you on every adventure you go on.

Of course, try to incorporate the element of surprise whenever possible by introducing something "new" to this solo date – a food you haven't tried, a place you haven't visited, or a country you haven't yet stepped foot in.

Travel somewhere else for at least a weekend – even if it's just to a bed and breakfast in a different town or state. This can give you a much needed escape that reminds you life will continue regardless of whether or not the narcissist is in it.

Less Cortisol

We'd prefer not to have more of this hormone. Author and coach Christopher Bergland (2013) suggests numerous ways to counteract the effects of this hormone, which include physical activity, mindfulness, meditation, laughter, music and social connectivity.

So why not take up a meditation and/or yoga class that will decrease these levels as you're healing? Here are some ideas:

- Join a daily or weekly Vinyasa Flow yoga class and/or incorporate a ten-minute breathing meditation every single morning to get those stress levels down.

- Watch more comedy shows and comedy movies to tickle your funny bone. Laughter lowers cortisol levels and this will also feed your reward system.

- Smile, even if you don't want to. Smiling releases endorphins that increase relaxation.

- Plan a weekly night out with some of your most supportive friends to increase social connectivity. Join a forum or support group for abuse survivors.

- Listen to music that expresses the different stages of grief and anger you may experience in the aftermath of an abusive relationship.

Self-Care Warrior Pro-tips ♥: If you let your tongue go limp in your mouth and open it slightly, this sends a message to your brain stem and limbic system to turn off cortisol and adrenaline. If you contract your muscles and take short, rapid breaths, you can also reduce cortisol levels for a quick pick-me up (Bergland, 2013). How neat is that?!

Relaxing and self-soothing are key to detaching from the narcissist in your life. They will also enable you to step back and resist your impulses if you're thinking about reconnecting with your narcissistic partner.

Boost Serotonin

To boost this powerful hormone that can cause ruminative addiction to your ex-partner when levels are low and can affect your impulsivity, ability to act on plans, emotions, memory, weight, sleep, and self-esteem, try these natural serotonin boosters, some of which are discussed by Alex Korb, Ph.D (2011) in "Boosting Your Serotonin Activity" on Psychology Today.

- **Sunlight** – Exposure to sunlight increases serotonin levels. Take daily morning and afternoon walks where it is likely to be sunny in order to get your daily dose.

- **B-vitamins** – Low levels of serotonin can cause depression. Taking Vitamins B6 and B12 can potentially lower the risk of depression. According to Cornell Women's Health, there has been a link found between inadequate amounts of B6 and B12 and depression. B vitamins are also found to be essential for the creation of both dopamine and serotonin.

- **Massage** – Research shows that massage therapy can help lower cortisol levels and boost serotonin and dopamine levels, especially among populations of need such as depressed pregnant mothers, those suffering from cancer as well as those with migraine headaches (Field, 2005).

- **Recalling happy memories** – According to Korb (2011), remembering happy memories can increase serotonin production in the anterior cingulate cortex, a part of the brain that controls attention. Look through old photo albums, old journals and home movies if you need help visualizing happy memories. By remembering happy memories, there's a dual effect: we increase serotonin while also preventing ourselves from ruminating over unhappy events.

Self-care warrior pro-tip ❤: Do not use this tip to think about or romanticize happier times with your abusive ex-partner. Instead, make a daily gratitude list of things that made you happy that have nothing to do with your ex-partner.

Therapy - Another way to tackle these trauma bonds is by talking to a mental health professional experienced in narcissistic abuse not only in relationships, but also in families. Someone who is well-versed and validating in this topic can help you uncover wounds beneath the surface you may not be aware. I'll talk more about the different types of therapy available in the section, "Traditional Healing Methods Explained."

Medications – There are, of course, medications that can help if you are struggling with severe, crippling anxiety or depression such as SSRI's. However, they are beyond the scope of this book to discuss. Please always consult your psychiatrist or mental health professional regarding the best medication for you to take. Do not ever "replace" medication you are taking with any of these tools, as they are meant as a supplement to your self-care regimen, not a replacement for therapy. You should always discuss with your mental health professional any change in medication you are currently taking, as there can be side effects.

Self-Care Warrior Pro-tips ♥: Exercise can target many of these bio-chemicals all at once. Doing jumping jacks, squats or running in place all allow a surge of neurotransmitters like norepinephrine, dopamine and serotonin. Exercise can lower cortisol levels as well. I highly encourage you to get a gym membership as well as a membership to your local yoga center if you don't have one already.

Whether you're currently in an abusive relationship, planning to leave, or have already started the journey to No Contact, any form of exercise – whether it be running on the treadmill, weight-lifting, dancing, yoga, walking, biking, Zumba – will act as a natural antidepressant and enable you to cope with your emotions more effectively at whatever stage of recovery you may be in.

Unraveling trauma bonds.

Much of our behavior is driven subconsciously and the bad news is, a lot of our programming comes from when we were kids. Bruce Lipton, Ph.D, author of *The Biology of Belief* (2007) tells us that even when we are in the utero we are aware of our environment - so much so that even as a fetus, we can be shown to react on a sonogram when we hear our parents fighting.

Imagine what it would be like for you, if you grew up being bullied or witnessing domestic violence, to be programmed with thoughts, beliefs, emotions and ideas that will affect you for a lifetime, especially if you're not conscious of them. A lot of us think we can get over the narcissist simply by learning more about narcissism and protecting ourselves when we see the red flags. Yet this is dealing with the neocortical part of our brains, not our emotional brain, our limbic system, which is actually the most susceptible to the narcissist's charm, especially if we've been abused in the past.

See, narcissists use our emotional, primitive brain, especially our amygdala, to trick us into falling in love with them and then increasing anxiety and fear so much that we're unable to think logically or see them accurately, especially when we're in the midst of the relationship. That's why people who have been in relationships with more than one narcissist need to look at our wounding - not to blame ourselves, but to *observe and change* ourselves for the better.

So many survivors unfortunately struggle with the symptoms of PTSD or complex PTSD. For survivors who do, I recommend continuing to gain professional support for your PTSD/complex PTSD and continuing to do your self-work through positive affirmations, meditation and exercise. The work never stops inside the therapy space, it just begins. Propelling your body in empowering movement can begin to combat paralysis and create a reverse discourse that can start to slow down the inner critical voice. Empowering music helps so much as well, as I'll describe in the next section.

The sad truth is, while knowledge is power, until you break the trauma repetition cycle and until you deal with your subconscious wounds, you can still be prone to gravitating towards narcissists and have narcissists gravitate towards you (remember, it's a two-way street!). Knowledge must be combined with behavioral changes and those behavioral changes must be supported by healing on the level of these subconscious wounds.

Important note about links

Throughout the book and especially in this chapter, you will find references to numerous links. This book is enrolled in the Kindle Matchbook Program which enables the reader to gain free access to the e-book version of the book and its hyperlinks via Amazon if they purchased the paperback version of the book on Amazon. Please visit the book's Amazon page for details on how to download your free e-book copy. I have done my best to provide full hyperlinks whenever possible, but there may be some full hyperlinks easily searchable on the web omitted for the sake of brevity.

You may also gain access to meditation links here: **http://tinyurl.com/selfcarewarrior** using the password "selfcarewarrior."

Healing Trauma in the Brain: Traditional Healing Methods Explained

Cognitive Behavioral Therapy

What is it? Cognitive Behavioral Therapy was developed in the 1960's by Dr. Aaron T. Beck as a therapy that focuses on challenging cognitive distortions and unhealthy thoughts which, as a result, feed into a cycle of maladaptive behaviors. It has been proven effective for a variety of disorders and medical conditions.

How does it work? After an abusive relationship with a narcissist, we will likely find ourselves ruminating over the lies the narcissist fed us about ourselves, our value in the world and our worthiness. Our beliefs about the world and ourselves can drastically change when we are met with the experience of any form of abuse and can cause us to engage in self-destructive thought patterns, feelings and behaviors (Bancroft, 2002).

CBT can be helpful in dismantling these distortions and false beliefs by enabling us to find healthier, alternative ways of thinking and feeling while pinpointing the connections among unhealthy thoughts, feelings, beliefs and behaviors.

Here are some resources that may help you on your CBT journey, hopefully along with the help of a validating CBT therapist:

Links

The Beck Institute – What is Cognitive Behavioral Therapy?
CBT Worksheets
Specialty Behavioral Health PDFS
Lynn Martin's Cycle of Maladaptive Behavior Client Handouts

Self-Care Warrior Pro Tip

Work in the therapy space is just the beginning. While in therapy, it's important to continue self-work and self-care through exercise, meditation and your own "homework" regarding what you've discussed in the therapy space. When not in therapy, you can start a supplementary practice that incorporates CBT techniques at home by making a simple list of the negative assumptions you have about yourself and the abuse.

These can include distortions like, "I am at fault for the abuse," "I am not worthy," "I deserved the abuse." Then, write down any and all evidence against these distortions. Next, write a "replacement" for the false belief or thought you've been carrying that incorporates this new, healthier way of thinking. This may be, "Abuse is the abuser's fault," "I am worthy and valuable," and "I only deserve love, compassion and respect." For more guidance on these types of exercises to banish negative self-talk, check out my meditation for Curbing Self-Talk and Self-Sabotage below:

Meditation Time ❤ Link: Curbing Negative Self-Talk and Self-Sabotage

Therapy and Healing Modalities for Complex PTSD

Effective therapies and healing modalities for C-PTSD can include the following:

Prolonged Exposure Therapy

Prolonged exposure therapy has four components: (1) education about the symptoms of trauma and the goals of treatment, (2) breathing techniques to manage distress, (3) real world exposure which helps you work on approaching safe situations that you may have avoided due to the fear of being triggered – as treatment goes on, you work towards exposing yourself to more distressing situations and (4) talking through the trauma, which involves addressing the painful memories you have been avoiding – as survivors continue to desensitize themselves to imagining and talking about these avoided memories, the fear of them lessens.

Cognitive Processing Therapy

Much like Prolonged Exposure therapy, Cognitive Processing Therapy involves educating the survivor about their PTSD symptoms. However, the emphasis on this type of therapy is on identifying maladaptive thoughts and feelings and then learning skills that help you challenge these cognitive distortions. This type of therapy also helps you work through changes in beliefs you may have had in your worldview due to the trauma, addressing your old and new beliefs about safety, trust, control, relationships and self-esteem.

Meditation as a Tool for Healing

Remember the discussion earlier about how trauma creates changes in the brain, often shutting down communication between the more emotional parts of our brain and the frontal lobes which control executive functioning, our ability to organize, plan, think and make decisions? And how trauma can shrink the hippocampus and the amygdala, which affects emotion, memory and learning? Well, research shows that meditation not only thickens the auditory and sensory parts of our brain, but also increases grey matter in the frontal lobes, regardless of how old you are (Lazar, 2005).

Abuse keeps us locked in the "fight or flight" mode – mentally and emotionally paralyzed. According to research done by a Harvard neuroscientist, a regular meditation practice for eight weeks can literally change our brain, making the amygdala which controls the "Fight or Flight" response, smaller, and thickening the hippocampus which helps with emotional regulation. The very areas of the brain that were once affected by trauma can now be rewired by meditation.

A forty-minute meditation practice every day can change the way you approach your emotions, your relationships and your overall sense of happiness and contentment. Meditation is free and can be done anywhere at any time. Contrary to popular myths, it does not require shutting off your thoughts but rather acknowledging them, accepting them, observing them and letting them pass. All you need is a willingness to focus on your breath and a space where you can sit quietly and reflectively.

Here are some podcasts and channels I follow, some of which are meditation channels and others that are specifically about healing narcissistic abuse. I have done my best to provide a web address whenever available in an accessible form; for links that are excessively long, please consult the free e-book copy of the book which you can access via the Kindle matchbook program on the Amazon page for this book, google the names provided or go to tinyurl.com/selfcarewarrior using the password selfcarewarrior to access some of the links.

Links

Meditation Oasis by Mary and Richard Maddux (This is my favorite meditation resource and the one that began my journey. Wonderful for beginners and experts alike) – www.meditationoasis.com

The Meditation Society of Australia (free mp3 meditations on their website) – www.download.meditation.org.au

YellowBrickCinema – Relaxing Music - www.youtube.com/user/yellowbrickcinema

Lucy Rising – Meditations for Narcissistic Abuse

Self-Therapy for Narcissistic Abuse Trauma/EMDR Sound Therapy

The Little Shaman Healing – Shamanic Drumming and Binaural Meditation

Joseph Clough – Self-Hypnosis Meditations

Michael Seeley – Self-Hypnosis Guided Meditations – www.youtube.com/user/michaelsealey

DBT

Dialectical Behavioral Therapy (DBT) combines cognitive behavioral therapy with Eastern mindfulness techniques. It is traditionally used for patients with Borderline Personality Disorder (although, as you have read previously, many victims with complex PTSD can be misdiagnosed with BPD). DBT offers a mindfulness approach that enables individuals to regulate and cope with their emotions, improve their interpersonal effectiveness skills and stay grounded in the present moment during crises.

The skills of DBT can be taught to anyone and everyone and are very useful for anyone who struggles with emotion regulation and toxic interpersonal relationships. It's important to remember that the majority of those diagnosed with Borderline Personality Disorder have suffered abuse and trauma in childhood – some people with BPD actually have narcissistic parents themselves. There is an overlap between the symptoms of Complex PTSD and BPD, so misdiagnoses of those suffering from the effects of narcissistic abuse is common. You don't have to be a Borderline to benefit from the skills of DBT; there are excellent websites that offer an overview of the skills and methods involved in DBT, such as DBTSelfHelp.com

Group Therapy

Group therapy led by a mental health professional can be a safe space to talk about your struggles, fears, and traumas while witnessing others doing the same. Research groups that focus on domestic violence, trauma, and/or any other areas you may be struggling with at this time. Expressing our emotions with others allows us to gain validation and support. It also increases social accountability for maintaining progress and self-care. Search for a therapy group here: https://groups.psychologytoday.com/rms/.

Support Groups

If you struggle with dysfunctional, abusive relationships and have trouble setting boundaries with others, there are support groups with other survivors that can help you. Some survivors have benefited from attending CoDA (Codependents Anonymous) meetings or Narcissistic Abuse Survivor Meetup groups in their local area. Go to Meetup.com to learn more.

A word of caution: If you are thinking of attending a meeting for Narcissistic Abuse, be careful and "test" it out first before you commit to anything – I once attended one where the group moderator had a very victim-blaming stance towards the narcissist's other victims; she also seemed baffled by anyone who had a pattern of abusive relationships, revealing a lack of knowledge about trauma repetition.

Remember that any support group, whether online or offline, can be triggering because the moderator or fellow members of the group may not be professionals licensed for group therapy, and may have narcissistic tendencies themselves. Much like the narcissistic abuse blogosphere, we have to be careful about the resources we consult. It's important to consume support groups in a way that is healthy and balanced.

Alternative Healing Methods Explained

EMDR

What is it? Eye Movement Desensitization and Reprocessing (EMDR) therapy is an integrative psychotherapy approach developed by Dr. Francine Shapiro, who noticed that eye movements can mitigate the intense effect disturbing thoughts have on us. It has been researched and proven effective, especially for the treatment of short-term trauma. While EMDR may not work for everyone, many survivors have reported finding relief after using it as a tool to process their trauma safely.

How does it work? Traumatic memories keep us "frozen in time." When we relive a traumatic moment, we feel as if it's happening all over again – retaining all the details from the first time we experienced it. EMDR is a complex eight-step process that desensitizes us to the negative emotions and thoughts associated with our traumatic experience through rapid eye movement and restores us with more positive feelings and beliefs. You can learn more about EMDR and find an EMDR therapist at the EMDR International Association here: emdria.org.

Emotional Freedom Technique (EFT)

What is it? Similar to acupuncture, EFT was developed by Dr. Mercola. It is a "tapping" technique using the same energy meridians used in acupuncture, but without the invasiveness of needles. Positive affirmations are coupled with using our own fingers to touch the meridians to reprogram the way we think and feel.

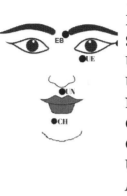

TH = Top of Head

EB = Eye Brow

SE = Side of the Eye

UE = Under the Eye

UN = Under the Nose

Ch= Chin

CB = Collar Bone

UA = Under the Arm

WR = Wrists

How does it work? There are nine tapping "points" some of which are shown above. Emotions like anxiety become trapped in certain parts of our body. EFT allows us to release these energetic blocks by allowing electromagnetic energy to flow more freely throughout the body. The affirmations are designed to validate and understand the function of the negative emotions, acknowledging their protective purpose while enabling the client to feel permitted to let them go. For more information about EFT, visit: http://www.eft.mercola.com/

Yoga

According to the Dr. Bessel van der Kolk, founder of the Trauma Center at Justice Resource Institute, yoga has been proven as an effective complementary treatment for chronic PTSD. Increasing a sense of mindful awareness, it enables individuals to experience "safety and mastery" over their bodies, giving them the resources to productively interpret intense physiological states of re-experiencing the trauma.

This is especially helpful to survivors of physical and/or sexual abuse. According to their studies, yoga has helped survivors ease dissociative symptoms, affective dysregulation and reduce tension throughout the body. I personally love hatha yoga, Bikram yoga, and hot vinyasa flow yoga. If you're a beginner to yoga, I recommend you take a beginner's class before moving onto more advanced classes. For more information about the effects of yoga on trauma, I encourage you to visit www.traumacenter.org.

Mirror Work

Self-help powerhouse Louise Hay talks about the effectiveness of looking into a mirror and saying positive affirmations rather than engaging in the traditional negative self-talk that arises when we normally look in the mirror. Mirror work may at first glance appear narcissistic, but really, it's about giving ourselves a healthy dose of self-love and self-compassion. Talking to ourselves lovingly and compassionately, while seeing ourselves reflected back, has the dual effect of conditioning ourselves with positive affirmations and associating those affirmations with our own self-image.

Art Therapy

Art therapy has been proven by research to be effective for victims suffering from PTSD, as trauma tends to shut down the part of the brain related to language (Broca's area) which renders us speechless. Art provides a medium through which we can begin a dialogue with our trauma by reconnecting us to the somatic and limbic aspects of the brain where trauma is encoded. Whether you use a sketchpad or a canvas doesn't matter. Pottery, sculpture, painting, sketching – it all counts. Get your painting tools, your colored markers or pencils and create something new.

If you currently reside in the U.S., you can find art therapists in your area on the American Art Therapy Association website at arttherapy.org. You will learn more about the role that expressive arts can play in my interview with Andrea Schneider, MSW, LCSW, located at the end of this chapter.

Reverse Discourse and Narrative Therapy/ NLP Reframing

As a graduate student at Columbia University, I studied the effects of life-course narratives and how they interacted with the life-course trajectories of bully victims. I explored how bully victims with a *resilience narrative* – those who reframed their experiences and rewrote their narratives as a powerful impetus towards success - were able to channel their experiences into a greater purpose.

The bully victims I interviewed actually returned to the site of the trauma to teach in classrooms themselves and raise awareness about bullying. This was a way to take back the often debilitating experience of severe bullying and instead use it productively as an experience that could leave a positive impact on future generations. This empowering narrative reframing enabled these victims to become survivors – it even made them grateful for the learning experiences of the adversity and most importantly, it gave them the motivation to change more lives as a result of what they had experienced.

Narrative therapy works on the idea that it is not our life events but rather our interpretation and narration of them, that affects our ability to solve problems in our lives. In addition, it attempts to rework trauma into a coherent narrative from disintegrated pieces that may be caused by dissociation. It places the client as the "expert" on his or her life stories and works to uncover skills, competencies, strengths and values to create "alternative" stories to the usual negative ones that often claim our perception of ourselves and our lives. Rather than narrating the same old story that we are not capable, for example, we may instead choose an alternative tale which recalls the multiple times we've survived and thrived through horrific circumstances.

This is why writing and journaling is so powerful to recovery, because we can literally change the narrative and talk back to the existing one. We can "reframe" the experiences we've had to benefit us. We can also reframe our perception of the abuser as powerful and invincible at any point by rewriting that old narrative so we become the powerful agents of our lives.

You witnessed my "alternative" story in my introduction. In my story, I reframed myself as a "warrior," who has tackled trauma throughout her life by channeling it into her transformation– rather than as a helpless victim repeating a cycle of trauma (although I certainly wouldn't deny that we can be both victims and survivors). I told a story of using my adverse experiences for the greater good, rather than talking about these experiences as being so powerful that they took over my life and defeated me. Rather than emphasizing my challenges, I refocused on my strength and spoke about how I used the experiences of trauma and abuse as a way to build a platform for survivors and give back to the survivor community.

Even if you're not working with a counselor who is trained in narrative therapy, you can change your narrative at any time while using a piece of paper and pen (or a good old laptop). Start by writing your old story of adversity (I was abused as a child, I felt hopeless and helpless) and then, write an alternative tale (Due to my abuse, I was able to help other survivors) right underneath it. What you'll find is that by creating a new, empowering alternative story, you start changing the negative self-talk, judgment, doubt, fear and self-hatred that is demonstrated in your old one.

For more information about narrative therapy, be sure to visit http://dulwichcentre.com.au/what-is-narrative-therapy.

Reverse discourse.

If you've read my first book, *The Smart Girl's Guide to Self-Care*, you should be familiar with what I mean by reverse discourse. "Reverse discourse" isn't something I necessarily learned in a psychology book or a therapeutic program. It's a series of techniques I developed and taught myself to decrease negative ruminations. In the work of Foucault (1988), reverse discourse was discussed as a medium through which power was reclaimed and redirected by challenging the normative discourses of sexuality and gender.

In the way I am using it (or adapting it), creating a reverse discourse involves a reclaiming of power, connotation and values of negative statements wielded at you by toxic people over your lifetime.

This is a method I've adapted and developed from my own real life experiences which has put me back in control of the language that has been used against me throughout my lifetime. This is an especially effective technique when you're recovering from verbal abuse.

This is also one of the most helpful techniques I found to release some of the rage I had towards my abusers and the cruel words they said to me. I used the technique to create a powerful reverse discourse that undermined every single abusive thing I had ever heard in my life. When I said we can become the narcissist's nightmare by empowering ourselves, I wasn't kidding. I've used reverse discourse to achieve big dreams and goals other people doubted I ever could, and to become the person I am today.

Reverse discourse helped me to become driven, confident and motivated to succeed beyond anyone's expectations. While it takes practice, when you regain control over how you define yourself and the language you use to reframe your reality, toxic people begin to lose their power and you begin to regain your own.

In short, methods of reverse discourse are creative ways you can empower yourself by taking back control of the language abusers or bullies have used against you. You can use reverse discourse by (1) "talking back" to your abusers, (2) replacing a word they used to disempower you with a new positive affirmation, and (3) reassigning degrading words with new, positive connotations that serve you.

1) Talking back to the abuser.

This is not about literally talking back, it's more about talking back to the ruminations over the abuse in your own mind. When talking back to an abuser, I find it most liberating when I allow myself to be as uncensored as possible when I write these down. It's the only safe space where I know I'll ever get to vent my frustrations freely without consequences. Feel free to unleash your rage onto the page. That's what it's there for, and it sure does beat pursuing literal revenge which could have real-life consequences. Related to this, you may also choose to create lists that outright challenge all the negative declarations toxic people have made about you. Creating this "reverse discourse" means writing down the concrete accomplishments or positive feedback others have given you, to counter snide remarks or abusive comments that you find yourself ruminating over.

If you're stuck, here are some ideas from my own use of reverse discourse:

Start by turning everything your abuser said onto them. Did they say you were unappealing? Write down how ugly and unappealing their outside is, as well as their inside.

Did they say you'd never achieve your dreams? Talk back to them and say just because you haven't achieved yours doesn't mean I won't achieve mine. Big ideas are not suited for small-minded people like you.

Did they say you weren't smart enough? Tell them you were smart enough to stop spending time with a dummy like them.

Yep, when I said harsh, I meant harsh. Let it out. Be a badass. Stop censoring your own anger. It's not as if the narcissist can hear you, so feel free to express yourself uncensored, to yourself. Connect with your authentic self, your authentic rage and your fighter attitude. So long as you do not act upon any of these thoughts or break No Contact by sending them any part of this new discourse, you're safe to release your anger in a healthy manner. In fact, according to Beverly Engel, LMFT, in her article, "When is it Better Not to Forgive?" attempting to stifle your anger while forcing yourself to forgive your abuser too soon actually impedes the healing process.

(2) Word or phrase replacement.

For the second component of reverse discourse, you can replace abusive words you've heard with new words or phrases whenever they come up in your mind or you find yourself ruminating over them. How you use this is up to you and your personal needs. Some survivors will find word/phrase replacement jolting, so for them, they might have to start small and begin to use positive words they have an easier time believing in that eventually lead up to the beliefs they want to have for themselves.

A survivor who has been criticized for her appearance may find more solace in replacing his or her rumination with something small like, "I am imperfect, but imperfection is beautiful," rather than right away saying, "I am so beautiful" without any belief in it. Assess where you're at and what you feel most comfortable saying – don't force yourself into extremes if you're not ready for them.

Other survivors, however, may benefit from extremes. I personally found it helpful to make the new word or phrase as hard-hitting and extreme as possible, because as an abuse survivor, I was used to hearing the other extreme end of the spectrum. For example, if your abuser constantly attacked your intelligence, replace any abusive phrase they've used against you with, "I am smart as hell" or "I am brilliant."

It may even be helpful to add an additional phrase that gives back the projection to your abuser – for example, "I am the smart one, you're just sad you aren't," is a great example of how to actively defuse the abuser's power while igniting your own. Whichever way you use this method, make sure that it caters to what you personally feel comfortable with. This can be an incremental process and there is no right or wrong way to do this method.

(3) Giving previously disempowering words a positive connotation and reframing their meaning.

In our society, words like "bitch" have been "taken back" with more positive connotations that refer to being a powerful woman, the most famous example being the new use of the word in Sherry Argov's book,

Why Men Love Bitches. There's no rule that says we can't apply the same principle to degrading words. If there is a phrase that you need to "remodel" to serve you and feel that you can without being triggered, all the more power to you.

For example, if a female narcissist emasculated you by saying, "You're not a real man, you're too sensitive," and this thought keeps popping back in your head, try remodeling this by saying, "If being a real man means taking your crap passively, sure, I am not your definition of what it means to be a real man. I am even better." It's powerful to recognize that while words can be destructive, they can also be taken back, reconstructed, rewritten and remodeled to revive your power.

(4) One of the most powerful ways you can use reverse discourse is by channeling every terrible thing someone has said about you into your highest good or the greater good of society.

I do this all the time. If someone insults your intelligence, you simply store that away as an incentive to prove them wrong in every single way. If someone tells you that you're not capable of something, you achieve it. You use what someone says degradingly as motivation.

You can also use this facet of reverse discourse to contribute to the world as well. For example, I've used all the victim-blaming statements of ignorant people as incentives to write blog posts that shed light on the factors that tether us to our abusers, make videos that dismantle stereotypes about abuse survivors and explore research that proves these people wrong regarding their misconceptions about abuse survivors.

Remember, only use these methods in ways that empower you and only if they make you comfortable. Reverse discourse is all about interrupting your usual thought patterns, taking back control over the language being wielded against you, and reframing words to serve your healing journey. It's not about embracing the abuse but rather reclaiming your power from it.

Neurolinguistic Programming (NLP) and Self-Hypnosis

If your abuser can brainwash you into thinking terrible, negative things about yourself, can you brainwash yourself into thinking empowering, positive ones?

Yes! I've done it many times – even when I was an eleven year-old undergoing severe bullying, I made sure I sat with myself and told myself very positive things about myself and soothed myself as if I was an adult soothing a child – even though I was a child soothing my child self! As I did not have any adults who supported me, I was forced to become an adult self to my child self. This is what helped me succeed even in the most impossible of circumstances with the whole world turned against me. I made sure to conquer my internal world before I ever battled it out to conquer the world outside of me. You could say I was born to create my own reverse discourse…and I want to teach others how to do it too.

The art of changing the internal landscape of your belief systems to affect your external landscape through your behavior is known as NLP (Neurolinguistic Programming). It was originally created by John Grinder and Richard Bandler in the 1970's to uncover powerful tools and skills for communication and change across a wide range of professional fields. Simply put, our use of language can literally "recode" our "programming," the way we automatically behave and react to certain stimuli. According to Anthony Beardsell, NLP Master Trainer, NLP is the art of "training yourself for excellence." It is all about reframing your internal representations and changing your physiological state in order to influence and improve your behavior.

This is what I'll call **re-idealizing yourself** after the devaluation and discard. That's right, I said it. You WERE worthy of being idealized, and just because the narcissist used that idealization for his or her own malicious agenda, doesn't mean the positive, loving things they said about you weren't absolutely on point. You *are* actually awesome and beautiful and intelligent and talented and powerful and unique – yes, you really are. You fell in love with the narcissist precisely because he or she made you feel exactly what you yearned to feel about yourself. You fell in love with the unconditional positive regard that you deeply desire within yourself. Now you just have to start giving that to yourself.

Meditation and Self-Hypnosis Time ♥

Kelly Jo Holly has an excellent meditation on this called <u>How to Heal Abuse Hypnosis</u>, on verbalabusejournals.com to begin to envisage your abuser as someone comical and childish.

Joseph Clough has a self-hypnosis channel to alleviate any fears or anxieties you're facing here: youtube.com/user/josephcloughhypnosis

Michael Sealey also has a terrific self-hypnosis channel that helps to raise confidence, improve sleep and mood. Visit him at youtube.com/user/michaelsealey.

*If you are suffering from severe symptoms of complex PTSD or PTSD, please consult a mental health professional to discuss if any of the meditations or self-hypnosis tracks discussed in this book would be potentially triggering for you.

Positive affirmations, is a technique mentioned throughout the book. They are part of many of the diverse healing techniques described, and using them is an important way to start heal subconscious wounds by reprogramming how we think about ourselves, our potential and the world around us. Affirmations are phrases that help us interrupt our normal thought patterns by instilling positive messages about ourselves and the world around us. Research confirms that positive self-affirmations can help improve problem-solving under stress (Creswell et. al, 2013) and psychologists suggest that positive affirmations also help us preserve our self-integrity in the face of threat, enabling our "psychological immune system" to defend itself (Sherman, 2006).

A common criticism of positive affirmations is that they cannot work for people with low self-esteem, but I beg to differ; they certainly won't work for everyone, but they can work. Given everything I went through in my childhood and adulthood, how much I've been able to overcome strikes me as miraculous. Positive affirmations and reverse discourse have been a cornerstone in my journey to becoming my best self and accomplishing what I set out to achieve, despite the traumas and doubts that suggested otherwise.

For those struggling with low self-esteem, PTSD or Complex PTSD, positive affirmations may have to be customized in order to prevent triggers. Or perhaps they need to be said in a way that gently and incrementally approaches the aspects of yourself that are being reworked, much like in reverse discourse. You may have to say things like, "I choose to be happy" rather than "I am happy" if you have severe doubts about yourself, suggests Daniel Perskawiec, a Certified Hypnotherapist and NLP Trainer from the NeuroIntelligence Institute.

Inner Child Work

What is it?

Inner child work is a therapeutic tool survivors can use to reconnect with the wounds of their childhood and deepen the relationship with the adult self. It can involve visualization, positive affirmations, and meditative/reflective work.

How does it work?

As cliché as it may sound, I truly believe that survivors of chronic victimization by narcissists have deep core wounds that exist in their "inner child." There is a part of us that is connected to that child, because when we are reacting to abuse in adulthood, the same wiring in our brain becomes reactivated and we literally regress back into infancy on a cellular level.

Many of us who feel unnoticed, unheard, and unseen due to other siblings or a toxic parent taking up all the space develop a sense of unworthiness early on - then, events in youth and adulthood tend to reinforce, retrigger and cement those wounds so deeply that we feel traumatized anytime we are placed in a "second place" position - and rightfully so. A series of experiences that led to feeling unworthy is, in fact, a chain of trauma that needs to be healed. Pain as historical and ingrained as this, needs to be addressed at its roots.

As discussed in the section, "Your Brain on Trauma," the trauma repetition cycle isn't something that can be logically processed and solved because it's not rational. The trauma repetition cycle is emotional and psychological. It is a cycle that is embedded in our thought patterns, our physiological reactions and our deeply ingrained beliefs.

It's our subconscious wounding that creates these types of patterns in adulthood - so the first step to overcoming the wounding is to become aware of these wounds on a conscious level. That is why I always recommend meditation, self-hypnosis and affirmations. These can all address the subconscious wounding that other sources of knowledge like articles, books, blogs and videos - while helpful - may not be able to access.

That's why inner child work – creating a dialogue with and visualizing comforting our inner child and the wounds that this child carries, may be essential to healing for survivors of chronic abuse. That is why it is important to do what Pete Walker (2013) calls "re-parenting" the inner child – by giving it the compassion and unconditional positive regard that we may not have received in childhood.

This means nurturing the child, soothing the child, giving the inner child a safe emotional space to express his or her feelings, and ultimately thrive, integrated happily in our adult body. As adults, we may have disassociated from the wounds of childhood because they were too severe for us to process. Connecting with our inner child gives us permission to address the pain we may have suppressed or numbed as a coping mechanism – allowing us to grieve and feel righteous anger at the suffering we experienced – both of which can be crucial to recovery.

For me personally, Melanie Tonia Evan's Narcissistic Abuse Recovery Program (NARP) was a cornerstone in my journey to addressing these subconscious wounds and detecting that they existed. Even if you do not believe in the Law of Attraction or any of the other philosophies related to the program, it can work as a healing meditation program that enables you to visualize your wounds, detect what wounds in childhood are creating a pattern of gravitating towards narcissists, and then also heal them. If you can't afford this program, you can try Inner Child meditations on YouTube – there are plenty of different ones online.

Link: Check out how to heal our inner child mindfully in Healing the Child Within here: http://www.mindful.org/healing-the-child-within/

Reiki Healing

What is it? Reiki is a Japanese spiritual non-invasive healing and stress-reduction technique which involves a Reiki practitioner using his or her hands to "heal" your body, based on the energetic blockages that may be present within your body. "Rei" means universal and "ki" means life energy.

How does it work? Reiki operates under the idea that negative feelings and thoughts are not just stored in your mind, but also in your body, your aura and your energy field which often result in illness. When our life-force energy is disrupted by emotions like depression, anxiety, anger - this results in us being sick. Energy flows through the practitioner's hands to where it is most needed during a reiki healing session, restoring balance and harmony physically, emotionally and spiritually. You can find reiki practitioners in your area here on the International Association of Reiki Professionals website at www.iarp.org. You may also wish to search on Yelp, Groupon and LivingSocial for centers and practitioners that offer Reiki.

You can also learn how to use reiki healing on yourself using the numerous resources available online.

Link: Watch this video on Reiki Healing here: http://tinyurl.com/reikimeditation

Acupuncture

What is it? Acupuncture is an ancient Chinese healing technique involving the use of needles at specific points of the body to heal a wide variety of physical and psychological ailments.

How does it work? There are 12 primary and eight secondary invisible lines of energy flow in the body known as "meridians." An acupuncturist targets specific points of the body to help resolve the physical and/or emotional ailment plaguing the patient.

In "Stories of Healing Emotional Trauma in My Acupuncture Clinic," acupuncturist Nicholas Sieben, M.S., L.Ac, writes, "People may recognize there are unresolved issues in their lives: "ghosts" from their past. But most are unclear how to go about resolving them. Many go to talk therapy. However, according to Chinese Medical theory, trauma lives in our bodies. It becomes stuck in our blood and bones where it incubates, causing various physical and mental symptoms. To fully resolve trauma, the body needs to be released. There needs to be a physical detox."

To learn more about acupuncture, visit NIH's page on acupuncture here: www.nccih.nih.gov/health/acupuncture. You can also search for an acupuncturist if you live in the United States here: www.aaaomonline.org/search/.

Chakra Balancing

What is it? Energy practitioners believe we have seven energy centers in our bodies known as "chakras." This energy map of the body was developed hundreds of years ago in India. Chakra balancing is still a practice today. These energy centers house emotional and physical well-being, and each chakra is associated with specific physical ailments. Trauma can affect each and every one of the chakras. To read how, visit: www.traumahealed.com/articles/check-in-with-your-chakras.html

How does it work? A compelling discussion in the narcissistic survivor community is the ability of a narcissist to energetically drain us, leaving us feeling depleted of our internal resources.

Keeping our chakras balanced and cleansed through visualization and meditation allows us to have a healthy mind-body connection that prevents both physical dysfunction as well as emotional difficulty. Link: To learn about each of the seven chakras and where they are located, check out: http://tinyurl.com/chakrameditate.

How to heal the chakras:

Start with a balancing chakra meditation. My favorite, and the most effective I've found so far, is:

Link: Michael Sealey's Chakra Balancing, Cleansing and Healing meditation, easily searchable on YouTube.

Self-Hypnosis is akin to meditation in that it helps to subconsciously reprogram your mind.

Michael Seeley also has very soothing hypnosis tracks that are incredibly calming and healing - very much like meditation. I highly recommend his Chakra Healing Meditation, Guided Meditation for Over-Thinking, and Sleep Hypnosis for Deep Confidence.

You can also help heal the chakras through aromatherapy, gardening, yoga, mantras, affirmations and sound. Here are some resources to help you identify the best practices for healing your chakras:

Links

Heal Yourself Now: The Best Healing Method for Each Chakra by Vicki Howie

http://consciouslifenews.com/best-healing-method-chakra/1133074/

7 Easy Ways to Spring Clean Your Chakras by Deborah King

http://www.healyourlife.com/7-easy-ways-to-spring-clean-your-chakras

Your 7 Chakras and How to Keep Them Balanced and Cleared
https://spiritualspaniagara.wordpress.com/2014/07/16/your-7-chakras-and-how-to-keep-them-balanced-cleared/

Cord Cutting

What is it? Cord-cutting is a spiritual exercise that enables you to cut your energetic bond with a toxic and negative person in your life. It can help you in detaching from that person or from a toxic interaction you've had.

How does it work? Cord-cutting can take on a variety of forms, but it usually involves visualization of the cord between you and your ex-partner, ending with the cutting of the cord. I have included a meditation for cord-cutting below which incorporates visualization and affirmations. A word of caution: if you are in a severely distressed emotional state about your narcissistic partner, it is best to leave this meditation for when you are in a calm and centered place in your healing journey, as you will be asked to visualize your partner in this meditation. Always consult with a trauma-informed counselor about any triggers you may experience for meditation.

Meditation Time ♥ Link:
Releasing and Cord-Cutting Meditation

Aromatherapy and Incense

What is it? Aromatherapy is an alternative healing method where the individual uses scents and essential oils as a way to help with emotions and health. Individuals can choose to inhale the fragrance or apply the oils directly on their skin.

How does it work? According to Suzanne Bovenizer, CMT, CST, our sense of smell is connected to the limbic system in our brain, where emotions and memories are stored. Scents stimulate that part of the brain, releasing chemicals that cause us to become more calm and relaxed. Aromatherapy can help a great deal with anxiety, which can be a key component of the distress victims of narcissistic abuse experience.

You can buy essential oils and an essential oil diffuser for your home so that aromatherapy is always accessible to you. You may also seek aromatherapy in alternative ways: some yoga centers offer yoga with an aromatherapy component, and many massages can also incorporate elements of aromatherapy in a session.

I recommend both essential oils and incense. Here are some links to purchase products for aromatherapy:

Products for Healing ❤ Links

Art Naturals Top Essential Oils

Essential Oil Diffuser

Aromatherapy Incense

The Complete Book of Essential Oils and Aromatherapy by Valerie Ann Worwood

Spirituality/Faith/Prayer

In the Survivor Survey, many survivors listed their faith as one of the key components that kept them going after narcissistic abuse. Faith in a bigger purpose, a higher being, a greater meaning, is very threatening to a narcissist who wants to be considered God. It is very threatening to a narcissist's God-like delusions of grandeur when we place our faith in something bigger than them - whatever faith or spirituality we may practice, a belief in a greater purpose and meaning is incredibly threatening to these predators because it enables us to believe in ourselves, our worth and our rights as human beings. Research shows a relationship with a perceived spiritual figure can serve a compensatory role in dysfunctional attachments we may have formed throughout our lives and that such a relationship may also have a moderating effect on low self-esteem (Reinert, 2005).

Have something you can do every day that connects you to whatever form of faith or spirituality you have. It could be a gospel choir or a mindfulness program – a church or a Buddhist temple. It does not matter what form this spirituality or faith in a bigger purpose takes. It can even just be faith in your own higher self, your inner guidance and intuition. For those who engage in prayer, combine prayer with meditation to get the added benefit of rewiring your brain – simply begin or end every meditation with a prayer that personally inspires you. Here are some examples:

"Thank you God for this meditation. May I heal from my terror and may I feel whole again."

"Thank you to my Higher Self. I pray that I am protected, safe, and strong during my healing."

"God, guide me through my meditation and help me gain everything that I may need from it. May it help my healing journey. Amen."

Important Note: For those victims who have suffered spiritual abuse, it's important to not force yourself to engage in anything that makes you feel uncomfortable or that triggers you regarding the abuse you experienced and how spirituality was used against you. When looking at various healing modalities, please always consider your own comfort level and your triggers first. When in doubt, consult with a licensed mental health professional who can help you navigate your triggers and work through the warped spirituality that the narcissist may have used against you.

The Power of Nature

Nature is a healing balm to a hurting soul, a powerful portal to more healing that is often overlooked and underestimated. Developing a daily connection to nature every day through hiking, walking or jogging in a natural environment has an incredible effect on our brains and can act as a restorative practice that enables us to refocus, reenergize and rejuvenate.

Scientific research proves nature's ability to lower cortisol levels, relieve stress, improve our ability to concentrate and improve our mood (Berman, Jonides, & Kaplan, 2008; Mayer et al., 2009). Even the act of walking barefoot on the earth during warmer months can improve overall wellbeing and sleep while reducing pain and stress levels; the theory of the benefits of "earthing" suggests that walking barefoot connects us to the earth's electrons. You can also do this through gardening, which is a very therapeutic and mindful activity that allows you to see the growth you want within manifest externally.

Some ideas for enjoying the daily benefits of nature may be: scheduling a morning or afternoon walk every day, taking a trip to a location with a beautiful natural landscape, taking a walk by a river, going to the beach, hiking outdoors, taking a jog in a park or the woods, taking your lunch break outdoors or picnicking frequently. If the weather is not warm, "access" nature in alternative ways: go camping and make sure to start up a fire; sit near a fireplace if indoors; open the window in the morning to let the sunlight in and hear the chirping of the birds; watch the snow fall or hear the rain. Listen to meditation music that incorporates the sounds of rainfall, a waterfall or the waves of an ocean.

Music Therapy as Catharsis

Music helps to regulate mood, reconnect with our authentic emotions, reduces heart rate and blood pressure, lowers cortisol levels which cause stress and helps to manage anxiety levels. It's no wonder that music can even be used in a therapeutic relationship to help an addict in his or her recovery, can help improve social functioning in patients with schizophrenia, and can reduce the side effects of cancer treatment.

For narcissistic abuse survivors, music can help us get in touch with emotions we've been suppressing, channel and release some of those emotions in a safe space of healing, and connect with someone else (the artist) through the lyrics, the beat of the music and/or the theme of the song. Music can also help lift a survivor from a mood of despair and powerlessness, gently guiding that survivor to feel happier and empowered while simultaneously giving their immune system a boost! Now that's what I call healing on the level of the mind, body and spirit.

You can choose to listen to the music you find most healing, or you can even seek out a certified music therapist at the American Music Therapy Association at www.musictherapy.org/about/find.

Links:

Here are some links to interesting studies on the effects of music.

CNN: This is your brain on music

http://www.cnn.com/2013/04/15/health/brain-music-research/

PsychologyToday: Does Music Have Healing Powers?

https://www.psychologytoday.com/blog/brick-brick/201402/does-music-have-healing-powers

Harvard Health Publications: Healing Through Music

http://www.health.harvard.edu/blog/healing-through-music-201511058556

Self-Care Haven's Music Library for Survivors

I created a playlist with some of the songs that have helped me on my recovery journey. There's a diversity of genres, moods, and emotions to connect with in these songs. Check out my YouTube playlist for survivors here: http://tinyurl.com/survivorplaylist.

You may also wish to check out an artist by the name of Twinkly Tus, who sings beautifully empowering songs about narcissistic abuse, on SoundCloud: www.soundcloud.com/twinklytus.

Self-Care Warrior Pro Tip: Hybrid Techniques

Practice Hybrid Healing Modalities to make these extra powerful.

Also what I like to call the **Dual Mind and Body Method** – Combining positive affirmations with movement (such as physical exercise) can also help to further reinforce them into your belief system. Record your positive affirmations on your phone or tape recorder and listen to them while you go for a jog or watch daily. This enables you to access multiple parts of your brain and reprogram both your mind and your body. It conditions you to associate your affirmations with movement, energy and vitality rather than the dark slumber of depression narcissists lure us into.

I love doing "hybrid" activities where I combine techniques. For example, I once attended a candlelit hot yoga class with music playing – it appealed to all of my senses and targeted various areas of my brain, allowing me to self-soothe and heal both mind and body at once.

There are plenty of ways to combine healing methods and make it fun! This might mean…

- Relaxing in a scented bath with an audio of positive affirmations playing on the background.
- Listening to positive affirmations you record yourself (or, as Louise Hay recommends, a loving caregiver or friend recorded for you) as you walk on the treadmill or go for a run.
- When doing yoga poses, repeat powerful mantras such as, "I love myself," "I am safe," "I am balanced" during each pose aloud or in your mind.
- While getting a massage, meditate or pray silently, allowing your thoughts to simply flow.
- Taking a walk on the beach while meditating to the sound of the waves.
- Viewing empowering videos like "Mind Movies" that help you visualize the situations you want while listening to soothing music or a meditation with binaural beats. These are easily searchable on Google and YouTube.
- Using a scented oil diffuser or incense while writing/journaling.

A note: if you do wish to experiment with hybrid techniques, make sure they're not interfering with each other and that these two techniques you're using truly complement one another. Sometimes, it's important to focus a great deal of our energy and attention into one single activity – such as meditation – for it to be effective.

Blogs and YouTube Videos on Narcissistic Abuse – A great deal of my surveyed survivors pointed out the helpfulness of validating blogs and videos they watched online in their healing journey. There was something about seeing a live person talk about narcissistic abuse, share tips and resources, and validate their experiences, that enabled them to heal tremendously. Even today, I receive comments on my own YouTube channel, Self-Care Haven, from survivors about how these videos have played a major role in their healing journey, sometimes even moreso than therapy.

Validation, resources and encouragement are key to healing, so I encourage all narcissistic abuse survivors to watch helpful videos on this type of abuse. You may wish to start off with videos that have gentle encouragement rather than triggering topics. Here are some helpful channels I follow from fellow survivors of narcissistic abuse who are insightful and experienced (you can find the full list in the Resources section located at the end of the book):

YouTube Links (All searchable on YouTube):
Lisa A. Romano, Adult Children of Alcoholics Life Coach
Shrinking Violet
Finally Free from Narcissism
Annabel Lee
Narcissism Survivor
Spartan Life Coach
Ross Rosenberg

Releasing the Assumption that a Narcissist is Just Like Us and We're Supposed to "Let it Go."

Do you ever ruminate about whether your narcissistic partner misses the relationship or why he didn't fight for you the way he should have? Or why you wish you had some sort of validation and acknowledgement from him that he mistreated you? Do you question why you can't seem to let it go?

It's because *you're not supposed to* - not yet anyway. Many people who haven't experienced this type of abuse are used to people telling them to "let it go," but this can be nearly impossible for a survivor of this type of crazymaking. We have to go through multiple methods of processing what's happened - including understanding the way narcissists think and why they act the way they do, before we even get to the tip of the iceberg. That is why healing and the No Contact journey, while rewarding, can be very challenging as well.

Many survivors ask why their narcissist doesn't hoover or "miss" them, but the reality is that the narcissist has no emotional capacity to be attached. A part of the narcissist closed off a long time ago for reasons and causes that were way before you ever entered the picture (which is why I stress it is *absolutely not your fault* how your partner behaves towards you).

Although I don't advise doing this as this can be triggering, looking at any online forum where people with NPD talk about their mindsets or reading a book by someone who is a sociopath and narcissist is alarming and devastating. The reality that survivors don't wish to believe because it is so heartbreaking...is that people with NPD feel a void where emotions would normally be and cannot experience real human emotions like love and empathy.

Narcissists feel a very shallow, watered-down version of normal human emotions except for rage and envy, which they feel with intensity. Narcissists will unfortunately never be able to connect to another human being due to this emotional numbness - he may "fake" it well in the beginning, but the connection will reveal itself to be false. If they have been emotionally and/or physically violent towards you, they will be violent towards another. If they have triangulated you, they will triangulate someone else. The abusive cycle never ends, but thankfully, you are working on breaking your own cycle with the narcissist. That is what is important and what will ultimately save your own life.

That being said, I can very much relate to and understand the addiction to wanting validation from this type of toxic partner, especially since this type of partner has worked very hard at managing you down and making you feel as if you are the person to blame for the problems in the relationship.

This is why we become so addicted to wanting and seeking approval. Narcissists don't work on our logical, thinking minds - they appeal to the emotional parts of our brains which are hard-wired to respond instinctively to avoid abandonment. We haven't evolved beyond the "If I am out of the tribe, I won't survive" mentality unfortunately - and the narcissist can target the very wounds that make us fear abandonment - tricking us into believing that their discard of us is a life and death situation. Unfortunately for many victims, it can be, and that is why I want to make sure you know that a narcissist's pathology is not your responsibility.

Your own body chemistry has been hooked through surges in chemicals and hormones like dopamine, oxytocin, adrenaline and cortisol and conditioned to seek the highs and lows only this partner can give you. This was also a person you spent a considerable amount of time with - our investment in such a relationship is often complex and nuanced - filled with love, anxiety, hatred, disappointment, grief and fear.

We hope for more even when we have grown accustomed to receiving crumbs. We become addicted to the abusive cycle which conditions us to associate love with violence. I hope you can remember this whenever you are feeling guilty about your feelings to reach out to your partner or desire for him or her to reach out to you.

The key is to accept your feelings while still allowing yourself to release your partner. Judging your feelings will not help you - but embracing them will. You have to say to yourself, "It is okay to have these feelings. I honor them but I don't act upon them."

We must own and see our pain before being able to release it more effectively - especially in a relationship where our pain was rarely seen or recognized as valid. One of the cruelest aspects of narcissistic abuse are the joys you used to cherish that were tainted by the toxic abuser. They have ways of even making what you love to do or things you love about yourself inaccessible.

Shutting down due to trauma and chronic anxiety are symptoms of the aftermath. It will take time. Small steps are easier than big steps. I just hope you know that a part of you can never be taken and destroyed. It's the same part of you that is still willing to survive and hope. Hold onto that part of yourself and keep adding to it every day. Meditate, adopt a mantra or affirmation, say a short prayer...start small and I have faith you will move onto the bigger actions when you are ready. You have to fight for the miracles that are ahead of you no matter how bleak it may seem now. It does and will get better. The best is yet to come.

Manifest a New Reality for Yourself

Let me preface this section by saying you don't have to believe everything about the art of "manifestation" to gain a new perspective. There are certainly components of manifestation that I still struggle with today and find victim-blaming as I fully believe that the accountability of abuse lies with the abuser. I don't think we "attract" abuse in any way – I think abuse happens to us because an abuser chooses to abuse us. I also don't wish this section to come across as victim-blaming, as I adamantly believe that *survivors are not to blame for abuse in any shape, way or form.*

There is a heated debate regarding Law of Attraction and manifestation in the survivor community. Some survivors find it victim-blaming, while others have utilized it (including through programs such as Melanie Tonia Evans' NARP program) to change their lives. From a sociological and psychological viewpoint, believing in the idea that we can create a new life for ourselves can help us increase our perceived agency and power. So whether you call it manifestation, the secret, or the Law of Attraction (LoA), or simply a desire to rebuild a new life, the label is less important than the fact that a belief in your own agency can be helpful as a template for pursuing your future goals and aspirations.

I firmly believe you should only use healing resources you are personally comfortable using and the resources that are not triggering to you – so if LoA triggers you in any way, avoid using any resources associated with it altogether.

I've selectively used what I can from the principles of manifestation in order to rebuild my own life. Sociologically speaking, adopting a mindset that you can "create your own reality" opens up new avenues and opportunities as your perceived agency and power receives a boost. I have personally benefited from experimenting with some of the principles of LoA to manifest incredible miracles and changes in my life, and so have incredible public figures such as Oprah, Jim Carrey, Tony Robbins and Marie Forleo. To each their own, however, and if you don't believe in it, you certainly do not have to. Not everyone will benefit from the idea that we can create our own reality. Everyone will have different perspectives on this.

For survivors who are open to manifesting, it can be a source of motivation and inspiration to address the agency you have in rebuilding your life. Experiment with increasing your vibrational frequency by cultivating positive emotions or moving from an emotion of complete powerlessness to more powerful emotions; watch mind movies that represent the love, wealth or abundance you want your life to have; reset your mood and negative self-talk often with encouraging statements as well as laughter, meditation and yoga.

However, do not forget to balance this with acceptance of your emotions and the fact that what you went through was traumatic; that your abuser is still an abuser and that you do not need his or her energy in your life; don't use manifesting principles to repress your emotions or prevent yourself from getting help. Emotional blockages actually deter you from rebuilding your life. This is only meant to be a framework to begin creating the things you do want to manifest in your life. Focus on what you want moving forward, create vision boards of the life you want, write extensively and specifically about the life you want, become aligned with the energy of your true self – these are principles that can be helpful to survivors who want to carve out a space of hope and inspiration for their future lives.

Survivor Insights

Healing Tools for Narcissistic Abuse

Question: What have you done to heal from narcissistic abuse? Here are some of the things survivors have tried:

"As much as possible! Cranial Sacral work, EMDR, Cognitive Behavior-type therapy, chakra balancing, new activities, reading blogs, doing research online to read about similar experiences (community is huge!), subscribing to useful newsletters... It has been all about putting my own health and wellbeing first, devoting time to myself to feel and accept the experiences and feelings, reaching out for help when needed, and doing as much as I could to learn, taking positives away from the devastation. It's putting one foot in front of the other, whether a day at a time, or just a moment or two." – Pasqualena, Survivor from Maryland

"I received counseling at various times but it was very ineffective and was not targeted at recovery from trauma, which prevented me from making much progress. At age 62 I had EMDR for the PTSD and have not had a reoccurrence. I first found CODA 26 years ago, attending meetings off and on, devouring books at various stages, etc." – Penelope

"Place an invisible shield around my body and don't allow the daggers thrown to penetrate my soul. Pretend I'm dealing with a mental patient and not my husband/best friend." – Debbie, Michigan

"I've continuously read books and that helped in the initial stages...Then, I started talking about my feelings and views towards narcissists' behavior on forums and reading other real peoples' views and that made me feel a lot better. That I wasn't alone. Talking to my best friends or family, even though they were very supportive and open minded didn't help because they couldn't understand the feelings of manipulation and degradation a narcissist can put you through...The most powerful tool I used was reading other survivor accounts. To have it verified...that my feelings weren't exaggerated or just felt by me." – Josephine, Survivor from Hong Kong

"I was with my last narcissist for a year and after the breakup, I looked back through my diary and wrote down a chronological record (with dates) of every abusive incident (eg "18/6/15 - Reyner suddenly went into a totally unprovoked rage and shouted insane insults at me. It was terrifying." Then, with those incidents fresh in my mind, I created a list, entitled "For When I Miss Him," summarizing everything awful about him eg. fake, emotional con artist, liar, cruel, heartless, remorseless, cheater, exceptionally manipulative, gaslighter, triangulater, stonewaller, full of fury, drug addict, etc. These lists remind me why I do not want to be with him!" – Aurla, Brighton, England

"Therapy and spiritual guidance. Reiki." – Catherine, Survivor

"Information was key. Once you begin waking up to what has been happening around you the whole time you can begin stopping the cycle which angers the Narcissist to an interesting boiling point." – Agent J, VA

"I found that distractions helped. Getting involved in my community, working and school helped me keep my mind free from sad thoughts or contacting that person. It worked as long as I kept my distance from her.

I also would make myself say to her things my mind knew were right but my heart didn't want to say. I would say she didn't have my best in mind, her actions tell me she doesn't care and so on. I knew this would make her mad and I didn't want her being mad the reason we'd stop talking. But I forced myself. We'd stop talking for months at a time. I seem to be fine, I still loved her, but my days were just fine." – T. Newton, Survivor from Tacoma WA

"Read up on the psychology of abuse. Listen to music. Being alone to process without chatter. Usually outside doing something physical, doing these things helps you believe you CAN do anything. Share my story without shame." – Karina T., Survivor

"Left him! Got a life. Rebuilt confidence painfully, day by day. It was terrifying but worth it. Forced myself to integrate back into the world and had the help of a close friend which was the most healing thing that happened. Also therapy helped." – Helen, Survivor from Australia

"First I had to decide that their lies were in fact, lies. Then it took me years to realize I needed to have boundaries. I had to finally move away and cut off communication with these toxic people. Currently I am re-creating my own support system/family. I hope to have a healthy relationship one day… I have an amazing faith (not church life, but true faith) and I also have to say all the self-help books and counseling aren't nearly as effective until you are ready to let go of THEM and fight for YOU! For me I had to realize I put all of them above God and above myself." – Taylor A., Survivor from WI

"Counseling, meditation listening to the words in my head and learning to turn them around from a negative to a positive." – Amanda, Survivor from Tennessee

"To heal, I instituted ABSOLUTE ZERO contact on that day and forever after. I have never broken zero contact since that day." – Michelle the Midwest Triathlete

"I have found the greatest aid in healing so far has been social support groups and educating myself about the healing journey. And my animals--horses, dogs, cats and livestock." – Laura, Oregon

"I have begun to look at my own actions, and patterns in picking partners. I am also working to understand boundaries and how to set them without compromising. I know that I err too often on the side of kindness, and make myself available to be exploited. I am working on developing a more healthy and realistic self-esteem. I also cherish trusted friends and family, and try to be more selective about where I put my energies." – Heide, Utah

"Therapy, yoga, screaming in my pillow. Somewhat helpful, but 2 years later I'm still a mess." – Natalie, Petaluma, California

"Thankfully, I found your blog and helpful articles/advice! I do my best to keep my distance from this narcissistic "former friend." This was a friendship (or so I thought), not a romantic relationship." – Lisa in New York

"I've watched many YouTube videos and read books on the subject of narcissistic abuse in order to feel that I'm not alone in my experience or 'crazy'. I've also written accounts for myself of each individual abusive act that I dealt with during that 3 year period in order to stay strong with no contact and to remind myself of what I'd been through." – Jobo, England

"I have researched, read, and uncovered the problem through what I have read. I thought my abuser had an anger management issue, and through research, I discovered the real problem by reading blogs, survivor stories, scholarly books, articles, films, Facebook groups, and anything else I could find that would verify, confirm, and explain what happened to me. These strategies have been very helpful, because this is basically where the information on this topic is. Most people don't get it. Many therapists don't get it, so it's up to me to research and discover information about what I can do to protect myself and recover from the abuse." – Anne, Indiana

"I have cut all contact with him. It has been a very effective strategy, but it's only been 2 weeks. I've done this before but he always came back. This time was different as I had evidence he couldn't deny or lie his way out of. It was not pretty." –Claudia, California

"It's been almost a year since we broke up, and I am still healing slowly but surely. I noticed behavior changes in him two years into our relationship and couldn't quite understand it. I used the internet to search on this strange behavior of his and it took me straight to a website on NPD. I took the test and the symptoms were most of him. I began to research more in to it and came across YouTube videos, such as yours and many others. I read plenty of articles and even a book or two. And because of that, this helped me come to terms with his condition. When we broke up, I was more ready that I would have been if I knew zilch about it. I'm glad I learned lots of information about this disorder before we split up. It has helped me to realize the reasons for our unhealthy relationship were not because of him as a human being, but because of this dreadful disorder." – Nyree, New Zealand

"No contact was the most effective way to heal from the abuse, as well as spending time with family and friends and filling my life with new experiences unrelated to the narcissist. There was no true "shortcut". All I could do was keep reminding myself that I experienced happiness before the narcissist, so I could do it again afterwards--and it just took some time." –ProudSurvivor, California

"I moved away. I saw myself perceived by different kind of people who did not know of him or what he said of me. I saw myself mirrored in healthier more positive people. It has worked." – Gloria, Mexico

"I have gone back to my own personal interests, like painting, performing music, reading, gardening and finding myself to be great company, without another necessary for that." – Gail S. Robbins, Colorado, USA

"My discovery of narcissism is fairly recent. The biggest thing I have done is to leave my marriage. This was facilitated by taking a retreat to a monastery where I was free to think calmly without his intrusions. In that environment I felt joy again and saw I was not totally damaged, I could still find myself. The joy of that discovery was intense. I missed being me rather than the person I was manipulated into being! I have moved exceptionally slowly in the separation from my husband because we share a son and I am trying to protect him. I also fear what would happen if my husband were threatened too much. In daily ways, I limit contact with him. We rarely speak on the phone and when we do I have made it clear that I will hang up if he starts attacking me, and I do. In written communications I try to be brief and factual. He criticizes my writing for being too legal, and I point out he is free to criticize but I am actually being professional. When he tries to lie and manipulate, I have been calling him on his "forgetting" things we agreed. I have been explaining in detail the potential negative impacts of things he tries to do on my son in writing.

Upon leaving our marriage and home I started to see that many of our friends were not my friends, they were not on my side. I have let these people go, which has been hideously hard and left me feeling lonely.

However, after several months I cherish my real friends more and they have been so wonderful. I am also back in contact with old friends and have cherished those connections too. I decided anybody who was making me feel like a bad person was part of the problem. On my own, I have been filling journals with my realizations so I have a record of what is happening. During the separation phase I found that little comforts like soft clothes, music, and scents were really important. I carried scented hand cream and had a little perfume on my desk at work. I listened to my favorite music wherever could.

The music has been crucial to my son who uses it as a form of self-expression since his own voice is often drowned out by our separation and the specter of his dad's anger or rejection. Material expression is also important: I cut my hair and stopped dying it, I threw out the clothes he bought me and got my own. I put up the curtains one of his supporters criticized, got rid of the used chairs I always hated, and am putting up a picture that he derided of a women reading. It reminds me of the poise of a person alone with their thoughts. These things have helped immensely. However, I can also say that professional counselors were not helpful until after I had already realized what was going on myself. They focused on my problems as if they were without cause (I had a mental diagnosis by then so that explained everything.) Regarding my husband, they focused on his alcohol use and not on his systematic use of anger to control me, etc. I felt blamed for not leaving, etc. So I think you have to be very careful with who you choose to trust. The counselor must understand what drives your responses." – Sandra, Washington

"Therapy, medication, support groups." – Mary, Washington

"I began, and continue, a year-long work of self-improvement, and teaching myself that the things my former wife managed to convince me about myself were mostly wrong." – Greg Tenney, Indian Hills, Colorado

"It took a ton of prayer. Constantly listening to Christian music, songs of faith, encouragement, hope, God's love...specific songs would come on the radio at the exact time I needed them "Stronger" and "Overcomer" by Mandisa. "Voice of Truth" is another that sticks out. My pastor, his wife and my church family were the greatest sources of strength and encouragement. I spoke to couples who went through the same thing. That was a great help as their experience was so similar to mine, I would often take their advice...hard as it was! And I pray daily for God's protection from him...from anything he might try to do to me. Knowing that it will impact my daughter if he goes after me, I pray for protection for both of us from him." – Shannon, Central Ohio

"I have read lots but after 2 1/2 years I am now starting to recover and find out who I am. I made a decision early that I owed it to myself to rediscover what I really liked against what I thought I liked. It's still hard but gets better every day and for the first time in my 60 years I now live on my own. That was my biggest hurdle!" – Michele, Melbourne

"I have read every book I could, therapy twice a week, and reached out to others that have experienced this through the internet. I will say you have to have a knowledgeable therapist or this could be dangerous." - Gaia

"Counseling - excellent way of 'telling the story' in a safe environment. Trustworthy friends - helpful and supportive. Reading books and online material about narc abuse - very enlightening and helps you to feel less alone in the aftermath. Meditation and mindfulness practice - calming and cantering. Exercise - helps with the depression." – Gemma, United Kingdom

"No Contact Ever Again, researching and reading up on narcissistic personality disorder plus other survivors' experiences, journaling, talking about it to people I trust, start doing the things I couldn't do whilst I was in the relationship, acknowledge the fact that it was never real and that it wasn't my fault that I was targeted." - Diyanah, Kuala Lumpur

"Prayer and self-care. Both are effective for me. Through prayer, I am able to thank God for creating me as a woman. For bizarre reasons, my abuser praised me when I would act masculine and would encourage it. After embracing my gender, I can take self-care steps to enhance my femininity, which at age 38, I am still growing into." – Ergsmith, Southern California

"I recently joined an online support group and I've spent a lot of time educating myself and journaling." – Pam V., New Jersey

Can counseling help or harm a victim of narcissistic abuse?

I believe that therapy by a professional who is trained and knowledgeable about this type of abuse can be incredibly helpful to abuse survivors – in fact, support from someone who understands this type of abuse is necessary to recovery and healing. Unfortunately, due to the lack of attention given to narcissistic abuse among mental health professionals, not *all* professionals are able to provide a sensitive and validating approach to victims of this type of covert psychological abuse. As a result, there may be a few professionals who unintentionally re-victimize their clients when they invalidate their experiences and ask victims to look at their part in the abuse – this is especially prevalent in couples' therapy, where both parties are told to change their behaviors and look within.

While it's certainly admirable to look within for self-improvement, this type of invalidation can also make victims feel as if the covert abuse they are experiencing is not legitimate – which actually further gaslights them into staying within the relationship to make things work. Many survivors can benefit from sharing their story with another survivor who has been through similar experiences in addition to seeking therapy from a trained professional.

There are wonderful counselors out there like the ones mentioned in my book who are validating and empathic, but there are also mental health professionals who may fail to acknowledge how traumatic abuse can be. Maintaining a neutral emotional expression/stance, for example, can be very traumatizing for a victim who simply needs validation of the horror and of the abuse. Lilly Hope Lucario has an excellent article regarding how neutrality from a mental health professional can harm and re-traumatize trauma survivors on her blog, Healing from Complex Trauma and PTSD.

There also needs to be further discussion of how therapists judge how survivors react to abusive behaviors that are not as well-known like triangulation, stonewalling, blackmailing, smear campaigns etc. and acknowledge the difficulty of leaving an abusive situation and recovering from its trauma. Too many therapists do not know enough about trauma and its effects, and are prone to judging the victim for staying too long/reacting in a certain way/feeling a certain way about the abuse.

A validating professional knows that an abusive relationship is not easy to leave and that psychological reasons like trauma bonding will interfere in moving forward. Many mental health professionals misunderstand how covert and insidious these behaviors can be and think that the victim is "projecting" or being hypersensitive. As a result, they try to refocus on how the client is reacting to the abuse, rather than validating the abuse.

The best therapy in my opinion is with a trauma-informed mental health professional who demonstrates empathy for the client's pain, is able to understand the depths of trauma in the client's life, and gently guide the victim towards self-compassion, which I personally believe is the root of true change – not judgment and timelines for healing. A client will be more likely to leave a toxic situation when they are validated in their pain and secure in the fact that there is someone who understands them.

Distinguishing Between a Validating vs. Invalidating Therapist

• When talking about an abusive incident, an invalidating counselor starts to draw attention to things that you did or said beforehand to potentially provoke the incident. They may unintentionally or intentionally gaslight you into believing that your issues are at the root rather than the narcissistic abuse – for example, pointing out that you should work on your jealousy issues if you are bringing up incidents of triangulation or infidelity. A validating therapist, on the other hand, will empathize with your pain, validate the abuse and address the internal "hooks" as well as obstacles that are in the way of detaching from your partner. They will provide a balanced perspective that acknowledges the manipulative behavior while also acknowledging any insecurities that may be retriggered in the abusive cycle.

• An invalidating therapist continually asks you to focus on your own behavior and take accountability for staying in the relationship, refusing to validate how difficult it is to extricate yourself from an abusive partner and saying things like, "But you choose to stay" without acknowledging factors like trauma bonding, financial dependence, having children with the abuser, etc. and how difficult it is to leave an abusive relationship. A validating mental health professional would focus less on the fact that you stay and focus more on how to best support you during this time, while tailoring resources that may help you to leave or at the very least, understand the signs of this form of abuse so you can begin to start the process to detaching from your abuser or plan to leave the abuser right away if you are in imminent physical danger.

• A counselor who is invalidating will often demonstrate no solid understanding of the effects of trauma and will consider emotional/psychological abuse as a normal "relationship" problem that both partners need to resolve together. Counselors who truly understand the complexities of emotional and psychological abuse are able to acknowledge that any form of abuse is unacceptable and detrimental to their victims. They don't necessarily have to interfere in their victims' lives in order to understand and address this.

• Invalidating counselors show an urgency in their attitude that signals to you that you have to "let it go" whenever you start to bring up flashbacks or ruminations over the abuse. A trauma-informed counselor knows that trauma cannot just be "let go" of, no matter how "small" an incident may seem to an outsider, because what is often happening is that a small trauma can set off triggers to a larger trauma that has been occurring for a long time beneath the surface. Trauma-informed counselors also know that an abusive relationship takes a toll on your sense of self-worth and perceived agency; they know about the addictive nature of the abuse cycle and they know that trauma has to be confronted in order to be healthily processed.

• An invalidating counselor questions whether the motives of the narcissistic partner are malicious and intentional despite reports and clear evidence of repeated devaluation and no improvement in behaviors. While a counselor is often encouraged to remain neutral, this neutrality can actually harm the victim.

• An invalidating therapist attempts to talk about the tender, loving moments in the abuse cycle as proof that the abuser is "trying" rather than acknowledging that the tender moments are a set-up for abuse – thus these loving moments are in fact abusive bonding. Counselors who are aware of the dynamics of abuse are well-informed about the fact that abusers rarely change - they do not attempt to feed into the victim's false hope; rather, they continue to provide support while redirecting the victim to stay grounded in the reality of the abusive relationship rather than falling into the trap of romanticizing their partner.

• Despite telling your therapist that you've been narcissistically abused, the therapist makes no effort to better understand this type of abuse or learn more about personality disorders. He or she minimizes the problems in your relationship as mere conflicts that must be resolved through the work of both partners. This is perhaps one of the biggest barriers between counselor and victim that needs to be addressed. A counselor who hears the word "narcissistic abuse" and does not look further into it to better understand what the client may be going through, is probably not a counselor you want to continue with.

• Defends the abusive partner and says their abuse wouldn't be so effective if it weren't for your own triggers – ignoring the fact that *abuse is abuse regardless of how you react to it*. Everyone has triggers that need to be addressed, but that does not discount the fact that the actual abuse has taken place and needs to be validated. A validating mental health professional understands the complex nature of abuse and how it can be retriggering while still acknowledging the abuse happening in the present.

• In sessions with an invalidating therapist, you start realizing you've spent more time in a session educating your therapist about narcissistic abuse than you have healing from it.

In a validating therapeutic relationship, the therapist and client should work together and co-create a relationship that benefits the survivor's healing. The survivor should not be doing all the work. The therapist should be able to guide the survivor to the appropriate tools to begin to process their trauma.

There are incredible therapists out there who *do* specialize in narcissistic abuse and the effects of trauma. Andrea Schneider, LCSW, and author of the terrific, informative book, *Soul Vampires: Recovering Your Lifeblood After Narcissistic Abuse*, is one of them. Andrea was sweet enough to take the time to answer my questions from the perspective of a therapist who is well-versed on narcissistic abuse and well-equipped to help clients. In the following interview with Andrea, she discusses her own experiences in treating clients suffering from narcissistic abuse as well as the current research and discourse which we've been discussing throughout this book.

Interview with Andrea Schneider, LCSW and Author of *Soul Vampires*

(1) While many survivors feel a great sense of relief from understanding what happened to them, others may feel reluctant to label their experiences as abuse because narcissistic abuse can be so covert, confusing and insidious. From your perspective as a therapist who has worked with many survivors, how would you define "narcissistic abuse"?

That's a great question. I find that with the vast majority of my clients, there is great relief in understanding what narcissistic abuse is. It's no fun to have to deal with diagnostic labels, but in this circumstance, information is empowerment for survivors. In my view, narcissistic abuse is emotional abuse perpetrated upon a person either in a love, work or family relationship (lover, parent, sibling, boss, friend, etc.). The individual doing the abusing is on the narcissistic continuum ranging from Narcissistic Personality Disorder (NPD), malignant narcissist, or psychopath (i.e. The Dark Triad described in forensic therapist Christine Louis de Canonville's book *The Three Faces of Evil*, 2015).

The person being abused, generally speaking, is deceived into a false relationship or connection at the service of the narcissist's/psychopath's ego. Whether the survivor is a child, a colleague, a friend, a spouse or a lover, the impact of the narcissistic abuse is profound and typically takes a good amount of time (sometimes many months to many years) to work through the elements of traumatic loss.

I want to emphasize that the abuse is NOT the survivor's fault. Pathological predators target healthy, emotionally intelligent people because the predator is lacking significantly in all of those "super traits" (strengths) of the target that Sandra A. Brown defines in her book *Women Who Love Psychopaths* (2010). Some, but by no means all, abuse survivors may have been raised in families where narcissistic abuse was the norm in their household (common in families with sexual/physical/emotional abuse).

In turn, some of those survivors do in fact experience a repetition of the cycle of trauma in future relationships because the connection with the new pathological person (i.e. a lover) is "familiar." In essence, there exists in some circumstances an initial blueprint from the survivor's family-of-origin, from which to base future adult relationships. Sometimes this leads to encounters with people exhibiting extreme narcissism in love, work, friendships, or family. That being said, regardless of the psychological history of the survivor, there is much hope that the survivor can work through these layers of trauma from the narcissistic abuse, heal and move forward to have new healthy relationships and live a full and fulfilling life.

Narcissistic abuse is typically an insidious, very covert form of emotional abuse which involves manipulations and deceptions by the perpetrator, including the emotional abuse tactics of gaslighting, lovebombing, hoovering, idealizing/devaluing/discarding. The resultant feeling in the survivor is that of cognitive dissonance, or holding two contrasting thoughts in one's mind (i.e. "I fell in love with this man, but why do I feel unsettled after he called me a whore?") The survivor develops, in many cases, a trauma bond with their abuser (particularly in love relationships or parent-child relationships) due to the deceptive emotional abuse (see Patrick Carnes' book *The Betrayal Bond*, 1997).

Due to the biochemical bonds discussed earlier in your book, trauma is encoded on a very physiological level. Bessel van der Kolk, neuroscientist and author of *The Body Keeps the Score: Brain, Mind and Body in the Healing of Trauma* (2014), discusses how abuse is encoded neurologically in the brain. Traumatic emotions are essentially embodied on a physiological level, whereby the resolution of the trauma requires the bridging of various parts of the brain and body into an integrated conversation (van der Kolk, 2014). Van der Kolk also draws upon the work of Bruce Perry, a neuroscientist who espouses a neurosequential theory of trauma recovery involving somatic, kinesthetic, emotional and cognitive levels of the brain (Malchiodi and Perry, 2008).

Narcissistic abuse is a complex form of emotional abuse which can bring about Complex-PTSD (extreme Post-Traumatic Stress Disorder), depression and anxiety in survivors. I equate narcissistic abuse to "soul rape" (Schneider, 2014). The survivor did not consent to being deceived, betrayed and abused. The perpetrator pretended, like a stage actor, to be someone they were not at the beginning of the relationship, much like a wolf in sheep's clothing. Eventually the survivor can see the abuser behind the mask, and once exposed, the abuser emotionally devalues and then cruelly discards/rejects the survivor. This disturbing fact is evident in circumstances where an abusive parent perpetrates sexual abuse on a child or when an adult falls in love with an extreme narcissist and is subsequently abused, discarded and abandoned.

2) How do you know when a client has been abused by a narcissist? Is there a set of symptoms they usually present? Can you discuss more about whether there is a relationship between narcissistic abuse and complex PTSD, especially for victims who have been raised by a narcissist or have had relationships with multiple narcissists?

Absolutely. Although to my knowledge, no concrete research has specifically drawn a correlation between complex PTSD and narcissistic abuse, the anecdotal evidence in clinical literature and online forums as well as from what I see in my own private practice is staggering. I do believe there is a direct correlation, and such research is currently being done by traumatologists in the field. So stay tuned, and I am certain we will be seeing the results of current studies in the field (see the list of traumatologists at end of article).

Drawing off the work of Pete Walker, author of *Complex PTSD: From Surviving to Thriving: A Guide Map for Recovering from Childhood Trauma*, when a survivor has been impacted chronically and over a long period of time by emotional abuse (and/or sexual and physical abuse), particularly by pathological individuals who exhibit extreme forms of narcissism or psychopathy, the survivor will often show signs and symptoms of what is termed Complex PTSD.

This term was originally coined in traumatologist pioneer Judith Herman's book, *Trauma and Recovery* (1992). Complex Post-Traumatic Stress Disorder (C-PTSD) typically looks like chronic, ongoing Post-Traumatic Stress Disorder (PTSD) manifesting in a range of symptoms that can include numbing, avoidance behaviors, hyper-vigilance, chronic depression and anxiety, panic attacks, flashbacks of abusive incidents, and dissociation. C-PTSD impacts functioning in relationships, work and day-to-day activities.

Most often the abuse is very covert and veiled in secrecy, such that the survivor is the only person privy to the abuse, and the outside world has a benign perception of the abuser. Thus, cognitive dissonance ensues for survivors and further exacerbates complex-PTSD symptomatology. For resolution, the survivor requires psychotherapy with a highly skilled therapist. This condition is basically Post-Traumatic Stress Disorder that occurs over a long period of time and with exposure to repeated sadistic trauma (not unlike a soldier returning from war but with added layers of abandonments by significant people in the survivor's life) (Schneider, 2015). Pete Walker also addresses the abandonment depression so common in survivors of this form of pervasive abuse, whether it occurred during childhood or adulthood, or both. Furthermore, he elaborates on the importance of doing the grief work associated with this traumatic loss(es) (Walker, 2013).

Survivors can also experience depression, anxiety, and stress related somatic complaints from the chronic surging of adrenaline/cortisol that the body is exposed to over a long period of time with narcissistic abuse. The body readies itself in fight or flight mode, prepared to do battle or flee from the perceived threat. Covert narcissistic abuse generates this physiological response in the survivors' body. And with that, trauma becomes not only a psychological hurdle but also a circumstance which requires release on a physical level.

The above work in the field of trauma lends credence to the notion that exposure to narcissistic abuse results in significant emotional pain (Brown, 2010). The longer the duration of the abuse, the higher the frequency, the greater the number of perpetrators, the more cognitive dissonance, the more likely the survivor will develop complex PTSD, resulting in added layers of trauma and grief work to wade through in the healing process.

3) Have you also worked with clients who have been abused by those on the far end of the narcissistic spectrum, such as sociopaths? If so, what are your observations about the similarities/differences in the ways narcissists vs. sociopaths operate and how they affect their victims?

I do work with many survivors of psychopathic abuse. Narcissism exists on a continuum, whereby an individual may possess "traits" of narcissism (i.e. a bit arrogant and self-absorbed) to NPD (Narcissistic Personality Disorder, a clinical diagnosis in the DSM) to malignant narcissism (extreme narcissism whereby the narcissist actively seeks to cause pain in his/her target in order to extract narcissistic supply) to psychopathy (see my infographic for a visual of this narcissistic continuum in my e-book *Soul Vampires, 2015*).

Individuals who are extreme narcissists (malignant narcissists and psychopaths) are the most dangerous emotional abusers. Although they may not be the Ted Bundy's (serial killers) of the world, they show no genuine empathy, remorse, or compassion for their significant others/family members/co-workers. Their mission in life is to extract narcissistic supply to fuel a vacuous psyche, most often in romantic, family or work relationships, attempting to exert maximum power and control. Romantic relationships are often the forum whereby such pathological individuals hunt for their prey and select targets who are either vulnerable (i.e. recently out of a relationship, depressed, etc.) and/or targets who possess certain qualities that the predator wishes to consume (emotional IQ, attractiveness, money, sex, nurturance, a successful career, beauty, etc.).

Researcher and therapist Sandra A. Brown (2010) calls such relationships those of "inevitable harm," which is a theory I also subscribe to. Whether in a relationship with an individual with NPD, malignant narcissism or psychopathy, there will not be a positive outcome for the survivor, as long as the survivor remains in the relationship with the abuser. Contact and exposure to the narcissistic abuse equates to pain and harm. The perpetrator is not able to change. The abuser's personality is fused and fixed, fossilized into an amalgam of Swiss cheese, a psyche with many holes and voids.

I am a strengths-focused therapist, but when we are discussing extreme narcissism, I am very clear that such abusers have extremely limited capacity for change, especially those far on the end of the continuum in the malignant narcissist/psychopath range. The only hope for healing for the survivor, in those cases, is to GET OUT of the relationship and go NO CONTACT. Once out of the relationship, there is abundant hope for healing, and eventually, thriving. It is a distinct honor and a privilege to bear witness to this transformation in my practice, as survivors soar to the place of thriving.

The more extreme the narcissist is on the continuum, the more extreme, frequent, intense and sadistic the abuse. Malignant narcissists and psychopaths do not have empathy, remorse, reciprocity, accountability, integrity, authenticity, honesty, accountability, compromise, trust or respect—all essential elements of healthy relationships. Those with NPD lack all of the above, as well, but may show less premeditated sadism in extracting narcissistic supply (compared to a malignant narcissist or psychopath). Their aim is to fuel their fragile egos, as well. Some individuals with NPD will attempt to extract narcissistic supply primarily through work or community endeavors, thereby obtaining adulation and praise for humanitarian works (think politicians, religious leaders, etc.).

Others on the narcissism continuum tend to lean moreso on relationships to extract narcissistic supply, and always, the targets of those relationships experience emotional pain from the power and control mechanisms imposed upon them by narcissistic abuse, often through seductive withholding of affection and intimacy (podcast, Walker and Schneider, 2015).

I would encourage the survivor to not fixate on what type of narcissist their abuser is, but instead, to identify that their abuser's behaviors are unacceptable, abusive and cruel. Ultimately, whether the perpetrator has NPD, is a malignant narcissist or is a psychopath – the abuser has an ingrained pathology in his/her psyche which renders them unsafe to engage in a relationship with. To continue to be involved in a relationship of any kind with such a disturbed abuser is to continue to be exposed to ongoing complex trauma and loss.

4) There are some survivors who may shy away from psychotherapy after being invalidated by a therapist who may not know as much about narcissistic abuse or how traumatic it is. Yet seeking guidance from a mental health professional is often necessary for victims to safely address symptoms of trauma. What advice can you give to survivors who are looking for a therapist like

you who can meet their needs and provide a validating perspective? For example, is there a type of therapy that may not be as effective for survivors (ex. interpersonal therapy vs. cognitive behavioral therapy) or certain specializations that may enable a therapist to more effectively address the victim's needs (ex. specialization in trauma)? What types of treatment and therapies do you believe are the most effective for survivors of narcissistic abuse?

What is absolutely essential for the survivor is to connect with a compassionate and competent helping professional who is licensed to provide psychotherapy and has a specialty in narcissistic abuse recovery and trauma work; who is strengths-focused (for the survivor) and exhibits unconditional positive regard and client-directed therapy.

The safe, healing relationship with the therapist is essential so that the survivor can restore trust and healing within themselves and the outside world. When a relational therapist creates a "safe holding environment" (Winnicott, 2002) for healing, the survivor is able to narrate their story of abuse and receive validation and confirmation of the truth of their experience.

Look for a therapist who works in positive psychology and trauma-informed psychotherapy. Survivors require hope that they can and will resolve their trauma, to connect with their resilience and post-traumatic growth (Malchiodi, 2014).If that helping professional in any way shape or form blames or shames the survivor, do not pass go! Find another helping professional immediately!

Survivors need and deserve a supportive, strengths-focused therapist who is compassionate and competent to treat C-PTSD, depression and anxiety stemming from narcissistic abuse. I personally do not believe that the labels of "codependent" and "love addict" are helpful or even applicable to the healing process. In some cases, some survivors may have a history of codependency.

However, not all survivors are codependent. And to make a blanket statement as such, labeling/shaming/blaming the survivor, is not only completely contradictory to some individual's stories, but having that label serves to further disempower the survivor to take on the blame and shame of the abuse. Often what looks like codependency or love addiction is really the aftermath of the trauma bonds with an extremely pathological abuser. I repeat, such abuse is NOT the fault of the survivor.

If I were to recommend "who" to look for in a therapist, I would emphatically declare that the following approaches are ESSENTIAL to the healing process of the survivor: The therapist must be strengths-focused, client-centered, interpersonal, relational, and humanistic. A survivor must feel empowered to co-create her own healing process with a helping professional who is skilled in trauma work and can walk her through the many layers of healing at the survivor's pace.

An excellent clinician will honor what the client brings to the table any given day and will provide the necessary tools and psychoeducation for healing of this traumatic loss to occur. The client is acknowledged as the source of their own agency and empowered to connect with their fierce survivor instinct within, eventually moving into a healing place of thriving.

So often survivors are reeling with cognitive dissonance (feeling they are to blame for the abuse, that they are the crazy ones, that they still love their abusers because of the trauma bond). When a client narrates their story and a compassionate therapist bears witness to this story, the client is confirmed and validated that her story is THE truth. Cognitive dissonance then begins to dissipate. There may be several sessions of "telling the story" (either verbally and/or through expressive arts) so that the client is able to "master" the trauma.

Some clients find verbal ventilation helps in this regard while the therapist provides unconditional positive regard and active listening, validating the client's experience and confirming for the client that THE SURVIVOR IS NOT TO BLAME. So often survivors have internalized the gaslighting perpetuated upon them that they feel they have misperceived the reality of what occurred.

Clients need to engage in trauma work once the relationship of safety has been established with the therapist and the client begins to share her story. The therapist should be versed in evidenced-based trauma-informed therapies which may include: mindfulness based cognitive therapy, grief work, EMDR (Eye Movement Desensitization and Reprocessing), somatic experiencing (see Peter Levine's work in resources), and trauma-informed expressive arts interventions (see Cathy Malchiodi's work in resources).

Much of the work is very relational and interpersonal, combined with the finesse of working collaboratively with the client and applying appropriate therapies described above which show merit in the traumatology literature from the stance of strengths-focus and client empowerment. I love the work of Pete Walker, Peter Levine, and Bessel van der Kolk, as well as pioneers in the field of expressive arts such as Cathy Malchiodi. Blending their perspectives in a neurosequential approach to healing trauma is cutting edge and the stuff of current research and healing.

(5) Are there other interventions for survivors that are helpful to their recovery and can enable them to work through the trauma?

I blend several approaches mentioned above by providing a safe environment for my clients to narrate their story. I then go about providing the necessary psychoeducation for my clients to understand narcissistic abuse and offer many recommendations for resources/websites and bibliotherapy.

This important step is essential to lower the cognitive dissonance so common in narcissistic abuse survivors. I work with my clients to establish No Contact boundaries with their abusers (or in some cases where the survivor shares custody of children, Limited Contact). The establishment of healthy boundaries is essential to the healing process of my clients. We also work on transmitting the "positive holding environment" of the therapy hour to the real world found in empathic social supports existing in the client's life.

We work on self-nurturing and self-soothing. My clients actively grieve their traumatic losses through mindfulness based cognitive therapies and expressive arts. Homework involves self-care practices that release trauma physiologically through mindfulness based meditation, yoga and other appropriate exercises. Survivors reclaim their self worth and move on to not only heal, but thrive. Some of the journaling and art exercises I do with my clients is found in my e-book, *Soul Vampires: Reclaiming Your LifeBlood After Narcissistic Abuse (2015)*.

If a client elects to do life coaching on the phone or by Skype, I would just recommend "buyer beware," as with working with any psychotherapist or life coach. Life coaching is not psychotherapy, so the life coach should not be engaging in the discussion of clinical concerns like depression, anxiety, C-PTSD, and interventions connected with those circumstances.

Survivors of narcissistic abuse and coaches can be invaluable in providing support and resources, acting as a crucial source of support, but should take care not to overstep the very thin line that moves into psychotherapy. I have seen helping professionals, whether licensed or laypersons, actually cause harm to survivors by victim-shaming and blaming. It concerns me greatly when that helping professional perhaps has not done their own healing work or is not educated in the strengths-focused approach of narcissistic abuse recovery; those "helpers" then unknowingly re-victimize the clients they claim to help.

Being that we live in an increasingly global world, I do believe phone consultations and Skype-type therapy are the wave of the future. At some point, psychotherapists will be able to be licensed across statelines but currently are limited to putting on a "life coaching/consulting hat" when working with clients outside of the state they are licensed for. That being said, a competent, compassionate licensed therapist who is also a life coach or consultant can be of invaluable help to survivors all over the world. We are out there, and we want to help (see Michelle Mallon's Facebook Support group and list of competent and compassionate providers).

Online support forums can be helpful as well. However, again, "Buyer beware." I have seen some really concerning re-victimizing of survivors on some well-known forums by facilitators/moderators who are not licensed or trained psychotherapists. That being said, some forums are really helpful and spot on. I would encourage the survivor to research online forums with their trusted therapist/life coach and enlist their helping professional's support in locating an appropriate and emotionally safe survivor support forum.

Resources/Works Cited:

Brown, Sandra A. (2010). Women Who Love Psychopaths: Inside the Relationships of Inevitable Harm with Psychopaths, Sociopaths and Narcissists, Mask Publishing.

Carnes, Patrick (1997). The Betrayal Bond: Breaking Free of Exploitive Relationships, HCI Publishing.

Curran, Linda (2009). Trauma Competency: A Clinician's Guide. Premier Publishing.

Herman, Judith (1997), Trauma and Recovery-The Aftermath of Violence- From Domestic Violence to Political Terror, Basic Books.

Levine, Peter (2010). In an Unspoken Voice: How the Body Releases Trauma and Restores Goodness, North Atlantic Books.

Louis De Canonville, Christine (2015). The Three Faces of Evil: Unmasking the Full Spectrum of Narcissistic Abuse, Black Card Books.

Malchiodi, C. (2016, March 3). Trauma-Informed Art Therapy (TI-AT) and Trauma-Informed Expressive Arts Therapy. Retrieved on March 3, 2016 from http://www.cathymalchiodi.com/Trauma Informed Art Therapy.html.

- See more at: http://www.cathymalchiodi.com/art-therapy-books/trauma-informed-art-therapy/#sthash.eXOwYJzB.dpuf

Malchiodi, C. (March 6, 2012). Trauma-informed expressive arts therapy.
New York: Sussex Publications/ Psychology Today.
See more at: http://www.cathymalchiodi.com/art-therapy-books/trauma-informed-art-therapy/#sthash.eXOwYJzB.dpuf

Malchiodi, C. and Perry, B. (2008). Creative Interventions with Traumatized Children, The Guildford Press.

Mallon, Michelle: Therapist in Ohio who has online support group and vetted list of providers of narcissistic abuse recovery:
https://www.facebook.com/NarcissisticVictimSyndrome/info/?tab=page_info

Schneider, Andrea (2015). Soul Vampires: Reclaiming Your LifeBlood After Narcissistic Abuse, Bookbaby.

Steele, William and Malchiodi, Cathy (2011). Trauma-Informed Practices with Children and Adolescents, Routeledge.

Van der Kolk, Bessel (2014), The Body Keeps the Score: Brain, Mind and Body in the Healing of Trauma, Viking Publications

Walker, Pete (2013). Complex PTSD: From Surviving to Thriving: A

Guide and Map for Recovering from Childhood Trauma, Create Space Independent Publishing Platform.

Walker, Kristin Sunata and Schneider, Andrea (2015) Podcast: everythingehr.com: Is Narcissism Psychological Viagra? http://everythingehr.com/is-narcissism-psychological-viagra-join-counselor-andrea-schneider-and-host-kristin-walker/

Winnicott, D.W. (2002). On the Child, Da Capo Press.

About the Author

Andrea Schneider, MSW, LCSW, is a licensed psychotherapist and life coach, with a private practice in Southern California. She has been practicing for more than 20 years, helping women, men, children, teens and families heal from trauma, loss, abuse and major depression/anxiety at various life transitions. Andrea received her MSW (masters in social work) from the University of Michigan, Ann Arbor, and her bachelor's in psychology from UCLA. She also has a Trauma-Informed Expressive Arts certificate from Cathy Malchiodi's Trauma-Informed Practices and Expressive Art Therapy Institute. She has worked in numerous clinical settings ranging from a domestic violence safe shelter, school-based counseling for children and teens, community mental health clinic, day treatment facility, a hospice and a psychiatric mental health clinic for a major HMO. She has been in private practice for more than 11 years.

Andrea also brings her expertise to supervising pre-licensed master's-level clinicians and enjoys training other therapists and medical practitioners in her areas of expertise. She provides in-person psychotherapy as well as telehealth support internationally. Andrea authored the book, *Soul Vampires: Reclaiming Your LifeBlood After Narcissistic Abuse*, available in ebook format at Bookbaby.com She has also written several articles on narcissistic abuse recovery for goodtherapy.org as well as her own blog, From Andrea's Couch. Visit Andrea's website and blog at andreaschneiderlcsw.com.

Social Media Platforms

Andrea's website and blog (From Andrea's Couch):
http://www.andreaschneiderlcsw.com/
Andrea's e-book: https://store.bookbaby.com/book/soul-vampires
(e-book can be formatted for smartphone, laptop or tablet)
Andrea's articles at goodtherapy.org:
http://www.goodtherapy.org/therapists/profile/andrea-schneider-20100917

Facebook: https://www.facebook.com/Andrea-Schneider-MSW-LCSW-125478894159044/

LinkedIn: https://www.linkedin.com/in/andrea-schneider-msw-lcsw-5b186a1b

Twitter: https://twitter.com/andrea_schneid

5 Powerful Self-Care Tips for Abuse and Trauma Survivors

Shahida here again. Being a trauma survivor is a challenging journey, but it is also an empowering one. Trauma acts as the catalyst for us to learn how to better engage in self-care and introduces us to endless modalities for healing and expressing ourselves, enabling us to channel our crisis into our transformation. Most importantly, it gives us access to connect with other survivors who have been where we are. It is in these validating communities that we tend to find the most healing, even outside of the therapy space. This chapter described the various traditional and healing modalities that are available to survivors. So as to not make the process overwhelming, I've selected some major self-care tips I think all survivors of trauma can benefit from.

Here are some tips that I've lived by that can benefit the healing journey of those who have been through trauma and abuse. This article was also featured on The National Domestic Violence Hotline.

છબ

As a survivor of lifelong trauma and abuse, I became a creative and active consumer of diverse methods to heal myself. I also learned, from a very young age, to speak to myself kindly and compassionately to counter the abuse I experienced. I didn't know it then, but I was essentially staging what I later dubbed a "reverse discourse" against my own trauma - rewriting the narratives of the various ways I had been traumatized into powerful tools for transformation. Today, I help survivors all over the world begin the journey I began many years ago.

1. Positive affirmations.

In order to reprogram our subconscious mind, which has undoubtedly been affected by the abusive words and actions we've undergone, we have to literally reprogram our brain and minimize the negative, destructive automatic thoughts that may arise in our day-to-day life.

These thoughts stir self-sabotage and hold us back from embracing all the power and agency we have to rebuild our lives. Many of these thoughts are not even our own, but rather, the voices of our abusers and bullies who continue to taunt us long after the abuse has ended. When we've been abused or bullied in any way, we continue to abuse ourselves with what trauma therapist Pete Walker calls the voice of the "Inner critic."

The most powerful way I've reprogrammed my own inner critical voice is through a system of positive affirmations that I engage in on a daily basis. These are positive affirmations that should be tailored to your particular wounds and insecurities. For example, if you have an insecurity about your appearance that your abuser has attempted to instill in you, a positive affirmation can gently interrupt the pattern of ruminating over such harsh comments by replacing the toxic thought with a loving one. A self-sabotaging thought about your appearance suddenly becomes, "I am beautiful, inside and out" whenever the harmful thought or emotion associated with the thought comes up.

One of the most effective techniques in engaging in these positive affirmations aside from saying them aloud is a technique from my larger method of "reverse discourse" which I discuss in my first book, *The Smart Girl's Guide to Self-Care*. Record all of your positive affirmations on a tape recover or a voice recording application and listen to them daily. Hearing your own voice repeating these affirmations daily - "I love myself," "I am valuable," "I am worthy," "I am beautiful" - is a potent way to rewrite the narrative abusers have written for you and banish that browbeating bully inside of your own head.

2. Heal the mind through the body.

According to trauma expert Dr. Bessel van der Kolk, author of *The Body Keeps the Score*, trauma lives in our bodies as well as our minds. It's important that we find at least one form of physical outlet for the intense emotions of grief, rage, and hurt we're bound to feel in the aftermath of abuse and trauma, in order to combat the paralysis that accompanies trauma, leaving us feeling numb and frozen.

I personally love kickboxing, yoga, dance cardio and running while listening to empowering music or listening to positive affirmations. Do something you're passionate about and love to do. Don't force your body into activities that you're not comfortable with, and do not exhaust yourself. Using physical exercise as an outlet should be an act of self-care, not self-destruction.

3. Breathe.

For abuse survivors who struggle with symptoms of PTSD or complex PTSD, mindful breathing exercises and meditation are especially helpful in managing what Pete Walker calls our fight, flight, freeze or fawn responses to flashbacks and ruminating thoughts.

As an undergraduate freshman in college, I learned how to meditate through my university's mindfulness programs. On my own, I also explored hundreds of different types of meditations available on the web and through podcasts - everything from self-compassion meditations to Chakra cleansing ones. I even taught others to mediate for the first time during a club meeting at college - and today, I create meditations for survivors of emotional abuse all over the world, to help them to heal. Meditation is and continues to be, one of the most powerful instruments in my self-care toolkit.

Taking time to observe our breath, whether it be for five minutes or an hour, can be immensely helpful to managing our emotions and nonjudgmentally addressing our painful triggers. In addition, meditation literally rewires our brain so that we are able to mindfully approach any maladaptive responses that may keep us locked into the traumatic event.

If you have never meditated before and would like to try it, I would highly recommend an app known as Stop, Breathe and Think, recommended for people of all ages. Find out more about this app here: www.stopbreathethink.org.

4. Channel your pain into creativity.

Art therapy is especially helpful to survivors of PTSD because it enables survivors to find modes of expression that allow them to create and integrate rather than self-destruct. According to van der Kolk, trauma can affect the Broca's area of the brain which deals with language. It can shut this area of the brain down, disabling us from expressing what is occurring.

Allowing ourselves to express the trauma in a somatic way is important because trauma and the dissociation that comes with it, can be difficult to process into words. When we are dissociated from the trauma, our brain protects itself from the traumatic event by giving us an outsider perspective to the trauma, disconnecting us from our identity, thoughts, feelings, and memories related to the trauma. The brain tends to "split" a traumatic event to make it easier to digest (Kalshed, 2013; Schuster, 2013).

Since trauma can disconnect us from both our minds and bodies through processes of depersonalization, de-realization, and even amnesia, art can help us reintegrate the trauma where we were previously disconnected from the experience. As Andrea Schneider, LCSW, puts it, expressive arts can be a way of "mastering the trauma" that we've experienced. Whether it's writing, painting, drawing, making music, doing arts and crafts - it's important to release the trauma in alternative ways that engage both our mind and body.

I have used my various traumas to paint, to draw, to write fiction, poetry and articles regarding abuse to help other survivors. When we create something, we also have the option of sharing our art with the world - whether it's a beautiful painting or a book. Harnessing our pain into creativity can be a life-changing experience - both for ourselves and for others.

5) Asking for help.

Contrary to popular opinion, asking for help does not make you helpless or powerless. It is in fact, a strong recognition of your own power to be able to seek help and be open to receiving it. Connecting with a group of fellow survivors helped me immensely to validate and honor my experiences. It fueled my ability to be self-compassionate and also gave me a passion for helping others on their healing journey.

Sharing your story with other survivors can be incredibly healing and cathartic, but if you are struggling with the effects of trauma, I also highly recommend finding a validating mental health professional who specializes in trauma and understands its symptoms in addition to finding a support group of fellow survivors.

Having the support of a mental health professional throughout the process can ensure that you are able to address your trauma triggers in a safe space. It is important to choose a *validating, trauma-informed* counselor who can meet your needs and gently guide you with the appropriate therapy that addresses the symptoms and triggers.

It is important that you are supported in a safe space with a trauma-informed counselor who can meet your needs and gently guide you with the appropriate therapy that addresses your needs. Some survivors benefit from EMDR therapy, which is a therapy that enables them to process their trauma without being re-traumatized in the process. However, a therapy that works for one survivor may not work for another depending on their specific symptoms, the severity of the trauma and the length of time a person has been traumatized. Be sure to discuss with your mental health professional what the right type of therapy is for you.

As a supplement to therapy, you may wish to also consult the resources on this excellent list, which includes free or low-cost mental health resources: http://greatist.com/grow/resources-when-you-can-not-afford-therapy.

Throughout this journey of healing from trauma and abuse, make sure you are being self-compassionate towards yourself. A great deal of trauma survivors suffer from toxic shame and self-blame. It's important that we are gentle towards ourselves during this journey, that we acknowledge we are doing our very best, and that we ask ourselves every day, "What would be the most loving thing I can do for myself in this moment?" in any circumstance. There is no time limit to learning and healing, there is only the power of transforming our adversity into victory, one small step at a time.

What happens when the survivor is a child "programmed" for narcissistic abuse? Life coach and bestselling author Lisa A. Romano shares her story on how we can transform our childhood programming into success. From childhood trauma survivor to adult thriver, Lisa has inspired hundreds of thousands of people with her books, her blog and her YouTube channel for children of narcissistic or alcoholic parents.

Healing The Childhood Programming That Makes You a Magnet for Narcissists by Lisa A. Romano

Life can be quite a roller coaster of a ride. Back when I was a child, I suffered from depression and anxiety. I understand this now, but when I was a child all I felt was crazy. I found it nearly impossible to fit in. I felt invisible at home, and in the way. My mother used to say that she and I could not get along because we had what she referred to as a personality conflict. I remember being seven years old, and feeling innately flawed. All I knew was my mother could not love me, and for some reason it was my fault.

It has taken me decades to recover from my mother's rejection. In our home, emotions were frowned upon.

As children, my siblings and I were encouraged to "suck it up" and to never "act like babies." We were told that we had no right to cry, to feel sad, or to complain. We feared our father as well as our mother. They were both disciplinarians, short-tempered, and verbally abusive. I remember tip toeing around my childhood home hoping that no one would see me, while at the same time feeling desperate to be seen on an authentic level.

After my first marriage fell apart, and I found myself battling the desire to finish my life out beneath the blankets on my bed, I realized that I needed help. It was an incredible act, to ask for professional help, considering that I had been brainwashed to believe that asking for help was a sign of weakness. My mother was an emotional stuffer, and deep within me I knew she disapproved of my efforts to make sense out of what was happening in my life. I knew one thing for sure. I needed to make certain that I would not pass onto my children many of the messages she had passed down to me. When I looked at my mother, I saw a woman who lived in fear of upsetting her husband, who had selflessly also given up her rights to imagine her own dreams for the sake of keeping a narcissist quiet.

My marriage was a carbon copy of my childhood, although at the time I could never have seen that. Caught in the eye of the tornado, it was impossible for me to gain an objective snapshot of the mirrored realities I was stuck in. Through tremendous self-analysis, I was able to put the pieces of the puzzle my life had become together. In therapy, I discovered that I had married my mother's emotional twin as an unconscious attempt to gain the maternal validation I never received in childhood. As I learned more about the children my parents were, the clearer my own childhood became.

Both of my parents are adult children of alcoholics. Neither of them have ever gone into therapy, and both still struggle with the trauma of their childhoods, although they'd never admit to that. My parents are the perfect dysfunctional couple. My mother is a poster child codependent, and my father is a textbook garden-variety narcissist. As many psychotherapists would agree, these two personality types attract one another like moths to flames. Narcissists need to be taken care of, and codependents find their worth in taking care of others. A match made in subconscious heaven.

In therapy, I learned to appreciate why my marriage fell apart. Programmed to worry more about what others thought about me than what I thought about myself, groomed me to be the perfect little codependent wife. When I met and married my husband, I wanted nothing more than to please him, and to make him happy. I would anticipate his needs, and see to it that he wanted for nothing. I never thought about myself, or considered what I needed. My life was all about ensuring that my man was satisfied, thanks to the downloads I received from my mother.

After my third child was born, my body began to shut down. A few years earlier I developed adult onset asthma, and started experiencing debilitating migraine headaches. I was suffering from panic attacks that often stopped me in my tracks. I began to be afraid to leave my house, because I was worried a panic attack would hit while I was driving on a highway with my children. In addition to what was happening in me internally, my body began developing rashes my doctors could not explain.

Entering into therapy was an act of survival, and if it were not for my children I am not so sure I would have had the courage to ask for help. Many years later, I am eternally grateful for the information I received about codependency, and ultimately the research I did on narcissism, because it was the knowledge I gained that saved my life. Understanding why I was the way I was helped me come out of my codependent brain fog, which allowed me to feel more in control of my life, and even my future.

Today I am a Certified Life Coach and bestselling author. It is quite amazing to me to look back on my life and remember the intimidated young mother I once was. One of my most painful memories is of my ex-husband standing over me yelling, as I was curled in a ball, wedged between the toilet bowl and bathtub. During our separation he stopped paying the mortgage on our home, and also stopped paying our credit card bills as well. In addition, he stopped giving me money to buy groceries. So terrified of him at the time, I waited until the last possible moment to ask him for money. The children and I had begun surviving on whatever food was left in the house on the day he moved out. When the last box of macaroni and cheese was gone, I had no other choice but to ask him for money.

At the time, I knew nothing about covert narcissistic abuse. My husband did not fit the stereotype. He was not boastful, and in fact presented himself as a humble individual. He did not overtly appear to be elitist. People loved him, especially my mother and father. On the outside, he was the life of the party, and he seemed able to gel with just about anyone. On the other hand, on the surface I was the one who was jaded, standoffish, and untrusting of others. Superficially, my husband appeared very much like a great catch, and from across any room, I was the bitchy wife.

In hindsight, I have great empathy now for the young mother I once was. Yes, I was angry, but I understand now I had every right to be. My husband had just as many personalities as he did suit jackets. I on the other hand, had one personality, and it was raw. I did not try to manipulate people into liking me the way he did. In fact, I understand now that his intention was to please as many others as possible, so he could gain outward validation. Knowing other people approved of him was a weapon he used against me whenever we had an issue. At the time the only person's opinion that mattered of me was his. My desire to gain his validation was the fuel that kept our dynamic going. And it was not until I stopped chasing his approval, that our dysfunctional tango began to unravel. It was also at that time that my Boy Scout of a husband began to turn into Mr. Hyde.

If I have learned anything in my lifetime about relationships, it is that until you truly love, respect and honor your right to have opinions and emotions, you cannot attract someone into your life that can love and respect your opinions and emotions. My husband was a mirror of my relationship with my Self. I did not know how to honor what I felt, and in fact I did not have a connection to my Self. For most of my life I was operating below the veil of consciousness, completely out of subconscious programming.

My recovery from narcissistic abuse hinged on my ability to understand why I was attracted to a man like my husband in the first place. Owning and accepting the fact that I was a codependent, allowed me to gain a much needed perspective about my situation that enabled me to make sense out of why I was the way I was, and why I attracted who I married. Crucial to my healing, was learning to understand who my parents were as children, as well as adults. As patterns of thoughts and beliefs, as well as behaviors began to emerge, the woman I had become made sense, in spite of how unhappy I was about being the codependent, emotionally crippled woman I used to be.

My husband fooled me with his Boy Scout Charm. I could never have known when I was twenty-one that I was dealing with a passive aggressive, covert narcissist who lacked the ability to see me. I could never have known that he lacked the ability to have empathy for me, as well as anyone else for that matter. What I witnessed with my eyes, although it never matched what I felt on a heart level, caused me to doubt my hunches about him. And because as a child I was brainwashed to disown my feelings, as an adult I did not know how to honor the intuition I had about my husband being abusive. Instead, I was easily swayed to believe what he and others told me about my feelings. "Your feelings don't matter Lisa. Focus on what you do have. Stop talking about how you feel. Your feelings are irrelevant."

As a Life Coach, I am honored to help others identify what they are feeling, and I help them come into alignment with their root instincts. I help emotionally neglected and abused adult children learn how to tap into their true Self, the one they were brainwashed to believe was irrelevant, and unworthy. I help codependents understand their childhood brainwashing for the sake of helping them clearly identify what they are doing wrong, for the purpose of helping them figure out how to do things right. I teach others about narcissistic abuse, and help them integrate their past pain with a promising future. I help others recover their ability to honor their divine rights over their own minds, and ultimately teach people the art of loving the Self.

I am grateful for the opportunity to add to this collection of work. It is my desire, that the message you received from my contribution is one that fills you with hope. If a narcissist or a codependent raised you, chances are you will attract a narcissist into your life as an adult. But the good news is, once you awaken to the program, you no longer have to, dear one. Remember who you are—you are enough!

About the Author

Lisa A. Romano is a Certified Life Coach who specializes in Mentoring Adult Children of Alcoholics who are seeking to move beyond their painful pasts. She is also a bestselling author, radio show host, and speaker. Regarding her work, she says, "I assist people conquer their limiting, unconscious beliefs about Self; the ones they were programmed to believe when they were little and impressionable. I help adult children from all sorts of dysfunctional homes and otherwise 'normal homes' to create new belief systems that serve to facilitate their personal growth. Through a co-creative coaching/mentoring relationship unconscious beliefs are made conscious and new beliefs about the divine Self are created. As children born to dysfunctional caretakers, we may have been brainwashed to believe we are not worthy, that our emotions don't matter, and that who we are is not valuable. Unless we learn to face these dysfunctional thinking patterns and then appropriately adopt new, healthier ways of seeing Self--we unconsciously recreate our pasts by attracting people and circumstances that mimic our childhoods. I have seen amazing transformations...I help adult children Master The Self-- so that they can finally put the demons to rest and live the lives they were born to live!"

Social Media Platforms:

Website: http://lisaaromano.com/
YouTube: https://www.youtube.com/user/lisaaromano1
Facebook: https://www.facebook.com/codependency101/
Twitter: https://twitter.com/lisaaromano1

Suffering from abuse at a young age often means we need to give ourselves what we never received in childhood. Ingrid Roekke, founder of the inspirational and empowering Show Boundaries YouTube channel and thought field therapist, shares her own incredible story of overcoming lifelong traumas and learning how to re-parent the abused child.

Re-Parenting the Abused Child by Ingrid Roekke

Narcissism. That's what all personality disorders boil down to - malignant *narcissism.* At the core of all antisocial personality disorders, we find hardcore narcissism. A narcissism hallmarked by an overall self-serving agenda, tainting the narcissist's every action and gesture. Completely stripped of empathy, the narcissist will get what s/he wants at any cost. Yet, most people don't know what narcissistic abuse is - unless they've come across this form of abuse firsthand, and need to figure out what the heck happened to them. In other words, learning about narcissistic abuse more often than not, occurs *after* one has been narcissistically abused in the first place. Too little, too late, right? This inflamed topic encapsulates my nemesis, my profession and my passion.

An abusive stepfather, and a fight-fawn mother raised me. My mother's abuse was narcissistic and martyred. It was physical and psychological. She couldn't make my stepfather be loving and compassionate, so she manipulated, shame-bashed and guilt-tripped us children to be her devoted followers. Always fighting for her pat on the head, her smiles and her affection. The role as the golden child was passed around, and so was the role as the scapegoat. We were always at her martyred debt. The first time I remember I hated myself for being such a burden to my mother, I was only five years old. I never remember anything *but* feeling like a burden and a mistake. My whole childhood revolved around avoiding scorn and beatings. It revolved around constant rumination about how I could crack the code to make my mother love me.

What personality did I have to use in order to make her notice me? To approve of me? It didn't take long before I generalized this perspective, and tried to crack the code for acceptance with anyone I interacted with. I had no personality. It was wiped out from early on. I morphed into the person that would be accepted in any given situation. If Carol liked me goofing around, I would be goofy. If John liked me to be serious and intellectual, I would be serious and intellectual. I didn't know how to be anything but a chameleon.

I actually ate strawberries till my late twenties's because I had been told all my life that everyone loves strawberries...*Well, okay, then*, I thought. *I love strawberries, too.* I really detest the taste of strawberries, though. I found that out in my late twenties. I had lived a whole life never knowing what I preferred. I didn't know that I didn't like strawberries. It simply was never a priority to find out what I preferred. My focus was never inwards, towards myself, it was always outwards towards other people's preferences. Today, however, I am the proud decliner of strawberries when someone offers them to me!

Someone recently told me that at a very young age I said, *"If my mother is happy, I am happy."* Plain and simple, and yet very devastating. There was no "me". Only mother. I had no personality of my own, no preferences, no agenda. Nothing other than to find out how to please mother. *

My stepfather abused me sexually. My father was absent for large parts of my childhood. My brothers were physically and psychologically abusive. Actually, I remember *one* brother's abuse in particular. Even now in my thirties, I think about it pretty often. All day, every day, he would systematically degrade me, down-talk me and use what I told him in confidence against me in blackmail.

Still, in this crazy circus that was my family, he was the only one I had *some* peaceful moments with, and I needed those moments so badly. I would flee into those moments with play and laughter like my sanity depended on it. I was neurotically naïve. I *needed* to see that my family loved me. I *needed* to understand that abuse was love, because if I didn't...

That would mean that my family *didn't* love me. It would mean that my *mother* didn't love me. A small child will be crushed under that kind of truth. The pain will be excruciating.

So - I lied to myself. It's was self-preservation 101. It was easier to digest that I was being an abomination, rather than acknowledging that my mother didn't love me. So the translation of a small child went as the following: Abuse *is* love. Abuse *is* justified. My mother *does* love me, she is just very upset because of how I behave. Because of who I am. It's *me*, the 5-year old, that's so evil and horrible that my mother has to pull my hair and press her thumbs into my eye sockets. She doesn't do that because she doesn't love me (because she does love me!), but she does it because *I* am bad. *That's* why she screams all those things to me. Because, *I am* being mean to *her* (*she* is not being mean to *me*... *she* loves me!). And she is *really* upset, which means that I must be *that* bad. Poor mommy that got a child so upsetting as I. To make this long story a little less long, we can sum up the reaction to childhood abuse in one sentence: *A child that's being abused by its parents doesn't stop loving its parents, it stops loving itself.*

Added with this mental response to abuse, you have the power of persuasion combined with the power in numbers. The more people abusing a child, the more the child will start accepting that this is *not* a coincidence - it's *the child* being in the wrong, for sure. An entire family can't be wrong, can they? As an educated adult however, I now know for a fact, that an entire family *can* be wrong. A family can be *that* dysfunctional that it's made of enablers, codependents and abusers. This family will find themselves that *one* scapegoat. You'll get a malignant family dynamic that's condoned, because very few people recognize abuse as something manipulative and psychological.

I didn't wake up one day and realize this, however. That's unfortunately not how this healing thing goes! I had to marry a malignant narcissist, be severely abused, discover that my child was sexually abused, have my child taken away from me in court while having my complex CPTSD misdiagnosed as borderline personality disorder and have a domestic relationship with a *new* narcissist, until I started getting my understanding straight (I'm one of those slow learners that make sure I get my lesson several times before I get the idea).

With that being said, I started the road to enlightenment when I was nine. Maybe even earlier. But I have my first memory of myself ruminating about life, abuse, meditation, reincarnation and the journey of my soul. In between this, I was cutting myself, trying to kill myself or writing suicide notes. Now, there you have a complex journey, for sure! The more desperate I was for pain relief, the more desperately I read about psychology and spirituality - or tried to kill myself! My point being, the healing journey is not easy, and it wasn't fast. It was a three-steps-forward-two-steps-back kind of process (yeah I know, that concept sucks a little…).

I've read hundreds, maybe thousands, of books about psychology, spirituality, personality disorders, complex PTSD and healing. I've spent thousands and thousands of dollars on education. I've cried endless bed sheets soaking wet. I've meditated. Many times I've been frantically crying *while* meditating. I've screamed and I've suffered. I've laughed of the abuse. I've made fun of it. I've prayed to angels and to God. I've cursed God. I've cut my arms till they bled. I've drank. Done drugs. Some of my techniques for handling my childhood pain were good and constructive. Some were not. So I navigated. Gradually. And I grew. Decade after decade. Shedding my pain, little by little. And in step with shedding the pain, I was also shedding my self-destructiveness.

Today, I specialize in manipulative and emotional abuse, with emphasis on the fact that this form of insidious abuse is widely condoned by court mediators, custody evaluators, judges, therapists, lawyers, law enforcement and the CPS. This is a very severe problem, as it morphs helpers into enablers. It turns helpers into proxy abusers. One remedy will be for us to never stay silent about narcissistic abuse. We must never stay silent about our meetings with ignorant judges and custody evaluators. Enabling psychologists and flying monkeys. We must keep talking about all aspects of narcissistic abuse until the phrase is as common as sexual abuse.

I've been working with clients one-on-one and also teaching classes. How to assert boundaries. What abuse is. How to recognize it. How to stop self-mutilating. How to control depressive thoughts. How to grow self-compassion. I took all my pain and abuse, and decided that *I* would use *it*, as I was sick of *it* using me. In other words, I took the bull by the horns, and decided to make a living out of what had nearly had killed me. This way I felt I got the last word, rather than just having to pick up the shattered pieces of myself after years of abuse, just to carry on with my life, with a limp.

I was the stereotypical story of a codependent. Going from abusive childhood settings and right into adult abuse. I had no referential frames to normal and healthy emotional templates. So there you have it summed up: an abusive parent-child relation will more often than not, predict a future with continuous abusive adult relationships.

How unfair is that? You would hope that adult survivors of childhood abuse would finally catch a break once they are physically out of their home. But, sadly many of them don't. Their physical body has moved out from their abusive childhood surroundings, but emotionally, they are still trapped in the mentality of the little child they once were - desperately trying to be worthy of their loved one's love and respect. (Been there, done that, bought the t-shirt!)

Today, when I recognize an emotional flashback, I show compassion for myself. I give love to the little girl who was traumatized so severely that even 30 years later, she's upset about it. The more intense the emotional flashback is, the more obvious it is to me how much my caregivers failed the little girl I carry inside of me every day. What if *I* were to kick *my* children in the back, while screaming at them to get out of my sight? My heart rots at the mere thought of it. They would be devastated and broken. It would be horrible if I did that.

And yet, someone did that to me. People mandated to protect me from the world, were actually the ones I ought to have been protected *from*. I was a fragile and helpless little child. That's messed up! That's *not* okay! I *acknowledge* that. And then I give myself compassion for having been wounded so severely. For having been completely helpless in the arms of abusers. And then I feel proud for growing up. I feel proud for being a loving mother.

And lastly, I feel proud for breaking the abuse cycle. It stops with me. All of the things I've mentioned have been part of my cognitive process, and every time I get flashes from destructive thoughts, depression or emotional pain and shame, I re-parent myself. So why do we have to re-parent ourselves? Your childhood setting might've been physically abusive. It might have been emotionally neglectful. It might have been psychologically terrorizing.

Or, it might have been all of the above. Still, we find survivors that suffered abuse in *different* guises, to have completely *similar* wounds in their souls. So what's the common denominator? The factor causing such great emotional and psychological injury is the message carried across to the abused child: *You are not worthy of affection or love.*

Different forms of abuse are simply a way of getting this message across, in different languages. Now, in childhood, the message that comes from abuse is extremely damaging, as the child's brain is evolving an understanding of "self" and of how "self" fits into this world. The child is being *programmed*. Moreover, it's essential and crucial for a child to receive unconditional love and affection from the parents. Thus, child abuse is a way of malnourishing the child, only on an emotional level, and more often than not, the child will develop psychological ailments due to this malnutrition. These malnourished conditions affect the child long into adulthood.

When a child is well-nourished, it will see itself as wonderful. A child's greatness and importance will be obvious to it. So, when the child experiences abuse or neglect, this will cause great confusion. This will cause a cognitive dissonance within the child, which is tremendously stressful and excruciating. It's the optimal inner tension. The child believes s/he is magnificent. But, at the same time, s/he *experiences* that her abuser strongly contradicts this understanding by constantly and systematically showing that s/he's *un*worthy of love and affection.

To tighten the gap between these two contradicting realities, (and thereby managing to lessen the cognitive dissonance) the little child has to give up on *one* of the beliefs: the little child will let go of the understanding of self as worthy of love. The child stops believing that s/he is wonderful. As the self-loathing becomes very severe, s/he might feel increasingly ashamed of once having thought that s/he was worthy of love. Morphing together with the abuser's mentality is a self-defense mechanism when one *physically* cannot get away from the abusive relation.

Later in life when the little child grows into an adult survivor of childhood abuse, s/he will be the ultimate gift to abusers, as the manipulative abuser will start re*activating* the destructive childhood understanding of self. Especially narcissistic abusers who will reactivate childhood scarring. Many of them will never lay a hand on their abuse-target, but will simply control the survivor via constant guilt-tripping and shame-bashing. They will hold the survivor accountable for their every emotion. They will refer to childhood abuse by claiming that they understand the abusers and why they abused you. This way they awaken the inner critic at full force. As the survivor has no reference to a relationship being any other way, they may live many years, even decades in abuse, not being able to fully *recognize* their relationship as abusive.

As the abuse-target gets depressed, self-mutilating and suicidal (a result of the ongoing abuse, of course…), their abuser will take advantage of the target's unawareness of what "normal" looks like. The abuser will therefore be able to get away with shame-bashing and guilt-tripping the abuse-target for "not being happy," for being "ungrateful" and for being "dysfunctional."

Thus, the victim feels extremely ashamed and guilty for their depression, even though it is a completely *normal* and healthy reaction to being abused. This is equal to a shooter blaming his gunshot victim for bleeding! This way their depression worsens, while at the same time, the abusive grip gets more severe. Of course, if the target had grown up with healthy references to relationship dynamics, they would've recognized the *ab*normal in being abused. But, most often narcissistic abusers choose the easier targets - someone that has been pre-abused and primed. Someone filled with crusted wounds that are easy to break open. Someone that has never been exposed to normal.

Now, who would find someone already traumatized from abuse, and eagerly abuse them further? Well, narcissists are happy to do just that. Literally. Narcissists are parasitic, lazy and have no ethical boundaries. Thus, it's a win-win situation in all areas for the narcissist, as an already abused person represents so much less work for them. They don't have to go through all the trouble priming their abuse-target. It's already been done, and it is so much easier to manage an abusive relationship with someone who has already had their boundaries annihilated.

When the abuse-target is completely drained of narcissistic supply (money, free housing, admiration, free food etc.), or they simply get bored, they just move on to the next target. Again, preferably, someone that was previously primed for abuse in childhood. Someone that will strive for love *while* they are being abused. Adult survivors of childhood abuse will often amplify their pleasing-tendencies parallel with the increase of abuse. The more rejected the target is, the more the target will strive to "earn" the abuser's love. This way, the narcissist will get to be increasingly brutal in their abusive ways, while at the same time they are increasingly being more catered to and spoiled.

Very often, the abuse-target has been childhood abused. Far from always, but nevertheless, quite often. However, there is no single defining common denominator in an abuse-target, other than them being extremely empathetic. They are helpers and fixers, and they are found in all layers of society. As you see, I focus on the abuse-targets that have been primed for abuse in childhood. The kernel in childhood abuse is the ruthless emotional incest, where the child is forced to act out the role of the parent, and the parent holds the child accountable for their every feeling, for their every situation. If something goes wrong, it's always the child's fault. If the parent experiences pain - it's again the child's fault. If the parent is out of a job or is having financial difficulties - it's the child's fault.

The child will be forced into a therapist role by the parent. It will be forced to take responsibility for the parent and everything the parent feels. Now, see how easy it will be for a narcissist that meets this kind of survivor to start puppeteering them around, using their own guilt, empathy and shame against them? Holding their abuse-target accountable for *their* adultery? For *their* anger and rage? For *their* abuse? This relationship is a one-way street where the abuse-target is held accountable for everything, has a long complex list of rules to follow and every minute is unpredictable. If one doesn't manage to follow the rules, one gets punished. Love and affection is taken away. Just like in childhood. The narcissist will just pick up where the abusive parent left off, and the survivor will fall right back into the role of the child obediently taking accountability for every aspect of every minute.

Just reflect a little... Is there a chance that your abuser is similar to your childhood abuser? I am not talking exclusively about romantic relationships here. Your abusive relationship might also be with a friend, a family member or your boss. Indulge me a little. Grab a piece of paper, and a pen. Write down all the words describing how you *felt* as a child under the so-called love of your abusive parent. In other words, describe how you felt in that supposedly loving parent-child relation. If you as a child were constantly being scorned, constantly held accountable for your father's feelings, or were always being guilt-tripped and shame-bashed by your mother every time you asked for help (*or* asserted healthy boundaries), there's a large chance that you are in one of those toxic relationships in your adulthood.

You will learn a lot about how you as an adult might interpret what loving relationships are supposed to look like. For example, to me, the equation would look something like this: *Parent-child relationship = I am unworthy. A burden. Annoying. I have to strive for affection. I have to strive for attention. I have to please others in order to be accepted. I have to agree with everything in order to be safe. Talking about my preferences will make people angry at me. Talking about my needs will make me lose love.*

I can compare this little note about what my childhood environment looked like, to a note I make about what love looked like in my marriage. The two notes describing childhood-relationships vs. the note describing adult-relationships would be identical. The abuser in your adult relationship will definitely take advantage of your childhood programming and your flawed emotional template. I like to refer to this form of abuse as manipulative abuse, when your adult partner re-activates childhood traumas, and it is *the* most *brutal* kind of abuse.

According to Sandra Brown, M.A. (2010), it's estimated that 60 million people are being seriously harmed by someone else's antisocial personality disorder in the United States. But still, antisocial personality disorders are a great taboo in our society, and is majorly not being acknowledged or accounted for in family court, in therapy, in the police force, in social circles or in the CPS. This shapes a society that enables highly manipulative narcissistic abusers to get off the hook, while their victims are being pathologized and scrutinized and further abused. Obviously, for the victim, having their abuse-experience discredited and invalidated by the legal system, the mental health care system and their social circle, is an enormous secondary trauma, compounding the devastating effects of the original abuse.

We must never stop talking about narcissistic abuse. Keep sharing those posts and keep commenting on those YouTube videos. One day, narcissistic abuse *will* be a common terminology. It may not be in *our* time, but maybe our *children* will reap the benefits of a society able to recognize abuse that goes beyond the physical. Maybe our children will have justice in courts, or gain validation in a therapist's office. Or better yet - maybe they will recognize all the red flags on the first date, and go No Contact before therapists and courts become a part of the equation. Let's do our job well, and refuse to stay silent about narcissistic abuse.

*The 60 million people affected by those with personality disorders estimate is from "60 Million People in the U.S. Negatively Affected By Someone Else's Pathology" by therapist Sandra L. Brown on Psychology Today: www.psychologytoday.com/blog/pathological-relationships/201008/60-million-people-in-the-us-negatively- affected-someone-elses

**I have a great relationship with my mother today. We have both co-healed and I have forgiven her for my lost childhood. Today she is as supportive and loving as a mother could be!

About the Author

Ingrid Roekke is the founder of ShowBoundaries.com, an empowering resource for abuse and trauma survivors and hosts the popular YouTube channel Show Boundaries to help narcissistic abuse survivors worldwide. She is a nutritional physiologist, specializing in emotional eating and behavioral addictions. She is also a mindfulness instructor and a thought field therapist. She is currently earning a masters in psychology.

Social Media Platforms:

Facebook: https://www.facebook.com/Show-Boundaries/
Twitter: https://twitter.com/ShowBoundaries
YouTube: http://www.youtube.com/user/showboundaries

Many people underestimate the impact of verbal and emotional abuse, but the fact of the matter is, words do hurt and the effects can last a lifetime. Founder of Ending Abuse Media, Alison Soroka, shares her thoughts about the power of language in the realm of abuse.

Sticks and Stones and Hurtful Words by Alison Soroka

We all remember the childhood chant "Sticks and stones can break my bones, but words can never hurt me." We had it wrong! Hurtful words can cause significant harm. Names will forever hurt, especially when parents do the name-calling.

Verbal or emotional abuse conveys that one is worthless, flawed, unloved, unwanted, endangered, or only of value in meeting someone else's needs. It includes:

- Belittling, name-calling, degrading, shaming, ridiculing, or humiliating.
- Making one feel unsafe by slamming a door, bashing an object, or threatening severe punishment.
- Setting unrealistic expectations with threat of loss of affection or physical harm if not met.
- Ignoring, being emotionally cold and unsupportive, withdrawing comfort as a means of discipline.
- Rejecting, avoiding, or pushing one away.
- Describing one negatively.
- Openly admitting dislike or hating the person.

Children who were verbally abused grow up to be self-critical adults who are more likely to experience depression and anxiety (Sachs-Ericsson). They had almost twice as many symptoms as those who had not been verbally abused. They were also twice as likely to have suffered a mood or anxiety disorder. Sachs-Ericsson studied more than 5,600 people ages 15 to 54; and surprisingly, nearly 30 percent reported they were sometimes or often verbally abused by a parent.

Emotional abuse occurs for many of the same reasons that physical abuse occurs. When one is stressed, they may lash out verbally and physically. Some who verbally abuse may have learned this parenting style from their own parents. They may be unaware of positive ways to motivate or discipline their children.

Verbal abuse can have long-term effects. Over time, one begins to believe the negative things they hear about themselves. They use those negative statements and thoughts as explanations for anything that goes wrong. One may use negative self-talk and believe "I'm stupid" or "I'm lazy" or "I'm no good." When the message is repeatedly conveyed by someone, the pattern of self-criticism and negative thinking follows oneself through one's life. Self-criticism makes a person more prone to depression and anxiety.

Research by Martin Teicher (2006) at the Department of Psychiatry, Harvard Medical School, shows that verbal abuse during childhood may have an impact on mental health that is even greater than other forms of abuse. Parental verbal abuse affects a child's developing brain and is also a powerful negative model for interpersonal communication that impacts a child's future relationships.

Physical abuse might leave physical scars, but verbal abuse leaves invisible scars that may never heal. The impact of verbal abuse on vulnerable, developing children lasts a lifetime. Sticks and stones will break our bones, but unkind words are even more destructive and enduring.

References

Sachs-Ericsson, N., Kendall-Tackett, K., & Hernandez, A. (2007). Childhood abuse, chronic pain and depression in the National Comorbidity Survey. *Child Abuse & Neglect, 3*, 531–547.

Teicher, M. (2006). Sticks, Stones, and Hurtful Words: Relative Effects of Various Forms of Childhood Maltreatment. *American Journal of Psychiatry Am J Psychiatry, 163*(6), 993. doi:10.1176/appi.ajp.163.6.993

About the Author

Alison Soroka is the Founder and Executive Director of Smiles and Laughter Entertainment/Ending Abuse Media which was established in March 2011 and is an innovative media organization with the goal to increase awareness and knowledge about domestic violence. We also assist the public in identifying and accessing the resources available to victims and their families. Smiles and Laughter Entertainment/Ending Abuse Media aims to stimulate action by sharing stories, providing referrals, connecting critical resources, assisting in how to identify the risk factors of domestic violence, and displaying where victims can go for help. We are aligned with the City of Surrey's goal to "Improve public awareness around the reality and perception of crime."

Alison's vision, "To leverage media to expose the crime of domestic violence, share vital resources, and encourage family peace," came from a combination of her experience in the film industry and being a thankful survivor of domestic violence. Being well-versed on the dynamics of this crime after having fled an abusive living situation (nearly losing her daughter's life and her own in the process) and also knowledgeable about media options, Alison is able to apply media as a primary tool of focus, using video, radio, print, and internet to reach the largest audiences.

It is through this avenue that she seeks to promote the organization's motto of "Together We Can Break the Cycle of Abuse." As a mother of three children and a human welfare advocate, Alison passionately wants to contribute to "breaking the cycle of abuse" while making communities safer, more informed, and prouder places to live. She is disciplined and committed to assisting in the eradication of domestic violence. She believes this is possible as long as we, as a society, unite with strong, active, unified, and persistent voices to expose and ultimately annihilate this cowardly act and crime. There are no communities that are immune; therefore, making it all that much more important for us to reach the largest of audiences and inspire every one of use to do our part. Our future generations deserve the opportunity to enjoy a childhood filled with peace and innocence; not pain, suffering, or emotional trauma. Every woman deserves a life free from fear.

Every child deserves to grow up knowing no threat of violence in their home. When we as a society can say that we feel safe and loved, then we know our work is done. Why we chose Smiles and Laughter Entertainment as our organization's name...because this is the aftermath of what can be if we work together in providing love, support, and assistance to victims of domestic violence. If you believe in this vision, or even if you are just willing to consider it, please support Smiles and Laughter Entertainment/Ending Abuse Media in whatever way possible so we can work together towards our common goal.

Social Media Platforms:

Website: http://endingabusemedia.com/
Facebook: https://www.facebook.com/EndingAbuseMedia/
Twitter: https://twitter.com/endabusemedia
Youtube: https://www.youtube.com/user/EndingAbuse

CHAPTER FOUR

The Game You Can Win

N arcissists are natural competitors. They suffer from pathological envy, so they're inclined to break down our greatest strengths and assets to win the game. They play games every day – they compete in conversations, in devaluation, in their discard of their victims. In the book *SuperBetter* (2015), Jane McGonigal presents a brilliant framework for how to gamefully live our lives – by setting up a reward system every time we engage in "power-ups," use our "super-strengths" to defeat the bad guys and score points every time we've undertaken a new challenge in life.

This is how I want you to approach any narcissist in your life, be they relationship partner, parent, boss, co-worker or friend. The narcissist is always competitive and treats everything in life like a game. From now on, you will too – but not a petty game for the sake of competition. A game where the stakes are much higher – a game where the stakes include the quality of your life and your happiness.

If the narcissist is your supervillain, there's only one way to "defeat" him or her. His or her ultimate goal is to destroy you, destroy the self-esteem and success you've worked hard to build, destroy your ability to trust in future relationships and your self-worth. You must take inventory of your existing "superpowers" as well as his in order to save your own life and that of your kingdom – everything you've built from your finances to your relationship with friends to your business. Every small victory scores a point and gets you ready for the final battle. It's time.

As you read the following superpowers and power-ups you can use when encountering a narcissist, complete the list. It's helpful to take inventory of both your strengths and weaknesses as well as the strengths and weaknesses of the narcissist. I've made an example list to help guide you as to what types of items would be best to place on the list.

An Inventory of Your Weaknesses.

Narcissists prey on these to ensure they keep you hooked in the relationship. Knowing your weaknesses will be helpful to learning what is being triggered when the narcissist attempts to "battle" you in any way. Once you learn what weakness is being triggered, you'll have an accompanying strength to combat it. List your own – at least ten.

For example, some of my weaknesses in past relationships might include the following:

- **My empathy for the narcissist** - I empathize with the narcissist, yet this makes me vulnerable to his or her attacks and the honeymoon phase of the abuse cycle because narcissists often fake emotions or feel shallow emotions.

- **My "love" and compassion for the narcissist** – Much like my empathy, my love and compassion gets me in trouble when it comes to the narcissistic abuser. The problem is that my happy memories with the narcissist are skewed because they were shared with a person who did not really care for me – so really what I am acting on is a love for a person who was a mask that hid the narcissist's true self, an imitation of who the narcissist really was.

- **My past** – The traumas of my childhood have "primed" me for narcissistic abuse. The narcissist works on my deepest fears of abandonment from childhood to keep me in the abusive cycle and working to please him or her, despite how badly he or she mistreats me.

- **Sexual chemistry** – The narcissistic abuser and I share a strong sexual chemistry that is unparalleled due to the traumatic and biochemical bonding discussed in Chapter 2. Connecting physically with the abuser often restores the relationship back to the original state. Essentially, it's like pressing a reset button.

An Inventory of Your Strengths

What are your strengths? We all have them. These are the badass qualities that ultimately make you a narcissist's worse nightmare. Some of them are the same weaknesses that make you susceptible to his or her traps. For example, some of my strengths, which other survivors also share, are listed below:

- **My empathy for other people besides the narcissist.** Empathizing with others is a gift, something the narcissist lacks and many narcissists wish they could feel. I can use my empathy to share stories with other survivors to help them. I can use my empathy to stop feeling jealous of the other people the narcissist triangulates me with and realize it is not their fault – they are also a victim/puppet just like me. I can use my empathy to connect more deeply with other people on a level the narcissist can't, creating social networks and relationships that the narcissist doesn't have to be a part of. This can make me stronger and able to leave.

- **My ability to use any situation and channel it into the greater good.** I can transform any adversity into incentive and I have been known to make incredible comebacks from trauma. That means I can use any painful experiences I have with the narcissist as fuel, as motivation, as a source of knowledge and wisdom – in order to give back to the greater good and speak more knowledgably about narcissistic abuse. My ability to yield this superpower allows me to transform any superpower the narcissist has used against me as a tool for self-transformation and changing the world. Every time I help another survivor with what I've learned from narcissistic abuse, I've spread more light in the world to combat their darkness.

- **My sense of humor, even during the darkest of moments.** Although laughter certainly has its time and place, I've always been able to use my sense of humor to "lighten the load," so to speak, on my journey of trauma. Viewers of my YouTube channel can attest to the fact that I try to be lighthearted whenever I can, while still acknowledging the seriousness of narcissistic abuse and validating the damage it can cause. This has enabled me to stay in touch with my humanity even when experiencing great darkness. It has also permitted me to see the narcissist as a predator whose antics are often absurd and comical.

- **My thirst for knowledge.** I don't take things at face value and I am always seeking to better understand my experiences as well as the intentions and motivations of other people. I've been researching narcissistic abuse for quite some time and I am now in touch with the reality of the abuse. Due to this, I'll rarely be satisfied with excuses for abuse or kid myself into thinking that an abusive incident wasn't abuse. Being educated on the narcissist's schemes and tactics allows me to step back from the abuse and see the narcissist for who they truly are rather than who they pretend to be.

The Narcissist's Strengths

- **Able to target your weak spots without remorse.** Narcissists and emotionally abusive partners spend a great deal of time "researching us," especially during the love-bombing phase when they are sharing their secrets with us and compelling us to share our own with them. They create customized "programs" if you will for each victim, which enable them to bring into conversation the very things that they know will hurt us the most, in a way that is covertly manipulative and abusive.

- In the same way they placed us on a pedestal by learning what we love to hear and what we've always longed for in a romantic partner, they also know how to thrust us off the pedestal and devalue us in the cruelest ways possible. They know your insecurities, your worst traumas, and your worst fears. Nothing is off limits for the narcissist. Without empathy, they feel no need to censor themselves or hold back on the strategies they've constructed to defeat us.

- **Charming façade to the outside world.** When you are planning to leave the narcissist or try to detach from him or her, be prepared for the voices and opinions of the outside world to interfere. Narcissists often spend much of their lifetime building a great image for themselves and victims often do not find validation for their decision to the leave the narcissist aside from a support network of fellow survivors. It is important to have a supportive counselor as well as a community of survivors to turn to when the voices of the outside world hinder our inner guidance.

- **Their instinctive knowledge of human behavior.** Narcissists and sociopaths have an advantage in that they have spent their whole lives studying others from a more emotionally detached perspective. They have spent time analyzing and researching what makes other people tick because they had to learn how to imitate human emotions. They understand what it takes to traumatically bond their victims to them and therein lies their ability to use their own unpredictable behavior as a "hook" to keep you anchored in their abuse.

The Narcissist's Weaknesses

- **Despite their air of grandiosity, narcissists hate and fear who they really are.** While many narcissists enjoy the fact that they have an upper hand over what they see to be "pitiful" empathic beings, deep down inside there are also many who despise their incessant emotional numbness and boredom. They are emotional vampires always dependent upon the lifeblood of their victims. They can only gain energy by being a virus to someone else's host. Their own energy is lifeless and they know it. They cannot generate their own power or energy. They fear how abnormal they are and detest the fact that while they can pretend to blend in with the rest of society, they will never really be a part of it. Knowing how different the narcissist is – and not in the special and unique way they desire, gives us the upper hand as we can feel the full range of human emotions and love in a way the narcissist can't.

- **Indifference is their kryptonite.** Narcissists cannot stand indifference. Hatred, they can take, because it gives them confirmation of their power to control and provoke and bring their victims down to their level of misery. Love, they enjoy for a bit especially during the idealization phase, because it validates how convincing their false mask is. Indifference? Indifference means there's no power, no reaction, no ability to ruin someone's life or their day – the victim moves forward without so much as a second glance, and that kills them inside, because they've lost a source of supply that they can no longer toy with. The game can only run for so long, especially for somatic narcissists who will eventually age and lose their youth and beauty. As they become older, narcissists lose some of the power and pull they once held over their victims. Without any treatment for their symptoms, or behavior modification, the people that once looked up to them now despise them; karma has a way of giving them what they deserve tenfold, even if you aren't around to witness it.

- **Their shallow emotions are no match for the deep emotional connections we can forge with the world.** It is my hope that all survivors one day form a deep lasting relationship with a healthy partner. Some already have and I love to see happy letters from survivors telling me about their new, gentle, loving and respectful partner so different from the last – but it is my guarantee that they are all capable and deserving of happy, healthy relationships regardless of their relationship status now. Unlike the narcissist who is unlikely to go to treatment, we are gifted and blessed with the ability to empathize with others and meaningfully connect to others – including other survivors. Our voices are strongest when we rise together. Many victims I've heard from move forward into healthier relationships and marriages that last the rest of their lifetimes. Despite the experience of narcissistic abuse, we have the grand ability to change, grow and evolve in a way that narcissists who are often emotionally stunted at a very young age, cannot. We have a power that they do not have. We are really the special and unique ones.

Build Your Immunity

Growing up, I loved watching the show *Charmed*. This show was about three badass sister witches who used their superpowers to vanquish demons, all while battling the normal human struggles of love, work and family. The show was inspiring and empowering to a teenager like myself who often wished she had magical powers to navigate her own traumas and bad guys.

At some point, I realized why I was so addicted to this show: being a Charmed One meant kicking ass no matter how big or bad the demon, creating "spells" that transformed less than ideal circumstances into something that could serve the world, and striving to follow your destiny no matter what.

This is what we have to do when we battle any toxic person in our life. We have to resolve to kick ass and build our own emotional, spiritual, and intellectual resilience. We have to "cast spells" in the sense that we must rewrite the story the narcissist has written for us – what any bully has written for us in our lifetime. Think of positive affirmations and mantras as your magical "spells" - building immunity against toxic bullies who attempt to tear you down.

We must rewrite our own narratives and recognize how extraordinary and unique we truly are, no matter what anyone else says or thinks. Building immunity to toxic people takes time, practice, persistence and commitment. We have to strive every day to continue forward with our destiny regardless of how many challenges we may face. We have to constructively channel our strengths as well as our knowledge of our weaknesses in whatever battle we may fight.

Here are some ways to start building your immunity to toxic people:

- Stop seeking their validation and approval. Validate yourself and congratulate yourself on a daily basis for every awesome thing you do.
- Start saying "no" to things you really don't want to do or don't have the time to do.
- Start standing up for yourself every time someone tries to bully you or put you down. It's not acceptable anymore.

- Have a sense of humor about your flaws and weaknesses while maintaining a balanced view of your strengths and values. That way, when someone tries to put you down, you can have a laugh instead of giving some toxic person satisfaction that they've hurt you.

- Use kickboxing or martial arts as a way to release pent-up anger towards the bullying you may have experienced in an abusive relationship or throughout your lifetime. Physically manifesting your power can go a long way in convincing yourself how powerful and strong you truly are.

- Spend enjoyable, pleasurable alone time and make it a non-negotiable part of your self-care contract. Whether it's a hot bath, a jog, a hot yoga class or time for writing, turn off your connections with the world and give yourself a "me" only date invite to something relaxing or somewhere new. Spend time with the most valuable person in the world – you.

Eradicating People-Pleasing Habits

Symptoms of being a people-pleaser include but are not limited to: saying yes when you really mean no, allowing people to trample all over your boundaries on a weekly basis without asserting yourself, and "performing" character traits or behaviors that do not speak to your authentic self. Can cause high blood pressure and stewing resentment that festers for years until the "last straw," at which point sounds of an explosion erupt. You're so tired of being Jekyll all the time you become the worst version of Hyde possible to let out all the steam that was simmering within all along.

Jokes aside, people-pleasing is becoming a sad epidemic in our lives, and it's not just restricted to peer pressure among teenagers. We've all done it at some point, and some amount of people-pleasing might even be necessary in contexts like the workplace. However, people-pleasing can be a difficult habit to eradicate if being compliant is something we've been taught is necessary to avoid conflict. Think of children who grow up in abusive households: if they're taught that whenever they displease authority figures they will be punished just for being themselves, they may be subconsciously programmed to navigate conflict similarly when it comes to future interpersonal relationships.

Adults can engage in people-pleasing to an unhealthy extent, to the point where they engage in friendships and relationships that don't serve their needs, fail to walk away from toxic situations, and put on a "persona" rather than donning their true selves because they are afraid of what people will think of them. This can keep us in overdrive to meet the needs and wants of others, while failing to serve *our own* needs and wants. People-pleasing essentially deprives of us of the ability and the right to engage in healthy self-care.

People-Pleasing, Abuse and Self-Care

People-pleasing, of course, becomes more complex in the context of abusive relationships where the dynamics are so toxic that it's difficult for survivors to simply walk away when faced with cognitive dissonance, Stockholm syndrome and gaslighting. At this point, it's no longer just people-pleasing, it's the misfortune of being caught in the midst of a vicious abuse cycle.

However, people-pleasing *does* make it easier to ignore the red flags of abusive relationships at the very early stages especially with covert manipulators. We can also become conditioned to continually "please" if we're used to walking on eggshells around our abuser. This is why knowing our own boundaries and values is extremely important in order to protect ourselves and listen to our intuition, especially when it's screaming loudly at us. Minimizing people-pleasing is also vital in the process of going No Contact with our abusers.

Part of healing is reframing the way we think about pleasing others versus pleasing ourselves. Here's a revolutionary thought: what if I told you that your needs and wants were just as important as the people you were desperately trying to please, if not more? What if I claimed that your entire existence – your goals, your dreams, your feelings, your thoughts were in some way valid and needed to be addressed? Just as valid as the friend you're trying to impress or the parent whose approval you seek?

People-pleasing and Rejection

We *all* seek approval at times and many of us fear rejection if we dare to show our authentic selves. By trying so hard to avoid rejection, we end up rejecting ourselves. The problem arises when this becomes a consistent habit and leaves us vulnerable to manipulation, exploitation and codependency. When you're not honoring your authentic self, you're depriving others of the chance to see the **real** you, the right to judge you on your own merits and not the persona you perform.

Remember that rule on airplanes about parents putting on their oxygen masks before they put the oxygen mask on their children? Well there's a simple reason for that – we have to take care of ourselves first before we can take care of others. If we exhaust our own reserves to the point where we have nothing left, we won't be helping others at all.

The first step to minimize people-pleasing is to radically accept the realities of how inevitable rejection is. We cannot and should not try to please everyone. Some people will like you. Some people will dislike you. Others will outright hate you for their own reasons and preferences. And guess what? That's okay. You have the right to do it too. You don't have to like everyone or approve of everyone either. You have your own preferences, judgments, biases, feelings and opinions of others too. Don't be afraid of that, and don't fear rejection. Instead, reject the rejecter and move forward with your life.

You cannot let people-pleasing detract from the real you – by working so hard to gain the approval of others, you inevitably risk losing yourself. You become a puppet led by the needs and wants of various puppeteers. In the most extreme cases, people-pleasing can cost you your mental health and take years off your life. So stop cheerleading bad behavior and start cultivating your authentic self!

Tools to Minimize People-Pleasing

Start to minimize people-pleasing today by getting together a list of your top boundaries and values which you will not allow anyone to trespass in intimate relationships or friendships.

You can use this boundaries worksheet to write down ways in which your boundaries have been crossed in the past and the actions you can take to protect your boundaries in the future: http://www.liveandworkonpurpose.com/files/Boundaries.pdf.

Here are some additional recommended readings on boundaries, values and people-pleasing which I hope will be useful to you:

21 Tips to Stop Being a People-Pleaser on PsychCentral
10 Ways to Say No on The Society for Recovering Doormats
12 Core Boundaries to Live by in Dating and Relationships on Baggage Reclaim by Natalie Lue
Five Ways to Build Healthy Boundaries on WritingThrough Life.com
Different Types of Personal Boundaries on PsychCentral
10 Ways to Practice Positive Rebellion on AllisonCrow.com

Recovery from Rejection

Rejection can send us spinning in ruminations over our self-worth and desirability. Whether you were rejected from a job, within a relationship, a potential romance, or a friendship, rejection can threaten our sense of self-efficacy, self-image and self-esteem if we don't learn to embrace and cope with it in healthier ways. Rejection can also maximize people-pleasing because we may feel like we are at fault for it and must try harder to win someone else's approval. Rejection by a narcissistic abuser? Forget about it – the likelihood of trauma makes our cognitive distortions about rejection even worse.

Here are some crucial ways we can develop a healthier relationship with rejection and cope with it in productive ways. I call it the "Three R's of Coping with Rejection."

The Three R's: Challenge the Rumination, Redirection to Something Better and Rejuvenating a Sense of Self

1. Challenge the Rumination

Challenge your irrational thoughts and beliefs. Rejection makes us vulnerable to cognitive distortions, inaccurate thoughts, or beliefs that perpetuate negative emotions. When we feel rejected by others, we may engage in "Black and White" distortions where we perceive ourselves or the situation as "all bad" or "all good." We may also participate in *filtering*, where we exclusively focus on the negative details of an event rather than the positive ones. Most likely, rejection will lead to some amount of *personalization* where we attribute the blame of someone else's negative toxic behavior to ourselves, as well as *overgeneralization*, where we interpret one event of rejection as evidence for a never-ending pattern unlikely to change.

Our "explanatory style" of how we respond to people who reject us, especially if they are abusive or toxic is important to our well-being. Whether we see these events as proof that something is wrong with us, or as proof that whoever has rejected and mistreated us has something about them that is incompatible with our needs and wants, is paramount to how we approach life moving forward.

What do you think happens when you carry around these false beliefs about rejection being equal to your self-worth? Most likely, you end up with a partial or full-on self-fulfilling prophecy, because cognitive distortions tend to affect our perceived agency in navigating constraints and opportunities in our daily lives. If we think we can't do it, we often don't even bother trying – we don't get the job because we don't believe we're qualified to even apply for it.

We don't achieve healthy relationships if we believe we're not good enough. We may end up having a never-ending pattern of bad luck in relationships because we sabotage ourselves in ways we may not even be aware of and maintain connections with toxic partners. **Rejection can**

prompt us reject ourselves under these false assumptions and subsequent actions.

Try this exercise. Start by writing down a list of ten negative, false beliefs you hold about yourself, the power of rejection, and its connection to your perceived self-worth. These can include beliefs like, "Rejection means I am a bad person," "If someone rejects me, it means I am not good enough," or "I need people's approval before I can approve of myself."

Next, write down ten reevaluations next to these beliefs. These include thoughts that challenge the beliefs or provide evidence against it, like, "Rejection is about the other person's expectations and preferences, not about my worth as a person," or "I can feel good about myself regardless of someone else's perception of me." If it proves helpful, try to think of examples where these challenges were true. For example, you might think about how someone else's expectations for a relationship differed from your own and shaped his or her rejection of you (or more accurately, the relationship itself).

Or, more importantly, you might remember a time when you yourself rejected someone, not because of his or worth, but because of your own needs, wants and preferences. Putting yourself in the rejecter's place enables you to gain a broader perspective that resists personalizing the rejection and helps you to move forward. You're essentially reminding yourself that everyone, at some point, gets rejected by something or someone, and it's not an experience exclusive to you or indicative of how much you're worth.

2. Redirection to Something Better

Rejection doesn't have to be a negative thing – it can be a positive release of your efforts and energy, and a redirection towards something or someone more worthy of you. What are the ways this specific rejection has freed you? Have you gotten laid off from a job and now have the opportunity to work on your true passion? Has the ending of a relationship enabled you to take care of yourself more fully and opened up time and space for friendship, travel, and new career prospects?

For every rejection, make a list of new opportunities and prospects that were not available to you prior to the rejection. Whether they be grandiose fantasies of what could be or more realistic goals, this will help train your mind into thinking of the infinite possibilities that have multiplied as a result of your rejection, rather than the limiting of possibilities we usually associate with the likes of rejection.

3. Rejuvenation of the Self

Remember there is only one you, and that a rejection of your uniqueness is a loss on the part of the rejecter. We've heard this phrase, "There is only one you," time and time again but what does it really mean? It means that your specific package – quirks, personality, looks, talents, dreams, passions, flaws – can never be completely duplicated in another person. You are unique and possess a certain mixture of qualities no one else on this earth will ever be able to replicate even if they wanted to.

Embracing our uniqueness, while depersonalizing rejection, enables us to remember that rejection can be a redirection to something or someone better who can appreciate us fully.

Whoever rejected you has ultimately lost out on your uniqueness – they will never again find someone exactly like you who acts the way you do and who makes them feel exactly the way you did. But guess what? It means someone else will. Another company will benefit from your hard work, perseverance, and talent. Another partner will enjoy the beautiful qualities that make you you – your sense of humor, your intelligence and charisma. Another friend will be strengthened by your wisdom and compassion.

You are a gem, and you don't have to waste your precious time attempting to morph yourself into anything else just to get someone to "approve" of your unique brand. You are who you are for a reason and you have a destiny to fulfill. Don't let rejection detract from that destiny. Let it redirect you to better things. Let it remind you of how special you truly are, and let it rejuvenate your sense of self rather than destroy it.

Link: Be sure to also check out my video on "Why Rejection by the Narcissist is a Blessing" on my YouTube channel.

A funny thing happens when we begin to radically accept ourselves for who we truly are: we begin to see people for who they really are rather than attempting to fix them or please them enough in order to convince them to change.

Once we've started eradicating the bad habit of people-pleasing and started cultivating personal boundaries, we'll find it a bit easier to come to terms with some of the harsh realities of toxic people and their agenda. When we have a healthier perception of boundaries, we begin to practice a form of healthy detachment that counters the enmeshment style of relationships that often leaves us merging our identity with the identities of others.

Healing challenges us to accept 7 Inalienable Truths about Narcissistic Abuse, and to practice a healthy detachment - something that is indispensable to recovery.

Let's Recap: 7 Inalienable Truths About Narcissistic Abuse

Your partner is unlikely to change if he or she is a full-fledged malignant narcissist or sociopath. A sense of entitlement and false sense of superiority is intrinsic to a narcissist's disorder.

No amount of love, compassion or empathy on your part will cause them to change. A narcissist must want to change for himself or herself and it often takes a breakdown for that rare occurrence to happen.

There will be times when you reconcile the cognitive dissonance about your partner by romanticizing the good aspects while dismissing the abusive ones. Aside from trauma bonding, this is what usually keeps survivors in the cycle of narcissistic abuse.

In order to truly detach from your narcissistic partner, you will have to do the opposite: reconcile the cognitive dissonance by seeing the abusive self as the true self, and the good aspects as part of their charming, false self.

You may be addicted to your narcissist through biochemical and trauma bonding, which can cause relapse, but recovery and healing *are* possible. In order to move forward, you must continue to forgive yourself while still remaining committed to your goals.

Although there are universal steps and milestones many survivors go through on their journey, there is no "one size fits all" plan for healing, nor is there a timeline for when healing should magically end. We are always learning new things along the way, and healing and uncovering new wounds. Each survivor has unique needs and it is usually a combination of both alternative and traditional healing modalities that tackle mind, body and spirit that enable them to heal some of the trauma.

You are not alone, although you may feel you are at first due to the smear campaigns, the isolation and the alienation you feel,as well as the invalidation you may receive from your supposed support network and society. There are millions of survivors out there, just like you, and many are rising to speak up about their experiences and using them to rebuild a better life.

Congratulations warrior, you're well on your way along the healing journey. Let's explore some of the superpowers you can use to conquer battles along the way.

SUPERTECHNIQUES AND "POWER-UPS"

Opposite Action: The Power of the Unexpected

Narcissists expect their victims to be reactive to their manipulative ploys and endless provocations. They expect to have power and pull. What they *don't* expect is indifference, happiness, joy, security or determination from victims encountering their torment.

Opposite Action is a self-care technique I mention in my first book, The Smart Girl's Guide to Self-Care, and it's meant to change the physiological state of an individual through the simple science of engaging in the opposite action in order to change one's emotional state – the most famous example being smiling when you're in distress, which actually reduces stress and enhances mood (Paul Ekman, 1990).

When it comes to narcissistic abuse, opposite action can be used in multiple ways across various contexts. It can be challenging for victims to implement but if implemented correctly, this "supertechnique" can be very effective in reducing stress levels. How? Well, any time the narcissist, whoever they may be and whatever context you may encounter them in, attempts to use one of their tactics on you, you serve them a big heap of Opposite Action. Here are some ways you can do this:

If they're **stonewalling** you, expecting that you'll come after them anxiously, you sit still and use that silence as a way to indulge in self-care or do a pleasurable activity. Refocus on a task that you have to get done and turn off the phone. Read books about narcissism and narcissistic abuse; watch YouTube videos; reach out to a friend; meditate deeply; go out and do something fun. Do the opposite of what the narcissist expects you to do, which is to grovel and beg for his or her attention, and use it as a way to practice No Contact instead.

If they're **triangulating** you, consider giving them a blank expression and changing the subject or exiting the conversation altogether rather than giving them an outraged lecture. Instead of adding fuel to the fire, end the conversation or redirect it to something else. If they are triangulating in person and it's a stranger (meaning it's not someone they're actually having an affair with, because otherwise this is not recommended), exude extra warmth to the person they're trying to triangulate with or excuse yourself – staying classy will not only circumvent the narcissist getting supply, the other person will notice your respectful behavior, as well.

Self-care warrior tip: The best way to tell if a narcissist is truly triangulating you is if you're in a group. If they are connecting with someone else excessively in front of you, turn to another person in the group and begin engaging with them instead, ignoring the narcissist's interactions with the other person completely. You'll be amazed at how quickly the narcissist's head suddenly turns towards you and this new person even though they were so engaged before with their new source of supply. This proves that their engagement with the other person is simply for show – a way to increase your insecurity and make you battle for their attention.

If they're **hoovering** you, the narcissist expects that you'll fall prey to their pity ploys or accusatory remarks, breaking No Contact like you always did before. Rather than giving in, you delete and block them from all platforms, including social media platforms. When they hoover, you engage in Opposite Action and ignore, ignore, ignore. Engage in some laughter therapy or some yoga. Do a little dance and get yourself in a happier mood. Each hoover is a signal that the narcissist is losing control and knows it. It's narcissistic injury at its worst.

Mirroring

Dating coaches often talk about mirroring our dating partners so that we don't fall into the trap of overinvesting in someone who isn't emotionally available for a relationship with us. However, we cannot afford to mirror back the shallow positive side of the narcissist which is ultimately false; I suggest we mirror back the attributes that make the narcissist so compelling to us, mainly the "cold" phases where they show their true self.

With narcissists, this type of mirroring has a dual intention: it enables us to cut back on our own investment, but it also helps us to prevent more trauma to the system as we plan the eventual break-up if we are still in the relationship. By withdrawing from the narcissist when the narcissist withdraws, by also "mirroring" back the cold phase they subject us to, we save ourselves a great deal of energy by not chasing a shadow that will always escape our grasp anyway.

Using Silent Treatments or Abusive Incidents as Periods of Self-Care and No Contact

If you're currently still in a relationship with a narcissist and planning to get out, this one's for you. Narcissists consume our everyday lives with their long texts, their overbearing phone calls, their flattery and praise in the idealization phase of the relationship.

During the devaluation phase, however, they will give you silent treatments, stonewalling and emotional invalidation up the wazoo. During those silent treatments, it is important for you to also continue to mirror the narcissist by withdrawing from them, as well. Spend less time with the narcissist - limit the number of dates per week, limit phone conversations, allow calls to go to voicemails, and spend that time on your own self-care, with friends and family who appreciate you, and with projects that deserve your time and effort.

Make a chart, if you have to, of all the types of communication with the narcissist you're limiting, and to the amount of time you're limiting that form to. If you need more help on how to do this, I recommend reading Zari Ballard's *The Little Black Book of No Contact.*

If you've already gone full No Contact with your narcissist, congratulations! Just apply these same principles to ruminating about them or thinking about them, instead. Whenever a thought pops back up, or a rumination, or their cruel voice in your head, engage in an act of radical self-care instead: meditate for an hour, take a hot, steaming bath, or pour yourself a cup of hot tea while reading a good book. You deserve it.

Prioritizing Yourself as Revenge

Remember all the times the narcissist picked someone else or something else over you? The many times they triangulated you, made you feel unimportant, made your contribution to the relationship feel worthless? Yeah, it's time for some good old revenge. Prioritizing yourself will be crucial regardless of what stage of the healing journey you're in. It will include saying 1) No to the narcissist and 2) Yes to yourself, your needs, your goals, and your dreams. For all the times the narcissist chose to make you second place to something or someone relatively unimportant, this is your chance to finally treat yourself like number #1. In Chapter 5, you'll learn more about how prioritizing yourself plays a huge role in maintaining No Contact.

Future Projection

While I normally advise people to be mindful of the present moment, there's a time and a place to think about the future. Narcissistic abuse survivors are constantly going back from past to present, shifting rapidly from ruminations and recollections to the trauma that jolts them back to the here and now.

Projecting into the future means thinking about questions such as the following: 1) If this form of abuse continues and gets worse, as it often does, how will my mind, my body and my spirit be affected? 2) What goals, dreams or aspirations may be thwarted as a result of me being exposed to this form of abuse, based on what this narcissist has already ruined for me? 3) What will marriage and raising children with this person feel like if I continue in this relationship? Or, if you already have children with this partner, how will my children be affected emotionally and psychologically due to witnessing this abuse or experiencing it themselves? And, my personal favorite, which may surprise you, 4) What will this person look like when they are very old, bald and out of shape?

Remember – if you're dating an attractive, somatic narcissist who takes pride in his or her looks, those looks won't last forever and doctors haven't yet mastered the art of personality transplants. Sorry to break it to you, but if the narcissist is an ugly person on the inside, no external appearance will make up for it over time. You'll probably find that the narcissist became more and more attractive to you during the idealization phase, and then incredibly unattractive during the devaluation phase because their true self came out.

This is not a coincidence – a person's true spirit usually shines through whatever exterior they're projecting – so time will eventually uncover the narcissist's true self, and your future projection of that may help give you a well-needed reality check about what exactly to expect in the future. All the external assets will eventually lose their shine, but if you're dating someone with character and kindness, you'll find that they'll become more and more attractive to you over time.

Future Projection can also be used after you've already ended a relationship with a malignant narcissist by celebrating all the milestones that you never reached with them, that likely would have ended in disaster, depression and depletion of your resources. This means saying things like, "Thank God I never ended up with someone who always made me feel terrible about myself," or "Thank God I don't have to raise children with someone who probably would've used them as objects," whenever you find yourself romanticizing the abusive relationship.

If you're still having trouble with this idea of Future Projection, I recommend reading books by survivors who've had lengthy marriages and children with narcissists or sociopaths. My favorite book in this category is *Husband, Liar, Sociopath* by O.N. Ward, which paints a vivid, horrifying portrait of what it's like to sacrifice your entire life for a person who has no remorse.

Limiting Social Media

Narcissists love to provoke through social media posts, creating different false selves through statuses, photos, and comments; they love knowing that you can see them flattering new and old members of their harems, pursuing their exes, and triangulating you with shiny new victims. During the detachment phase, I recommend withdrawing from using social media to "stalk" the narcissist in any way. Chances are, if you're reading this book, you've already experienced enough of the narcissist's emotional and/or physical infidelity. No need to follow their crazymaking tactics. Deactivate your Facebook, uninstall your instagram, and take a break from Twitter if you have to. Trust me, over time, the relief will far surpass your need to "check in" with your abuser. It will also help heal your addiction to the narcissist.

Meditation and Yoga

I remember when I was dating my narcissistic boyfriend, I had won a raffle to attend an exclusive gym for free. During one of my free weeks, I took advantage of every type of yoga that was available in that luxurious gym. It was so powerful the way the yoga counteracted the effects of the abuse - even though I was still in contact with the narcissist during the time and was experiencing many of the red flags that he was abusive, I felt calm, collected and ready to handle the day each and every time. Applied to the No Contact journey, meditation and yoga will help to provide spaces where you can heal, process and come to better understand your own perceptions about the abuse. Both will allow you to recuperate during this period of detachment and keep your head on your shoulders.

Stop Rewarding Bad Behavior

If narcissists are emotionally like children, the last thing we want to do is give them candy every time they walk in our houses with dirty shoes. If your narcissist is hoovering you after discarding you horrifically, the best satisfaction would be to give them nothing but silence. Complete withdrawal and indifference is what destroys the narcissist and keeps them up at night. If your narcissist did not appreciate your presence, why not give them your absence? If you are dealing with a narcissist you can't avoid, don't indulge them in their grandiose fantasies. Stop giving them so much air time with your people-pleasing habits. Don't invest more energy than you need to. Every ounce you give the narcissist is energy you could be using to better yourself. Remember, it's time to idealize and supply yourself – not the narcissist.

Are they turning on ridiculous crocodile tears and the pity ploy to get you to stay with them – an act you've seen a million times before right after an abusive incident? Try not to laugh and tell them they're being way too emotional before packing up and leaving. Are they bragging about their latest purchase? Give them a blank stare and blink as if they've just grown three heads instead. Are they texting you about how much they miss you, while they have their new partner in bed with them? Screenshot the message to document it in case you ever need it, and then delete, block and forget. Resist the urge to give them a lecture, fall prey to their re-idealization of the relationship or triangulate you with their new source of supply. The game is over. Finito. No going back.

Quit the People-Pleasing and Reconnect with Your Authentic Self Every Day.

As we discussed in the section about people-pleasing, it's important to ask yourself the question every day, "What do I need today? What does my body, mind, heart and spirit need?" and do it, unapologetically. In Bronnie Ware's book, *Top 5 Regrets of the Dying*, she notes that her patients in palliative care had a common regret: not living a life true to who they really were, rather than who others expected them to be.

No matter how long or short life may be, it is truly worth pursuing your own authentic self rather than society's "bootleg" sugar-coated, watered-down version of who you ought to be. Take it from someone who's always been a bit of a rebel: I don't like doing things "traditionally" or going down a certain path just because it's considered the "normal" for most people. My life path is unique because I set it up to be that way and I decided to go after my dreams rather than doing what other people expected of me.

You might have days where you feel the world is against you. There are negative and cruel people in this world, and it seems the more you are victimized, the more negative events appear to follow like a domino effect. The world can be a hostile place for trauma survivors who are routinely retriggered by events and people who demonstrate the sort of cruelty that survivors have already experienced in the past. You might feel pressured to "harden up," "get over it," "move on," when you're not ready, or you may feel invalidated in your experiences, your choice of career, your decisions in work, family, and relationships.

The key is to find ways to stop seeking validation from the outside world and give the validation you really need to yourself. Start to create your own joy and be mindful of the things you are grateful for - even when it's just the basic things like your ability to see, hear, walk and the fact that you have food and shelter. Positive affirmations, meditation, exercise, writing, laughter, social connectivity with people who you trust and put you in great spirits - these are also great ways to pull the focus back to you and reconnect you with the divine self-worth that the world taught you didn't matter.

Documentation.

An abusive narcissist who also happened to be an alcoholic once stupidly harassed and abused me while drunk through Facebook messages. I saved all of these messages, of course, and while I would never release them, they served as potent reminders of why I was never going back. The lengthy pages of word salad, cursing at me, putting down women, demeaning my abilities, calling me names, all of which were unprovoked and came after an innocuous discussion about a comedy show - these would all ruin his reputation as a public figure in a heartbeat, sure, but for me, it was the act of documenting the act that really saved me a lot of misery down the road. Since he was quite charming and kind in public, it was one of the few sources of "proof" I had aside from my own accounts about his abuse. If I ever had any inkling of breaking No Contact or any urge to go back to the narcissist, I would simply consult these messages or talk to one of my trusted friends who I had shown them to.

Make sure you save any abusive texts, messages, e-mails, voicemails - not for the purposes of smear campaigning, mind you, but for the sole purpose of reference any time you have an urge to feed your addiction. In addition, this evidence can help you in court if you are in fact in a legal battle with a narcissist. Keeping in check with the harsh reality of the abuse, while traumatizing, can save you years of future heartbreak and dependence on these lethal people.

Journaling.

Journaling will be a great way for you to write your "shit list" about the narcissist, the crazymaking behaviors and words which kept you up at night and ultimately addicted to their pathological mind games. Your journal is a private space which the narcissist won't have access to so make sure you keep it out of sight in a place he or she would never look. Journaling about what happened during dates, inconsistencies, incidents of emotional and/or psychological violence, gut instincts and weird feelings will keep you in tune with your intuition and separate you from the gaslighting tactics of your abuser, grounding you in your sense of reality. To get a "No Contact" journal, you can visit zazzle.com/selfcarehaven* and begin tracking your journey.

Mantras and Positive Affirmations.

For those who feel stifled by silence or feel oppressed in a situation where silence is the best course of action, hear this: your voice matters and it will resound in the spaces and places where it is most important and most needed. Not with your abuser, but with other survivors and the world you were meant to leave an impact upon.

Traumas and conflicts are likely to feel threatening to our psyche. On harder days when we're struggling with addictive behaviors, self-defeating thoughts and urges to break No Contact, we can make the choice to meditate, reflect and look at ourselves compassionately. Rather than continue to invest or waste energy on the people and situations that are draining us, we can channel some of that energy into our own self-care, self-love and self-compassion.

As mentioned before, mantras and positive affirmations allow us to redirect our attention from ruminations and refocus on our inner power, strength and motivation. They help to reprogram distorted ways of thinking and perform important inner work that will enable us to achieve our desires, goals and dreams. You'll learn more about the superpower of positive affirmations in *Chapter 5: The Journey of No Contact*.

CHAPTER FIVE

The Journey of No Contact

Making yourself a narcissist's nightmare may be an easier task when it comes to cultivating your badass characteristics of strength, resilience and can-do attitude, but overcoming the addiction we develop to narcissists is an entirely new monster. How do you cure a drug addiction?

There's no simple answer. It takes consistent, daily effort and a healthy relationship with your craving. You may relapse multiple times. You may have to fall off the wagon to get back on it. The addiction we develop stems not only from a biochemical attachment filled from the oxytocin-craze we developed during the idealization and even the devaluation phases (remember when the narcissist immediately sprinkled in some physical affection in between devaluation sessions? Yeah. Intentional.), but also from low self-esteem, a low sense of self-worth and self-defeating behaviors akin to self-injury.

We break No Contact when we feel there is no other way to cope. We break No Contact because we feel we lack coping resources, even though there are plenty of resources available, online and even offline. We break No Contact because we have an illusion of control and believe that keeping tabs on our narcissist magically enables us to control the outcomes of their lives and the karma they're bound to face…right?

Whether or not your narcissist ever faces karma is not a question I am qualified to answer. Personally, I believe in karma and do believe narcissists will get their share of it, whether or not we get to see it. Many narcissists age terribly and somatic narcissists who once relied on their looks find that their supply is scarce and their remorse high. They are left with no authentic connections, let alone a sense of personhood. Hopefully, by that time, we'll no longer care, regardless and will have moved forward with our lives.

I also believe in a Higher Power, and I believe that preserving our own moral integrity means keeping people out of our lives who demonstrate a lack of it. However, the idea of karma may haunt us. We may never see justice served. Yet the only thing we have control over is ourselves. We control whether we break No Contact or keep moving forward with our lives, despite how difficult the struggle may be. We control how much we allow the trauma to disable us. We control what resources we utilize, what books we read, what forums we visit, what types of people we maintain friendships and relationships with.

Don't be fooled: you will always have the power to say no to this drug, no matter how many times you relapse or how challenging your journey has been. You always did have the power. Knowledge of your inner power is a crucial element of battling your drug addiction to the narcissist, for it really is a drug. Each dose of cyberstalking or texting serves as a temporary "fix" before we're back in the depths of hell trying to crawl out of the graves we've dug ourselves in after leaving. We've seen what cold, callous people they are, how they devalue and smear us to others, and yet we can't seem to stay away. The urge to get our next fix seems too great, too powerful.

The impetus behind addiction is the craving for our drug of choice. We must radically accept our cravings if we want to commit to our rehab. Does this mean acting upon our craving? Absolutely not! It means taking a nonjudgmental stance on our cravings. It means accepting that cravings will come and go. They will subside, and they will sometimes drive us to the brink of insanity.

Meditation Break

Try this exercise whenever you're facing the urge to break no contact. Sit with your legs crossed and your palms facing upwards. Close your eyes and take four deep breaths, elongating the exhale for a few more seconds each time. Imagine your craving as having an ebb and flow of sorts which follows the rhythm of each breath– there is a strong peak as the craving reaches its zenith – and then inevitably ebbs away as if it were never there, only to appear again.

Accept that this is the natural cycle of craving. Accept that all you can do is to allow the feeling to subside. Don't act on the craving. Don't self-injure. Don't self-harm. Don't reach out or react. Simply accept that this craving exists, that it may be here for a long time, that it may subside and then come back again. It's a natural cycle and it's even more difficult when first detoxing from the narcissist.

The Time Will Pass Anyway

Survivors may find it challenging to begin filling up the space that the narcissist once filled in their lives. Yet we have to understand that time will pass anyway; you may as well use that time rebuilding yourself rather than trying to mend a broken relationship built on a false foundation.

As you pass the time, be proactive and productive. Write on online forums for survivors about your cravings which will reinforce your No Contact regimen via encouragement of people who've been there. Contact your friends and family members who may be supportive and discourage you from contacting the narcissist. Distract yourself with pleasurable activities or immerse yourself in work. This rewards our brain's Behavioral Reward System (BAS) and makes us more optimistic about the future.

Whatever works for you, do it. Take a long walk. Wait at least one hour for the craving to subside. If it doesn't, keep looking for things to do. Refer to your physical documents which talk about your break-up and the unhealthy dynamics of your relationship, over and over again.

Reread them. Reinforce in yourself the image of the true callousness and cruelty that resided in this person you dated or married.

Know that this predator, whatever he or she is doing or whoever he or she is with, is still the same. They will not change. But you have. You will keep on changing. They don't know the new you yet. The new you is the real you, the one that has been waiting to emerge all along. The one who is not a drug addict. The one whose recovery is on its way. The one for whom the best is yet to come. For every addict, there is the hope of recovery. Even if you relapse, there is still hope and resources out there to assist you when you get back on the wagon. Accept your past relapses and commit yourself to a bright new future.

A future without the narcissist. A future which does not require the narcissist at all. A bright future in which new, beautiful people are waiting to meet you – new friends and potential love interests. New goals and new successes. A clean slate. Close your eyes again and take four new deep breaths. With each breath, imagine a new possibility. Will you have a new job? Will you get married someday? Will you do a new project? Maybe you are imagining that vacation you've been yearning to take. In your mind's eye, take it. You can see that future. It's so close. It's so achievable. Without the narcissist, you are truly free. This freedom has responsibilities, of course. You will no longer define yourself as an addict. You will no longer be defined by your addiction. You will develop a healthy relationship with your craving.

And most of all, you will start being the narcissist's nightmare when you stop being his or her supply. For the narcissist, too, is a drug addict with his or own demons…their drug is new and old supply. Their drug is attention and superficial relationships. Their drug is anything and everything that distracts them from endless boredom and emotional numbness. Do you wish to be an addict like them? Breaking No Contact to seek the drama-filled chemical upsurge of cyberstalking or texting or hooking up only to feel used once more? Didn't think so. So drop the bottle and have a seat. It's time to stop creating new scars and start healing the old wounds.

What No Contact is and what it isn't

No Contact (NC) is not a game or a ploy to get a person back into our lives; this technique has been misrepresented in many dating books and blogs. We should not desire to have people who have mistreated us back into our lives. On the contrary, No Contact is a way to remove this person's toxic influence so we can live happier, healthier lives while cultivating our authentic self and minimizing people-pleasing. As shown by the image above, No Contact is the key that locks out that person from ever entering our heart, mind, and spirit in any palpable way again.

Why We Establish No Contact in the Context of Abusive Relationships

We establish No Contact (NC) for a number of reasons, including preserving a healthy mind and spirit after the ending of a toxic, unhealthy or abusive relationship or friendship. NC gives trauma bonds, bonds which are created during intense emotional experiences, time to heal from abusive relationships. If we remain in constant contact with the toxic person, we will only reinvigorate these trauma bonds and form new ones. No Contact also gives us time to grieve and heal from the ending of an unhealthy relationship or friendship without reentering it. Most of all, we establish No Contact so that toxic people like narcissists and sociopaths can't use hoovering or post-breakup triangulation techniques to win us back over. By establishing No Contact, we essentially remove ourselves from being a source of supply in what is clearly a non-reciprocal, dysfunctional relationship.

How to Execute No Contact Effectively

Full No Contact requires that we do not interact with this person in any manner or through any medium. This includes in-person and virtual contact. We must thus remove and block the person from all social media networks, because the toxic person is likely to attempt to trigger and provoke us through these mediums by posting updates on their lives post-breakup. We must also block them from messaging or calling us or contacting us via e-mail. Avoid the temptation to find out about the person's life via a third party or in other indirect ways. Remove triggering photos, gifts and any other reminders from your physical environment and from your computer.

Always refuse any requests to meet up with this person and ignore any places the person frequents. Should the person stalk or harass you by other means and you feel comfortable taking legal action, please do so. Your safety comes first. If you are in a situation where you must remain in contact with an ex-partner for legal reasons or because of children, keep in low contact (minimum communication) and use the Grey Rock method of communication if this person has narcissistic (NPD) or antisocial (ASPD) traits. You can find out more about the Grey Rock Method by Skylar on Lovefraud.com or the 180rule.com.

I also highly recommend cutting contact with the friends of the abusive ex-partner if possible, as well by removing them from your social media sites. I understand you may have established great friendships with these people during the course of your relationship but if you did date a narcissist or sociopath, he or she has likely staged a smear campaign against you and you will likely not get any validation or support from these people.

Unfortunately, the narcissistic harem or fan club is ultimately convinced by the illusion and false self of the charming manipulator. Think of your ex-partner's "friends" (more like supply) as being kept in a *perpetual idealization phase with no discard* - they are not likely to believe your accounts of the abuse and may even be used by the narcissist or sociopath to hoover, triangulate, trigger or manipulate you in some way. It's best to cut ties with them completely and create your own support network that is separate from the abuser.

If your friends became enamored and reeled in by the narcissist and they refuse to believe in your accounts of abuse, go No Contact with them immediately. These people are not your real friends if they are more captivated by a stranger than by someone they've known all along. You've just been given a hidden blessing of knowing who your real friends are (who knows, they may even be narcissists themselves). Trust that if they are good people, they will see the mask slip in time, even if it takes years, and that your energy is better spent finding new networks that are completely separate from this person.

Sticking to No Contact

If NC is a struggle for you, there are many ways to ensure that you stick to it. Make sure you have a weekly schedule filled with pleasurable, distracting activities, such as spending time with friends, going to a comedy show, getting a massage, taking long walks, and reading helpful books such as *The No Contact Rule* by Natalie Lue. As I discussed in Chapter 3, you're going to need to create new reward circuits in your brain that have nothing to do with your narcissistic partner.

Take care of your physical and mental well-being by exercising daily, establishing a regular sleep schedule to keep your circadian rhythms in balance, doing yoga to help strengthen your body and relieve stress, as well as engaging in a daily meditation practice of your choice. I offer a Healing Meditation for Emotional Abuse Survivors on my YouTube channel, Self-Care Haven and Meditation Oasis (meditationoasis.com) is also an excellent resource for guided meditations. You may also experiment with alternative healing methods such as Reiki, acupuncture, or aromatherapy.

Do yourself a favor and look up online forums that relate to unhealthy and toxic relationships; joining such a forum ensures that you have a community and support network that enables you to remain NC and support others who are struggling just like you. It will also help validate some of the experiences you went through during the friendship or relationship with people who have also been in similar situations.

Do not resist your grief during this process, because you will have to face it at some point. The more you resist negative thoughts and emotions, the more they'll persist - it's a fact. Learn how to accept your emotions and accept the grieving process as an inevitable part of the healing journey. I recommend trying the grieving exercises and abiding by the No Contact rules in the book *Getting Past Your Breakup*, written by certified grief counselor Susan Elliot.

Most of all, develop a healthier relationship with your cravings to break NC by practicing radical acceptance and mindfulness to the present moment as we discussed earlier in this chapter. Remember that relapse may be an inevitable part of the addiction cycle and forgive yourself if you do break NC at any point. After practicing this self-compassion and forgiveness, you must get back on the wagon after falling off of it.

It is helpful to track your urges to break NC in a journal to curb acting upon the urges. Make sure that before you act on any urge, you give yourself at least an hour to collect yourself. It will get easier once you realize that breaking NC often bears no rewards, only painful learning experiences.

Links: See my videos for more <u>Tips on Maintaining No Contact</u> and <u>No Contact: Healing From Narcissistic Abuse</u> on my YouTube channel, located at youtube.com/user/selfcarehaven.

No Contact's Healing Power

The ending of an unhealthy relationship often leaves us reeling and feeling unable to cope. Even though we logically know we did not deserve the abuse or mistreatment, we may be tempted to stray from this when our emotions get a hold of us. As discussed previously, trauma bonds, bonds to people that are created through intense, shared experiences, often keep us tethered to the abuser, as well as other factors such as codependency, low self-esteem and feelings of low worth, which may have been instilled in us from the abusive patterns within the relationship or may have kept us in the relationship in the first place.

No Contact is a space for healing and reviving yourself, apart from the belittling influences of your former partner or friend. It is an opportunity for you to detach completely from the toxic person while moving forward with your life and effectively pursuing your goals. It enables you to look at the relationship honestly and productively from the realm of your own intuition, perceptions, emotions and thoughts, apart from the gaslighting, projection and manipulation of the former partner.

Remember that anyone who has treated you with anything less than respect does not deserve to be in your life, so NC helps you to resist the temptation to invite them back into your life in any manner or form. Many survivors find it helpful to track their progress on a calendar, blog or journal. You should celebrate and take note of your NC progress, as it is both a challenging and rewarding path to self-empowerment.

Narcissists love an audience. They crave any attention, positive or negative. That's why they tell provocative jokes, to send you into a tailspin. They love seeing the machinery in your head work as you struggle to defend yourself against their criticism and bullying. That's also why they love-bomb you, so they can later become the recipient of your reciprocating affections and love.

They love seeing how sappy you get with just a few of their lines and just a hint of their crumbs in the devaluation phase. It's all a ploy to maintain your attention while also using devaluation to deprive you of their own attention towards you. Sure, they will triangulate and bring in others to give them supply as well, but removing yourself as a source of supply is essential to becoming the narcissist's nightmare.

Once you take yourself out of the equation and maintain absolutely no contact with the narcissist - this includes looking them up on social media or finding out things about him from a third party – you free yourself as a potential source of supply and audience post-breakup.

Maintaining No Contact also has many beneficial results besides removing yourself as a source of supply:

You move forward in your own life. Without the tales of knowing what the narcissist is up to, or his or her new victims, you force yourself to move forward and consider the possibilities of meeting new people, trying new hobbies, working on existing and new goals. You carve out a space for the future where the narcissist no longer resides, no longer belongs and no longer can enter. In this projected future, *you* are the powerful one. You control who you invest in. You give more time to the most important person in your life – yourself.

You give trauma bonds time and space to heal. Ever heard of Stockholm Syndrome? Trauma bonds are very much at the root of Stockholm Syndrome. Narcissistic abusers know all about how these bonds work – even if they don't know the technical knowledge of how they work. They just know from years of experience with manipulating people that pain and pleasure create a bond stronger than pleasure alone. They sense that their hot and cold behavior will create that "frustration-attraction" experience Dr. Helen Fisher proved was the case. They're incredibly intuitive about what bonds their partners to them – the hot and cold cycle, the bodily contact, the rush of chemicals and hormones, the intermittent reinforcement, the pathological mind games. They've spent their whole lives mirroring others and faking empathy, so they have no problem convincing you that they are just like you and that they can change.

At the root of their idealization and devaluation cycle, they make sure to throw in just enough sweetness to throw you into doubt and question your diagnosis of them. Yet this sweet and mean cycle of abuse never fails to create a biochemical addiction and attachment to the very trauma that's being endured. By maintaining No Contact, you prevent new trauma bonds from forming, which they surely will if you are dealing with a narcissist.

Remember: a narcissist is the type of person that suddenly makes his or her social media posts public in an attempt to make you emotionally unstable post-breakup, with happy stories about him moving forward with new women (or men) and new successes. Please, don't believe the hype. These are all attempts to appear as the "winner" of the breakup, but we all know who the real winner is.

The person with empathy and conscience, the person who is capable of love, respect and compassion – that person is you. Narcissists live in a state of eternal boredom and no amount of success or sex is ever going to satisfy them. A male narcissist, for example, could have the most witty, engaging, beautiful, funny woman on their arm and he will still end up resenting how charismatic she is, how much of a failure she is at being a doormat, and how she takes away the spotlight from them because she's far too successful! Same for a female narcissist. They are never satisfied and they will constantly blame you for their dissatisfaction.

They will never be satisfied with what they have, unless they have a complete doormat that turns a blind eye to their affairs, crimes and indiscretions. And even when they do have that doormat, they end up abusing and exploiting that person regardless, treating that person with contempt for being so "foolish" as to believe in them. You're damned if you do and damned if you don't when it comes to a narcissistic partner. Do not feel envious of the new victim. They are now committed to a life of pain, suffering, and the shallow illusion of a relationship.

You leave yourself open to heal and move onto healthier relationships. Healing cannot happen if the source of the wound is constantly picked at and added onto. You cannot have the possibility of a new, healthy relationship in the future if you continue to keep tabs on your old one. This goes for any relationship, whether it's one with a narcissistic abuser or not. Do you think a healthy relationship partner won't be able to sense that you're still hooked on your ex-partner?

Think again! I've had a few "first dates" that never turned into second ones because I noticed right away that the individual began talking about their ex and their history. This is a clear sign of emotional unavailability, and sometimes even narcissism if they tend to smear their ex. While you may be able to hold it together in the first stages of dating, your insecurities, your wounds and triggers will inevitably come out. This may lead to rejection which is a normal aspect of life, albeit hurtful, and rejection at such an early stage of healing can compound existing wounds greatly. It's much better to wait, start healing rather than plunge right into the next relationship. You could be either scaring a healthy partner away, or gravitating towards another unhealthy one.

You can work on your dreams. Without dating an abusive partner, I had extra time and energy to write books, support other survivors, pursue my education, travel and live out my dreams. Think of all the time and energy you spent trying to get an abuser to change. Did it lead to any productive outcomes? No! Nothing except a learning experience. Now that you have all that extra time and energy, use it to fuel your dreams and make your goals come to life. That album you've been thinking of producing? Do it. The film you want to direct? Start it. That book you've been thinking of writing? Write it. That school you've been wanting to apply to? Apply to it. That job you've been searching for? Look for it. The possibilities are endless and there is no better time than now to accomplish all of your dreams and goals. Forget what the narcissist has told you about your competence, aptitude or skill set – remember that narcissists are often pathologically envious of their partner's assets and are constantly attempting to bring them down so that their partners don't surpass them. Well, now it's your time to shine!

You can help the community. You spent all that time supplying, engaging with and paying attention to a brain-dead jerk who likely only helped others in order to show off that he or she did it. Since it was a nonreciprocal, dysfunctional, abusive and non-normative relationship, you essentially performed charity work with all your love, generosity and thoughtfulness on someone who was inhumane and undeserving of it. Reconnect with the sides of you that the narcissist will never have – the compassionate side, the side with empathy and appreciation for other living beings. Give back to the community and reconnect with your humanity. What are some of the causes you care about? Many survivors find that after undergoing such a painful, traumatic experience as this, they want to give back to the communities that are suffering in a similar way – so they end up volunteering at domestic violence shelters, suicide hotlines, and some even become counselors, coaches and researchers themselves as a result of these experiences.

If you're comfortable, I recommend that you share your story with other survivors on online forums or private Facebook community groups you trust – this is not only extremely cathartic, it will add on to the knowledge of the larger community and validate the experiences of other survivors who have suffered similarly. Encourage other survivors to maintain No Contact while you're on your journey. Write blog entries and articles about what you've learned about narcissism. Recommend books and educational resources to others. If you have friends in emotionally abusive relationships, offer them a hand and a listening ear. Make sure they know you've been there. Volunteer to help with events that raise awareness about all forms of domestic violence. Donate to organizations whose missions you support. Give back to a community that really deserves it and needs it. It's a better use of your time and energy than giving too much to someone who will never be able to give you anything in return. Supply those who really deserve it and need it – and in doing so, you also supply yourself with a more enriching, fulfilling life filled with new support networks that likely understand your own struggles.

By establishing No Contact, you are ultimately staging your own victory and exploring your strengths, talents and new freedom with more ease. I invite you take the first steps to recovery and success by challenging yourself to at least 30 days of NC if you are doing it for the first time.

Then, once you've reached the 30-day mark, continue towards your goal of 90 days which is the recommended time for drug addicts in rehab. Keep a calendar to celebrate every day you've spent away from your abuser (or in Low Contact, if you can't go Full Contact).

Make sure to focus on what you have accomplished and not ruminate too much on judging yourself for where you think you are failing. Remember, those reward circuits in our brain need us to feed something other than the narcissist – so reward and supply yourself. A lot. You deserve it. Throw yourself a huge celebration at the end of each month by splurging on something you've always wanted to do – whether it's a spa day or a trip to a new country. I remember I used to have an actual celebration on the anniversary of my breakup with a narcissist because it reminded me I was free. Hell, I still do! No Contact or Low Contact is an accomplishment and it deserves to be celebrated.

No Contact or Low Contact will provide a detoxifying period where you can start to heal in a protective space of self-care and self-love, enabling your mind and body to repair itself from the abuse. Utilize the resources I've mentioned here in order to maintain No Contact and purge your life of the toxic influences you were once tethered to. The journey to No Contact is just the beginning, and the best is yet to come.

111 Alternatives to Breaking No Contact

Struggling with No Contact? Here are 111 Alternatives to Breaking No Contact whenever you get an urge to do so. From the silly to the productive to the downright weird, these actions can help you engage in what motivational coaches like Tony Robbins call **"pattern interruption"** – interrupting a pattern of rumination and obsession every time you get an urge to reach out to or respond to your narcissistic partner. You can use anything from this list or create one of your own – the content of what you do is less important than its significance and impact in your life, as well as its ability to constantly interrupt that pattern and anchor a new habit in its place.

I've drawn these methods from my own life, research and journey into No Contact in the hopes that it will help your journey!

1. Go for a refreshing walk or jog outside – without your phone.
2. Go to the gym and run on that treadmill. Release all the pent-up frustration and some endorphins to boost your mood. While you're at it, increase your social connectivity by challenging yourself to talk to at least three other people at the gym.

3. Walk in a circle five times around your room or as many times as possible. While walking in that circle, remember that all you're doing is continuing the literal cycle of abuse if you choose to reengage.

4. Brush your hair and count to 100 while doing so. When you reach 100, remember that you've probably had the same number, if not more, of arguments with your toxic ex-partner. Why add one more?

5. Take a hot shower. Or a hot and cold alternating shower. Not only is this rumored to boost your immune system, it's way more preferable and relaxing than the hot and cold tactics of a narcissist.

6. Record or write down what you want to say to your abuser rather than calling or texting them.

7. Shop online for clothes you need or books you want to purchase. Use your money to splurge on something you always wanted to buy – it's time to treat yourself.

8. Cook a new recipe. Cooking something new can be a "mindful" activity that prompts you to focus on adding the right ingredients. If you're not a good cook, this method works even better because you're focusing moreso on how not to set the kitchen on fire. It always works for me!

9. Call a validating friend to chat about something other than the narcissist (unless you're in need of a really good vent. Then chat away and afterwards, go back to work).

10. Text someone you haven't spoken to in a while to catch up. Do this if a narcissist hoovers you as well – instead of responding to the narcissist, you begin a new conversation with someone else. Use detachment from a narcissist as a way to connect with other people.

11. Do fifty jumping jacks wherever you are.

12. Put on your favorite energetic song and dance your butt off.

13. Sign up for a fitness class or browse online for one.

14. Write on a survivor's forum about your No Contact challenges and lend a listening ear to another survivor.

15. Meditate to soothing music like this track.

16. Look up a YouTube video of your favorite baby animal. Watch at least three videos.

17. Cuddle with a pet.

18. Don't have a pet? Go to a pet store and pet a soft animal.

19. Cuddle with a stuffed animal (yes, I know you have one. No need to be ashamed.)

20. Record a set of six positive affirmations and replay them over and over to yourself until the urge passes. "I am in control" and "I am the most powerful person I know" are two of my favorites.

21. Write the beginning or a chapter of a book – pick any genre you'd like to write about.

22. Write a synopsis to a book you'd like to write or even one you wish you could read. Get those creative juices flowing.

23. Download a new book on Kindle about something you always wanted to learn more about.

24. Watch a comedy or a non-triggering thriller.

25. Watch videos of skydiving or other dangerous activities.

26. Plan a tattoo you'd like to get and look up designs.

27. Think about a pleasurable childhood memory.

28. Look in the mirror and say, "I love myself," until the urge passes.

29. Listen to a new genre of music. Pro-tip: EDM music really helps clear your mind.

30. Catch up on the news.

31. Read articles or empowering stories about people in adverse circumstances.

32. Watch a TED talk on a topic you know nothing about or are interested in. Go to ted.com/talks.

33. Get up and do a long stretch.

34. Do yoga on a mat if you have one or sign up for a yoga class online.
35. If you have kickboxing gloves, use them to punch a punching bag. Alternatively, punch a pillow.
36. Make a cup of your favorite tea or coffee and wrap yourself in a blanket.
37. Read a good book.
38. Rewrite the lyrics to your favorite song.
39. Write a fanfiction based on your favorite television show or book series. Or, read fanfiction that's already out there.
40. Use any paint supplies you have to paint or draw a picture.
41. Write a poem.
42. Write a short story.
43. Write an unsent letter to your abuser declaring your best qualities. Do not send it.
44. Call or email your therapist and/or coach.
45. Watch a mind movie based on what you want more of in your life.
46. Play a game of Angry Birds or solve a puzzle. Choose games that are very visual. Tetris has been proven by research to reduce the symptoms of traumatic memories before they're fully consolidated, for example.
47. Download games you enjoy on your phone and start playing them.
48. Take four deep inhales followed by exhalations counting to eight.
49. In warm weather, take a trip to the beach.
50. In cold weather, build a snowman or sit in a cozy, warm café.
51. Go to a beautiful place and take pictures of it.
52. Write a blog entry on a subject you need to do more research on or a subject you already know well.
53. Leave a supportive comment on someone else's blog or YouTube channel.

54. Make your own YouTube channel or if you already have one, upload a video that can help someone.

55. Watch a reality television show – brainless entertainment can in fact be a great self-care activity when you find yourself overwhelmed with ruminations or too much work and too little play.

56. Pin pictures to your Pinterest board or start a brand new bulletin board, pinning pictures of what you want more of in your life.

57. Make a literal board in real life. Cut out pictures of things you want to put from magazines and paste them on your vision board.

58. Share a post of an interesting news story on Facebook.

59. Create your own survivors FB page or FB group. Or join a new one.

60. Follow survivor advocates on Twitter as well as motivational speakers. Tweet at your favorites.

61. Send a thank you card or note to someone. Gratitude enhances social connectivity and helps to lift your mood.

62. Go out shopping.

63. Buy a gift for someone.

64. Make a gift for someone.

65. Go to the library and browse your favorite section for books.

66. Take a hot relaxing bath with scented candles and your favorite meditation.

67. Visit someone who lives in a different city or state.

68. If you have a car, drive somewhere you can see a gorgeous view. Or take the bus.

69. Drink a glass of water. This helps to reenergize you and gives your immune system a pick-me-up.

70. Walk up and down the stairs until you feel tired.

71. Join a Meetup group. Go to Meetup.com to search for fun groups, activities and events in your local area.

72. Go to a Meetup event based on your interests and hobbies.
73. Take the train to somewhere you've never been.
74. Go to a free museum and check out their new exhibit.
75. Go to the zoo.
76. Take a long walk from your house to somewhere you usually take the bus.
77. Write a list about things you admire about yourself.
78. Write a list of accomplishments and miracles.
79. Draw beautiful designs on yourself using a pen.
80. Lift weights, or heavy books if you lack weights.
81. Play a sport, weather permitting.
82. Take a walk to your local park.
83. Go to your local church and sit in meditative silence or pray.
84. Go out dancing with a friend.
85. Go out to eat.
86. Say a prayer for yourself or someone else.
87. Write down a prayer you want to come true.
88. Make a budgeting plan.
89. Brainstorm a business you'd like to start. Then, write a name for the business and a rudimentary business plan.
90. Go to the grocery store to buy essentials.
91. Make a delicious smoothie out of your favorite fruits.
92. Clean out your closet and donate old clothes to Goodwill.
93. Sign up for a volunteer project around your area.
94. Plan a vacation. Find pictures of your dream vacation and pin it to your vision board or Pinterest board.
95. Write a letter to your favorite author.
96. Sign a petition for a cause you care about.
97. Record yourself singing.
98. Do karaoke with friends.
99. Play or learn to play an instrument.
100.   Do twenty sit ups.
101.   Do twenty push ups.

102. Count backwards from 100.
103. Say the alphabet backwards.
104. Go through a photo album filled with good memories that have nothing to do with your ex, online or offline.
105. Paint your walls your favorite color.
106. Go to the science section of the news and read something new.
107. Make a bucket list of things you've always wanted to experience.
108. Make a goal list for the rest of the week or month.
109. Create a "gratitude" jar and start putting in pieces of paper with things you're grateful for written on them.
110. Buy an intricate coloring book and color images in.
111. Say to yourself, "I am finally free and I deserve to stay that way" as many times as it takes before the urge lessens or passes away.

SELF-CARE WARRIOR CHALLENGE FOR NO CONTACT – *Self-Care Haven Coaching Exclusive*

Find one self-soothing activity you can engage in whenever you are triggered or stressed out when struggling with urges regarding No Contact. Here are some examples of self-soothing activities:

- Take a 20-minute walk to release endorphins.
- Listen to soothing music.
- Take a nice, long soothing bath with scented candles.
- Write or say a positive affirmation or mantra that calms you (ex. "I am safe." "I am loveable." "I am worthy." "I am valuable.")
- Attend a yoga class of your choice.
- Do a ten-minute meditation or listen to the meditation video provided in the beginning of the e-mail whenever needed.
- Cuddle a pet or looking up videos of cute animals.
- Watch a comedy stand-up or a funny movie.

Here are some powerful ways the examples above can work for self-care when you are being triggered by memories of your narcissistic partner. Think of this as a game - make it fun and not stressful. It's not about winning or failing. It's simply about gathering points. Every time you do a self-care activity, jot it down in a journal and give yourself a point for the day.

▶ **Choose one powerful mantra or positive affirmation you can use to ground and center you.** This is a statement that can counteract any anxiety you're feeling. Write it down on a piece of paper and carry it with you wherever you go. The trick is that you must feel comfortable saying it. Words like, "I am beautiful," "I am worthy," "I am calm," are powerful and true, but you must be willing to feel that they are true. Choose something you can say and feel the truth of as you say it. You may start with something like, "All is well," or "I am safe" before moving onto more specific affirmations.

▶ **Turn off your phone and all electronic devices for one hour.** Listen to soothing and calming music of your choosing and make sure you are not able to be disturbed. As an alternative, you may also wish to take this time to meditate, reflect, pray or engage in another type of spiritual practice. You may also wish to do nothing but observe your own breath. Whatever you choose, allow it to be a time with no distractions - a space and time carved out only for you and you alone.

Make no apologies or excuses for this act of self-care. Allow yourself to let go of other priorities and focus on yourself as a priority.

▶ **Do one type of physical exercise you truly enjoy.** You may wish to start by taking a brief walk and building up to longer walks over time. You may also wish to engage in a different type of physical activity. This could be yoga, jogging, dancing, kickboxing, taking a walk - it does not matter what the activity is so long as you feel rejuvenated and joyful after engaging in it, whether it be for thirty minutes or an hour and a half. Now is a great time to gather together a "joyful" playlist - an empowering playlist featuring music that makes you feel energized and ready to take on any challenge.

▶ **Play a game on your computer or phone that is visually demanding**. Research shows that when we play a game that involves a great deal of visual detail (such as a game like Tetris), we can block off centers of the brain that process pain and even prevent the number of traumatic flashbacks we have after a traumatic event.

▶ **Watch a video of your favorite comedian or watch your favorite comedy movie.** Look up parodies or funny channels on YouTube. Laughter helps us lower levels of the stress hormone cortisol. It is medicine for both the body and the spirit. Give yourself an excuse to laugh at least once every day.

▶**Indulge in pampering yourself with a soothing, hot bath.** While it sounds very simple, it's an effective self-care tool that helps to both nurture and pamper you. One of my favorite self-care activities includes taking a hot bath using scented candles while putting some relaxing meditation music or a positive affirmations audiotape. Being surrounded by water connects us back to a sense of safety and security. You can also use this any time you're feeling triggered or upset.

Use your favorite bubble bath and really allow yourself to relish the luxury of this experience. Give yourself permission to lay back and soak it all in. Listen to calming words, see the bright lights of the candles, smell the beautiful scents around you and feel the physical and energetic "cleansing" of your body. Even just an hour long bath like this does wonders to give you a much needed reprieve!

Releasing Self-Judgment

Do you know what one of the biggest setbacks of No Contact with a toxic partner can be?

It's not the relapses we may have, or the mistakes we make during the journey.

It's the self-judgment we put ourselves through when we feel we haven't taken care of ourselves as much as we should. We ask, "Why did I do that, yet again? I know better!"

Yet this lack of compassion towards ourselves can be detrimental to our recovery. Judgment leads to negative self-talk, which actually perpetuates the destructive behavior we're trying to break. We seek out the toxic partner as a source of comfort, ironically because we're ashamed or feel guilty. Part of the reasoning is that we figure we've already made the mistake and we're not worthy of trying to do better in the future.

So instead of observing the thoughts and emotions that led to the behavior, we start to judge our own thoughts and emotions instead. A more productive exercise would be non-judgmentally keeping track of times you've broken No Contact and what happened right beforehand - as this is a very useful exercise to better understand your "trigger points" and find an alternative to how you react to them in the future.

It's only when we have radically accepted our cravings, urges and setbacks that we can begin to make the necessary changes to ensure we have a better life in the future.

In the videos below, I talk about regaining power and control and how doing so is also about embracing the recovery process, flaws, relapses and mistakes - everything that seems imperfect, and yet is likely to surface on the journey ahead.

I hope this helps you re-frame anything that seems less than ideal that has happened this week - whether it's a rumination that doesn't go away or an urge you gave into - or even if it's just a sense of self-blame for the trauma that you've experienced.

You're not alone and you're not at fault. Narcissistic Victim Syndrome and Complex PTSD can lead to many symptoms - and judgment, shame and self-blame can be at the core of them due to the gaslighting, projection and put-downs we have experienced.

It's my hope that this knowledge will help you to practice more compassion towards yourself...because self-compassion is the root of recovery from any addiction.

REFLECTION TIME: To learn more about our judgment and lack of compassion towards ourselves, be sure to check out *From Toxic Shame and Self-Blame to Self-Compassion: The Survivor's Spiritual Journey* **on my YouTube channel, Self-Care Haven.**

What about in the case of co-parenting with a narcissist – a situation where contact is inevitable? Kim Saeed, bestselling author of *How To Do No Contact Like a Boss* and founder of Let Me Reach, a platform that aids millions of narcissistic abuse survivors around the world, shares her insights with co-parenting with a narcissist below.

Co-Parenting with a Narcissist by Kim Saeed

Is there really such a thing? Not really. There's "parallel parenting," which is more akin to sending your child off into another dimension while you are forced to let go of questionable goings-on over there. You have to find a way to release your need to influence when your children go to bed, whether or not they brush their teeth, or what they see on TV. Expect that there will be attempts at last-minute changes in the schedule and spontaneous cancellations from your ex. Even worse, the Narcissist being the sort of person he is, may be handing your children over to babysitters and blasé family members while he continues his agenda of securing new supply, partying, traveling, or he might busy himself in some other way simply because he can't be bothered to fulfill his parental obligations.

In other cases (or simultaneously), the Ex will try to continue his oppressive tactics of calling and texting at all hours, showing up unannounced at your residence, and forcing himself onto your property and into your home uninvited as if he is still very much a part of your life. And if you're not assertive enough, you'll stand aside, uttering a feeble, half-hearted protest, while you watch him bull his way into your child's room and/or rip their report card off of the refrigerator – blaming your child's "C" on *your* "below-standard parenting practices." Although it may go against your nature to insist that he not come into your home, this is of utmost importance if you want to gain any sense of freedom for your future and that of your children.

Being one step ahead of the narcissist is crucial in order to pull this co-parenting thing off successfully. It entails acting in ways you wouldn't even consider under normal circumstances – and not only towards the ex. You also have to develop the ability to stop obsessing about what's happening when it comes to your child being under the care of the Narcissist. (Please note – if you suspect any kind of physical or sexual abuse, you should report it to the authorities immediately).

First and foremost, it's essential that you stop trying to be nice to the narcissist. This approach might work with people who actually possess the ability to acknowledge and appreciate your generosity; but you are dealing with a Narcissist. When you try to be nice to him, he sees it as an invitation to keep taking advantage of you…and to continue his tyranny and dictatorship over your life.

If this is the parental situation that you find yourself in, then it's time to overthrow this oppressive regime and take your life back into your own hands. Following are some basic steps to stop the madness and begin experiencing a sense of stability in your life:

1. You don't have to answer the phone every time he calls. Let it go to voicemail and then determine if you need to respond. Most of the time when the Narcissist calls, it's to blame and shame you for some fabricated sin. If he's not doing it for purposes of exercising control over you, then it's done in order to look like a concerned parent in front of a new partner or even in front of your kids. Never mind that he hasn't paid child support for seven months and that he removed the kids from his insurance plan (no one knows about that except you)! You suck and they rule. That's the general order of the day when he reaches out to call. Why participate in that? If you do engage in conversation, hang up the moment the focus deviates from the kids or the Ex turns abusive. You can offer a warning the first few times, but simply hang up after that. No further explanation is needed.

2. Consider changing your cell phone number and require that they contact you by email. If you suffer from out-of-the-blue or semi-automatic text messages from the Narc that catch you off guard (or cause anxiety from never knowing when you'll be attacked), then try the following strategy. (I did, and it cut down on the stress and surprise attacks BIG TIME). Typically, you only have to provide one method for the Narcissist to reach you regarding your children. This could be a cell phone, a land-line, email, or even a court-supervised email system. Change your cell phone number and don't give the new number to your Ex. Let him contact you by a land line or email instead. The latter is especially nice since most everyone has their email set up to go to their phone, anyway. This way, you can read the email and decide whether you need to respond right away. It also cuts down on ambushes because emailing takes more effort. Texting, SMS, and messaging platforms are venues that allow the Narcissist to attack at will. Cut out those options for him. Of course, he will throw a hissy-fit, but who cares? Not only will it decrease the number of stealth attacks by the Narc, you will also have some nice email documentation to present to the court if you ever have to file a harassment order or simply want to demonstrate his instability to your attorney.

3. Let today be the day you decide he doesn't walk through your door <u>ever</u> again. Your home is supposed to be a place where you feel safe – it's your haven, your sanctuary from the world. Don't allow him to continue to desecrate your sacred space. You have every right to demand that he no longer enters your residence. Notify him that you have made this decision. If he attempts to disrespect your request, inform him that you will notify the authorities if necessary. Then, follow through. Feel the fear, and do it anyway. The purpose of doing this is not only to implement a new way of life for you, but also to eliminate the under-handed tactics often employed by the disordered personality to stay in your head and keep you feeling off-balance. These tactics might include planting spyware on your computer and/or in your home, stealing heirlooms and other valuables (including cash), or raiding your home in search of evidence of a new partner, which is absolutely none of their business.

4. Don't feel that you have to go along with their requests for schedule changes. Does your Ex often make last-minute plans that don't involve the kids – during *his* time with them – and want you to jump in and smooth things over? That's not up to you. Even if you'd prefer to have the kids with you on these occasions, don't allow your Ex to get into the irritating habit of expecting you to be on board when he decides his parental obligations aren't important. If you agree to do it once, it will become a regular part of your life going forward. These schedule changes not only upset your kids' routines, they open the door for your Ex to continue taking advantage of you. If you do make any exceptions, then it should only be in the event that the Narcissist is experiencing a *confirmed* illness or injury. Are they claiming that they've broken a toe-bone? Been diagnosed with a crippling disease? Request documentation from the hospital. Lastly, your Ex needs to make their personal plans during the times your kids are *with you*. Not the other way around. If you cave each time this happens, it makes it more difficult for you to have a case in the event you want to file for a modification of custody later. Don't set yourself up for that.

5. Document everything. It's important to document *everything* in shared custody situations with a narcissist, and you don't need to tell him you're doing it—even when your guilty inclinations arise. Record all missed visitations, requests for schedule changes, missed doctor's appointments when your kids are with the narcissist and photograph any physical injuries your children may come home with. Share this information with your attorney if you believe the situation requires a modification of the custody arrangement you have with your Ex.

6. Summon the Law of Attraction when it comes to your kids. It's easy to fall into the insanity of obsessively wondering what's happening with your kids while they are with the Ex. Create a vision board and place index cards on it with quotes such as: "_____" (insert child's name) is always safe and healthy; "_____" knows I'm a wonderful parent; "_____" is always happy. Write down whatever is applicable and relieves your anxiety. In spite of your worry, try to visualize your kids being nurtured and loved. Place happy pictures of them on or near your vision   board.   Place   their   well-being   into   the   hands   of

God/Source/Divine Intelligence and be the best parent you can possibly be when they are with you. Embrace what you *can* control and let go of what you can't.

It's important to remember that you have to deal with a Narcissist in a different way than you deal with others. You want to be fair, do unto others what you'd have done unto you, and all of that. The problem is that these normal principles of human decency don't work with Narcissists! You must implement a different set of rules with them and learn not feel guilty about doing so. Remember, you wouldn't be forced to do all of these things if not for who *they* are. Stand up for yourself and your right to a calm and predictable environment inside your own home.

One last bit of advice about co-parenting with a disordered Ex - don't talk badly about him in front of your children. They will eventually see your Ex for who he is, anyway. When a parent talks badly about their Ex to their children, it causes frustration, confusion, and resentment in them. We need to be the shining example of maturity and emotional control because our children are already dealing with enough turmoil. That's not to say you should never show any emotional reactions in front of your children. We're only human, after all, and we should let our kids see that emotions are a natural part of being human. But we should be mindful to express our emotions in a way that doesn't make us look bad as their role model. Then, when you're in a private setting with a trusted friend or family member, you can say all you want about what an epic loser your Ex is if it helps relieve your stress.

Below, I share some tips from other survivors of narcissistic abuse who have had to co-parent with a disordered ex:

Tips from the front line (other survivors):

- *My suggestion for 'co-parenting' with a narcissist is this — find a good lawyer and file for divorce — find a good counselor for yourself and your children — and then just let yourself heal.*

- *I set up a monitored email after being harassed by texts, emails and phone calls even though we have been divorced for almost 2 years. I no longer have to deal with his 2,000 word rants. He is also only allowed to email once a day with an emergency over-ride stated in subject line if need be. By bringing in people to help, he has become a perfect little angel. It has slowed him down and put him in his place. The funny thing is that I hadn't been responding to his rants for over a year, but now those same words were being said back at him and it put him in his place. I am just thankful I have found something that is working. I literally thought his harassment was going to kill me. I don't know what I would do without my support group.*

- *After two years, what I refer to as "counter-parenting" is becoming abnormally normal… My ex decided that if I needed to give him information, I would have to call him personally (he canceled his texting plan and claimed he no longer knew how to email)… I didn't cave - I write info notes about dr visits, illnesses, date it/ sign it/ cc to file, and stick it in the kid's travel bag. I have lived to regret every time I have let my "niceness" get me suckered into doing something. I am still very much working on thinking what is the best for the kids, as they come home displaying signs of emotional and sexual abuse…that is another issue in itself.*

- *I have done everything, attorneys, judges, police, mediators, etc. He always runs his game on them. I finally, DON'T CARE! They will always be my children, they know I love them. I am the safe place, Daddy is crazy town. He has these kids so angry, they don't WANT to be with him now, whose fault is that? He always insisted on having his way, now he is hanging himself with his own rope.*

- From a male victim - *I have blocked all communications but one…and I just let my Narcissist ex leave a message. Kinda helps. She still can't go a week without a phone call (or three). Most are ignored which drives her insane…but her issues aren't related to our kids. The court orders are not favorable to her and she is always trying to change them. I can't let her email me because she writes novels…then her husband kicks in and writes harassing emails. I literally have three binders full of her emails.*

In closing, it's important to keep in mind that the ultimate power trip for a Narcissist is to be the most important person in your life, even more important than your own children. This seems to be especially true if you form a relationship with them and you already have children from a previous marriage or relationship. If you have older children, it's not uncommon for the Narcissist to try to convince you that you have spoiled your child(ren) and that they need to move out and learn to live on their own.

Don't fall for this scam. The Narcissist does this for numerous reasons such as wanting access to financial resources that you may offer your children, not wanting to be bothered with caring for another individual within the household, and, sadly, to see if they can push your boundaries past all reasonable limits, such as you kicking your own children out of the house. The result will be that your relationship with your children will be damaged indefinitely and you'll be left with a very dysfunctional relationship with a Narcissist who will never offer even a morsel of common decency.

Remember, you cannot control the narcissist's actions—only your own. The best you can do is show your children how much they're loved and be the emotionally competent parent since they won't get that from the narcissist. Minimize contact as much as possible, do not engage, and try to communicate via email or text only. Phone calls will only lead to "he said, she said" if you ever have to go back to court.

About the Author

Kim Saeed is a recognized relationship and narcissistic abuse recovery expert. Her articles, interviews, and guest appearances assist victims, survivors, and thrivers world-wide. She has influenced people from all over the globe by helping them leave their unhealthy relationships, overcome their limiting beliefs, and empowering them to rise above their destructive patterns so they can live the joyful lives they deserve.

Kim released her first book in March 2015, and it quickly rose to best-seller status. *How to Do No Contact Like a Boss!* explains the reasons for going No Contact and takes the reader from the initial planning stages, exit strategies, the moment of No Contact, what to expect in the days that follow, and how to deal with a persistent and/or abusive ex who refuses to respect one's request for No Contact.

Social Media Platforms

Website: http://www.letmereach.com
Facebook:
http://www.facebook.com/LetMeReachwithKimberlySaeed
Twitter: http://www.twitter.com/kimsaeed

Shahida here again. While I highly encourage people to speak out and speak up about their stories, I find that with a narcissistic abuser, silence can be the most powerful voice. A manifesto of mantras/positive affirmations for No Contact follows. Read them aloud whenever you feel the urge to break No Contact or whenever you need strength during a time of distress.

Mantras/Manifesto/Positive Affirmations for No Contact: Why Silence Can Be the Most Powerful Voice

My silence does not mean my endorsement of your cruelty nor my defeat. My silence often speaks more volumes than my wasted energy. Instead of attempting to argue with a fool, I will regroup, I will channel my hardship into fuel, I will refocus productively and as always, when least expected, I will make an even bigger comeback than the last, because that is what I do best and I will continue to do it. I will continue to speak my voice where it is counted, not discounted. I will continue to change the world with my voice. And yes, my voice will resound in the places it deserves to be heard.

I choose, every day, what I put my energy into. I can choose to waste time on the people who bring me down or the beautiful ones that raise me up. I can choose to meditate and reflect rather than absorb the choices of others. Their actions do not take away the good I have left to give to the world. Every day, I make my choices as if I truly, unconditionally love myself. In times of darkness, uncertainty, and struggle, I return to that self-love. In times of psychological warfare, I will fight for my right to peace of mind and happiness. I will win. And in doing so, I will inspire in others the courage to do the same.

Only I can define myself and I choose to define myself with power, strength and resilience. What I crave is only my addiction and my mind's mirage, but who I really am is who I choose to be. I choose to listen to myself, my intuition and what my inner guidance tells me. Despite the dark voices of others, I choose to remember who I really am. I am a force of great light, power and my divine inheritance is love. I am a survivor, I am a warrior, and I have made myself greater by the struggles that have shaped me.

I choose to re-channel my strife into my success, my crucifixion to my resurrection, my chaos into catharsis. Each obstacle is a portal to a wound that can find healing. Adversity is an opportunity for transformation and every crisis offers new knowledge for an awakening. I fought hard to live, thrive and transcend. I fought hard to establish myself and to achieve my dreams.

No one can take away from me what I have worked hard to build. No one can take away who I really am or the love I have within me. I choose to pursue all my dreams and the life of joy I truly deserve. I no longer hide myself in the shadows. I use my silence towards my abuser as a powerful key to freedom, and I use my voice with the world because I am now truly free. I am worthy. I am valuable. I am loved. I am precious. I am brilliant. I am beautiful. I am powerful. I am seen. I am heard.

Hear the audio version of this manifesto on my YouTube channel at youtube.com/user/selfcarehaven.

Survivor Insights

Surviving No Contact

Question: Have you gone No Contact with your narcissist? Have you had any relapses?

"Although I have not had any relapses (believe me the five other women did it for me - and those are just the five whose names I actually know). Where there is smoke there is fire. However, I did make an initial error. I did not understand that the narcissist keeps his constituents and his harem in place for triangulation purposes and continued abuse. So in the early stages I did continue to communicate with and even meet with a few girlfriends we had both known. It was not for months afterward that I realized I was technically not in zero contact since his minions were doing the recon for him. At that point I went zero contact with all minions, harem members and associates of the cheating lying narc." – Michelle the Midwest Triathlete

"I feel like I can't go "no contact" completely because we have over 50 friends / work acquaintances in common. I stopped following this person on social media, but every once in a while I receive a text from her. I reply with a very polite, yet brief response. I have not spoken to her in over 6 months. I do not text, call or reach out in any way. Unfortunately, a lot of people think we are still good friends so they might "tag" us together in photos from last year or comment to both of us. I cringe when this happens." – Lisa, New York

"During the period that I was with this destructive person, I did no contact 3 times before I finally stuck to it. My last communication with him was in the middle of November of last year and although he remained on Whatsapp for a good 2 months even though I'd blocked him, I stayed strong and feel very proud of myself for protecting myself and my self-respect." – Jobo, England

"I have gone no contact and most gladly so. I had no problem doing this because I had previous experience with physical abuse, (and a former malignant narcissist that I didn't even realize was one, until this time around). I had no problem throwing him out of my house and my life after he hit me. I should have thrown him out a long time before, but I didn't realize how much I was being manipulated and lied to. I have not really had a relapse, unless you count when he actually had the audacity to send me a friend request on Facebook. I watched him for a while, and observed his tactics of collecting people on Facebook. I was amused by this and somewhat validated by seeing his pattern play out. Then I stopped watching, deleted the friend request and blocked him. Then I unblocked him because I am not going to let him affect me one way or the other. There is no way that I would ever communicate with this person ever again. If I see him in public, I am prepared to act as if he isn't even there." –Anne, Indiana

"Yes. No relapses. What has stopped me is I no longer feel any desire for him. I don't want him back and I know I never will again. I found solid evidence this time and now I can believe myself over him." – Claudia, California

"Because my ex-narc left me (high and dry) he has never contacted me since then. He broke up with me over the phone. At the time, I had recently moved to other part of the country we both live in and it was three months after the move that he wanted out of the relationship. It's been almost a year. I have contacted him once since then and he told me he had moved on and is now in a new relationship. I guess that is the most hurtful part for me, having to be told by him he has someone new. And I am so sure he was with her before we even broke up!" – Nyree, New Zealand

"Yes, I have gone No Contact, and I have maintained it for more than a year (actually, almost two years). In terms of what's stopping me from relapsing, what helped was reading other stories about people who experienced trauma after reconnecting with their narcissist. It reminded me that it was bound to end badly if I ever relapsed. Furthermore, I now have a truly healthy relationship with a wonderful man, and don't want to spoil that by going back to a toxic one (however, I would encourage any fellow survivor to please NOT jump into another relationship too quickly. I only entered another one after a LOT of self-reflection and healing first)." – ProudSurvivor, California

"He is the one who cut contact. Sometimes I call him but I hang up without saying anything." –Gloria, Mexico

"I have gone NC with him many times, once for 18 months before I knew he was a narcissist. Since then I've only gone to 49 days, with many relapses. I have found it essential to block him from all social media." – Gail Sarah Robbins, Colorado, USA

"We share a son and I cannot go No Contact. What I do is not see him in person, limit phone calls and hang up when he is rude, and not reply to his flurry of emails and messages immediately. I often craft my responses over several days. Regarding relapses, we had a phone call a few weeks ago and it triggered a shocking relapse in physical symptoms including extreme neck tension mimicking asthma, insomnia and chest tension. I had to teach myself not to answer immediately and cater to his many quibbles." – Sandra, Washington

"I can't go complete No Contact because she's my mom and she's got PTSD due to losing my twin. I'm as close as she can ever get to him still being here. Plus I'd get bombarded by my other siblings if I cut her out completely. I'm good with the small amount I see her now...though I need to reiterate the fact that she can't just try to walk in my apartment unannounced like she keeps trying to do." – Alex, Townsend

"After 6 months this time, no contact. We were divorced for 5 years and kept in touch then got back together for 2 years before he discarded me." - Mary, Washington

"Yes I have gone no contact. He keeps trying to contact me and get at me through others." –Susie, Missouri

"I cannot, because she is the mother of my child. I have majority residential and legal custody of our son, but he is still with his mother 2 - 3 times a week." – Greg Tenney, Indian Hills, Colorado

"We can't go no-contact because we share a 5-year old daughter. But I've taken steps to minimize contact and I'm still working toward this goal. I don't answer all his emails and texts. I filter them (and my replies if it's needed) through my current boyfriend. He is level headed, generous and very loving. He's teaching me how to not respond or respond with short, simple answers instead of lengthy responses. Not responding also helps with not leaving a "paper trail." He is constantly on the prowl looking for something to trap me, catch me in a lie or something. Ironic since he is the perpetual liar." – Shannon, Central Ohio

"Yes totally. But only having learned the perils of not doing so in past experiences with narcs. No contact is imperative (but very difficult as it feels addictively all consuming to want to make contact)." – Gemma, United Kingdom

"Yes, definitely. And yes, multiple times - the last time was on Christmas when I called him while I was in his city. Found out he was fucking his new girlfriend and I felt indifferent, probably slightly disgusted - he had the cheek to ask me if we could talk next weekend... I knew he was going to use me as intellectual/emotional supply while he gets physical supply from his girlfriend, so I decided to go No Contact once and forever." - Diyanah, Kuala Lumpur

"I have just gone No Contact after several months of low contact. My abuser is the man who adopted me (previously known to me as "Dad"). He is chronically I'll and lives with a 24 hour caregiver. My precious mother died 10 years ago. For these reasons, it took awhile to go No Contact. What keeps me No Contact without exception at this point is the fact that I am pregnant and refuse to expose my baby to the stress." –Ergsmith, Southern California

"Yes. Yes. The excitement in the relationship, I dislike boredom." – Stephanie, Winnipeg, Canada

"I went NC with my sister about 2 years ago after she went Narc Rage on me for the thousandth time. She hoovered me with flattery and gifts which I ignored. Her hoovering did trigger "reaction" in me and I was very upset. I'm not sure how to stop this pattern. Also I have a real problem with my mother who is enabling her, and acting as flying monkey to me, mother is guilting me for daring to draw boundaries and be "done" with the abuse. Mother wants me to remain in the role I played for 40 years. Mother is making it impossible for me to escape my narc. Not sure what do to." – Laurel, San Francisco

"No contact. Yes, relapses in the form of nightmares and panic attacks." -Anonymous, Location Undisclosed

"It is not possible. There are common minor children." - S.N., Location Undisclosed

"No relapse. When he tried to reach me I blocked all social media and calls so he did get the point. I remind myself when I get nostalgic, I remind myself of the toxic life I was living. Giving up all of me just to please and keep him." –Kathy, FL

"Tried to a few times and relapsed when he got bored with his current girl and came back to me with promises of change and undying love. Blah!" - Donna, Chattanooga TN

"No contact has accidentally happened. He works two weeks out of town every month. I no longer tell him what I do when he calls me every day from out of town. I no longer tell him who I'm with or where I go. I make major decisions on my own instead of including him in the mall. This is my way of protecting myself from getting used and taken advantage and taking advantage of so he can use me for his purposes in manipulating me into not doing what I want to do with my life from day to day. Because he tries to manipulate me emotionally." – Carla, Location Undisclosed

"I tried various times to go n/c. Usually, I would weaken; several times he came crying to me for help with some emergency (exaggerated or false, as I would later learn)- just the relief of having contact again broke my determination- I would be so ashamed with myself and feel so incapable of self-control." – Janet, Nashville, TN

"I've gone No Contact. Block then unblock , block and unblock .... I can randomly block and unblock he will always be there calling and texting. Yes I relapse .... All the time." –Michelle, Northern California

"Yes, I am in No Contact at present. I had many relapses in the past but sought my own closure. So during the Hoovering end-phase, I ended it with the Narcissist by not calling on his Birthday, not picking up the phone when he called, and slowly removing myself. I also tested his insatiable supply needs by saying goodbye, which of course he responded with the Silent Treatment. So for over a week I waited to text and apologized as it was only a drunk text (wasn't) and to ignore it. He bit and was hunting me down the next morning. Then I sent him a final goodbye text. He currently calls every week but also stalks and rides by my house revving his motorcycle. Last one was Saturday and I am still in No Contact. Forever." – Kari, South Florida

"YES. It surprised me how long it took me to block his number. After discovering his rampant infidelity (we're talking hookers in Vegas and multiple GFs) I only sent him 2 text messages. One to express my pain and suggest he seek therapy on his own. To which he tried to justify himself by blaming his FOO and then blaming me. He then wrote me in the middle of the night frantically saying he needed help and for me to not abandon him. I sent him the number of a spiritual counselor and a therapy line. Then, I didn't initiate contact in any way but I didn't block him. I think I was hoping for remorse or begging or insight or...something. I kept him unblocked for 2 weeks after kicking him out of my home. And the only thing he did was to "check in to say hi and see how I am doing." No ownership of fault, no serious apology. Nothing. I think my mind still hoped that maybe somewhere this was a mistake. But I am SO LUCKY that neither this man, or the narcissist I was with in 2011 initiated extended attempts to keep me. They discarded me after realizing I was serious about moving on. So, I guess I'm "lucky" (?) that I didn't have a long residual tail of either of them in my life." – Anonymous, California

"Yes, I've gone no contact. No relapses. She will not change and I cannot put myself through that again." -Marie, New Orleans

"I went no contact with a narcissist and he began hoovering me and the hoovering started to turn into stalking and harassment. Four months ago I was granted a five year no contact restraining order by a judge based on the evidence I provided. I have gone no contact with a narcissist but he still Hoovers me with phone calls and messages every single day even though I have changed my number 2 times and blocked his phone number. I even downloaded an app which intercedes blocked calls but this doesn't stop him from leaving me messages through voicemail. What stopped me from communicating with him was knowing that he is such a phony and every single word he says is manipulative, every single touch movement word and thought is manipulative. These were extremely difficult times to come to but I have to face this reality and face the truth in order to move on and heal, and I'm grateful that I accepted the fact that he is a phony." –Maria M., Location Undisclosed

"Yes. That was 3 months ago, no relapses. My inner voice has stopped me. And I realized I feel much better now. Even if sometimes I still miss her." -Jen, Baltimore, Maryland

"I try to maintain no contact on an emotional and social level, but I have children with them and mentally have to distance myself from that person when they see the children. Most of the time I do not initiate contact with them and they do not extend themselves to see the children. On occasion when he feels it is convenient for his life." – Ms. L, Idaho

"I have gone no contact, but I have to willingly bring myself to not text him." Meredyth, New York City

"No contact with ex-partner. I see him around and feel sick when I do see him. Emotionally manipulative and possible narcissist. Diagnosed as bi-polar and on lithium medication. I was very vulnerable when I was in this relationship and couldn't bear being alone. He took advantage of my vulnerability, gossiped about me behind my back and made me feel very insecure and 'dark' inside. This was preferable to being alone at the time as it provided me with a social life. I never loved him nor was I attracted to him and I doubt he found me attractive. It was all about codependency. He had a strange sexual fetish called BDSM which he kept from me. I knew something was wrong and when he told me about it, it was pretty disturbing. I dumped him after he told me he had cheated. I had also cheated so the facade was officially over. I am still angry at myself for allowing this emotional predator into my life. I have been single for six years and would be very reluctant to give up the peace of mind I now enjoy." –Heather, Location Undisclosed

"After we divorced, I could not stop texting him daily. I tried but could only go a day or two without texting. Over two years, I tried to go NC almost every day and failed. My first success was a week, second was two weeks, third was three weeks, fourth was two months. Final and current is eight months NC. What stopped me from maintaining NC is that I could not bear the thought that the narcissist had forgotten me. He forgot I existed and I had to remind him I still lived and I still suffered and it was all because of him. I needed to keep reminding him what an evil monster he is and how karma will get him. I wanted him to feel my hatred every minute of the day for what he did." –Debbie, Michigan

"Yes I have gone no contact since September 2015. I had a relapse at the end of December 2015. Trying to get back on track now with going back to counseling." S., Wales

"No contact for 9 months, I have not taken him back since because I now know he is a narcissist, anti-social, and scores high as a psychopath." - Healing Vibe, Location Undisclosed

"We have shared custody so I am using grey rock technique." - VCK, Germany

"Not complete NC. More grey rock. I only respond when I need to keep the peace. Plus, I can't be that mean even though I know anytime she tries to be nice she's probably done something evil or shady, is doing something shady or about to do something shady. She lies so much and is so manipulative that I find it near impossible to trust what she is saying. I'm probably a co-dependent/empath so it's hard to go complete NC. We're not divorced yet so I need to play the game with her." - Billy Z., Chicagoland

"I went no contact before I knew what it was called. The day after he left I severed all social media connections. This caused an angry tirade of emails/texts. I politely requested that once all financial matters were settled that we no longer speak to each other and could any further contact be limited to such. This caused another set of angry emails which I think were supposed to make me feel bad about me? Eventually I called in the police and I let him know this was happening via email. He hacked my emails, deleted all the vicious nasty threatening ones before I'd realized what he was doing (I had kept hard copies). After that I never heard from him again. He is now blocked from all means of communication and he no longer knows where I live or work." - Magpie, UK

"I did finally manage to go no contact. I had to trespass him from my house as he continued to show up at all hours of the night. I had the paperwork for a protection order after he showed up at my work. Thankfully he gave up when I refused to attend a meeting with him and my church pastors. It was the hardest thing to do when I still loved (was addicted to) him. Learning about trauma bonds helped through a great website esteemology." - Lilly, Auckland, New Zealand

"No. I have lost my employment, and I am physically disabled due to chronic pain."- Cinde, Idaho

"Yes. I had one or two relapses of extremely short duration, just a few days until I realized I was being set-up again, and there was no REAL caring behind the facade. I also noticed that when I spoke up about my needs or asked questions I got the familiar blank look, followed by irritation." - Faye, FL

"We still live together because divorce is expensive, and even when I did file, I was told he had the right to remain in the house as long as he didn't do anything that required police intervention." -Anne, New York

"Yes, no contact, Yes, some relapses, but oddly enough the no contact is successful because they refuse contact with me." - Hope, Arizona

"I'm as close to No Contact as I can be while co-parenting. I initiate communication with him only via text and occasionally email." -Evelyn, Midwest, USA

"Yes, 25 years ago. One relapse when I confronted my mother about my father's sexual abuse." -Amanda, Massachusetts

"Yes to no contact. Yes, I have had relapses. I have this desire to call him out, to tell the truth. What stops me is the learning that he will only be satisfied by that." - Lou Ellen, Location Undisclosed

"As we are working together, I can't go on No Contact, but on a private level, I am successfully without contact. We worked with the Silence Treatment for many, many years, always ending with me giving up or giving in, so, yes, many many relapses without any effect. Now, I really guard myself. No complaints about him, no remarks on how much he hurts me or what I would wish for, just no remarks. Completely focusing on myself. This helps me most in the moment." - Gabriele, Japan

"I tried. I find that my pattern is to constantly replace my partner with another narcissist." - Kara, Indiana

"The first narcissist I met raped and impregnated me at 14 and I went no contact for obvious reasons. The second one walked away from me and I never heard from him again. I think he thought I was not good enough because I was a young, single mom. The third one was so sneaky and manipulative, that it took me 1 1/2 years to realize he was damaging me and I wasn't going crazy. I went no contact with him. It seemed very painful to do so and that is when I slipped into severe depression and stopped taking care of myself for a long time. There have been others, too. But, I started fighting back so much after that third one. I didn't know these men were narcissists. I thought men in general were just disgusting, hateful and selfish and I had to be on guard with them. That was the majority of my experience with them. My father must also be a narcissist. He was always a selfish and controlling person when I was a child." - Rhonda, Salt Lake City Area

"It took me a long time to stop checking the dating website where we met, and checking some groups he belongs to, but eventually I realized that he certainly wasn't following MY movements because I kept a very low profile for months after the relationship ended." - Judy, Colorado

"Yes, no contact for 3 years. I had relapses in the first year but none since then. I realized that nothing was going to change and that he would always be able to put me back into that situation if I communicated with him." -Mel Jan, Location Undisclosed

"No but not talking or seeing him. Fear of retaliation." –Kenlee, Alabama

"I wish. We have two children together, so it is not possible to go full No Contact, but that would be amazing if I could. My version of No Contact with him is to converse ONLY via Our Family Wizard or via my attorney. I do not respond to texts or phone calls. My attorney has been very helpful in coaching me on my written responses to him. I still catch myself feeling the need to defend myself against his accusations and with her help, I am learning to be short and simple in my responses." – Amy, Seattle

"Yes. absolutely NO contact and I am better off because of it. No relapses." - Jennifer from Ottawa Ontario, Canada

"Yes, No Contact with former husband. When he was at the point of death I emailed him letting him know that I hoped the best for him. Then started 6 months of emails - I saw that it was the SAME games he was using to entrap me emotionally. Never again. And he is still alive." - Dawn, Michigan

"YES! NO CONTACT IS VITAL! Stand your ground and remove the toxicity - it DOES GET BETTER! You can do it. You DESERVE joy, support, and TRUE love." – Pasqualena, Maryland

"I went No Contact multiple times and for good on October 16, 2014- I never contacted him again after that day but he continued to harass and stalk me over the last year which cost me a lot in court dates and lawyer fees." –Jill, New Hampshire

"Yes I have and then I went back so many times thinking it would change, but I knew deep down I'd be right back to the beginning again. I felt like I failed myself every time I went back." M., Chicago

"With other narcissists, abusers in my life but have been with a few and have relapsed. Some dependence has stopped me, feeling I am not good enough or financial reason." –Tina, Massachusetts

"No contact at all and blocked everywhere. No relapses, but there have been men that resembled him in behavior that I have been attracted to. I have not gotten involved though. My practicality stops me as well as lessons learned." Charlotte, Olso

"Yes I have, although I bombarded him with emails in the beginning trying to explain all the hurt and frustration. Big mistake as he just used that to confirm that I was crazy and unable to communicate. It is unfair to my children to be the go between but there is always a punishment if I do not do what he wants or some form of manipulation to get done what he wants." –Amanda, Tennessee

"Yes, I did have relapses in the beginning, but not for several years now. When you don't understand narcissism you honestly believe them when they show back up. It's very confusing at first." - Shawna Levonne in Ripley, WV

"Yes I have finally gone no contact with my ex-partner, I did not at first, but I learned in a big hurry that was the worst thing I could have done, because it opened the door for him and his friends to abuse me more." –Dawn, British Columbia, Canada

"Yes, I changed my phone number and moved 600 miles away." Deb, South Carolina

"As much as I can. But we own two businesses and share two dogs so I have not had that luxury, unfortunately. The no contact that I did enforce when I attempted to divorce him in 2012 resulted in 5 months of constant harassment and emotional terrorizing. He called me repeatedly, refused to give me space, created drama and financial problems that he thought would motivate me into action back in this direction. Eventually, he used an accident that happened with a friend as an opportunity to emotionally melt down, escalating the situation to the point of threatening to commit suicide if I didn't go to "marriage counseling" with him.... After spending 10 years declining my requests for counseling. I was so exhausted and worn down by this point, I caved and went to counseling just so he would give me a break. I was in the middle of working on my PhD and he created so much chaos and distress that I was at risk of destroying my academic career. I had to give in to his will at that point." –Hallie, Kentucky

"I have and he keeps finding ways to manipulate me back into his life. I'm going to change my Facebook, my phone number and my email." – Kay, Texas

"Yes. Yes, relapses. But this time for no contact, I'll keep it really no contact because it's one of the last wishes my dying mother said to me. It had been 5 years with 3 major break ups from the narc, all because of other women, commitment issues, I wasn't the right one for him issues. And my mother was just devastated to see me giving it such hope each time, trying so hard and then getting kicked to the ground again and again." –Josephine, Hong Kong

"I´ve been no contact 2 different times in the last two years. First time I was no contact until I contacted him and ended up returning to him. I was sure that everything that had happened was my fault and I was doing everything in my power to make the relationship work. It was like a job. I was thinking and planning everything around him like he was a God. I imagined him being the best man that I could ever have. Nothing worked. All the effort was in vain. He started devaluing me and threw me away just like he had done the first time, even worse than that. After that I went no contact for 2 months and broke it when he called me for my birthday. I am in contact with him again. I know it is wrong but I am convincing myself that I have the upper hand and control over the situation." –Dzana, Stockholm

"I can't because of children." - Lara, NH

"He recently placed an order of protection against me. It has been the best thing since sliced bread. Doing this he can no longer call me or text me. My life has been much improved. I used to dread the onslaught of hateful messages. It has given me freedom to live my life. He can't come ask me what I'm doing, why or who with. I have a boyfriend who was afraid of what Tom would do to either one of us if he found out I was dating. Now it would draw attention to him in a negative light if he attempts to harass me. This has been a Godsend." –Karina Tulloss, Location Undisclosed

"Yes, but it took me almost three years and one protective order later to have no contact." - Jen, Baltimore, Maryland

"I have gone almost no contact. We have children and I have to see him and discuss certain things. However, I do not engage him in small talk and I walk away when he tries. I also do my communication through text. That way things are in writing and I don't run the risk of him trying to twist my words." –Ava, Tennessee

"Yes and it took years to actually break the ties. At first I was too scared without their constant input in my life. Then when I was truly sick of it and was ready to be alone, these people 'upped their game' to try and keep me down and under their control." – Taylor Amell, WI

"Yes I have tried no contact. Yes I relapse often." - Brianna, Tennessee

"We have 3 kids together so I keep communication to a minimum." – Adele, Cabada

"Yes, no contact for months at a time. I have relapsed; tragedy, holidays or missing each other would bring us back in contact. We would start talking again and it was like no time has passed, we're in love again." T. Newton, Tacoma, WA

"Yes, I went No Contact. Her husband rang approximately 10 months after, which brought up anxiety so I changed my phone number." - Mikala, Euthulla, Australia

"I finally went no contact a year after the discard and terrorization. It's been 2 years! I'm afraid, if I ever see him again. I will be a widow in the women's prison!" –Tara, GA

"I relapse every time he calls. I wish I just couldn't answer but I do." – Susan, Indiana

"I am unable to go fully no contact yet because of the frequency of seeing the kids, but in general, yes I am no contact." – Dawn, Memphis

"I have gone No Contact with my only two living family members who are both malignant narcissists - my brother and my aunt. And I also moved across the country from NY to California to get away from them." – Maria, California

"I was able to go no contact thanks to him being out in prison for violent crimes against others after I left him, it made all the difference in the healing process, because I have children to the narc, I now see him only for visits with the children and that's it, it's still hard and I can still feel him trying to draw me back in to his web but I am so much stronger now that I'm able to resist and have kept threatening and disparaging messages he sent so I can go over them and remember the treatment and pain he caused." – Danielle, Melbourne, Australia

"I finally decided to block both him and the girl who appeared to be his next victim on social media. I had low-contact before and a post I saw sent me reeling and I had a bad nightmare. That's when I said "enough." I haven't relapsed, I think the threat of another nightmare is keeping me from doing so. Perhaps it isn't perfect- we run in the same social circles and I know I will see him again at events. Sometimes friends of mine will send me screenshots of his Facebook posts or messages he has sent them." –Anonymous, Syracuse, NY

CHAPTER 6

Pathological Narcissism in the Family, Friendships, Workplace and Society

Female Narcissists in Friendships

The DSM estimates that 75 percent of narcissists are male and the remaining 25 percent are female (APA, 2013). Now, these statistics may be skewed as there may be a gender bias in diagnosing women as borderline rather than as narcissists. Whatever the numbers may be, you are likely to encounter a female narcissist at some point during your lifetime - you could be a heterosexual male who's dating one, you could be a female who has a friend that is a narcissist, you could have a narcissistic mother, a relative or a coworker...the list goes on.

In my personal experience, I've befriended females with narcissistic traits and qualities. I would say a couple of them were on the high end of the spectrum of pathological narcissism - so self-absorbed and so covertly cruel that you would need to have researched narcissism in order to understand the breadth of their cruelty and the fact that they did, indeed, intentionally wish to hurt you.

Although male and female narcissists both share the traits of lack of empathy, haughty arrogance, self-absorption, and use the same techniques such as gaslighting, triangulation, smear campaigns and present a false self to the world, we have to remember that females are socialized differently than males in our society.

Depending on the culture we're talking about, psychopathology can present itself in different ways, especially given differing attitudes towards women in each society. Here are some differences I've observed among female narcissists:

Self-absorbed and vain, relies on sexuality and appearance.

Female narcissists, like somatic male narcissists tend to be incredibly superficial, vain and overly concerned about their appearance. Most likely, this is due to society's emphasis on a woman's physical appearance rather than her other attributes. Unless the female narcissist is a cerebral narcissist who primarily focuses on her intellect, the female narcissist will likely be incredibly conventionally attractive and fit. Research indicates that male narcissists have been shown to be the ones who tend to have an overinflated assumption regarding their appearance, while both male and female narcissists have been shown to overestimate their intelligence (Gabriel, Criteli and Ee, 2006). Though I am sure that not every female narcissist fits into this mold, the female narcissists I've met were attractive, charming and presented a very well-polished appearance to society.

Flatters and idealizes people based on her own point of power.

This trait applies to friendships as well as relationships with female narcissists. Since their point of power is often appearance, female narcissists will often flatter you depending on what they themselves would consider flattering to them and/or things they know you will enjoy being complimented on. This idealization phase takes place not only in relationships but also friendships. Narcissistic female friends will "hook you" much like they hook their dating or relationship partners by gushing over how beautiful, talented, and accomplished you are - when in reality, they just want to set you up for failure and their covert put-downs later on.

They will engage you in a "bond" that at times feels very special, unique, and different. This is a "partners-in-crime" mentality that flourishes in healthy friendships, but falls flat in ones with a narcissistic friend who has the agenda of sabotaging your success. Nobody is allowed to be more talented, beautiful or more accomplished than them in their mind. If you are, and if you are well-liked in your group of female friends, watch out. The narcissist is grooming you for covert abuse that will attempt to sabotage your friendships and it is targeted to bring you down for the very qualities they flattered you for in the first place, because they have what Christine Louis de Canonville calls in her article, "The Typical Narcissistic Woman as a Friend" an "insatiable need to covet" what they don't have (2015).

Needs to be the center of attention at all times.

This is related to the above point. Narcissists cannot stand anyone outshining them and they need to be the center of attention at all times. This means that when you get a job promotion, they will somehow attempt to outshine you and take the attention away from you. These can be through both covert and overt methods. For example, if a narcissist is particularly overt in her behavior, she may start talking over you and mention her own raise at work before you've had a chance to finish your sentence about your job. She will use any point of conversation to turn any news, good or bad, back to her and her own life.

However, if a narcissist is a particularly covert one, she can put you down in ways you won't even fathom. She may pretend to be very happy for you and your job promotion, but come the time that you have a celebration party, she will find some way to sabotage your happiness by bragging about herself, undermining your accomplishments to your other friends, or placing the attention on another friend that she's grooming as new supply.

Uses sexual prowess to get her way and show her status.

Christine Hammond, LMHC (2015), writes that male and female narcissists seduce their victims differently. According to her article, "The Difference Between Male and Female Narcissists," male narcissists tend to hook their victims with charm while female narcissists tend to use their bodies; unlike histrionic females who tend to be overtly provocative in their manner of dress, female narcissists tend to wear provocative clothing selectively for a specific goal or occasion.

Many, but not all, female narcissists can be hypersexual just like somatic male narcissists. In society, women are often unfairly judged and shamed for their sexuality, so some female narcissists may not be as open about their hypersexuality whereas others will be. Others may go to the other extreme, donning a self-righteous attitude of "purity" as they show contempt for those who are more sexual. Female narcissists can use their sexuality or lack thereof as a powerful tool to gain control in relationships and also achieve status in friendships like males.

They may brag about their sexual conquests, flaunt their body, wear provocative clothing even in contexts where it may be deemed unprofessional, and "modestly" boast about all the men (or women) that secretly or overtly want them. They will "complain" about all the times they get hit on, flirt with others even when they are in a long-term committed relationship, and engage in infidelity, even with partners who are already committed to others.

It gives them a sense of satisfaction to be the "mistress" or other woman who can take a man (or woman) away from their partners. They delight in being "the other woman," because to them, they can never have enough supply. Even if they had adoring male partners who treated them well, I knew many female narcissists who would engage in this type of behavior, emotionally and/or physically cheating on their spouses or partners.

Beware: if you suspect someone is a female narcissist, remember that they do not have boundaries. They may also flirt with your significant other. Although your significant other may not fall for it, remember that the female narcissist purposely does this not only to gain his attention but also yours: she's very well aware of how it may hurt you that your boyfriend or girlfriend is interested in them. That's why it's important to detach early when you detect narcissistic qualities in someone, so you don't get too heavily involved in the love triangles female narcissists tend to produce, even outside of their own relationships with their primary partners.

Engages in relational aggression in female friendships.

Gossip, slander, sarcasm, condescension are part of the arsenal of weapons every narcissist possesses, but the female narcissist takes it to a whole new level within the realm of female friendships. Remember that when it comes to bullying, females are shown in the literature to be more relationally aggressive, and research has shown that female narcissists tend to be a bit more subtle and indirect than males in their bullying tactics because it is less socially acceptable for them to aggressively assert their superiority over others as it is for males (Morf and Rhodewalt 2001). They employ their tactics moreso by affiliating with others of great social power to get their needs met.

Never trust your secrets with a female narcissist, as they will be told to your friends within twenty-four hours. The embarrassing moment you went through? Your other best friend will already know it. Your reputation? Slaughtered. Smear campaigns, especially if you "injure" the female narcissist in some way or invoke her envy, are likely to follow. The condescending smirk as the narcissist compliments you, then puts you down, will catch you off guard and make you doubt yourself about whether she really is a friend or an enemy (frenemy, anyone?). She will never allow you to feel secure, especially if you are proud of yourself. Like male narcissists, female narcissists are also pathologically envious and competitive, but even moreso towards other females because of the way she has been socialized to behave.

Highly materialistic.

Much like male narcissists, female narcissists tend to be materialistic as well as superficial. They want the arm candy, the new car, the best designer purses, and the expensive dresses and shoes. They may generate these items on their own through their own income, or they may also use a partner or a friend to associate themselves with success. Whatever route they take, they will find a way to feed their need for excess and glamour, as they are more likely to spend money than they are to actively obtain it (Hammond, 2015).

Tends to be incredibly envious of others.

The female narcissist engages in put-downs and shapeshifting to maintain control and curb her envy. She may present herself as your best friend to others and may even associate herself with your success, but behind your back (and sometimes laughingly to your face), she will do everything she can to humiliate you and put you down. She feeds off your insecurity and likes to provoke your jealousy.

She is highly competitive and prone to giving backhanded compliments like, "You look so good for your age," or "Wow that guy must really like you! He looked at me too, but I guess he has a preference for bigger girls." The female narcissist's cruelty is covert or overt depending on her personal interpersonal style. I've met female narcissists who were loud, highly opinionated, obnoxious and physically aggressive. I've also met female narcissists who were arrogant, haughty, materialistic, and laughed at you rather than with you with backhanded compliments. There is variety in this group, but they all share a common mission: to take your friends, your partners, your sanity and your feeling of security.

Narcissistic Family Members and Parents

Narcissistic abuse can happen in any context, whether it's family, friendship, a relationship or the workplace. In family situations where one or both parents are narcissistic, their children are seen as objects/trophies and are subject to narcissistic rage if the children dare to live independent lives outside of the control of their parents. One child can be made to be the scapegoat or the black sheep of the family while the other sibling is the "Golden Child." Family members who are the scapegoat are devalued and endure smear campaigns while the golden child is placed on a pedestal and idealized. In the case of siblings, if a sibling is narcissistic, they will do everything in their power to devalue and sabotage the sibling that threatens them.

I am blessed (and cursed!) to know about narcissism from all different angles - from relationship partners to friends to coworkers to family members. I always joke that God put me on some holy assignment of sorts – a research endeavor into all forms of narcissism – one I certainly didn't ask for, but glad I received. At least, that's one way of reframing it. That's why I know how devastating it can be to be raised by a narcissist and how the cycle can repeat when you find yourself gravitating towards those who share the same qualities and traits as your parents.

Here are the main traits of narcissistic parents to watch out for:

Narcissistic parents treat their children like trophies.

Like the parent who lives vicariously through their child, narcissistic parents view their children as objects who exist only to do their parents' bidding – they are "supply," nothing more, nothing less, and they are treated with contempt unless they can be used strategically in a smear campaign against the parent who is the victim, a divorce proceeding or custody hearing. I often hear from survivors whose narcissistic ex-spouses become suddenly interested in their children during the divorce.

Author Tina Swithin also speaks about this dynamic in her blog, One Woman's Battle – Divorcing a Narcissist at onemomsbattle.com. This is deliberately engineered as a ploy to hit the victim where it hurts: the narcissist or sociopath is likely to suddenly morph into an amazing parent once they realize they might lose supply. They know how important children are to the victim, so they will use children as ammunition to fulfill their agenda. Children who are caught in the throes of a divorce with a malignant personality often find that they are "love-bombed" by their narcissistic parents and met with rage if they don't follow the proposed protocol of choosing sides.

In some cases, narcissistic parents may take objectification to a whole new level. Think of the show "Toddlers and Tiaras," where mothers pathologically objectify their children in order to live out their own dreams of being a beauty queen. This type of behavior may also be amplified in families where children are taught a high sense of entitlement, especially in higher socioeconomic classes. They see their children as extensions of themselves to a pathological extent and want them to achieve what they could not. While normal parents can do this to some extent too, the narcissistic parent subjects their children to verbal beatings and emotional battery, sometimes even physical abuse, in order to get them to comply with their needs and desires. There are even narcissistic and sociopathic parents who sexually abuse their children because they have no qualms about overstepping boundaries. In addition, female narcissistic mothers tend to be jealous of their daughters and treat their daughters as competition, rather than family.

When they lose control of their children, narcissistic rage precedes any empathy or compassion.

Children are not taught to pursue what makes them happy, but rather that they must pursue what makes their parents happy and if they don't, they will be put-down, abused, and verbally, emotionally and psychologically berated. Much like narcissists in relationships, narcissistic parents engage in this type of rage to maintain control as their kids grow older and begin to forge their independence away from the family. They are more likely to be idealized as children when they are fully under the control of their parents, though they can certainly be devalued and abused in numerous ways as children as well, depending on the circumstances.

They are hypercritical and rarely provide you with emotional validation. They also tend to follow an enmeshed family style.

Narcissistic parents put down your goals, downplay your achievements, remind you constantly of what you have yet to achieve, and put you down as much as possible so you never have the sense of worthiness and security that all children have a right to have as soon as they are born. They rarely validate your emotions, and they neglect to provide you with appropriate emotional support. When you are crying, they will criticize you for crying. When you are laughing too hard, they will berate you for being loud and inappropriate. Much like narcissistic dating partners, they hate to see you happy - unless it's due to an accomplishment they can show off to others. Yet their style of parenting tends to be incredibly engulfing, controlling, and overbearing. They may micromanage each aspect of the lives of their children, or, on the other end of the spectrum, they may struggle with issues such as addiction that they use to excuse rageful attacks and overall neglect of their children.

They only care about their own image.

Narcissistic parents can be incredibly charming, generous and likeable in the public eye. They are heavily invested in impression management. To the outside world, narcissistic parents look like the perfect father or mother, but behind closed doors, it is an entirely different story. As children age and begin to pave the path to independence, they are likely to pursue goals, careers and relationships their parents may not agree with. While respectful disagreement is one thing, narcissistic parents will go so far as to sabotage your success in attempting to build your own independent life outside of what they want for you.

The reason the narcissistic parent has their own plan for your life has to do with their agenda - many of them want to look good to the outside society and their relatives and friends. They want to brag about how little Tommy became a doctor or how sweet Sarah is marrying one. They don't care if Tommy wants to be an artist or that Sarah's doctor fiancé is abusive towards her. All they care about is how your behavior reflects upon them, which is why they feed their children a skewed version of perfection and punish them for not living up to it. This distorted version of perfection is used to belittle their children into never feeling good enough, worthy or deserving of respect and love.

*There may be differences between female narcissistic parents and male narcissistic parents. Psychiatrist Mark Banschick, M.D. has written excellent articles discussing the dynamics with both narcissistic fathers and narcissistic mothers on Psychology Today. Check out his articles titled, "The Narcissistic Mother" and "The Narcissistic Father."

Narcissistic Co-Workers and Bosses

It can be very difficult to maintain calmness in a situation where the narcissist is a co-worker or boss. I've definitely had experiences battling a full-fledged narcissist in a toxic work environment and I know how devastating it can be, especially when you rely on a job to provide you not only your income but your professional development. Workplace bullying and harassment is a serious problem, especially when it comes to narcissistic predators that seamlessly "fit into" the work environment by being their charismatic selves, while bullying their targets and blameshifting to make their targets look as if they are the ones victimizing them.

Narcissistic co-workers are often in cahoots with their bosses (who may or may not be narcissistic themselves) and are able to sabotage the professional development of anyone they find particularly threatening, due to their pathological envy.

Overt workplace narcissists tend to display aggressive, haughty, bullying behavior that shows contempt for your perspectives and ideas. They are less likely to have an adoring harem and more likely to have people who fear them at work. They tend to be intimidating, rather than charming and impressive.

Covert workplace narcissists are more likely to have a fan club and a more convincing façade. They may praise you to your face while they steal your ideas, sabotage your success, spread misinformation about you, and triangulate you with superiors to make it seem as if you are a source of trouble. Some co-workers or bosses may use their power to even sexually harass or intimidate you. A hostile work environment can take a toll on not only an individual's self-esteem, motivation and productivity, it can lower company morale.

In any toxic work environment where stressors and sabotage are likely to come up, I recommend the following steps:

(1) Mindful breathing. Meditation and yoga can seriously save your life. I hate to beat you over the head with these two, but if you practice meditating daily, you will be able to access that part of yourself that can make it through anything and can mindfully address your triggers. Use these to your advantage, especially if you are in a toxic work environment where your livelihood depends on it and you're still searching for other opportunities. Calmly breathe through and when in doubt, *remain as professional as you can be under the circumstances*. If you need to set boundaries, do so firmly and respectfully.

(2) Remain as professional as possible and document everything. Avoid sharing your best ideas with colleagues that are likely to rip you off. Whenever possible, communicate important business information respectfully through e-mails which can be saved and documented – this is very important because if there is any misinformation spread about you, you can at least back it up with proof that cannot be denied. This is also helpful if you are forced to share any ideas with a co-worker who may later steal them, so you have proof of "origin." If you are forced to always communicate your ideas face-to-face, why not just send an e-mail shortly after saying something along the lines of, "Thanks for discussing my idea of…with me, and for the encouragement!" just so you have it for your records? It certainly cannot hurt as long as you make it clear that you were the one with the idea.

Narcissists look to provoke actions within you, in order to depict you as the unprofessional ones – they may even provoke you in person as well as through e-mail. Remember that anything you say or do, even if it is trying to tell your side of the story to your boss, may be used against you. If the narcissist is well-liked and has duped your superiors in the workplace, it can be dangerous to attempt to smear them in any way because the narcissist will use this as fuel to sabotage you further. Being overly emotional about the bullying you're experiencing will be used to depict you as the unstable one, much like the dynamic of a narcissistic abuser and his or her victim in an intimate relationship.

(3) Refocus your anger/frustration into doing your best work. Avoid gossiping about that co-worker or boss because there are likely to be supporters in the company that may feed them the information. Keep your energy balanced and your emotions in check using the self-care tips, tools and healing methods we discussed in Chapter 3. Seek professional help if you aren't doing so already, because having a validating therapist or coach on your side while you vent about work can be very empowering, especially if that professional can help you sort out the ways in which you may be handling the situation in a maladaptive manner. A mental health professional or coach can also work with you to brainstorm healthy solutions to the situations that are arising.

(4) Reframing the experience to benefit you and taking action. What can this experience teach you about your current situation? Is it time to seek a healthier workplace environment? Look for other opportunities? Or can you use the emotions you have about the situation to access an even more motivated version of yourself? If the structure in that workplace is so toxic that it seems you never get ahead because of the brown-nosing narcissist, it may be time to use those experiences to fuel your search for other opportunities. On the other hand, if you think this experience can be used as an opportunity in itself to surpass your own best work, use it to benefit you and your own performance/advancement. Meditation and yoga can also help maintain calm and lower ruminating thoughts about these types of situations.

To learn more about workplace bullying, be sure to check out Dawn Marie Westmoreland's website on workplace bullying on www.dawnmariewestmoreland.com.

How to Deal with Narcissists You Can't Avoid: Six Ways to Skillfully Respond

If you're in a relationship with a narcissist or are currently dating one, I highly recommend going No Contact as a default response after detaching and ending the relationship using one of the methods for breaking up with them. Don't play games you can't win, especially if those games cause you emotional trauma. However, sometimes interacting with the narcissist is a necessary evil, especially if we have to encounter one in the workplace, a family reunion or if we have children with the narcissist and instead have to maintain Minimum or Low Contact as a result.

Remember that in work-related situations, if the narcissist is not a boss, they will often have what one of my YouTube subscribers, Asjah, astutely called a "hit man" - someone with more power that the narcissist feeds false information to in order to ultimately take you out. This can be a woman or a man depending on the type of organizational setting and is common with a malignant workplace narcissist. So be very wary of the information you give to both the narcissist as well as anyone that might be on their side – it can and will be used against you.

Here are six possible ways to respond to the narcissist that saves you a great deal of energy in the long-run should you encounter one and are forced to interact:

1. Gray Rock Method.
Narcissists get excitement primarily out of provoking you and seeing you respond in anger, confusion or despair. Since their emotional lives are so flat and bland (unless they feel the rage of a narcissistic injury), witnessing human beings have emotional reactions is like getting tickets to a free show. The puppeteer loves watching his or her puppets perform, after all.

The Gray Rock method, which basically consists of having very flat or boring responses to usual provocation or triangulation tactics, leaves narcissists with very little supply and excitement. It's like taking away a kid's favorite treat when you look at them with a poker face during their usual antics. It also saves you a lot of energy and gives you the satisfaction of knowing you've withheld their usual supply. Most importantly, it makes it less likely that the narcissist will continue to pursue you as supply once they know you can't give them the reactions they're desperately looking for.

2. Avoid triggering subjects and derail catastrophic conversations.
Narcissists enjoy using circular conversations, meaningless word salad and countless contradictions to mess with your mind, deflect your attention off their abuse and keep you off balance. They'll deny saying something, they'll contradict something they said earlier, they'll bring in irrational arguments and they'll continue to break your boundaries in a

way that leaves you inevitably frustrated. This keeps the focus off the narcissist's actual behavior and leaves you wasting precious energy and time trying to figure out what's actually being said. Think of it as looking through garbage trying to extract gems. Except, there are no gems. You're just becoming a hoarder of the narcissist's useless "crazy-making" tactics.

To prevent this from happening, you can derail a provocative conversation immediately by doing one of the following:

- **Changing the subject to a harmless topic the narcissist is genuinely interested in, something he or she is *likely* to want to talk about.** Something that satisfies his or her need for attention and admiration without harming you in the process. In fact, try to make it a topic *you're* interested in so you'll still be spending your time wisely. "Hmm, that's interesting. Oh! But, can you tell me more about that new business venture you're working on?"
- **Cutting off the conversation abruptly with an excuse.** "Wow, that's *fascinating.* Sorry, I have to go to a meeting/bed/dinner/another planet now. Talk to you later!"
- **Acknowledging the statement positively or making a joke.** "You know, you're right. I could use a better sense of humor! Thanks a lot for pointing that out." (This is especially useful in interacting with internet trolls, who seem to go away once they get their daily ego stroke).

3. Make the narcissist a source of *your* supply.

This technique is not for everyone and I am mainly suggesting it for the workplace or for a professional connection. If you find you feel guilty by doing this and would prefer to not gain anything at all from the interaction, you should honor that. I include this suggestion only as a way to offer a variety of options.

Since the narcissist uses you for supply without remorse, and this post is geared towards superficial/forced interactions with narcissists, you can also try to think of ways the narcissist can benefit or help you since he or she is out to exploit you anyway.

If you're dealing with a narcissistic coworker, think of ways that this coworker can serve you since you have to interact with him or her anyway. Do they have special skills or talents that you can learn from? Is their network big enough to help you make new connections? This is highly likely since narcissists in the workplace enjoy building harems and surrounding themselves with special people.

Be very careful and selective with whom you use this suggestion, as some narcissists will make you feel indebted if they give you something and you happily receive. I am not suggesting you become a narcissist yourself - not at all. If you do decide to practice this, don't think of it as narcissistic or stooping to their level when doing this - think of it as *quid pro quo*. The narcissist uses you for attention, and since you are forced to interact with him or her, you might as well gain something from it in the meantime.

4. Opposite Action.

As I mentioned previously, this technique can be used quickly and effectively when emotions threaten to get the best of us. It's very simple: when you feel like getting angry at the narcissist's provocative statements, smile instead. Your brain doesn't know the difference between a real smile and a fake one, so chances are, your emotions will soon follow your facial expression. Your mood will improve and you will feel less stress than if you did not perform this action.

You'll be more calm and relaxed, while the narcissist scratches his or her head wondering why you're not responding in the usual way. There are other ways to perform opposite action. When you feel so overwhelmed and want to cry, laugh instead. Laughter is great medicine and decreases stress hormones.

If the narcissist is trying to provoke you through triangulation or put-downs, react by being nonresponsive or laughing. Enjoy yourself as if you were watching an absurd comedy because in actuality, you are. Narcissists are comical and absurd in their antics. Your pleasure and dismissal throws them off because they expect anger and sadness in response to their manipulation tactics. Maintain control in the face of the narcissist's attempts at provocation, and who knows? You may even be overlooked for another, more "entertaining" source of supply that is more reactive to the narcissist's ploys.

5. Validate your feelings and establish your boundaries.

This is so important and vital to responding to the narcissist out of a place of personal security, self-respect and self-love. We must validate our feelings to the narcissist and resist their gaslighting. Our trouble arises when we view narcissists as "legitimate" people like us rather than as master performers. We see ourselves as victims of the narcissist's techniques, but really, we are more powerful than we think once we are armed with adequate knowledge of the narcissist's condition.

Once you start viewing narcissists as "predictable" characters with unpredictable masks and as shapeshifting chameleons that will stop at nothing to get a reaction, you will understand the need to step back and see the narcissist's ploys as what they truly are, rather than focusing on the emotional reaction you have to them. This will make it easier to establish firm boundaries with them without making excuses for their behavior or invalidating your own feelings in the process.

Make a list of boundaries you absolutely need the narcissist to abide by. Boundaries like, "Do not call me after midnight" or "Do not speak to me in that condescending tone." Since narcissists will try to break boundaries, take control by making sure you are not receptive to this boundary-breaking when it occurs. When the narcissist speaks in a certain tone, smile, make an excuse and walk away before he or she continues. When the narcissist calls you after midnight, turn off your phone and don't be available. The key is finding ways that you can establish your boundaries without having to force the narcissist to honor them, since he or she is unlikely to do so.

6. Reframe your thoughts.

Once you accept the fact that your idea of the narcissist is different from who the narcissist actually is, you'll be much happier and accepting of coexisting with all the narcissists you'll inevitably encounter in this world.

Narcissists are pathetic performers, precisely because they are dependent upon us as supply. They are like emotional leeches and they need us to survive.

Any time you find yourself ruminating over something the narcissist said or did, stop. Step back. Observe your feelings. Accept them and validate them. However, do not internalize the narcissist's projections of you. Understand that this is an abuser who is toxic and exploitative, and that their cruel tactics are deliberately geared to cause you pain. If you accept this, you will gain more mastery over your emotional reactions and be more able to skillfully approach situations with narcissists without losing your dignity in the process.

Cyberbullies and Online Predators

Cyberspace provides narcissists and those who have antisocial traits with easy access to victims through minimal effort on their part. This is especially rampant with the rise of new online dating applications such as Tinder, OKCupid, and PlentyofFish where victims are literally one "swipe" away from being targeted. Outside of the online dating sphere, narcissists, sociopaths and psychopaths roam for supply on online forums meant to help survivors as well. There are even some narcissistic "gurus" who pretend to be victims as a way to feel a sense of power and control over a victim that has been retraumatized.

Cyberbullying and trolling are strategic ways for narcissists who lack adequate narcissistic supply_or who are experiencing boredom to get a quick "fix" *without being held accountable for their abuse*. A recent study showed that online trolls demonstrated high degrees of sadism, psychopathy and Machiavellianism (Buckels et. al, 2014).In the context of intimate relationships, survivors of narcissistic abuse may be stalked, harassed and cyberbullied for years even after the ending of the relationship, *especially* if they were the ones to discard the narcissist first.

When a narcissist suffers from a narcissistic injury, this can lead to narcissistic rage. This rage is a result of an injury to their ego when something or someone threatens their delusions of grandeur and "false self." Since survivors often implement No Contact with their abusers, narcissistic abusers feel a loss of power and attempt to regain that power through tactics like provocation, hoovering and post-breakup triangulation techniques.

On a larger scale, narcissists and those who have antisocial traits employ similar manipulation tactics in cyberspace to provoke and harm complete strangers. This should come as no surprise to anyone who has encountered trolls or cyberbullies – they are notorious for attempting to provoke people in order to derive sick feelings of satisfaction that they apparently can't get anywhere else.

Bullying in any form, especially anonymous bullying, can lead to devastating results. Research indicates that cyberbullying in schools leads to a higher rate of suicidal ideation and suicide attempts in victims of cyberbullying (Hinduja and Patchin, 2010). There have been a number of suicides that were triggered by the words of anonymous sadists – the suicides of many teenagers, for example, were a direct result of cyberbullying. Cyberbullying and trolling leave such a terrible psychological impact that there is even a movement against anonymous comments sections on media outlets.

Since there is little accountability for cyberbullies and the laws against it in each state may not protect victims entirely from emotional abuse, it often goes unchecked and unpunished. If cyberbullies are ever reprimanded, it is usually *after the fact* of a tragic suicide or in the event of publicity. In the case of the recent death of Robin Williams, for example, people became outraged when they heard that trolls on social media outlets were harassing Robin Williams' daughter and had caused her distress during a time of intense grief and loss. Usually, however, the sadism of these bullies goes unnoticed except for the people who have to endure the harassment.

THREE WAYS TO DISTINGUISH A SADISTIC CYBERBULLY FROM A PERSON WHO'S PROVIDING CONSTRUCTIVE CRITICISM

1. They stage personal attacks rather than present logical arguments.

Rather than engaging in healthy debate and respectful disagreement, cyberbullies and trolls distinguish themselves from normal people who disagree by staging personal attacks on character instead of providing evidence against the argument that they claim to have problems with. Instead of saying, "Research proves you wrong, here's the source," they're more prone to verbal diarrhea which consists of insults, name-calling, word salad, circular logic and provocative overgeneralizations deliberately aimed to get a rise out of you. They may even bring up personal details or assume things about you that have nothing at all to do with the matter at hand. A cyberbully is, like many narcissists in intimate relationships, a *perpetual boundary-breaker.*

2. They persist.

Some cyberbullies give up eventually if they don't get the response they were looking for, but others will keep hunting for more of a reaction and provoking you, even on multiple accounts. Like narcissists in intimate relationships, they use the anonymity feature of cyberspace to employ triangulation techniques with their "fake" accounts to show "support" for – who else -themselves.

3. Stalking.

When you do respond in a way they're not accustomed to, they suffer a kind of narcissistic injury and resort to low blows and attacks. Some cyberbullies are satisfied when you give them a quick ego stroke, like a "You're right" to their insult and go away. Others are much more malicious. When you give them radio silence or choose to report their harassing behavior, they come after you.

I've had cyberbullies follow me all the way onto personal social media accounts in an attempt to silence my voice on important issues or because they suffered a narcissistic injury when I didn't respond. They weren't persisting to try to respectfully get me to see their point of view, either – they were outright insulting me and making assumptions about me that had little to do with the topic at hand.

THREE WAYS TO HANDLE CYBERBULLIES AND TROLLS

1. Don't engage or feed the trolls unless necessary.

Depending on the forum or website that you're being harassed on, there may be an option for you to report harassment or block the person. This is especially useful for cyberbullies who are attacking you personally and taking a toll on your mental health. This is sort of like going No Contact – except, instead of someone you were in an intimate relationship with, you're going NC on a stranger out to harm you. Find a way to remove them from your presence with the least amount of effort. They're simply not worth the time and energy that it takes to stage a rebuttal. Remember: narcissists always need an audience and a source of supply. By removing yourself as a narcissistic source of supply, you refuse to give them the attention they're looking for. By default, you win. However, if they are continually harassing you and stalking you, or if they are threatening you, you can take legal action if feasible.

2. Be strategic about your privacy.

Different forums and websites have different policies, so be strategic depending on what platform you're using. Most social media platforms allow you to block or report anyone who's harassing you, so take advantage of whatever you can do. Next, explore the privacy settings on whatever platform you're using. If you feel comfortable and it's available, take on the option that will enable you to share the least amount of information with the public. This will prevent cyberbullies and trolls on the hunt from finding out the personal details of your life. If you find it feasible, consider limiting the number of social media accounts you have so that you only use the ones you absolutely need for your professional and social life.

If you're a blogger and are being trolled or cyberbullied, websites like WordPress take it one step further and allow you to see the IP address of the person commenting. This enables you to watch out for multiple "fake" accounts cyberbullies may be using to troll your blog or website and you can block one specific IP address from commenting on your blog altogether and just be done with it.

Should cyberbullies ever threaten you with physical harm, you can use this IP address to find out where the troll or cyberbully resides, so you can report them with more accurate information. Simply copy/paste the IP address into a geolocation website such as www.iplocation.net. This will yield identifying information that you can have in case the cyberbully or troll ever threatens you or if you suspect the cyberbully may be someone you know, such as your toxic ex-partner.

3. Refocus your energies on productive outlets.

Trolls and cyberbullies will never have the final say on your self-worth or your abilities. Why? Because they're literally spending their time trying to tear people down. Don't you think that if they were fulfilled in their own lives, they'd find better things to do? Thankfully, *you do* have better things to do than to ruminate over the narcissists and sociopaths in cyberspace. You have a blog to run, a website to manage, a Twitter feed to update, a Facebook page to update, and a story to share.

Continue to use your voice and make it heard. Only engage with respectful people and save the debate for people who can disagree with you in a manner that's not pathological. Let the cyberbullies motivate you to make waves for social change and to continue to speak out on behalf of the underdogs.

If you're at any point feeling overwhelmed by these bullies, shut down the computer, unplug the devices, and *tell someone*. Stand up for yourself and do not let this go unchecked. You deserve to be heard and validated. Also help others who may be going through similar struggles.

The more you spread awareness about this important issue, the more likely change can happen.

Important Note: If the cyberbully is someone you know, like a friend or former romantic partner, make sure you go No Contact with the person immediately, document any text messages or incriminating phone calls and report them to online service providers or law enforcement agencies if they violate your state's anti-bullying laws on stopbullying.gov. In that scenario, their anonymity no longer protects them from the consequences of their harassment.

Remember: bullies can be adolescents *or* adults. Though they all share the same mental age of five, they can be dangerous to us at any age group. Let's take a stand against bullying and harassment in all forms – from text messages to forums, from social media to blogs. We do not deserve to be violated or disrespected – even online.

Stay safe and take care. Here are some additional resources for cyberbullying which may prove helpful to you:

Links

Top Ten Tips for Adults Who Are Being Harassed Online

Top Ten Tips for Teens Who Are Being Harassed Online

Reporting Cyberbullying from StopBullying.gov

How to Spot Blog Trolls and What to Do by Kristen Lamb

How to Stop Caring About Trolls and Get On With Your Life

CHAPTER 7

Healing from Emotional Trauma and Rebuilding Your Life

T ime is traditionally used to inform us of appointments, allocate hours to work, and track our progress. We use time to remember to go to the doctor, to go to the office at a certain hour, to track our progress at work or school. We can use time for reflection as well as daily tasks: time motivates us meet an important deadline, but it also tells us that we've spent several years in a certain relationship, helps us to celebrate one-year anniversaries with significant others, and acts as a marker of *investment and energy*. If we feel we haven't spent our time in a productive way, we feel our investment and energy had little return. We feel overwhelmed with regret and a sense of learned helplessness that threatens to disable us from making necessary changes in our lives.

Survivors of abuse and emotional trauma have a special and significant relationship with time. I've heard numerous stories end with, "I can't believe I wasted this amount of time on this person," or, "These years of my life have been wasted!" It is a painful realization when we recognize we've given our precious time and energy to something that deeply wounded us.

Sometimes it takes a horrifying diagnosis or the ending of a relationship to force us to reflect on the time we have left, but we can be mindful of the present right now, *at this very instant.* Although we cannot go back in time to change the way we've spent it, it's important that we stay mindful of the time we still possess, in the here and now.

In order to spend our time more constructively, we can do the following:

Allocate more time for healing rather than ruminating.

Excessive rumination may be the initial response to the ending of an abusive relationship or after a significant trauma. Survivors of trauma may suffer from symptoms related to PTSD or acute stress disorder, like numbing, dissociative symptoms, recurrent nightmares, flashbacks, hypervigilance and intrusive thoughts. While it's extremely important to be patient with ourselves and not rush the healing process, it's also necessary to make active changes in our lives in order to make progress.

For the sake of our mental health, addressing our painful emotions and assessing what happened is necessary to moving forward, and we eventually come to the stage where we have to set aside time for what is necessary to heal ourselves. That means being proactive by seeking out professional help, setting boundaries such as low or No Contact with an abusive ex-partner, maintaining a strong support network and engaging in self-care that nourishes our body, spirit and mind.

Challenge

Set a "time limit" for excessive ruminations. If you find yourself ruminating for three hours a day over a particular situation for example, set the time limit to one hour and then spend the rest of the time doing something else like exercising, working on a project, watching a favorite television show, meeting with a friend to do something fun, or writing a poem.

You may still have distracting thoughts during that time, but at least you will be spending more time doing an activity that benefits you rather than spending more time than is necessary reevaluating scenarios you've revisited too many times. Whenever these intrusive thoughts come up, try not to feed them. Step back, observe, and radically accept them, just as they are. Engage in pleasurable distractions or cross another thing off your to-do list. Allow yourself the right to feel all of your emotions, but do not get stuck and permit them to hold you back from enjoying your life.

It's inevitable that we will think about the trauma and have strong feelings about it. There is absolutely nothing wrong with that - it's a normal response to trauma. I make this suggestion to end excessive ruminations not to invalidate the legitimate feelings and thoughts about trauma that may surface, but to acknowledge that your time here on earth is precious and finite, and you want to spend it in a balanced way.

If you want to move forward, spending excess time overanalyzing situations rather than actively engaging with your life will only deter you from living your life the way it was meant to be led. You must spend some time assessing your trauma, but don't forget to spend time healing from it as well. **Take breaks to relax, work on your goals and live life.** This goes back to maintaining that delicate balance between owning both our status as survivor as well as our agency.

Take the time to pursue your unique destiny.

In *The Seven Spiritual Laws of Success*, Deepak Chopra speaks about the "Law of dharma," which is the unique destiny we're meant to fulfill. Chopra argues that our "dharma," our "purpose in life," manifests best when tied to serving humanity and the larger world around us. We have to ask ourselves, how much time am I spending on cultivating this destiny? What do I do every day to serve humanity? Is my current job fulfilling me? Is there volunteer work or another line of work I can pursue to make better use of my talents? Is there a talent I am wasting rather than sharing with my current efforts?

Challenge

Write down two or three talents or skills you feel you haven't used in a while, or haven't used at all in public. Next to each one, write at least five things you can do to cultivate that talent. If possible, pay special attention to how that talent may serve others. These things can be big or small in the way they help others.

For example, if one of my hidden talents is photography, I could volunteer as a wedding photographer to capture the meaningful moments in my friends' wedding or start a project that involves taking photographs for a social cause I care about. If my hidden talent is nutrition and fitness, I could volunteer to teach fitness classes at a local community center or start a YouTube channel to help people to change their diets and lifestyles. If I have a great sense of humor, I might use it to regularly brighten someone's day or I might join an improv comedy group and participate in shows that entertain hundreds of people in need of a daily escape. If I have a passion for mental health and loved to write, I could start a self-help blog or write a self-help book (sound familiar?)

You get the picture. There are so many creative ways to use our talents and put them into use to serve humanity. In the midst of this exercise, you might even come across what you were meant to do all along. This is a better use of our time and it permits us to change the world rather than to focus on what we *can't* change - the past.

Enjoy and be mindful of the present moment.

Be grateful for what you still have now in the present moment. From basic things like food, shelter, our vision, our ability to walk, to good friends, a stable job and access to health care and education. Cultivating this habit of lifelong gratitude brings us to a place of mindfulness that is beneficial to our health and appreciation of life. Remember: time spent on remorse detracts from time spent savoring what we still have. Nothing lasts forever, so focus on what is still here.

Challenge

Start to replace unhelpful thoughts and cognitive distortions about the past with positive statements about the present. Whenever a judgmental statement like, "I shouldn't have done this" or "I regret what happened," arises, replace it with, "I am grateful to have survived and learned from this experience."

If this is too difficult because of the extent of trauma you've endured, try to remind yourself of something you still have despite the trauma, like "I still have my health and that's what's most important" or "Now I have the freedom to pursue my dreams without interference." Not all "alternative thoughts" will work to diffuse ruminations over the past, but making a significant effort towards a more positive attitude about your life experience will help you become more resilient to obstacles in the long-run.

It is also helpful to keep a gratitude journal to remind yourself of all you have to be thankful for in this life. The more time you spend being grateful, the less time you spend being resentful and the more likely you'll have an increased sense of perceived agency in your life. You'll be more likely to see challenges as opportunities for growth rather than as dead ends, and more likely to constructively channel your life circumstances into life-changing awareness.

Put an end to toxic interactions and relationships.

These are the nonreciprocal, unfulfilling interactions or relationships that leave you emotionally drained and exhausted. They include: relationships that are past their expiration date, friendships that leave you feeling terribly about yourself, and other interactions with people who mistreat or disrespect you. This helps us to refocus our time on healthier, fulfilling relationships that will make us happier in the long-run.

Minimize people-pleasing and cut ties with the people who don't accept you for who you are and who don't appreciate what you have to offer. This is necessary in order to make the most of our time and use it wisely. Should you need to maintain contact for whatever reason (for example, this could be a family member who you're forced to interact with on a weekly basis) it's important to at least significantly reduce the time and energy you spend interacting with this person or ruminating over your interactions with them.

Challenge

Think of a person in your life who you've spent unnecessary time with and energy on recently. What can you do to reduce or end the interaction? Is there a way you can set a boundary so they don't contact you as often? Do you need to stand up to them and make it clear that you no longer want them in your life? Whatever you must do, do it now. Save yourself future pain and the heartache of having to endure a relationship or friendship that isn't serving you by ending it now or detaching from it. These unfulfilling interactions only hold us back from the destiny we're meant to fulfill.

As survivors of trauma, our best bet is to keep moving forward and focus on our self-care and self-love. Only by doing so can we fulfill that destiny. As we learn to make better use of our time, we have to remember that healing is a lifelong journey. We may encounter several traumas on this journey, but recovery can be a productive process in that it makes us mindful of the time we've spent and the time we have left.

Every single one of us has something we can do to change the world while changing ourselves for the better. Whatever you may call it - destiny, dharma, mission or fate, start asking yourself today: what's yours?

Survivor Insights

Tools to Transcend the Narcissistic Abuse Experience

Question: What has been the most powerful tool you've used for healing?

"A narcissist will seek the prey with the highest ratio of reward to effort. They are basically lazy, cheap people but they still want a beautiful, smart, fit, sexually evolved partner. So if you are at a low point in your life or suffering some sort of loss - maybe you have an elderly parent or a death in the family or have just ended your marriage. These life circumstances are what they love." - Michelle

"My friends and family have been my anchors. Recently I have begun to reach out and search for support from other victims and survivors. I look forward to learning how to reprogram my patterns, to learning to positively cope with the PTSD, and to living my life as MYSELF again."
– Laura, Oregon

"Energy healing and energetic trauma clearing starting with the abuse from the narcissistic parent." – Jane, Massachusetts

"Watching your YouTube videos, reading your articles and also those by other experts such as Show Boundaries and Assc Direct and The Spartan Life Coach and Narcissist Support and Beverley Banov Brown etc. Being reminded that I'm not alone and that there are a huge number of people who do understand the horrific nature of narcissistic abuse has been enormously helpful. I'm finding it fascinating and liberating to learn more about NPD. I look forward to learning about how to overcome CPTSD. I also want to use reverse discourse / talking back / empowering mantras, as suggested by you." – Aurla, Brighton, England

"Honestly, the first codependent book I picked up when my world crashed around me in 1989, "Healing The Child Within" by Charles L. Whitfield MD; followed by many, many books on co-dependence and then your video on narcissistic abuse...which I had never heard of. I was finally able to figure out that not only was he bipolar (which he tells everyone about), but narcissistic, paranoid schizophrenic and probably a psychopath."

"Cognitive therapy. I want to try EMDR." – Kelly, California

"Telling my truth to a safe person and crying about this experience. After three years I am ready to start my life again. Adding in exercise and fun activities. I want to add meditation because I think our neurochemistry is changed by this experience. I also want to start art activities. I believe the creative part of us is very much harmed by these experiences." – Angelina M., Ohio

"Honestly, your blog has been the most helpful!! It's comforting to see that others have been through similar situations (and that I was not imagining things). Also, unfortunately, my work colleagues and our common "friends" think this person is great and wonderful. When I'm asked about her, I just say something neutral and then try to change the subject. So far, that works. I have one other friend who I have confided in, but I don't dare mention the truth to any "mutual" friends." – Lisa, New York

"The most powerful tools that have helped me in my healing have definitely been YouTube videos (yours in particular) so thank you so much for all your work. I also kept his last poisonous text message to remind myself (should I ever need it) of what he really is." – Jobo, England

"Reading, communicating online and watching videos have been the best healing tools for me. I read the stories of other people who have gone through what I did, I can participate in forums, blogs, Facebook etc. It has been great to be able to actually message other people who understand narcissistic abuse (and abusive psychopaths/narcopaths). It is also an important part of the healing process to be able to give support to others who are at varying stages of the healing process. And to receive support from them as well, when I have moments of pain, frustration, or other angst." – Anne, Indiana

"Watching your YouTube channel." – Anonymous in Virginia

"Google! A simple Google image search has turned up even more truth of who he is. The more truth I've seen the more apparent his lies. And just being busy and active! Staying busy and active keeps me from thinking about him much. Suddenly it's been a couple weeks and I find myself thinking less and less and less about him each day!" – Claudia, California

"Websites, books, videos of peoples experiences about the narc and turning to the Lord and reading the true word. These things have truly helped me overcome my narc in so many ways and to be honest I am happy he left me when he did, because it made it easier for me to get on with life and the positivity of my life a it stands now! I think that sums it up for me." -Nyree, New Zealand

"No contact, because once I was away from his toxic influence, I gained a more objective perspective on what I went through. Getting into a healthy relationship now has also been a big help for me." – ProudSurvivor, California

"Meditation. Writing. Performing spoken word at open mics." – Gloria, Mexico

"No contact, expressive arts (painting, performing music, gardening, learning new skills, sleeping better, calmness." Gail S. Robbins, Colorado.

"Learning about gaslighting is new and powerful for me. This allows me to systematically assess what went on and understand why I declined as I did. It also offers self-forgiveness because the responses are survival instincts." – Sandra, Washington

"Not living with her has done wonders for both me and my step-dad. I've recently learned about NPD by chance. I was buying socks on Amazon and I don't know how, but I came across "Children of the Self-Absorbed...A Grownups Guide to Getting Over Narcissistic Parents." That came in last night, so I'm looking forward to reading it, taking notes, and sharing it with my siblings...the less brainwashed ones anyway. All day, I've been listening to videos on YouTube about the topic. I finally have the correct terminology to describe her and our situation." – Alex from Townsend, MA

"Reading and learning. I need to understand something before I could readily accept things and move forward. I'm going to therapy soon too." – Good2BeFree, NJ

"Support groups, positive feedback have been so helpful. My medication was an important kickstart. I'm not sure where I will be going from here, but I'm sure it will continue to be up." – Mary, Washington

"No contact, trying to stay physically active and trying to do the things I know I used to enjoy. I am looking forward to looking forward to things again...I miss my "Joy." – Susie, Missouri

"God; introspection; physical workouts and health." – Greg Tenney, Indian Hills, Colorado

"Having God, spiritual guidance from my pastor and friends, having a boyfriend who is the opposite of narcissistic. Basically, having guidance from others to help me think differently, react differently and change the way I view myself." – Shannon, Central Ohio

"The most powerful healing is my children and my friends who have stuck by me. I have no contact with him even though sadly my son works for him. That breaks my heart but it was my son who first alerted me to what his father is! I am about to start yoga to help my mind and my body!" – Michele, Melbourne, Australia

"Reading about other people's experiences - so helpful and validating. Basically just getting on with your life and not letting them destroy your future." – Gemma, United Kingdom

"Again, No Contact! The silence is so comforting. Journaling is another powerful tool - our recorded memories are our truth - journaling helps me make sense of the chaos and validate my own experiences. Guided meditations and soothing sounds (EMDR, ASMR, et cetera) have also been incredibly helpful for me. Also, I doll up and work out to reassure myself that I am beautiful and desirable. I have also begun to read and think for myself and formulate my own opinions - I feel a lot more intelligent and clear-headed than I was a few months ago during the devalue and discard phase." – Diyanah, Kuala Lumpur

"Did a lot of astrology, to analyze her- 'very big ego', 'not interested in other persons' a..s.o. But the healing came from the very many clips on narcissism on you tube. Those helped, giving practical insight and confirmation of behavior I had been seeing." – Peter Klein, Netherlands

"Prayer and self-care. I am looking forward to building friendships and a support network beyond my wonderful husband. It has been difficult for me to keep friends over the years due to the trauma of abuse. I am excited to think about having a friend." – Ergsmith, Southern California

"The most powerful tool has been to educate myself about narcissistic personality disorder and to talk it through and journal about it." – Pam V., New Jersey

"An understanding of narcissism, knowing that it is not my fault. I need to strengthen myself now." – Rebecca, Washington

"YouTube videos and blogs on this topic have been very helpful. Like the stages of grief, I want through the anger phase where I was getting comfort from the snarky, sarcastic and "pissed off" tone of many memes on this topic, made for survivors of narc abuse. Those were emotionally satisfying for going through the anger stage." – Laurel, San Francisco

"I will continue to educate myself about this behavior. I never knew there was a specific behavior pattern. When I found this out, I was shocked to find out that strangers could identify him without ever meeting him. It validated a reality I never knew." – Kathy, Florida

"Putting distance between us and asserting my new found dignity. Future - make more friends." – Donna, Chattanooga, TN

"Group meetings; talking to trusted friends (but they get tired of it); reading a lot of books about Narcissism, and co-dependence- also several websites have given great comfort- knowing other women have been sucked into this horror as well." – Janet, Nashville, TN

"Learning about attachment theory has been huge. I turn most often to internet self help as it's available in the moments I'm the lowest. I am looking forward to shaking down to the floorboards to finally, really understand my self esteem and FOO issues that are at the root of my partner choices. I'm looking into CoDA and truly understanding love addiction/limerence. If I'm honest, I'm scared. I don't know if I will enjoy or want love that doesn't give me that rush. But I have to be healthy. I'm turning 30 this year. Mistakes will turn into desperation in a few years. I have to fix this." – Anonymous, California

"The videos on Youtube have been very helpful. I am continuing to read books." – Marie, New Orleans

"The most powerful tool has been to be really honest with myself and other people and the narcissistic recovery community about who he is and what my part in the situation was and how I'm learning from this. The most effective healing tool has been my connection two other people who have suffered and are still suffering from narcissistic abuse." – Maria M., Location Undisclosed

"Yours and other YouTube channels. Spending time with supportive people. Walking in nature, some meditation. Still seeking a good coach...or support group." – Anonymous, Location Undisclosed

"Spartan life coach seminar, Pete Walker book "CPTSD from survival to thriving." – VCK, Germany

"Listening to my intuition. Find something to give you at least one belly laugh daily. I will continue to use self-help videos and online books/blogs as well." – Solo Happy, Chicago

"What helped me is to ACCEPT that he had no conscience. This was the biggest road block to healing: To accept that the apple is blue on the inside when you've only known apple that were yellow on the inside - your mind will not accept it at first." – La grande guerrire

"Talking, or rather writing and friendships. Reclaiming the parts of me that I had lost, reclaiming my life." - Magpie, United Kingdom

"Hard to pick out one but my favorites are Melanie Tonia Evans, Spartan Life Coach, Esteemology, Lisa A Romano. I just read everything and anything I could find. Fell asleep listening to affirmations every night for weeks. I started going to church as my family ceased contact with me. I'm going to go to al-anon meetings and see if those help." – Lilly, Auckland, New Zealand

"Finding ways to enjoy my own life. I still hope to be ready to date again, and do feel more confident about recognizing a healthy potential partner." – Faye, FL

"The support of friends, and spiritual studies: both of which lead me to have a better understanding of my strengths, as opposed to the weaknesses he constantly pointed out to me." – Anne, New York

CHAPTER 8

Ten Life-Changing Truths for Abuse Survivors

The journey to healing from emotional or physical abuse requires us to revolutionize our thinking about relationships, self-love, self-respect and self-compassion. Abusive relationships often serve as the catalyst for incredible change and have the potential to motivate us towards empowerment and strength, should we take advantage of our new agency.

Here are ten life-changing truths abuse survivors should embrace on their journey to healing, though it may appear challenging to do so.

1. It was not your fault.

Victim-blaming is rampant both in society and even within the mental landscapes of abuse survivors themselves. Recently, the victim-blaming and the mythical "ease" of leaving an abusive relationship has been challenged in the public discourse. Accepting that the pathology of another person and the abuse he or she inflicted upon you is not under your control can be quite challenging when you've been told otherwise, by the abuser, the public and even by those close to you who don't know any better.

Abuse survivors are used to being blamed for not being good enough and the mistreatment they've suffered convinces them they are not enough. The truth is, the abuser is the person who is not enough. Only a dysfunctional person would deliberately harm another. You, on the other hand, *are enough*. Unlike your abuser, you don't have to abuse anyone else to feel superior or complete. You are already whole, and perfect, in your own imperfect way**s.**

2. Your love cannot inspire the abuser to change.

There was nothing you could have done differently to change the abuser. Repeat this to yourself. Nothing. Abusers have a distorted perspective of the world and their interactions with people are intrinsically disordered. Pathological narcissists and sociopaths are disordered individuals who have specific manipulation tactics as well as behavioral traits that make them unhealthy relationship partners.

Part of their disorder is that they feel superior and entitled; they are usually unwilling to get help and they benefit from exploiting others. A lack of empathy enables them to reap these benefits without much remorse. Giving your abuser more love and subjugating yourself to the abuser out of fear and out of the hope that he or she would change would've only enabled the abuser's power. You did the right thing (or you will) by stepping away and no longer allowing someone to treat you in such an inhumane manner.

3. Healthy relationships are your birthright and you can achieve them.

It is your right to have a healthy, safe, and respectful relationship. It is your right to be free from bodily harm and psychological abuse. It is your right to be able to express your emotions without ridicule, stonewalling or the threat of violence. It is your right not to walk on eggshells. It is your right to pursue people who are worthy of your time and energy. Never settle for less than someone who respects you and is considerate towards you. Every human being has this right and you do too. If you are someone who has the ability to respect others and are capable of empathy, you are not any less deserving than anyone else of a relationship that makes you happy.

4. There is still hope for a better life.

Healing and recovery is a challenging process, but it is not an impossible one. You may suffer for a long time from intrusive thoughts, flashbacks and other symptoms as a result of the abuse. You may even enter other unhealthy relationships or reenter the same one; this is not uncommon, as a large part of our behavior is driven by our subconscious. Still, you are not "damaged goods." You are not forever scarred, although there are scars that may still remain.

You are a healer, a warrior, a survivor. You do have choices and agency. You can cut all contact with your ex-partner, seek counseling and a support group for survivors, create a stronger support network, read literature on abusive tactics, engage in better self-care, and you can have better relationships in the future. If you suspect you were the victim of emotional abuse, you can read about the manipulation tactics of emotionally abusive people and understand how pathological individuals operate so that you can protect yourself in the future. All hope is not lost. You can use this experience to gain new knowledge, resources and networks. You can channel your crisis into transformation.

5. You don't have to justify to anyone the reasons you didn't leave right away.

The fear, isolation and manipulation that the abuser imposed upon us is legitimate and valid. Studies have proven that trauma can produce changes in the brain. If we experienced or witnessed abuse or bullying in our childhood, we can be subconsciously programmed to reenact our early childhood wounding.

The trauma of an abusive relationship can also manifest in PTSD or acute stress disorder regardless of whether or not we witnessed domestic violence as a child. Stockholm syndrome is a syndrome that tethers survivors of trauma and abuse to their abusers in order to survive. This syndrome is created from what Patrick J. Carnes, Ph.D calls "trauma bonds," which are bonds that are formed with another person during traumatic emotional experiences. These bonds can leave us paradoxically seeking support *from the* source of the abuse. Biochemical bonds can also form with our abuser through changing levels of oxytocin, dopamine, cortisol and adrenaline which can spike during the highs and lows of the abuse cycle.

The connection we have to the abuser is like an addiction to the vicious cycle of hot and cold, of sweet talk and apologies, of wounds and harsh words. Our sense of learned helplessness, an overwhelming feeling that develops as we are unable to escape a dangerous situation, is potent in an abusive relationship (Seligman, 1983). So is our cognitive dissonance, the conflicting ideas and beliefs we may hold about who the abuser truly is versus who the abuser has shown himself or herself to be. Due to the shame we feel about the abuse, we may withdraw from our support network altogether or be forced by our abuser to not interact with others.

These reasons and more can all interfere with our motivation and means to leave the relationship. You may have been financially dependent on your abuser or feared physical or psychological retaliation in the form of slander. Therefore, you never have to justify to anyone why you did not leave right away or blame yourself for not doing so. Someone else's invalidation should not take away your experience of fear, powerlessness, confusion, shame, numbing, cognitive dissonance and feelings of helplessness that occurred when and after the abuse took place.

6. Forgiveness of the abuser is a *personal choice, not a necessity.*
Some may tell you that you have to forgive the abuser to move on. Truly, that is a personal choice and not a necessity. You might feel forgiveness of the abuser is necessary in order to move forward, but that does *not*

mean you have to. Survivors may have also experienced physical and sexual abuse in addition to the psychological manipulation. You may have gone through so much trauma that it feels impossible to forgive, and that's okay.

It is not our job to cater to the abuser's needs or wants. It's not our duty to reconcile with or forgive someone who has deliberately and maliciously harmed us. Our duty lies in taking care of ourselves on the road to healing.

7. Forgiveness towards yourself is necessary to move forward.

Self-forgiveness is a different matter. You do have to demonstrate compassion towards yourself and forgive yourself for not leaving the relationship sooner, for not taking care of yourself better, and for not looking out for your safety and best interests. These are all things survivors tend to struggle with in the aftermath of an abusive relationship and it can take a while to get to this point.

Remember: You didn't know what you know now about how the abuser would never change. Even if you had, you were in a situation where many psychological factors made it difficult to leave.

8. You are not the crazy one.

During the abusive relationship, you were gaslighted into thinking your perception of reality was false and told that you were the pathological one, that your version of events was untrue, that your feelings were invalid, that you were too sensitive when you reacted to his or her mistreatment of you. You may have even endured a vicious smear campaign in which the charming abuser told everyone else you were "losing it."

Losing it actually meant that you were tired of being kicked around, tired of being cursed at and debased. Losing it actually meant that you were finally starting to stand up for yourself. The abuser saw that you were recognizing the abuse and wanted to keep you in your place by treating you to cold silence, harsh words, and condescending rumor mongering.

It's time to get back to reality: you were not the unstable one. The unstable one was the person who was constantly belittling you, controlling your every move, subjecting you to angry outbursts, and using you as an emotional (and even physical) punching bag.

Who are you? You were the person who wanted a good relationship. The one who strove to please your abuser, even at the cost of your mental and physical health. You were the one whose boundaries were broken, whose values were ridiculed, whose strengths were made to look like weaknesses. You attempted to teach a grown person how to behave with respect - often fruitlessly. *You were the one who deserved so much better.*

9. You do deserve better.

No matter what the abuser told you about yourself, there are people out there in healthy relationships. These people are cherished, respected and appreciated on a consistent basis. There is trust in the relationship, not the toxic manufacturing of love triangles. There are genuine apologies for mistakes, not provocation for attention or quick reconciliation.

Consider this: aside from the experience of trauma, these people in healthier relationships are not drastically different from you. In many ways, they are just like you - flawed, imperfect, but worthy of love and respect. There are billions of people in this world, and yes, you can bet there are plenty out there who will treat you better than the way you've been treated before. There are people out there who will see your wonderful strengths, talents, and who will love your quirks. These people wouldn't dream of *intentionally hurting you or provoking you*. You will find these people - in friendships and in future relationships. Perhaps you already have.

10. It may have seemed this relationship was like a "waste of time" but in changing your perspective, it can also be an incredible learning experience.

You now have the agency to create stronger boundaries and learn more about your values as a result of this experience. As a survivor, you've seen the dark side of humanity and what people are capable of. You've recognized the value of using your time wisely after you've exhausted it with someone unworthy. With this newfound knowledge, you are no longer naive to the fact that there are emotional predators out there. Most importantly, you can share your story to help and empower other survivors. I know I did, and you can too.

Survivor Insights

Chasing Dreams and Rebuilding Your Life After Abuse

Question: What is one thing you hope to achieve after this experience?

"I would like to have personal peace and get my confidence back regarding friendships. (Working on it!) I still feel bad about the situation and I dread running into this person at a business function. I definitely don't want to ever be alone with her. I wish I could "move on" and not be worried about such things, but the whole situation still makes me very uneasy. I'm sure with time the feeling will lesson, but I think I will always need to be on my guard, especially with this narcissist." – Lisa, New York

"True liberation - from the traumatic memories. To be able to look back at the Narcissist and everything to do with him with total indifference." – Diyanah, Kuala Lumpur

"I grew up in a deeply loving family and my parents shaped my character. Not everyone grows up this way. So I hope to impart wisdom to my children so that they realize that everyone does not have the same character as their mother and to watch and recognize warning signs of narcissists." – Michelle the Midwest Triathlete

"I still intend on being the sweet, kind, empathic being that God created me to be in spite of everything that I've been through and I hope that one day when I'm fully healed, I'll meet a lovely man who is worthy of all I have to offer in a relationship." – Jobo, England

"I hope to be able to get out of debt so I can take care of some of my own needs for a change. I need a new car and can't even afford to buy one right now because I paid off all of HIS bills, and took care of everything he didn't have the responsibility to take care of. In the process he had to have this, and that, and he sat home while I worked to pay for everything. I played in his band on the weekends, so he did make money that way, but that money wasn't near enough to cover his expenses. So I hope to get out of debt, take care of my own needs, and have a nice life in spite of all the damage he caused." – Anne, Indiana

"I hope I have gained the wisdom to not let this happen again without becoming bitter." – Claudia, California

"To move with life and follow happiness wherever it may take me and not to linger on the past. I am at present still working on this feeling I have of disappointment. I'm finding this much harder to overcome than I did my anger. I think it's because I'm more disappointed with myself than anything else. Even though it's not pulling me apart, it's just the thought of it still there and I need to work on how am I going to remove it from my life." – Nyree, New Zealand

"To learn more about myself and to never repeat this ever again." – ProudSurvivor, California

"Greatness." – Gloria, Mexico

"To feel fine being by myself. And if there is an authentic, healthy person out there for me, someday, then I wish for that as well." – Gail Sarah Robbins, Colorado, USA

"My journey is still in front of me since we are not yet divorced, my son is suffering and in trouble at school, and my job is on the line. I am just going forward with the faith that now that I have myself back and can see what is happening to protect my child, that is enough to carry me through." – Sandra, Washington

"Travel. I've been all over the US and a few different countries (thanks to the military), but I want to land all over the globe." – Alex Townsend, Location Undisclosed

"I still have nightmares. I can't imagine trusting another man in my life. I want desperately to get over that." – Mary, Washington

"I want to find my JOY....I want to continue to compete in my sport and become a professional athlete....I want to be a world champion. I will be a world champion." – Susie, Missouri

"See my son grow into an honorable and kind young man." – Greg Tenney, Colorado

"Preserving the sanity of my daughter. So far I've been successful in keeping fights from her. When he tries to start an argument in front of her, I cut him off. I won't answer him with anything except "We're not discussing this in front of her." Maintaining this is high priority." – Shannon, Central Ohio

"A healthy and honest relationship with trust and integrity." – Gemma, United Kingdom

"Helping other survivors." – Ergsmith, Southern California

"I'd like to use what I've learned to help others." – Pam V., New Jersey

"A healthy relationship." - Anonymous, Location Undisclosed

"I want to learn how to progress with healing and recovery with the unfortunate factor of having a primary relative play enabler/flying monkey/accuser/ blamer/shamer/guilter."

"Going to the grocery store without a panic attack and retaining a job." - Anonymous, Location Undisclosed

"Find peace and healthy love." – Kathy, Florida

"Forgetting the past." – Donna, Chattanooga, TN

"Offer yourself permission to give to yourself. I don't know how to answer this question. I still want intimacy with the partner of the companionship building a life together that is healthy and fun. I am anxiously living my life with anxiety every time I hear his voice now. Every time he walks into the room and comes to where I am, I am conscious now of the reason. He is trying to get something from me. Asking me questions etc. It's not because he genuinely loves me and wants to know how I'm doing. He lies to me and tells me he wants to know how I am doing so he can use me - it's not because he genuinely loves me and wants to know how I'm doing. He lies to me and tells me he wants to know how my doing so he can use me for his use of what he wants now. I deserve love instead of this." – Carla, Location Undisclosed

"Freedom in my mind. My mind still cannot concept how cruel people really can be. I'm nothing like that, so my mind has a hard time understanding wolves in sheep clothing." – Sarah Pearce, California

"Look for a calm companionship- avoid being seduced sexually- it will give a man power over you." – Janet, Nashville, TN

"To come out a better person ... This experience has propelled me to become a better person. I have to keep my self productive and take myself out of my comfort zone just to raise my vibration." – Michelle, Northern California

"To advance awareness about NPD in a more broad, national venue to aid in prevention and to provide me with my own vindication, in a more conducive and supportive environment. But more importantly, to never make this mistake again and come out more confident and stronger than ever, which is happening now. Don't know how I am going to achieve this, but I will." Kari, South Florida

"Peace. The ability to trust a man ever again. I seriously have no idea if that will ever happen." – Anonymous from California

"Calmness and understanding, which leads to taking proper care of my physical and mental health." – Marie, New Orleans

"One thing I have achieved after this experience is knowledge about highly manipulative people. Since I am a person of integrity and have a huge heart I assumed others were the same. When I met the narcissist he seemed like such a passionate genuine person that I truly trusted him and his actions. I have learned to trust my intuition and not to doubt myself. I have achieved knowledge that I didn't have before about manipulator people who Gaslight and what gas lighting is." – Maria M., Location Undisclosed

"No more flashbacks." – Anonymous

"I would like to achieve spiritual and mental strength to pull myself in the right direction away from things that negatively weigh me down. I think of it as my spiritual weight plan that will shed the toxic people out and invite a good healthy life both mentally, spiritually and physically." – Ms. L, Idaho

"To fully heal and be stronger and better if I ever run into him or his family again." – Meredyth, New York City

"Financial security. I would love to start my own business and not have to work for someone else, specifically a narcissist boss!" – Heather, Location Undisclosed

"I want the complicated mind of NPD's to be academically researched much more and I want mainstream media to expose NPD to the world in an accurate manner." – Debbie, Michigan

"Strength/understanding of the experience. To make me a better person for the future. I am a survivor now." – S. from Wales

"Self worth and success as a Christian and human, as a mom, grand mom, family member and allow the boy now man in my life as I should have from the onset instead of the path of self destruction and lacking self-worth my ex used to say 'the truth shall set you free" as he was lying the ultimate lie- - - the funny thing is the truth is what you need to accept if you really want to be free of abuse and destruction of life and humanity." – Tammy, South Florida

"There is a tiny part of me that still kind of believes in romantic love. Would I like a healthy relationship? Hell yeah. Do I think it's a probability? No way. I'd just like to get my life back, what's left of it." – Lilly, Auckland, NZ

"Happiness without looking over my shoulder." – Cinde, Idaho

"I can share my experiences with other people, so they will be more aware of narcissistic abuse." – Ryn, Jakarta, Indonesia

"To pass on some of what I have learned to others in society, and especially to my children and grandchildren so they are better equipped to protect themselves, by recognizing what is happening early on in a relationship. To take a relationship slow and not be swept up by it. That "what you think is infatuation may be an intricately executed seduction strategy to hook you into an abusive relationship." – Faye, Florida

"I hope to teach my daughters that they do not have to be perfect to be loved, nor is it their responsibility if someone behaves badly." – Anne, New York

"A healthy relationship and remarriage." - Evelyn, Midwest, USA

"Restore my identity and self-esteem." - Diane, California

"Total no contact. Getting back/finding myself again." - Blueeyes, Indiana

"A loving relationship with a person who is not a narcissist." - Lou Ellen, Location Undisclosed

"Trust, love, happiness, feeling worthy." - Madie, Ireland

"I have a new relationship now with someone I met as a child before the first narcissist and we were torn apart by my parents for unknown reasons. We are happy together, although I am ostracized by most my family because of being with him. But, I want to achieve a trusting relationship with him. He is not a narcissist (believe me, I have put the poor guy to the test because of my fear and lack of trust) and I don't need him. But, I do want be with him for the rest of my life and he is loyal to me. So, I hope to eventually let go of my anxiety and put more trust in him, our relationship and in my own judgment." -Rhonda, Salt Lake City

"Waiting for Karma to bite him in the ass. I still dream of have a beautiful marriage, the way God intended it to be, a partner in this life and helpmate." -Kristina, Oregon

"I would like to do some of the things this man and I discussed when we were still talking about our "future together." Things like travel, climbing mountains, exploring new places. But with nicer people." - Judy, Colorado

"I wish I could find the ability to have a normal relationship."

"Courage and confidence to be free to serve God and not the narcissist." - Kenlee, Alabama

"I hope to achieve peace, true happiness and true love one day." - Lakita, Texas

"Emotional strength." - Glenda, Tennessee

"Getting healthy again physically and gaining real confidence for once." -Galina, Michigan

"Complete mental freedom." - Julie, Location Undisclosed

"Complete detachment from his opinions." - Amy, Seattle

"I hope to achieve happiness from within and remind myself that I AM WORTH IT!" - Jennifer, Ottawa, Ontario, Canada

"I hope to rebuild my life somehow- right now I am raw and weak so it does not feel like I have it in me." -Wendy, Albuquerque, New Mexico

"To live a life free from such manipulation, gaslighting and drama. I hope for peace and I am now experiencing it as God changes the landscape of my life." -Dawn, Michigan

"I am thankful beyond words because it has cleared my lenses...and they have been foggy for a good three decades!" -Pasqualena, Maryland

"I still hope to find love someday." - Jill, New Hampshire

"Experience happiness, live life loving me, get the old me back." -M., Chicago

"I'm still working on my self confidence. I've also been a victim of verbal abuse and sexual abuse as a young girl. I'm 51 and learning all over to make my way in the world which is very difficult." -Tina, Massachusetts

"A life I like." - Charlotte, Olso

"Freedom, self-worth and happiness with life." SF Snipers Wife, North Carolina

"Not to be too naive and trusting and pay attention to my inner senses and not to give people too much benefit of the doubt and not share too much too soon." - Leena, Calgary, Canada

"Peace and contentment and happiness whether alone or with a partner. I would like to be able to trust again so that I might be open to a relationship. I become addicted to a relationship easily." - Amanda, Tennessee

"I hope to achieve a peace of mind and confidence that I lacked even before the psycho broke me. There is beauty in this journey. That beauty is discovering who you are and just how intrinsically valuable and unique you are and feeling good. Teaching my children that their self worth belongs to them." - Teresa, Australia

"Restoration of my sense of self." - Cricketts, San Francisco

"I'm a happily married woman now. Honestly I believe it helped me realize what I need and deserve. I've always been happy alone, so why did I tolerate such abuse, I've achieved happiness with another. Completely." - Shawna Levonne, Ripley, West Virginia

"The one thing I still hope to achieve from this experience is to help other people heal from narcissistic abuse, in any way I can offer my assistance. I also know I will never ever venture down this road again. Even if it means staying alone for the rest of my life. Because, now I love me, and I love my own company. I am at peace. Something I never had before all this happened." - Dawn, British Columbia, Canada

"To shut down our businesses, attempt to alleviate some of the debt incurred and to move forward with this divorce within the next three months. I want to rebuild my life, my career and my finances, have a child and move on to a different future." - Hallie, Kentucky

"Trust in relationships again." - Kay, Texas

"Normalcy." - Ginny Lou, Alabama

"I'll never get trapped in a narcissistic or relationship that requires me to do more work to keep it going." - Josephine, Hong Kong

"To love myself. To accept myself. To respect myself. To learn how to set firm boundaries. To learn from the message of this. Everything is in me. I don´t need no one outside myself to validate me. Trust God." - Dzana, Stockholm, Germany

"Realizing the dreams that I have and set aside because it was all consuming." -Adele, Canada

"I still love this person and it is a cycle for me. I need to fully walk away and work through my feelings." - T. Newton, Tacoma WA.

"Not be dependent on, or miss men!" - Helen, Australia

"To be able to trust again." -Mikala, Euthulla, Australia

"To feel like myself again. To not feel all the negative emotions I feel all the time." -Sarah, Ohio

"Justice! But it won't happen." -Tara, Georgia

"I need to learn to trust again." - Susan, Indiana

"That I will return to the old person I was before I met this purely evil man." - Allison, Georgia

"Trusting men." -Dawn, Memphis

"To help other people recognize the signs and avoid or get out of a relationship with a toxic personality." -Carla, South Africa

"I want to heal." - Karyn, Australia

"I want to reach all the goals that I couldn't before due to the narcissist's abuse." - Miss Diane Emery, Texas

"Self-confidence." - Maria, California

"Live out my time to work with my children, Horses and Nature." - Melly, Ohio

"I'd love to say my goal is to help others in this situation but right now, being fresh out of it, I just hope to heal, to feel better about it, to see my pain subside." - Anonymous, Syracruse, NY

"A knowledge and understanding of narcissists so that you can avoid them and happiness within pure happiness and love for yourself ." - Danielle, Melbourne, Australia

CHAPTER 9

Owning Our Power and Agency

The Distinction Between Victim-Blaming and Owning Our Agency

Victim-blaming is a touchy subject for many survivors, and rightfully so. Survivors of emotional and/or physical abuse are sickened by victim-blaming. I am, too. Why wouldn't we be? We have been in relationships where we were constantly gaslighted, mislead, invalidated and mistreated. The last thing we need is the outside world blaming us for not leaving soon enough, or for getting into the relationship in the first place. It's a whole other degree of invalidation that survivors simply don't need. It hurts us even more that the world refuses to acknowledge how difficult it is to leave an abusive relationship when you're in the midst of it, because you're experiencing so much cognitive dissonance that you don't even know whether to trust your own perceptions and realities. Abusive relationships severely hinder our perceived agency, overwhelm us with a sense of learned helplessness, and make it difficult for us to navigate the seemingly impossible constraints imposed by these toxic relationships.

I wholeheartedly understand this, and sympathize. However, I want to draw a distinction between victim-blaming versus acknowledging that we do we have the power to change our lives. I feel this gets lost somewhere in our resistance to concepts that may challenge us to evaluate and examine ourselves during the healing process or may appear to be blaming us for the abuse but can actually challenge us to move forward towards self-improvement and fulfillment. I feel, as both victims and survivors, we have a tendency to belittle or demean any concept, idea or helping resource that tells us to also look inward when unraveling our own relationship habits. I understand why this would be the case – we might perceive these resources as being patronizingly ignorant. We might think these resources are telling us that we somehow asked for the abuse, or that we attracted it.

Some resources are in fact victim-blaming, but we have to learn to distinguish between what is victim-blaming versus what is encouraging us to own our own agency. Only when we learn this distinction can we also own our "surviving" and thriving status as well as our legitimate victimization by the toxic partner.

I know that there are many survivors out there who had never experienced interacting with a narcissist or a sociopath before they had this experience. They feel strongly about the fact that their relationship patterns were healthy before they met the narcissist or the sociopath. Still, even for those survivors, we can learn a lot about our own strengths (and weaknesses) from this experience. Not because those weaknesses justify the abuse, but because all human beings have imperfections and vulnerabilities, and emotional predators tend to prey on these. If we tend to enjoy flattery and equate it with genuine care or love (which most people do!), we now have the power to change that perspective and acknowledge that the next time someone tries to excessively "lovebomb" us, our experiences have taught us that it is not necessarily equivalent to sincerity, and that it may actually be a red flag.

Acknowledging that we have the ability to now see red flags and recognize them, is not victim-blaming, but owning our agency and ability to protect ourselves. It is true that emotionally abusive people can hide behind masks for so long that we may never know we're with one until years later. However, that is why it is so important to create strong boundaries early on so that no one person can dominate your life. That is why it is so important to spend time alone before you enter new relationships, to get accustomed to enjoying yourself, so that should these red flags come up, you know you have the choice to leave, and the threat of being lonely will not stop you.

For survivors who do have a pattern of getting involved with pathological partners and remaining with them, I do not believe it is blaming yourself to try to understand yourself better as a result of this. Whether it's acknowledging that you had a toxic parent that may have influenced your own relationship with a Narcissist or whether it's examining how the relationship took a toll on you, it really is beneficial to always reflect upon what happened, how it affected you, how it may have triggered past traumas.

This reflection shouldn't be confused with blaming the victim or saying that the victim "wanted" the abuse – it's about recognizing the impact of the trauma bonds that kept us tethered to this person while still maintaining our ability to heal ourselves. It's about recognizing any insecurities or any people-pleasing behavior that may be holding us back from fully healing and owning our full potential while knowing that we were unfairly mistreated. It's also about acknowledging our strengths – our empathy, compassion, the beautiful qualities of humanity that the narcissist or sociopath lacks, and recognizing that these were taken advantage of.

It's important to acknowledge that you cannot change or control the pathology of the other person, but that you can make positive changes in your own life by initiating and maintaining No Contact or Low Contact, engaging in taking care of yourself fully and holistically during the healing process and afterwards, and pursuing your dreams while moving forward.

As I noted in the various myths about abuse survivors, No Contact *is* difficult and so is leaving an abusive relationship. There are plenty of trauma and biochemical bonds that keep us attached and effects such as PTSD or complex PTSD that require professional treatment. However, healing in the aftermath is all about you and your choices, as the abuser is no longer part of the equation. If you even have the slightest form of willingness and hope to rebuild your life, you will find yourself taking the small steps needed to pave the path to bigger outcomes.

The 3 Steps to Owning Our Agency and Power After Narcissistic Abuse

1. Recognizing the power and agency you do have in the situation, even if there is a discrepancy between your perceived agency and actual agency due to the abusive and traumatic nature of the relationship.

What is the agency *you* do feel you have (not the agency others think you have, because they aren't the ones in the relationship, and they don't know what it's like)? What are the small changes you can make in your life, right now, that can help you engage in self-care and healthier boundary-setting with others? This could be minimizing contact and interaction with your abusive partner, seeking our resources online or in your community, incorporating small self-care breaks in your weekly routine – the sky's the limit and small steps can lead to bigger milestones.

2. Asking for help.

Contrary to what many people think, asking for help is not a sign of weakness or powerlessness – it's a sign of immense power. Asking for help is a sign to the universe that says, "I am ready to be served, I am worthy and valuable of receiving the guidance and support of others." Ask for help from a validating and supportive mental health professional or coach, ask for help from a supportive friend or family member. If you feel you are socially isolated because of your abuser or because of social anxiety stemming from the abuse, use technology to your advantage. Ask for help online, through survivor forums or mental health professionals who you may be able to reach through e-mail.

3. Change your belief systems.

Use the healing modalities we've discussed in Chapter 3 to target and challenge your belief systems through healing modalities like CBT, meditation, self-hypnosis and positive affirmations. Reframe your experiences and rewrite the negative narratives you hold about yourself. When you change your beliefs about yourself and your perceived agency, you can change your world and act on your actual agency, owning your true power.

This is about owning our story and owning our agency. This is not saying that anything the narcissist or sociopath did to you was your fault; not at all. It is saying that you are STRONGER than what he or she did to you, and that you will use this opportunity to reflect, return any blame to your perpetrator, and acknowledge that in the future, you now have the power (and now the resources) to walk away from what no longer serves you.

The reason I am writing this section is because I don't want our resistance to victim-blaming (a perfectly legitimate protest) to be confused with not acknowledging our remaining agency and power, something we felt was threatened or even lost completely due to the abuser's control over us. I get many comments from people that are quite threatened by this idea that we can be victorious after abuse, that we can rebuild our lives, by those who feel they are forever damaged.

I understand this feeling, and my book is in no way meant to invalidate your pain or suffering. You have a right to all of your emotions, all of the pain that you are feeling and expressing, the right to own the traumas you've experienced. My mission is not to invalidate this pain, but rather to motivate and inspire you to channel it in your healing journey. I fully believe each survivor has a part of them, no matter how tiny it may be, that is still hopeful and willing to heal. It is that small whisper within them, guiding them to a resounding roar. Do not give up, even on the darkest of days. Keep listening to that inner voice to continue forward.

We do not have the power to determine the terrible things people do to us; but we do have the agency and power to turn to constructive outlets for healing. We do not have the power to stop ourselves from being a victim of a crime; but we do have the agency and power to help other survivors by sharing our story. We do not have the power to change a narcissist or sociopath or control the degree to which they abuse us; but we do have the power to detach, hopefully cut contact with the narcissist if possible, take the time to heal and not enter a new relationship until we're fully ready to do so.

Our choices still exist. We are simultaneously victims and survivors; we have regained our agency and power from the abusive relationship, and this enables us to thrive and heal in ways we must recognize and acknowledge. Our interactions with narcissists give us an immense opportunity to look at what needs to be healed within us (whether these wounds were created via the relationship, past traumas or both), what boundaries we need to be more firm about (for example, not letting a partner communicate with us only via text and stay in contact 24/7 can protect us from what is likely the love-bombing from an emotionally unavailable con artist), and what values we hold most dear (if someone doesn't share our values of loyalty, fidelity, and integrity, we now know these are deal-breakers even if we tried to negotiate this in the past). We may have lost our sense of agency and power when we were struggling in a relationship with an abusive partner, but now we can take back the control.

These experiences remind us what is most important: self-love and self-care. It is not victim-blaming to look at what positive changes we can make in our lives to better ourselves, nurture and heal ourselves from the abuse we've endured. Not because we're "asking" for these people in any way, but because we DID in fact experience harmful relationships with them. We are not perfect, but we did not in any way deserve or invite the abuse. We can improve ourselves without having to blame ourselves. This means that we have to be proactive about healing without victim-blaming. There IS a distinction, and there is power in acknowledging that distinction.

My discussion on the distinction between victim-blaming and owning our agency was featured on Harvard-trained clinical psychologist Dr. Monica O'Neal's website on www.drmonicaoneal.com.

CHAPTER 10

Writing Your Way to Recovery and Closure

As I discussed in Chapter 3, writing can be an incredibly powerful tool for healing and empowerment. It seems fitting that the book should end on that empowering note, as writing for both me and countless survivors has served as a portal for us to create a reverse discourse to the abuse and trauma we have experienced.

I hope I can speak on behalf of many victims of abuse in this chapter by sharing a letter I've written to all abusers. I also invite you to also write your own "Dear Abuser" letter. Please do not attempt to send this letter to your abuser, as this will interfere with No Contact. The purpose of this exercise is simply to empower you with a creative outlet for your emotions.

Although I addressed this letter to abusers, I truly wrote it to empower and validate victims themselves - to motivate them to express themselves through other outlets and gain their own closure through exercises like writing the "unsent" letter. I have included my own letter, which is addressed generally to the abusers I've met, as well as those I know are out there, as an example below.

A Letter to All the Abusers Out There

Dear Abusers:

You may not know me, but I know you. I've been involved with you, and though you come in many different appearances, shapes, sizes and backgrounds, you are all more similar than you think.

You feed upon the insecurities of others. You make cutting sarcastic remarks to belittle others, because you will never know the joy of elevating others or respecting them the way they deserve to be respected. You are condescending in tone, manner and attitude, because you want so desperately to believe you are the powerful one in every interaction. You are physically aggressive, emotionally depraved, sadistic, destructive and poisonous.

Here's news for you: you are powerless. You are powerless without supply. Powerless without a victim to believe in your lies. You derive your sense of superiority from another's subjugation. Your power is dependent upon a victim's psychological investment in your false image, not your true self.

Each victim you come across, each victim you use as an emotional or physical punching bag, will eventually leave or be left by you when you realize you can no longer control him or her. The victim that stays will be the unlucky one, forever enslaved to your mind games. Even so, little by little, you will have to up the ante on the power ploys in order to maintain power and control.

How exhausting it must be to try to play puppeteer to someone whose strings you've entirely manufactured; you will never have the pleasure of receiving love and affection from a pure source of willingness, but rather from a place of fear, a place of trauma, of enslavement, of necessity. Your audience or harem does not count, as no one besides your victims know the real you. Even if they have caught glimpses of who you are, they do not love who you really are. How difficult it must be to realize that you will never be truly loved, and that you will never truly love another person.

You so desperately want to believe that within every relationship, you are a "catch," more intelligent, more attractive, more desirable and more accomplished than the victim whose energy you drain every day like the emotional vampire you are.

The truth is, you are none of these things. Every victim you target is inherently morally, spiritually, and intellectually superior to YOU. That is because victims of abuse do not have to abuse others to gain a sense of self-worth or importance. They already feel whole just as they are. They derive fulfillment not from harming others, but from helping others. They feel joy in showing compassion, respect and empathy for their fellow human beings. They give love without hate. They know we are all interconnected, and that hurting another hurts themselves. They have genuine, authentic accomplishments and successes they don't need to defend or boast about in order to feel good about. They have a conscience you can only imitate.

You, on the other hand, live in a world of brokenness, of false pride and fragile egotism. You realize you are truly alone, on the inside, regardless of how much power and pull you think you have over others. Surrounded by adoring fans who know nothing about your true intentions or your malice, you start to recognize that they, too, only care about your prestige and your appearances.

One day, your false image will shatter and the world will see you for who you truly are, and not who you pretend to be. One day, your victim will walk out the door. One day, you will look at yourself and realize that had you spent more time healing and loving, rather than fighting and hurting, you would be one with this world and not a destructive force within it.

Survivor Insights

Question: What is one thing you would advise to a fellow survivor going through narcissistic abuse?

"There is nothing you cannot overcome if you commit to it at a soul level." – Michelle, Midwest

"You are stronger than you think. You survived this. You know yourself better now than you ever did. You are not alone. You are loved. You are brave. You are a great person because you saw what needed to change; it was the hardest thing you've ever done, but you took the steps you needed to change it. Little by little, one step at a time, you changed it. That takes a tremendous amount of courage." - Elle, Virginia

"The problem is HIM not YOU. He is the crazy one, not you, you have been violated and spiritually raped. He took your love and your trust and made an absolute mockery of it. He shows no remorse for that and even gets a sick and twisted thrill out of it all. He is off making someone else's life a living hell so don't waste a tear on him, concentrate on yourself. Don't go around peeking through his keyhole trying to see how "happy" he is with his new "love" because he will never be happy and he hasn't a clue what love is. He has wasted enough of your precious time, go out there, heal yourself from this debacle and get on with your own life and watch out for the red flags, these predators can scope us out in a heartbeat." – Anne, Washington

"Don't attempt to get revenge on him, no matter how hurt or humiliated you feel. If you do something drastic like I did, you will look like the mad person, not him. Also, never get involved in arguing a point. He or she will argue black is white in order to win, and logic will not help you at all. They just love winding you up, especially about the things you feel most strongly about or your most deeply held beliefs. They themselves have no beliefs and care about nothing, so will change sides and change the goalposts at the drop of a hat. They particularly love beating intelligent and educated people in arguments, as this makes them feel superior, even though they are usually uneducated and have got a chip on their shoulder about it and envy you because you did the hard work to get your qualification." – Ålice A., England

"This is one of the hardest experiences you will ever have, but you will come out of this stronger, better, wiser. The abuser has not stolen your light. This is like a war and you must protect your light from a very, very dark energy in the form of a person." – Christa, Toronto, Canada

"It was not your fault that you were treated abusively." – Aurla, Brighton, England

"I suggest they read your "Five signs" blog carefully and take the advice seriously. Don't fall for anyone who comes across as "too charming" or flatters too much. Seems like this should be common sense, but I see a lot of others falling under the "spell" of this charismatic person, and it's really frustrating to watch the deception. Basically, she's super nice to people who can do things for her." – Lisa, New York

"Pick yourself right up. If they did it without a single thought of you, then you do the same. If you can't cause you are hurting, then think this: think about every bad thing they have done since you parted. Learn and believe their actions, not words." –Good2bfree, New Jersey

"I would always say 'listen to your gut instinct', it's never wrong and it is there for a reason, to protect you from nasty predators who are purely out to use and abuse you." – Jobo, England

"Read a lot or watch videos about this topic so you figure them out. It is one of the most important defenses, because as long as you close your eyes from the train that is coming towards you, you can not take action. You can only take action when you know what's going on. And never give up hope. However many people those monsters will infiltrate and use as marionettes, you are not a marionette. You are not the bad things they did to you or that you were pushed in to. You are not responsible for what they did or do to you. Only these cowards are responsible and they will never take responsibility for it, because they are not ever and will never be so strong and such a good person like you." – Helen, Berlin, Germany

"Don't fall for their stories, lies, excuses. Don't allow them to call, visit, email, send messages, nothing. No Contact is the best way. If they try to get in touch with you, they are just trying to suck you in again. That's it. Stay away, don't look back." – Anne, Indiana

"Listen to yourself! The first time your instincts tell you something is wrong listen. The second time they tell you RUN! Don't worry about hurting his feelings, listen to your own." –Claudia, California

"If you want a healthier, happier, enjoyable life without the narc in your life, a better way to find it is to leave when it's safe to. If you are a child with a narc parent, find help from a responsible adult or a family/friend member that you can trust and will be willing to help you to move to a safer environment." – Nyree, New Zealand

"You might have survived a storm yesterday, but you'll have a sunny tomorrow. You do NOT have to let this experience define you forever. Many other people have survived this before, and you will too." – ProudSurvivor, California

"It is not your fault. You are not what your abuser says you are. You did your best." – Gloria, Mexico

"They cannot authentically love anyone. They will often tell you they love you, but it is just a play on your emotions to get you to do what they want, so they can receive what they want for supply." – Gail Sarah Robbins, Colorado, USA

"Just listen to the little voice within that has been crushed down. Protect it like a candle flickering in the wind. You can go slowly and be protective. You can do silent things to cope. Put a flower petal in your pocket." – Sandra, Washington

"Accept that you're never gonna get an apology, because they're incapable of feeling like they've ever done anything wrong." – Alex, Location Undisclosed

"You aren't alone and it isn't your fault. When I talked to survivors, I was amazed at how many could tell my story word for word. They spoke of what happened, of how they stayed in spite of the torment, of how they went back because they knew it would be better - he told them it would. Some of us put decades into "getting it right" because we knew that if we loved him enough he would have no choice but to love us back." – Mary, Washington

"People like my husband suck the life out of you....I felt like I was dying....if you suspect your loved one is a narcissist...RUN!" - Susie, Missouri

"Just because you're a "man who won't hit a woman back" doesn't make you worthless, and you should not accept that kind of abuse either." - Greg Tenney, Indian Hills, Colorado

"If possible, go no-contact. If that's not possible...minimal contact. It seems impossible at first but once you "get it"...you'll see how beneficial it is." - Shannon, Central Ohio

"Read a lot, learn to love yourself again as I am sure everything you loved or did is a distant memory. Start to revisit your old passions and hobbies. Long walks, learn to love yourself again." - Michele, Melbourne, Australia

"Therapy and more therapy. Find others that have gone through this because the average person does NOT understand how we allowed what we did." - Gaia, Location Undisclosed

"Look after yourself as you will probably be suffering from PTSD for a while - be safe and sensible, do lots of nurturing things. Don't rush into another relationship, however tempting it might be, for distraction or to soothe the pain. Need to follow a natural path of healing by reconnecting with your lost or diminished sense of self." - Gemma, United Kingdom

"It wasn't your fault - be gentle on yourself." -Diyanah, Kuala Lumpur

"Even if you are still involved or have contact, endeavor to live your life for God and yourself. Doing so in the smallest ways can become a healthy habit to bolster your immune system and spirit." -Ergsmith, Southern California

"It isn't you, it's them! The narcissist is so adept in manipulating you that you think you are the one with the issue. You need to acknowledge that the person has narcissistic personality disorder and the behaviors that go along with it and that those behaviors are toxic to you. You need to put yourself first, and you need to stand up for yourself." - Pam V., New Jersey

"Do not engage the narcissist in verbal confrontations. You will lose. Walk away from the conflict." - Rebecca, Washington

"Believe in your heart and yourself, only you know who you truly are." - Stephanie, Winniepeg, Canada

"Watch out for the "fan club"; the enablers and flying monkeys! They will make it very difficult to progress with healing and recovery." -Laurel, San Francisco, California

"Build your support group and then run for the hills. Change your phone number, block Facebook, etc." -Donna, Chattanooga, TN

"Learn to truly love yourself and all the time and energy you would give to them, give to yourself and it's okay to be single and discover who you were really created to be." -Laurel, San Francisco

"RUN. If it seems off, RUN. RUN. RUN. RUN. RUN. Don't have sex with him until you truly know him. Listen to your body because it can feel it when a man is dangerous or faking. Read self-esteem and boundary books like your life depends on it. Because it might." - Anonymous, California

"Trust your gut feeling and if you go no contact you will indeed feel a void. But it will improve because you don't deserve to be mistreated or lied to." -Marie, New Orleans

"This is truly not your fault and you cannot change a narcissist. Your love will never be enough for a narcissist and you will remain emotionally, mentally, and spiritually bankrupt as long as you continue to engage with this person. It doesn't matter who this narcissistic is with, they will abuse whoever they can and whoever allows them to abuse. Don't be that person you're worthy of much more." - Maria, M., Location Undisclosed

"Work on the spiritually weak areas of who you are, listen to your gut feelings, and take time to know people. Meet other people so you can compare who is good for you and what will bring you trouble. Don't devote all your time to those negative people because you limit your ability to say no to them, won't find yourself trapped. People who love you and care about you will not seek to break you down or make you feel emotionally alone. The Golden Rule - love your neighbor as you want to be loved/treat others the way you wish to be treated, and do they reciprocate the same?" Ms. L, Idaho

"It's very very hard, you're not alone. The first few weeks will be the toughest but you deserve and you will get better." - Meredyth, New York City

"Get counseling. Find a low-cost/no cost option if money is an issue. Make sure you feel a good connection with your counselor and if you don't, keep going until you do. Feel the pain until one day you won't feel it any more. It will all be worth it in the end." -Heather, Location Undisclosed

"Once you realize what you're dealing with and how many survivors faced the same things, it opens up a whole new world of understanding." -Debbie, Michigan

"Focus all the negative into something positive. The narcissist might think he has won, but he will only do what he/she has done to you on their next victim. They will never change." S., Wales

"You are the black sheep because you have something special. Utilize the special trait and run forward." - Elizabeth V., San Marcos, California

"Either go no contact and or stay no contact, educate yourself on narcissism and disconnect from toxic people in general. Only then will you return to you." - Healing Vibe, Location Undisclosed

"Read Pete Walker's book "CPTSD from surviving to thriving." -VCK, Germany

"Listen to your intuition. Remain no contact. Do what makes you feel happy and loved. Avoid anything and anyone that brings you uneasiness." -Diyanah, Kuala Lumpur

"Read books on psychopath and narcissists, watch YouTube, read forums, join support groups, don't insulate yourself because you are ashamed. There is no shame to have." - La grande guerriere, Location Undisclosed

"Time will heal. There will be ups and downs but everyday gets better. Keep notes on every time you see, feel, hear the abuse or feel something is wrong. You'll want the info later when the shit hits the fan. It will also help you remember why it's okay to call it quits." - Billy Z., Chicagoland

"It gets easier, the person you fell in love with doesn't exist, accept that first! Work on your boundaries and remember, what YOU like doing, if you can't remember then go find out." Magpie, UK

"You can find peace and self-worth, find what works for you and screw anyone who wants to tear down your self-repair." - Tammy, South Florida

"Winnie the Pooh says it best, "Promise me you'll always remember: you're braver than you believe, stronger than you seem and smarter than you think." Oh and you'll find out real fast who your friends are. Don't waste your time explaining yourself to people who are determined to misunderstand you. It's ok to stop seeing people who don't want to see you grow."- Lilly, Auckland, New Zealand

"I hate to say the rote, 'Time will heal', because it does take work to sort through the immense pain, and you will continue to carry some of it with you. But it's not all bad, because it protects you from ever finding yourself blind-sided again. There is far more enjoyment in my life than I have ever experienced before. So in many ways my life has improved from what it was like even before the abuse. I enjoy every minute much more intensely, with greater awareness. Be merciful with yourself -- don't blame yourself for his behaviors! - Anne, New York

"It is not your fault and you deserve better." - Candice, KY

"Just get out. You will eventually find your new normal." -Evelyn, Midwest, USA

"It can be very subtle grooming. Take off your rosy glasses. It's not you. You're not crazy." -Diane, CA

"Please listen to family and friends. The bond is so addicting and we don't want to believe anything bad about our significant other." - Blueeyes, Indiana

"Understanding how manipulative a narcissist is, helps. No contact is best. Narcissists are like worms that get in your brain." -Lou Ellen, Location Undisclosed

"Look hard and deeply into yourself. See yourself as a story you've allowed someone else to create. Recreate your own story. Be responsible for yourself." - Kara, Indiana

"Once you are free from him (or her) don't concern yourself with what that person is now doing with their life, how he/she won't have anything to do with you or your children or how happy they seem to be. Get as far away from them as you can. Start as fresh as you can. Get a new job or go back to school if possible. Move away if you have to and are able to. Don't be afraid to make changes. You will be so much better off if you look ahead and not behind you. Forget him. Forget him. Forget him. If anyone you thought was your friend (or family) insists on maintaining contact with him/her, forget them, too. You don't need that. There are interesting and non-harmful people in the world you can connect with. Most of all, forgive yourself for your mistakes, for letting them in your life, It is not your fault. You were conned, probably by a very slick and practiced manipulator. It's okay to hurt for a while. In the end, you will be renewed and whole again." - Rhonda, Salt Lake City Area.

"They are not going to change…and you are NOT the chosen one." Vickie, South Bend, Indiana

"Remember the strong, confident, beautiful person you were before you met him/her. That person is still there, alive, vibrant and wonderfully made. YOU CAN DO THIS, one day at a time." - Kristina, Oregon

"There is an incredible sense of relief when you finally leave the relationship. There will be painful moments, but when I broke up with this man, I felt like a 12 ton weight had been lifted from my shoulders."
- Judy, Colorado

"He feeds on any slight crack of vulnerability or self-doubt; keep seeking resources to fill your cracks; fear not love makes our vulnerabilities torture zones." -Kenlee, Alabama

"No contact and seek a trauma therapist." -Lacey, Florida

"Run away as fast as you can. Keep a bank account they know nothing about." - Elizabeth, NC

"Not sure if I can give advice right now as I am still in the midst of the struggle, but in hindsight, I would say to hold on and not give up. There's joy up ahead...Don't take it upon yourself to get or take revenge, it'll only make him stronger and it won't make you feel better because you are better. Leave the revenge to God." - Lakita, Texas
"The opinions of others mean nothing, value yourself." -Glenda, Tennessee

"That if you have been abused before, and have any indication of anything that sets off a red flag, you should take extra special care to pay attention and protect yourself...and not make excuses for the person who is acting strange." Galina, MI

"Don't ignore abuse of any kind. Get away. It never stops or gets better."
-Julie, Location Undisclosed

"Talk to close friends, ideally the ones that knew you before you knew him. They will help you get back to the person you used to be (if you want to be her again, that is) and they are usually more willing and able to help you sort through the crazy. Also, remember that other people can see through their act, they can only fool people for so long and most likely you were the exception for being fooled for as long as you were." -Amy, Seattle

"Stand up for YOU because in some cases, YOU is all you have. Don't accept abuse and recognize it for what it is. Also, don't feel sorry for the abuser. Feel sorry for yourself that you didn't stand up for YOU when you should have." - Jennifer, Ottawa, Ontario, Canada

"Don't allow anyone to make you feel less than you know who you are. They have bigger problems that have nothing to do with you. Move on and don't look back." - SS, Location Undisclosed

"To be VERY patient and gentle with oneself- even when no one else believes you or understands." - Wendy, Albuquerque, NM

"WATCH for RED FLAGS. Educate yourself on what to watch for in these relationships and do NOT proceed if you see any of the narcissistic characteristics. One-sided loving relationships will suck the life right out of you and go on and on and on." -Dawn, Michigan

"KNOW THAT YOU DESERVE GOOD THINGS! You deserve RESPECT, COMMUNICATION, SUPPORT - you deserve to be loved the way YOU love others. You deserve to be cherished and should settle for nothing less. Believe it. With all of you. It takes time, and it hurts...but it WILL get better every day. You. CAN. DO IT!" - Pasqualena, MD

"I would tell them that they will heal and it will take time- find strength in others to find the strength that does lie within yourself." - Jill, New Hampshire

"Choose yourself, love yourself and understand that they're sick individuals who have no soul and don't care about you. They are incapable of loving anyone or anything. Run from them." - M., Chicago

"No contact and try very hard to understand that it's not you. That is the hardest thing for me because he looks so normal, happy, and has said that he never realized how little we had in common, so I blamed myself for all of it. Icing myself has been the hardest thing I have been able to overcome. No contact is the only way to avoid manipulation or comments that will hold you back from becoming a whole person again." - Amanda, Tennessee

"Save yourself! Get away from the narc abuser and stay away - your life may depend on it." -Wolflady, South East England

"You are beautiful. You are worthy. You are strong. You must love who you are. Find who YOU are. The narcissist is weak, a liar, a thief and will never take your soul. It is still there. You can find it. I promise. You were chosen because of your beautiful good qualities." -Teresa, Australia

"Taking from my own experience, where I became so depressed and felt so worthless, I felt I did not deserve to live (the narcissist makes you believe this). My advice is to try to not be alone with your thoughts for too long. Turn to your friends and people who know who you really are. You will shed many many tears through the process of healing. Surround yourself with positive happy successful people. Rid yourself of the negative Nellies that take the wind out of your sails. Be thankful for all the good in your life. It does get better, and you will find yourself again. I am not sure how long that will take as every individual is different. For me, 5 years later, I am now finally seeing the light. I have positive happy people in my life who respect me for who I am. It will happen for you...just BELIEVE." - Dawn, British Columbia, Canada

"Hang onto yourself, your experience and your feelings as YOUR truth. Do not let an abuser talk you out of your feelings or get away with telling you that you're crazy. If you don't fiercely fight to hang onto YOU, then they will have complete and total control over your emotions, your life, your future and even your identity. It happened to me, and I'm a very strong, educated woman. Little by little, he broke me down until I was a shell of a person and he used me as a slave to his emotional and psychological schemes. Whatever happens, fight to maintain any sense of your own self.... even if it's tiny and backed into a corner in the depths of your mind. You need you in order to fight back." Hallie, Kentucky

"Trust yourself and when something doesn't look, sound or feel right believe it!" -Kay, Texas

"If it feels wrong, listen to your intuition." -Lara, NH

"It's not your fault. You are enough. Love yourself. It's ok to cry." - Karina, Tulloss

"Get out right away because they will never change." - Jen, Baltimore, Maryland

"Don't stay afraid. Flex your muscles and see how strong you really are. We have to be incredibly strong people to survive at all for any length of time in a relationship like these. Use that strength to get and stay out!" - Ava, Tennessee

"Surround yourself with people who love you and be kind to yourself. This is not your fault." -Adele, Canada

"Realize who you're dealing with and untie yourself from the guilt they place on us." -T. Newton, Tacoma, WA

"Love yourself. You are not what their sick mind has invented." -Mikala, Euthulla, Australia

"Run. Run like hell. Do not look back. Accept it for what it is and be kind to yourself. You are worth more and didn't deserve this pain. -Sarah, Ohio

"Once an abuser, always an abuser! They don't change, so don't fool yourself." -Tara, GA

"Follow your gut! It doesn't lie." -Susan, Indiana

"Don't allow this evil person to change who you are--you are not defective ---they are!! Also, THE BEST WAY TO HEAL IS TO STAY AWAY FROM THE PERSON TOTALLY!!!!! Don't allow them back into your life for any reason." - Allison, Georgia

"Find someone who knows and understands what happened to you - really understands – i.e. - they went through it themselves." - Karyn, Australia

"It does get better, don't give up!" - Miss Diane Emery, Texas

"Make sure you have someone to confide in that is a neutral party and not friends with any of the narcissistic abusers. My family members have a lot of flying monkeys - who I thought were my friends and I tried talking to them about my problems and fears related to my Narcopath brother and they went right back and told my evil brother everything I said. And my Narcopath aunt had my brother take her to her lawyer to have me cut me out of her will and left everything to my brother. And I'm the only one in the family that is authentic and compassionate." - Maria, California

"Do things for yourself, start thinking about yourself, go out with friends, have fun, find your confidence and independence in these things. It's time for YOU!" - Danielle, Melbourne, Australia

"Never give YOURSELF away in the process." -Melly, Ohio

"Do everything it takes to leave as soon as possible." - Anonymous, Syracuse, NY

"Listen to your gut the FIRST time you feel something is not right and then don't doubt yourself when you see the first red flag." - Stef, Texas

"You can get through this." - Bridget, New Zealand

A Closing Love Letter to Abuse Survivors

I hope this book inspires readers to transcend their experiences and channel them into revolutionary transformation in all aspects of their lives. We all have a unique purpose and destiny to fulfill...reconnecting with who we are, and our calling is essential to moving forward with our lives and changing the world. I am sending every survivor reading this book all my best and infinite blessings to you and your healing journey. You are worthy, valuable, beautiful and deserving of all that is good.

Always remember there is a fighter and warrior inside of you that can transcend anything and everything. You are part of the revolution for changing the world, so continue to use your voice for the greater good no matter what. When you do not give up and continue to believe in yourself, your divine worth, and your incredible value - you are bound to be victorious.

Love, light and blessings to you, warrior –

Shahida

FAQ: FIFTY SHADES OF NARCISSISM

The following questions and answers are derived and adapted from real comments on my blog as well as my "Fifty Shades of Narcissism" Q&A in which readers granted me permission to use their questions and my subsequent answers in my book. No identifying information is included to protect the confidentiality of survivors.

Why do we gravitate towards narcissists? Is there such a thing as chronic victimization - a person who can have relationships with multiple narcissists and be primed to get into yet another one? How do we prevent that pattern?

We are drawn to narcissists because they tend to be charismatic and charming. Their false self is usually constructed of the very traits and characteristics we've been longing for – the love, validation and respect we may have longed for in our childhood but never received. A recent study by Haslam and Montrose (2015) showed that women who are looking for a marital partner, even if they had previous experience with narcissistic types, actually preferred narcissistic partners over non-narcissistic ones. That just goes to show that no one is immune – even if you have been with a narcissist before, that won't necessarily prevent you from gravitating towards another one in the future. Narcissists deliberately mirror and mimic our deepest desires and values, which makes them incredibly convincing and tempting to us. Narcissists also have a devil-may-care attitude that draws us in because they seem unfazed by anything – that's because they aren't.

It's important to remember that their false self is often the self we fall for - the true self of a narcissist does not unravel until they have hooked us into the relationship, so it is very difficult to identify that there may be any pathology present until we've invested fully in the relationship. By that time, their hot and cold tactics (also known as intermittent reinforcement) begin to take hold of us, creating that psychological and biochemical bonding that keeps us attached.

There is also such a thing as chronic victimization – when you find yourself being victimized by one narcissist after another. Unfortunately, many of us can be "primed" for narcissistic abuse due to the subconscious programming instilled in us from childhood – Research shows that those who witness domestic violence are more likely to become victims or perpetrators themselves - this can cause victimization by multiple narcissists throughout our lifetime, starting with experiencing narcissistic abuse in childhood.

There's a great book on early programming by Dr. Bruce Lipton – it's called The Biology of Belief (2007). He talks about an incredible study where a fetus on a sonogram can be shown to visibly respond to a fight between father and mother. Yes, programming can start as early as in the mother's womb! Imagine how traumatizing it must be for a child, if the only models of love they receive in their childhood, are models based on codependency (or as Ross Rosenberg calls it, Self-Love deficit disorder), abuse and disrespect. Trauma can have a significant impact on early brain development, interpersonal effectiveness and emotional regulation.

A large majority of our behavior is subconsciously driven – which means we ourselves may not even know the reasons for why we're addicted to the narcissist until we dig deeper into trauma from adolescence, childhood or even adulthood – trauma can happen at any time but most especially, it can rewire our brain significantly in childhood. If we've witnessed domestic violence or experienced any type of abuse or bullying that traumatized us, we are more susceptible to becoming attached to narcissistic partners in the attempt to resolve the trauma – this is what Dr. Gary Reece calls "trauma repetition" or "trauma reenactment."

For those of us who have a pattern of being with multiple narcissistic partners throughout our lifetime, it's important for us to look at the root of the original trauma – whether it was in childhood, adolescence or even young adulthood. There is something within us that needs to be healed in order to break this reenactment. Being with multiple narcissists is what I call "trauma upon trauma." We hide one trauma with another – we go from one narcissist straight into the arms of another – which makes it very difficult to step back and break the pattern, because we don't cease the pattern long enough to reevaluate and disrupt it. It's important that survivors address their subconscious programming as well as the programming instilled in them by their narcissistic partner – because it's very possible that our narcissistic partner is not only manufacturing new wounds in us but also reopening old ones. Addressing our wounds means we have to go deep within – usually with the help of a counselor – and we may even use methods like meditation or hypnosis to better access these deeper parts of our brain.

How do I break the cycle and stop getting involved with people who turn out to be narcissists?

This is an excellent question and one I think all survivors ask. I want to tell you that you've already taken the first crucial steps and should be very proud of yourself. You've learned about narcissism, you've ended relationships with narcissistic partners, and you've probably even taken a break from dating to work on yourself. You're on the healing journey. Everyone's journey to healing will be different, and unfortunately, there is no magic pill or a due date as to when you'll be fully ready to engage in a healthy relationship with a non-narcissistic partner. Having a narcissistic parent, as well as a series of narcissistic partner traumatizes us deeply – it shapes the way we look and interact within the world, the extent to which we trust others, and can have an impact on the way we look at ourselves in ways we're not even fully conscious of.

Healing does not have a time limit when it comes to that type of situation – we are always evolving and finding different ways to heal ourselves spiritually, emotionally, physically and psychologically. Survivors engage in different healing modalities – different types of therapy such as CBT or EMDR, acupuncture, aromatherapy, prayer, Reiki healing, meditation, abuse survivor groups, writing about their experiences – all of which can be helpful to them on their journey. Some survivors use Narcissistic Recovery Programs such as the popular one by Melanie Tonia Evans; others prefer more traditional methods. Only you can decide which combination of methods will be most useful for you, as each survivor has his or her own unique needs, beliefs and values that will need to be addressed. I highly recommend seeing a counselor who specializes in abusive relationships, if you haven't already, because that can be an incredibly validating and helpful experience as well in breaking the pattern for good.

I believe the moment we are actually ready for healthy, nourishing love is the moment when we stop looking for that healthy relationship with another person and start flourishing in a healthy relationship with ourselves. That takes a commitment to multifaceted healing on all levels of our being and deep engagement with self-care and self-love practices.

How do I tell the difference between the normal highs/lows of a regular relationship versus the idealization, devaluation and discard phases in relationships with narcissists?

Normal ups and downs in a relationship don't have abusive aspects to the extent that I've described. A non-narcissist, for example, would not need to stonewall/invalidate/smear campaign/gaslight/triangulate you constantly. Normal partners may have their flaws, may have different moods from time to time, but they don't persistently carry on affairs, deny they've said/done something they know they did, shut down every time you bring up a legitimate complaint, provoke you with belittling and insulting comments, attempt to stage a smear campaign against you or displace blame onto you. Normal partners have the ability to empathize and see your point of view – even if they disagree with it. They have the ability to feel remorse when they hurt you. They don't gain sadistic pleasure from constantly provoking you and making you feel badly about yourself.

That being said, you are the only one who knows the answer to what you're asking. You are the one who knows what your partner has done and said, and how that has affected you. If you're not getting what you want/need from a normal partner who is not abusive, that's a compatibility issue that needs to be addressed via communication.

If you're not getting what you need/want from a toxic partner, that's a whole other ball game because you're dealing with someone whose behaviors are unlikely to change. Not every partner is a narcissist, but not every partner is compatible with you either. That is something only you can answer.

What is the difference between a substance abuser who is emotionally abusive and a narcissistic abuser?

I've answered this question earlier on in the book but I think it warrants reiteration. I believe there is a difference between an alcoholic who has become dependent on his or her addiction and a narcissistic abuser who uses alcohol as a means to abuse and escape accountability - this means that their substance use is comorbid and co-exists with their narcissism.

Many survivors meet narcissistic partners who used alcohol or drugs as an excuse to engage in verbal and psychological abuse. Narcissists can abuse drugs in order to fill the void and perpetual boredom and numbness they feel. The difference lies in whether the abuser carries out their manipulative behavior and self-centeredness outside of his/her addiction, and narcissists most certainly do.

I want to stress that there are people with legitimate addictions to alcohol and they need help, support and compassion. What's important to remember is that there are many people who abuse alcohol or other drugs but do not abuse others when they do. Those who abuse alcohol and abuse others are often the ones who are using their addiction as an excuse to hurt others without having to be held accountable for the abuse they dish out while under the influence.

The truth of the matter is, curing a narcissist of his or her addiction will not cure his or her lack of empathy. There's a great book by Lundy Bancroft, author of Why Does He Do That?: Inside the Minds of Angry and Controlling Men (2013) who speaks about this. Bancroft worked with many abusive partners who still made conscious decisions while abusing substances. Their abusive behavior also continued outside of their substance abuse, even if it was in more covert and subtle ways.

It is not a distinction that's discussed often enough, but the overlap between substance abuse and narcissism must be discussed because victims may stay in relationships with narcissists if they are addicted to something, believing that if they help the narcissist cure his or her addiction, they will help to resolve the abuse. Nothing could be farther from the truth. So be very careful if you're dating someone with signs of both narcissism and substance abuse – especially if they're not willing to get treatment.

Should I tell a new partner about my experiences with narcissistic abuse? How can I tell the difference between someone who is sincere and trustworthy versus someone who is looking to love-bomb me?

In terms of dating new partners, especially if it's after a recent breakup with a narcissist, I would caution you to not reveal too much about your past relationship unless you've spent more time together, getting to know one another. If this man or woman is sincere, he or she will understand your need to take things slowly.

Someone who is love-bombing you would want to know about your past relationship patterns because they are trying to understand what you will accept/what makes you tick so keep that in mind. Fast-forwarding in the early stages of a relationship is often a red flag regardless - it prompts you to wonder whether the person is really into who you are and interested in taking the time to discover who you are versus enamored with who they think you may be. This could open the floodgates for emotionally unavailable people and/or other toxic partners like narcissists to subject you to more mind games than you need right now and put you on a pedestal only to push you off once their illusion of you is shattered even in a small way.

I suggest taking space and time to heal before getting into a relationship or even disclosing too much about your previous relationships to anyone. Watch your partner's actions and see whether it aligns with their words. Only time will tell.

That being said, I also don't advise approaching everyone and everything with suspicion either. Regardless of your fears, everything in moderation. Be open to whatever comes – whether it's red flags or true love. Take what you've learned to establish appropriate boundaries with others and honor your instincts.

Can narcissists change or be cured by therapy?

Whether a narcissist can benefit from treatment is highly dubious. I've heard from survivors that narcissistic/sociopathic abusers actually learn more manipulative tactics within therapy, thus exacerbating the abuse. They can also use couples' therapy to continue to project their false self onto their therapists and manipulate them into believing that the abuse is truly just in their partners' heads. There's still a debate on whether NPD can be fully cured. I personally believe narcissists can become more aware of their own narcissism, but due to their lack of empathy, I am not sure to what extent they benefit from treatment if there isn't an intrinsic motivation to change their behaviors. Perhaps successful treatment would need to address how becoming less narcissistic would benefit them in other ways that appeal to their self-interest.

There is a risk that therapy could also provide a site where narcissists actually learn to sharpen or practice their manipulation tactics. I've heard this can happen especially in couples' therapy, where the narcissist uses triangulation and the false self to gain control. Since they are clever wolves in sheep's clothing, it can be hard even as a mental health practitioner to assess the true motivations of the narcissist unless he or she has already been diagnosed. They may simply tell their therapists what they want to hear rather than having a genuine interest in improvement, and this can further invalidate the abuse victim's experience.

I believe that instead of focusing on trying to cure the narcissist, we must practice enough self-love and awareness to assess how to detach from one and move forward with our lives. Focusing on our own healing brings us to a healthier and more positive place and enables us to see that we do deserve better.

What are the differences between a partner who has Borderline Personality Disorder and Narcissistic Personality Disorder?

There can be clinical biases in diagnosing females as borderline and males as narcissistic. Thus people are likely to be diagnosed based on their gender even if they do have one or the other disorder. For example, a borderline male can be misdiagnosed as narcissistic because of a clinician's bias, while a narcissistic female may be seen as borderline or histrionic because of stereotypes of females being more emotional. There are actually some clinical distinctions between BPD and NPD. While BPD and NPD are both cluster B disorders with many, many overlapping symptoms (including manipulative tactics, a chronic sense of emptiness, a need for external validation and inappropriate displays of intense emotions such as rage), one thing they differ on is the degree of empathy they experience. BPD people, because they struggle with such overwhelming emotions, I would argue are capable of empathizing with the emotions of others moreso than people with NPD.

This is a very important question, as Borderline Personality Disorder (BPD) and Narcissistic Personality Disorder (NPD) have often been used interchangeably among survivors. Many people on my blog or YouTube channel share their story of a BPD partner, believing that narcissism and BPD are one and the same. It is actually Antisocial Personality Disorder that is closer to Narcissistic Personality Disorder than Borderline Personality Disorder because antisocial personalities demonstrate a high lack of empathy in addition to a disturbing lack of conscience and a high level of criminality with their interactions with others. Of course, abuse is still abuse regardless of the specific disorder, if any, a partner may have. However, I find it helpful to distinguish between the two so that survivors who are dealing with a BPD partner can better contextualize their experiences because it can be different than being with an NPD partner.

Contrary to popular belief, there are actually some clinical distinctions between BPD and NPD. BPD and NPD are both cluster B disorders with many overlapping symptoms including interpersonal manipulation, a chronic sense of emptiness, a need for external validation and inappropriate displays of intense emotions such as rage. However, one thing they differ on is the degree of empathy they can experience as well as their motivation for the way they behave interpersonally. BPD people, because they struggle with such overwhelming emotions, are capable of empathizing with the emotions of others more so than people with NPD. In fact, research shows that BPD individuals are actually more discriminating of mental states than people without BPD. Read "Borderline Empathy Revisited" on Psychology Today for more information.

According to Dr. Bessel van der Kolk, people with BPD are victims of trauma and do not deliberately enjoy hurting others to the extent that narcissists do. In fact, it has been stated by trauma expert Pete Walker that individuals with disorders such as Complex PTSD are often misdiagnosed with Borderline Personality Disorder because of how similar the symptoms can be in the realm of emotional dysregulation.

If you've met a BPD with severely narcissistic traits, it's possible that they have both disorders rather than just BPD, or have been misdiagnosed due to a bias in gender. While research states that 75 percent of NPD individuals are male, it's very possible that there is a high percentage of females with NPD who are being misdiagnosed as Borderline or Histrionic Personality Disorder because of gender stereotypes. Male rage is more normalized in society, while a female's narcissistic rage may be considered as "hysterical" and overly emotional. In addition, as female narcissists tend to be overtly sexual and vain, they can be misdiagnosed with Histrionic Personality Disorder. If you've met a Borderline who is all too similar to a narcissist, consider that they may just have Narcissistic Personality Disorder.

BPD individuals have difficult relationships with others for different reasons than NPD individuals. Individuals with BPD are more likely to fear abandonment, while narcissistic individuals are more likely to initiate abandonment, especially in the "discard" phase of their relationships. While narcissists often get a rush out of provoking their victims and harming them emotionally, which gives them "narcissistic supply" in the form of negative attention, BPD people are more likely to be emotionally manipulative because of their overwhelming fear of abandonment as well as chronic sense of emptiness and loneliness. BPD people are more likely to self-injure than to harm others. In fact, self-injury and suicidal thoughts/plans are a key component of BPD.

The emptiness that BPD people feel is a bit different – they do "need" people for validation, much like narcissists, but they are driven by the fear of abandonment in relationships rather than the need for supply – many can and do fall in love as well as empathize with their partners but the way they express that love can be demonstrated in incredibly manipulative, unhealthy and pathological ways due to their fears and inability to effectively cope with their extreme emotions.

The origin of BPD arises often in an incredibly invalidating family environment and/or trauma, which interacts with their biological predisposition to be hypersensitive, whereas the origin of NPD is still unknown. Theoretically, then, borderlines are more likely to be the victims of abusers – some of them may have even been raised by narcissistic parents – and later re-victimized because they are codependent and susceptible to emotional manipulation due to their need for validation from others. They feel emotions on an intense level, whereas narcissists often only feel intense emotions like rage due to narcissistic injury or a loss of supply. Most of the emotions narcissists experience are rather shallow – they feel emotionally numb most of the time and have a chronic sense of a void within themselves.

In addition, narcissists are unlikely to seek out therapy because a sense of superiority is intrinsic to their disorder. The majority of narcissists do not feel the need to change their behavior because it rewards them. They want to protect the image of their false self – not just from others but also from themselves. BPD people, on the other hand, tend to be hospitalized due to their suicide attempts/self-injury and can benefit from therapies such as Dialectical Behavioral Therapy, which enables them to regulate their emotions better, adopt healthier coping methods and learn skills for interpersonal effectiveness.

It's interesting, because if you have a relationship with these two types, you'll find that they are complementary in their dysfunction – the NPD individual often fulfills the BPD individual's worst fear of abandonment. With a BPD individual, an NPD individual can find a steady stream of supply. While abuse can cut both ways in this type of relationship, it's more likely that the NPD individual will be the aggressor because he or she has that cruel lack of empathy, while BPD individuals feel that the emotional effects of the abuse are magnified.

For readers interested in learning more about Borderline Personality Disorder, I would recommend reading Crowell and Marsha Linehan's "A Biosocial Developmental Model of Borderline Personality Disorder" to understand more about the origins and behaviors associated with BPD.

Why do Narcissists come back and try to contact you even after the relationship has ended? Is it possible that they miss me?

Many abusers stalk their victims months, even years after the relationship has ended, especially if the victims left them first or if they see that their victims are moving forward with their lives. If a victim left the narcissist first or he or she has moved on, this threatens a narcissist's sense of control that they once held over the victim. Also known as "hoovering," (named after the hoover vacuum) this is a way to manipulate or "suck you" back into the trauma of the relationship. It's actually a good sign because it means the narcissist knows he/she no longer has the power he once held over you.

Ignoring the hoovering tactic will only prove your strength and power, so maintain No Contact as much as possible. If the narcissist tries to provoke you or win you back by calling or texting you, instead of responding, engage in a different pleasurable activity – go for a run to release endorphins, soak in a relaxing bubble bath, text a friend who knows about your situation – do whatever is possible to be as unresponsive as possible while engaging in a form of self-care. Kill two birds with one stone – do something good for yourself while avoiding something that's ultimately poisonous to your mind, body and spirit.

Remember, due to the biochemical bonds, we feel cravings and urges that are very much like a drug addiction if the narcissist tries to hoover us or if we break No Contact in any way – including looking them up on social media, where they are likely to try to provoke us or flaunt their new target. No Contact means severing all ties and preventing the narcissist and his or her harem from contacting us in any way, including social media, which is often a narcissist's playground of provocation. So it's important that we reengage in self-care and do whatever we can to get back on the wagon – even if it's just a five minute meditation to center ourselves.

For readers who are interested, I have a new No Contact coaching program which I offer on my blog which helps survivors to radically accept those cravings while not giving in - and really start to mindfully tackle this challenging process of recovery. While relapse can be inevitable in the addiction to the narcissist, it is possible to get your life back after narcissistic abuse. You just have to be committed to recovery no matter what happens, regardless of the number of "relapses" you may have.

Should I tell the narcissist that he or she is a narcissist?

I have had some people share my articles and videos with their narcissists in an attempt to get them to admit they are narcissists. I highly recommend against this because will cause a narcissistic injury. True narcissists will defend themselves adamantly and become "triggered" and overly defensive when confronted with the truth, i.e. via a narcissistic injury - this results in narcissistic rage, which is a disproportionate amount of anger towards a perceived slight, disagreement or criticism that serves as a blow to the narcissist's ego and constructed false self. This will only continue the pathological mind games and narcissists will most likely become incredibly defensive in ways that can be even more traumatic. Knowing that they are narcissists are enough - no need to confront them with what you know.

When narcissists suffer a narcissistic injury from a perceived criticism, they will often respond with rage and aggression. Many people with NPD don't wish to accept accountability for their abuse and many rarely will. They would rather project and blame others than accept that they have a false self. Attempting to "shed light" on their condition often proves fruitless and only strengthens their defense mechanisms. I always recommend that survivors focus less on what they can do to change their abusers, who probably can't be changed, and refocus on their own self-care.

Link: You can read more about narcissistic injury from a diagnosed narcissist   himself,   Sam   Vankin,   here: http://samvak.tripod.com/journal86.html or if you prefer a source that's not a narcissist, here: http://thenarcissisticlife.com/the-narcissist-and-rejection/

My child is demonstrating narcissistic tendencies including lack of empathy. Is he or she a narcissist?

Children are just beginning to grasp the ability to empathize by age six or seven - although it might still be too soon to tell and I would caution against labeling a child before they've developed. It may be difficult to confirm whether it's NPD or something else at work until she gets older as children can go through many different phases of identity development, but that doesn't mean we can't notice narcissistic tendencies in children and work proactively with them. I would stress the importance of early intervention. As a concerned parent, you're already recognizing the signs, which means you can also help to build her social skills - through a combination of modeling, perhaps a child therapist if you feel it is necessary, interactive games, discussing hypothetical situations with her such as,"How would you feel if someone took something away from you? Well, Rebecca would feel the same way", etc.

Link: I recommend reading this article for more information about narcissistic tendencies in children.

Does a narcissist use sexuality and sexual withholding as a tactic? Why do I have such powerful sexual chemistry with the Narcissist?

Sexual withholding can definitely be one of the techniques a narcissist uses, and I've heard a similar tale about sexual prowess from survivors of narcissistic abuse across forums. Since narcissists do enjoy building harems, it's very possible that they've built up those skills over time precisely because they do have the knowledge of what works and what makes their victims addicted to them. They "mirror" what they've learned about their victims inside as well as outside of the bedroom.

There have been questions as to whether or not our sexual chemistry with a narcissist is all about the skills of the narcissist, or our own body's reactions to the narcissist – the chemicals in our body responding to the lovebombing and subsequent inconsistency/intermittent reinforcement, for example, which are making the narcissist seem irresistible to us. The highs and lows must make for an incredible cocktail of chemicals like dopamine, adrenaline and oxytocin as I've discussed in my book. During the idealization phase, narcissists can reel in their victims so convincingly that they feel quite high and this can then translate into very powerful sexual interactions with them. I believe it's a combination of a lot of factors at work, but it's a fascinating topic to explore and something to look out for, as well. Healing from the sexual component of the relationship is also vital to moving forward and maintaining No Contact.

My Narcissist is such a good person and generous to the outside world. Yet he or she is abusive to me. What does this mean?

Narcissists carry a false self and usually possess a stellar reputation as being charming, generous and loveable to others. Thus they almost always have a harem from which to gather a steady stream of supply because the harem is unlikely to believe the accusations of their victims. Some of them may even be involved in public service, charity work, and appear to love helping others. This is the way they receive the gratification, attention and admiration they so desperately desire and need.

Many abusers are seen as the pillars of their community. It's how they convince others that the stories of the abuse victim are false. Being empaths makes us quite vulnerable to rationalizing/justifying the abuse because we tend to feel emotions so strongly that we may fall into the trap of sympathizing with the abuser or even believing in the abuser's gaslighting claims that we are too "sensitive," especially when we see how everyone else believes in the narcissist's false self. However, they show their true self to the most intimate people in their lives because they know they can "hook" those people with a certain amount of emotional/psychological investment in the relationship as well as the trauma victims have experienced through their pathological mind games. This true self is who the narcissist REALLY is, so please do not be fooled. All acts of generosity are in fact, quite selfish mechanisms of obtaining supply and fostering the false self. Coming out of the nightmare, we recognize how that harmed us more than helped us, and that our emotions in reaction to the abuse were, in fact, valid.

Fifty Shades of Narcissism Q&A

My father and one of my more recent partners are textbook abusive narcissists. I see those qualities in myself at times. Is it possible for us to change if we actually want to? Or are being *aware* of being an abusive narcissist and *being* an abusive narcissist mutually exclusive since denial and cognitive dissonance are integral to narcissism? (I feel like I'm a living paradox sometimes, and my cousin would like to know if her abusive bf can change, too). Also, how long does it usually take to get out of the reality that an abusive narcissist constructs for you, and do you have any tips for self-care after you manage to get out? And speaking of getting out, what tactics do you recommend for that? My mother and I figured out that convincing them you're not worth keeping works well... although it takes a toll...

You're right that denial, specifically in the individual's devotion to the "false self" that they present to the world - is central to narcissism – the type of narcissism that gets you a diagnosis for the full-fledged personality disorder. It sounds like your awareness of your own narcissistic behavior and your willingness to look at that honestly will be one of your greatest strengths in healing and improving and it is one that distinguishes you from your father, and I assume also your partner. This type of awareness and the desire to change is rare in narcissists – so I am going to guess that you're not one, even if you do identify with having narcissistic traits.

Being raised by a narcissistic parent can unfortunately lead to us modeling victim or perpetrator behavior – sometimes even embodying traits/behaviors from both "identities" depending on the context. It sounds like you are acting out both simultaneously. Might I suggest that the qualities you see in yourself are not necessarily full-fledged narcissism, but reactions/defenses to experiencing trauma? (Disclaimer: I am saying this without knowing too much about the behaviors you're referring to.) Narcissistic traits can also overlap with other disorders as well – disorders which arise from traumatic experiences.

It's very difficult to undo the years of "programming" and conditioning from the effects of narcissistic abuse. I have met many other children of narcissists and I see them – unfortunately – display these same traits. It's usually on a spectrum, but some are eerily narcissistic themselves, or appear to be – the problem is, they don't realize or recognize it in themselves. I see it, as an outsider being familiar with what narcissism looks like, but they don't see it. When speaking about the trauma, they will usually mention their parent only and focus on the parent – not themselves/how they may also have narcissistic traits.

Yet they appear to lack empathy, they are envious, and they are also self-absorbed. They enjoy talking about themselves and don't seem to be genuinely curious about other people. They play mind games and stage pity ploys (and to someone who doesn't know the signs, this can escape their notice). Again, their awareness of this behavior also appears to be lacking (or if they are aware, they do not care). So your self-awareness is already the first step in self-improvement. The second is developing a better connection to your shame as well as empathy. Deep shame is often at the root of narcissism.

It is what narcissists attempt to hide themselves from – the self-loathing, even though paradoxically, they feel entitled and superior to others. Learning to empathize with other people – something you may or may not struggle with – is also central to narcissism and narcissistic behaviors. Do I believe that abusers can change? I think it's rare and I would not recommend to any of my readers to stay in an abusive relationship or attempt to change an abuser – change can only come from a person who wants to change, and full-fledged narcissists and sociopaths usually do not. However, I believe that a self-aware individual, specifically, children of narcissists, who are committed to changing for *themselves* – not for anyone else – can improve and learn to better model healthier behaviors, if they should wish to do so. Many narcissists do not have the capacity to seek help or improvement, as they do not think they need it. That's why I wouldn't rush to call yourself a narcissist considering your background, especially if you DO feel you have the ability to be empathic – the lack of empathy is one of the most significantly distinguishing factors of narcissistic individuals.

Time is not as much of a factor in getting out of the reality as what you do with the time. At least 90 days of No Contact is necessary in order to start "detoxing" from the narcissist and start to come back to your own perception of what reality is. But the journey can be a long one and there isn't a time limit to healing or recovery, because the effects of narcissistic abuse also enable us to look at past traumas and wounds that were retriggered by the narcissistic partner – these wounds may be so deep and go back far into childhood. So if they exist, those need to be looked at, as well.

Think of healing from narcissistic abuse as healing from a LIFETIME of traumas – one "advantage" of going through this journey is the ability to look within and understand what allowed us to form the attachment to a narcissistic partner, what traits make us "compatible" with that partner, and how to ultimately improve ourselves so we can start detaching from the toxicity of the relationship. I am not saying this to blame victims – quite the opposite – I am saying that many victims already have previous histories of abuse before they even met the narcissist.

Narcissistic abuse, as excruciating as it may be, gives us the portal to finally look at those traumas as well and begin to heal. As for self-care during this time: I recommend yoga, meditation, journaling, sharing your stories with other survivors through forums and blogs to form a support network. Seeing a trained professional who is experienced in narcissistic or emotional abuse can also be vital to your recovery. Find a therapy that seems right for you, whether it's individual or group, Cognitive-Behavioral or EMDR – there are many – research them and find something that is a fit for you and your current needs. Survivors can use a whole range of other alternative healing methods: I've heard success stories from survivors who use aromatherapy or Reiki healing in addition to traditional healing modalities.

Getting out from a narcissistic relationship can be incredibly difficult and painful. There are many reasons why survivors stay far beyond the expiration date. The first step is to get in touch with reality. As I mentioned previously in the book, Zari Ballard has a great book called *The Little Black Book of No Contact* which I recommend all survivors read. She suggests that we use the narcissist's silent treatments as "No Contact" for ourselves to reconnect with our authentic experience and emotions about the abuse. Journaling is a great way to reconnect with that reality as well. The second step is develop or reconnect to the life you had outside of the narcissist. Engaging in new hobbies, pursuing your own goals and meeting new people outside of your relationship is crucial – I found it very helpful to be with people who appreciated my personality and gave me the type of validation I needed to finally leave.

A tip for abuse survivors who engage in people-pleasing: Stop lying to other people/minimizing the abuse – talk about it to people you trust because you need support right now. Good friends can remind you of how special and awesome you really are – and plus, if you're going on new adventures, you have less time to ruminate over what the narcissist thinks of you and more opportunity to understand what makes you so damn great (a type of confidence that the narcissist has been trying to whittle down throughout the entirety of the relationship, no doubt!) The third step – and the hardest – is leaving.

You can choose to use the Grey Rock Method (see link below) and hope he leaves you first – or you can make the decision to leave yourself and go No Contact. While I always recommend the second to avoid the inevitably harsh discard, the decision is ultimately yours – but remember that if you do the former, you must fully commit to detaching from the narcissist using the tips I've already suggested. Hope this helps!

This happened to me a few months ago. We met through a mutual friend for networking purposes because were both artists and have similarities in work. However, we were both living on different sides of the USA. After months of talking and being showered with compliments that I was talented and seemed genuine and the girl he'd like.. I decided I'd go meet him even though I was warned by the friend he has a 'intense' personality with girls. If we became friends that would still have been fine with me. I arrive and meet him, something from the beginning threw me off. He talked only about himself but I figured it was normal to be excited to share things with me in person the first day.

He also abruptly tried to have sex with me a few hours into our meeting, and by abrupt, I mean not in a good way. Immediately after I was treated with the silent treatment, I'd even jokingly try to say "Hope I'm not boring you" and he'd roll his eyes and tell me to stop. A few days in I started to feel vulnerable and thought I did something wrong and doubted myself and was confused. I finally brought it up to him and he said "You make it seem like were breaking up" in an annoyed tone.

I am usually very confident in myself but it was the strangest experience to blame myself and cry and be consoled by him telling me his glory travel stories. I left and he gave me smirk and said see you soon. Months later with no contact he will send me links to his art shows wanting approval, not even asking how I am. It's the strangest thing I've ever had happen to me. Girls/guys never let someone put you in this position.

Thanks for sharing your story. You may be surprised at how common your experience is. A narcissist can turn even the most confident person in the room into an insecure mess - all by the covert manipulation tactics they use to covertly demean, invalidate and confuse their victims into doubting themselves, their experiences, their abilities, their accomplishments, and their identities. It does not matter how talented, attractive, self-aware or intelligent you are (in fact, that makes you even more attractive to certain narcissists looking for a challenge), you can still be duped because the narcissist operates on our unconscious needs, wants, desires and insecurities on an emotional and psychological level.

Often by the time we understand and process what's happened, it already has. We have to remember that we are dealing with someone who does not have empathy - who is self-absorbed and genuinely uninterested in us beyond as a source of supply - so they will always have the emotional advantage in exploiting us, unless we learn to see the red flags for what they are and take firm action. Of course, we'll also be thrown into high cognitive dissonance like you experienced when we remember the idealization phase and doubt our intuition and perceptions based on the confusing experiences when encountering the narcissist's hot and cold behavior. All of these things play perfectly into the narcissist's schemes of maintaining power and control over all aspects of the relationship.

What is the prevalence of NPD? Is it different for men vs. women?

Not many studies have examined the prevalence and treatment of narcissistic personality disorder. We have to remember the numbers can be skewed as narcissists are unlikely to seek help in clinical settings due to their sense of superiority and the nature of the disorder itself. The DSM-5 estimates that NPD occurs in only about 0.5-1 percent of the general (not clinical) population, with a higher range (2-16 percent) in the clinical population. Of those diagnosed with narcissistic personality disorder, 50%–75 percent are male (and don't get me started on how bias in diagnosing people based on gender - a woman who does have NPD being misdiagnosed with BPD or Histrionic Personality Disorder due to gender stereotypes - may play into this statistic!)

One study in the Journal of Clinical Psychiatry places the lifetime prevalence of NPD (as defined by the DSM IV, not V) at 6.2 percent, with rates greater for men, 7.7 percent than women at 4.8 percent in a sample of about 35,000 people (Stinson et. al 2008). Studies also point to a growing epidemic of narcissism in the United States - it is more likely to appear in western cultures and a study by Twenge and Campbell (2009) show that the rate had increased over the past ten years especially among the younger generation - in 2006, for example, 10% of 50,000 college students studied were said to meet the criteria for NPD.

Even given this data, it is hard to pinpoint how many people actually have NPD as narcissists are unlikely to seek out treatment because they do not believe anything is wrong with them (they've constructed the false self very convincingly, even to themselves) and feel they are superior to others. Those who do end up in therapies, such as couple's therapy, are likely to try to project their false self to the therapist and manipulate therapists into believing that they, not their partners, are actually the victims. It's a disorder that requires a lot more research.

I have been no contact with an abusive ex for some time but out of the blue he msgd me. Firstly he blamed me for him being nasty. Then said he was confused about what he wanted. Finally said he wanted his cake and also to eat it. He made some apology and told me to move on. I am confused as to why he chose to say those things so long after it all happened. I was with him four years. He was great at first, then the psychological and verbal abuse started. Then the cheating. Do you have any insight into why now?

Basing this off your message alone, I would say your abusive ex is using what is known as the "hoovering" technique. This is when a narcissistic/antisocial/otherwise toxic ex feels he/she has lost control over their previous victim because the victim has moved forward, is lacking in adequate "supply" (i.e. praise, attention, sex, etc.) and wants to check in to see that they still have control over devalued sources of supply. His conversation with you is ultimately nonsense - it's circular word salad (basically crazymaking interactions) meant to keep you on your toes so that you're left thinking about him again. Don't fall for the trap. I recommend blocking him off all social media and text messaging apps. Stick to No Contact! Anything else will lead you back into the vicious cycle and thinking about him is just what he wants. Put the focus back to YOU! Best of luck and take care -- hope this helps. Link: Read more about hoovering here.

Thank you for your thoughts on low contact, traits vs the actual disorder (which is not been officially diagnosed in my spouse) and your vulnerability and honesty about your experience with your father. I admire your work to face it and grow. I will look forward to your future videos and blogs. I might post more later when I gather my thoughts'; some of which are swirling around in my head about how my own triggered escalation can be just as harmful to my children's development; thus why low contact (less incessant/ insidious triggers) which makes myself less vulnerable to melt downs would be healthy for me and our children. The difficult person pushing my buttons has whittled me down or up to a hypersensitive to everything-- curious if you can relate with your experience as a child of a narcissist (or a father with traits). I am not a perfect parent, however I do 'see' my failures and work on them with professionals etc. I don't see this though with people on certain spectrums.

I can definitely relate in terms of both being the child of a narcissist who witnessed such interactions (the parent being provoked by abuse, the reactions) as well as having been in relationships with narcissistic partners. However, I think in the context of abuse, it is rarely hypersensitivity and moreso a culmination of normal emotional responses to abnormal, abusive behavior and trauma. As you know, narcissists are very skillful at provoking their victims deliberately with their manipulation tactics and put-downs - victims might bite their tongue, might repress their emotions for a while, but eventually, they may begin to react to the horrific abuse they've experienced - and each incident of abuse will grate on/provoke flashbacks of previous abusive incidents, which will lead to a more stressed out response as time goes on.

Think of it as having literal wounds on your emotional "body" - narcissists pick at those wounds with their continual abuse, and when they bleed, they quickly step back, act shocked that you've reacted, gaslight/project onto you the blame, and convince everyone else you're the problem, not them. This is very easy for them to do as they wear a charming mask in public, so any time you react, you may even get labelled as the pathological one - the public not knowing, of course, that in the past week, you may have endured many verbal/emotional/physical assaults at the hands of this person and are just beginning to express yourself. That's why Low Contact or No Contact, I believe, is the most emotionally safe place to be when it comes to dealing with the narcissist when it comes to having children with them.

As you said, it removes the possibility of emotionally charged interactions with them which are highly likely (but I would say not your fault - again, you are an empathic human being reacting to traumatic abuse). In the case of small children, witnessing or being part of such a trauma can have lingering effects on the development of the brain and their coping mechanisms for dealing with such trauma can unfortunately be maladaptive as they grow older. I hope this helps and I admire your strength in addressing this situation. It's a very difficult one and can get very complex when there are children to consider.

As a daughter of a covert narcissistic mother who has gone no contact for over 3 years I have been doing a lot of research on the topic and stumbled upon your videos on youtube which lead me to your blog and Facebook page. Your videos are FANTASTIC!! thank you so much for making them. I have a question for you for your 50 shades of narcissism Q&A. Sometimes I think about how I would feel if my covert narcissistic mother passed away and I did

not say goodbye because I remained no contact and if I would regret that. What are your thoughts on that?

I understand those feelings completely and it is a very personal choice to remain in contact (I still recommend Low Contact if you do wish to have any contact) with your parent when you become an adult. In my video regarding narcissistic parents and their children, I was referring to a situation where the mother had young children with the narcissist, where early brain development is even more likely to be affected/shaped by trauma. So I was sharing my insights with the mother regarding Low Contact to reduce the effects of the trauma that witnessing domestic violence in the home can have on a child. Of course, what I didn't say in the video is that once the child grows up as an adult, he/she will inevitably make his/her own decisions about whether to reach out to the narcissistic parent or establish a relationship with said parent.

Needless to say, reengaging with a narcissistic parent can also be a traumatic experience as an adult because it also re-triggers and adds onto childhood traumas. If you are already No Contact and it is benefiting you, it is your personal choice as to whether you want to engage in Low Contact instead, if that is your fear. For example, if a narcissistic parent is ill and you wish to reach out to them, I personally don't think there is a right or wrong answer to that. You should do what is comfortable for you and what feels right to you in that situation. There is no clear-cut solution to that problem because as empathic, compassionate beings, we will inevitably struggle with that kind of moral dilemma, which, however, does not mean you sacrifice your boundaries or values in the process!

What I do advise against is reestablishing Full Contact (the type of frequent contact you used to have with the parent as a child/adolescent), because you may also have regrets regarding the mind games/manipulation you'll have to endure. So I would not recommend interacting with a narcissistic parent more than is needed or is safe for your mental health. I believe that if you do transition to Low Contact, you should still maintain healthy boundaries with anyone who can potentially affect your self-care, especially if it's a relationship with psychological/emotional abuse. Prioritize your own needs when it comes to any situation in which a narcissist is involved..

When it comes to family, No Contact in general can be a more difficult area to navigate, but I have heard stories from people who have done either No Contact or Low Contact with parents as well as siblings successfully.

How often are they aware of what they are doing? Do they realize how sick they are? Or do they live in oblivion and fully believe they are not the abusive ones? Is the calculation cognizant when they discard and move to another target?

They try very hard to keep that type of information from themselves via their false self. Remember that their lack of empathy makes it harder for them to understand the painful emotions of others – in some ways, they like to provoke strong emotions in others. I believe that in some sick way, it alleviates their sense of emotional numbness.

Once the narcissist has moved on to new supply, does s/he ever think about the old supply? I was in a relationship (an extramarital affair, actually) for 26 years on-and-off, but after the final 5 years when we got very, very close he abruptly broke it off when, unbeknownst to me, he'd hooked up with another woman. How can a relationship of such longevity and intimacy just be summarily wiped from the narcissist's memory banks? I'm having a difficult time with this. Thank you.

If the narcissist does think about old supply, it is mainly in thinking of ways that he or she can use him/her in the future. The longevity of a relationship is not as important to the narcissist as control, power and how much he or she has over his or her various sources of supply – whether they be devalued sources of supply like ex-lovers or current sources of supply like present girlfriends. They are notorious for cheating, having affairs and having a harem.

They are not committed to anyone but themselves because they cannot feel love and empathy in the same way that other humans do. They are emotionally numb and are wired differently from regular, empathic beings. Thus, their commitments are always about the supply's loyalty to them and the supply's ability to be compliant and cater to his or her needs, wants and desires. If the supply stands up for his or herself, the narcissist will pull back to maintain this control.

I don't think my narcissist wanted me as supply because he blocked me from a social media site/cut off contact with me first.

Supply is not just about continuing the relationship with the former partner. It's about deriving a sense of power and constantly reconfirming that power. Praise and admiration, for example, are emotional sources of supply that narcissists often get from their harem. Any attention that he gets from your reactions to him blaming you/projecting blame onto you could be considered supply in that it reconfirms his own power and grandiose image of himself. It gives him the emotional satisfaction of knowing that you are probably having an emotional reaction to him blaming & blocking you and it also allows him to displace any guilt of any behavior he engaged it that would warrant it.

Consider blocking you as an assertion of power. He's not blocking you because he wants nothing to do with you - he's blocking you because he knows it's likely to get a reaction and that's the type of thing he needs in order to feel back in control. An excellent book I would recommend about this type of situation is The Little Book of No Contact by Zari Ballard...she explains the dynamics perfectly. Don't be fooled by it...it's likely the hovering will begin again, especially if you don't give him the reaction he's looking for (i.e. asking him why he blocked you, etc.). Cut off all supply, physical and emotional, and resist breaking No Contact. Hope this helps!

Having a hard time accepting the abuse went on, and I still struggle with the thought that he will treat the next girl better. He

was so gentle and charming at first and totally won over my trust - that I still can't comprehend his switch. Do they change very often for the next girl? Thanks. Wish I believed in Karma...

The narcissist does not change for the next victim; she is undergoing the idealization phase, as I assume you once did as well. Remember that how he treats her in public, also, is not a good indicator of how he treats her in private. What the narcissist seems to be doing is clear triangulation - he may have fed her lies or stories about you to create a "triangle" where misinformation is used to smear you. He gets a sense of power being able to show off his new relationship to you and intimidate you with this public image of being a good, respectful partner to instill this idea that you were somehow less than - when you are just as worthy of his respect. She is blissfully ignorant (or maybe a narcissist herself, who knows) to his manipulative ploys and may believe in his lies.

How do I get over the fact that the narcissist used me for sex?

I am sorry to hear you're experiencing this. I understand why you would feel distressed about this especially given the relationship likely meant more to you. The key is to reframe the experience: just because he doesn't view sex meaningfully does not mean that you yourself did not have a meaningful experience. Your sexuality is a part of you and it is not something to be ashamed of or disgusted by. Of course you may feel disgusted if you felt someone took advantage of you, but remember that your sexuality and your wholeness do not belong to him. They belong to you and you alone, and one day you will be able to share this gift with someone truly worthy of you. I recommend really accepting this part of yourself fully as well as the experiences you've had in order to move forward. View it as a learning experience, one that emphasizes how important it is for you to connect emotionally as well as sexually in a relationship with a person who does see it as meaningful.

Is it normal to be attracted to other narcissists after being in a relationship with one?

Yes, it is very common to be "primed" for narcissistic abuse right after another abusive relationship, especially after the length of the relationship as you've described. When we get accustomed to a new normal of traumatic highs and lows and the drama of an addictive relationship like this, basic respect and decency do feel foreign to us and we don't get the same "high." That's why it is important for us to do inner work and experiment with healing modalities that can address the trauma and subconscious wounding, in order to enable the brain to heal from the abuse.

Many of us are prone to seeking love quickly because we want a safe haven after the toxicity we've encountered - unfortunately, without healing our wounds, we often end up in the arms of another narcissist. This is because we've been subconsciously programmed to seek someone with similar traits as a way to "resolve" the wounds our past partner(s) have inflicted on us.

My ex-partner always commented on the looks of others. Is this triangulation or am I just being insecure?

While finding others attractive while in a relationship is normal, commenting on it constantly, especially if you've brought it up as something that bothers you, is not. Think about the way you've acted in the past in relationships when you found someone else attractive. Did you rush to tell the person you were with about it? Did you feel the urge to comment on it constantly, risking that the person you were with might feel insecure?

Toxic people have a habit of making their partners feel insecure - regardless of how beautiful and valuable their partners may be. In fact, the more attractive their partners are, the more they feel the need to put them down covertly so they begin second guessing themselves and doubting themselves. They do this in order to feel a sense of superiority and power over their significant others/supply. The more self-doubt they can make their partners feel, the less likely the partner will feel able to leave the relationship or think they can do better.

My observation is, more often than not, respectful partners tend to acknowledge who they find attractive in their thoughts and keep it to themselves when around their romantic partner. It's not a big deal to notice someone else is attractive - all of us do it and it is natural to notice people - but your ex seemed to deliberately point it out frequently which is quite rude and uncalled for. To talk about his interactions with other women is a little much and downright unnecessary. Noticing and verbalizing are two different actions and a respectful partner would limit it to the former. It is disrespectful to not appreciate your own partner while constantly commenting on the looks of others.

You deserve a partner who makes you feel desirable and doesn't feel the need to make you think you have to compete with other women for him. Nobody is that special and you shouldn't ever have to compete with anyone in a healthy relationship.

Additional Resources on Narcissistic Abuse

My journey would not have been complete if not for the extensive reading I did looking into this subject from talented professionals and survivors (including some self-declared narcissists and sociopaths who give us some insights into their own minds!). For readers who wish to learn more about the specific behaviors of narcissists and sociopaths, I recommend reading the following.

You can also access these books through my Amazon Survivor Bookstore here: www.astore.amazon.com/selcarhav-20

In Sheep's Clothing: Understanding and Dealing with Manipulative People by George Simon, Jr. Ph.D;
The Sociopath Next Door by Dr. Martha Stout
Psychopath Free by Jackson MacKenzie
Complex PTSD: From Surviving to Thriving by Pete Walker
The Body Keeps the Score by Bessel Van der Kolk, MD
Stop Spinning, Start Breathing by Zari Ballard
Without Conscience: The Disturbing World of the Psychopaths Among Us by Robert D. Hare, Ph.D
Soul Vampires by Andrea Schneider, LCSW, MSW
The Human Magnet Syndrome: Why We Love People Who Hurt Us by Ross Rosenberg, M.Ed
Narcissistic Lovers: How to Cope, Recover, and Move On by Cynthia Zayn and M.S. Kevin Dribble
Malignant Self-Love by Sam Vaknin
Confessions of a Sociopath by M.E. Thomas
Help! I'm in Love with a Narcissist by Steven Carter and Julia Sokol
Unashamed Voices: True Stories Written by Survivors of Domestic Violence, Rape

and Fraud: Exposing Sociopaths in Our Midst by Paula Carrasquillo and Lisa M. Ruth

Blogs and websites that also have helpful information on narcissistic behavior, abuse and the effects of trauma include:

Pete Walker – Complex PTSD

www.pete-walker.com/

Psychopath Free

www.psychopathfree.com

After Narcissistic Abuse

www.afternarcissisticabuse.wordpress.com

Narcissistic Behavior

www.narcissisticbehavior.net

Michelle Mallon's Facebook Community: Narcissistic Victim Syndrome

www.facebook.com/NarcissisticVictimSyndrome

Psychopaths and Love

www.psychopathsandlove.com/

The Narcissistic Life

www.thenarcissisticlife.com

Mental Health News Radio Interviews with Narcissistic Abuse Advocates

www.everythingehr.com/category/mental-health-news-radio/

Andrea Schneider, LCSW

http://www.andreaschneiderlcsw.com/

Shannon Thomas, LCSW - Southlake Christian Counseling

www.southlakecounseling.org/blog/

Healing from Complex Trauma and PTSD

www.healingfromcomplextraumaandptsd.com/

Emotional Impotence

www.emotionalimpotence.com/

YouTube channels I follow on narcissism and emotional abuse include:

Lisa A. Romano, Adult Children of Alcoholics Life Coach
www.youtube.com/user/lisaaromano1
Narcissism Survivor
https://www.youtube.com/user/NarcissimSurvivor
Spartan Life Coach
https://www.youtube.com/user/spartanlifecoach
Psychopath Free
https://www.youtube.com/user/PsychopathFree/videos
Ross Rosenberg
https://www.youtube.com/user/clinicalcareconsult

Channels Searchable on YouTube:

Finally Free from Narcissism
Annabel Lee
Shrinking Violet
Ollie Matthews
Understanding Narcissists

References

Bancroft, L. (2002). Why does he do that?: Inside the minds of angry and controlling men. New York: Putnam's Sons.

Bardenstein, K. K. (2009). The Cracked Mirror: Features of Narcissistic Personality Disorder in Children. Psychiatric Annals,39(3). doi:10.4135/9781412950510.n565

Bergland, C. (2013, January 22). Cortisol: Why "The Stress Hormone" Is Public Enemy No. 1. Retrieved from https://www.psychologytoday.com/blog/the-athletes-way/201301/cortisol-why-the-stress-hormone-is-public-enemy-no-1

Berman, M. G., Jonides, J. & Kaplan, S. (2008). The cognitive benefits of interacting with nature. *Psychological Science, 19,* 1207-1212.

Brown, S. L. (2010). Women who love psychopaths: Inside the relationships of inevitable harm. Penrose, NC: Mask Publishing.

Buckels, Erin E., Paul D. Trapnell, and Delroy L. Paulhus. "Trolls just want to have fun." Personality and Individual Differences. 67 (2014): 97-102.

Brummelman, E., Thomaes, S., Nelemans, S. A., Castro, B. O., Overbeek, G., & Bushman, B. J. (2015). Origins of narcissism in children. Proceedings of the National Academy of Sciences Proc Natl Acad Sci USA, 201420870. doi:10.1073/pnas.1420870112

Carnell, S. (2014, May 14). Bad Boys, Bad Brains. Retrieved from https://www.psychologytoday.com/blog/bad-appetite/201205/bad-boys-bad-brains

Carnes, P. (2013). The Betrayal Bond: Breaking Free of Exploitive Relationships. Health Communications Incorporated.

Choi, J., Jeong, B., Rohan, M. L., Polcari, A. M., & Teicher, M. H. (2009). Preliminary Evidence for White Matter Tract Abnormalities in Young Adults Exposed to Parental Verbal Abuse. *Biological Psychiatry, 65*(3), 227-234. doi:10.1016/j.biopsych.2008.06.022

Crowell, S. E., Beauchaine, T. P., & Linehan, M. M. (2009). A Biosocial Developmental Model of Borderline Personality: Elaborating and Extending Linehan's Theory. Retrieved from http://www.ncbi.nlm.nih.gov/pmc/articles/PMC2696274/

Creswell, J. D., Dutcher, J. M., Klein, W. M., Harris, P. R., & Levine, J. M. (2013). Self-Affirmation Improves Problem-Solving under Stress.PLoS ONE, 8(5). doi:10.1371/journal.pone.0062593

Field, T., Hernandez-Reif, M., Diego, M., Schanberg, S., & Kuhn, C. (2005). Cortisol Decreases And Serotonin And Dopamine Increase Following Massage Therapy. International Journal of Neuroscience, 115(10), 1397-1413. doi:10.1080/00207450590956459

Fenichel, O. (1945). The psychoanalytic theory of neurosis. New York: W.W. Norton & Co.

Fertuck, E. A. (2009, July 29). Borderline "Empathy" Revisited. Retrieved from https://www.psychologytoday.com/blog/science-the-border/200907/borderline-empathy-revisited

Foucault, M., & Hurley, R. (1988). The history of sexuality. New York: Vintage Books.

Gabriel, M. T., Critelli, J. W., & Ee, J. S. (1994). Narcissistic Illusions in Self-Evaluations of Intelligence and Attractiveness. J Personality Journal of Personality, 62(1), 143-155. doi:10.1111/j.1467-6494.1994.tb00798.x

Georgia Health Sciences University. (2011, February 28). Brain's Reward Center Also Responds to Bad Experiences. Retrieved from https://www.sciencedaily.com/releases/2011/02/110222121913.htm

Harvard Health. (2007). Drug addiction and the brain: Effects of dopamine on addiction - Harvard Health. Retrieved from http://www.health.harvard.edu/press_releases/drug-addiction-brain

Hammond, C. (2015, July). The Difference Between Male and Female Narcissists. Retrieved from http://pro.psychcentral.com/exhausted-woman/2015/07/the-difference-between-male-and-female-narcissists/

Haslam, C., & Montrose, V. T. (2015). Should have known better: The impact of mating experience and the desire for marriage upon attraction to the narcissistic personality. Personality and Individual Differences, 82, 188-192. doi:10.1016/j.paid.2015.03.032

Haslam, C., & Montrose, V. T. (2015). Should have known better: The impact of mating experience and the desire for marriage upon attraction to the narcissistic personality. Personality and Individual Differences, 82, 188-192. doi:10.1016/j.paid.2015.03.032

Hinduja, S. & Patchin, J. W. (2010). Bullying, Cyberbullying, and Suicide. Archives of Suicide Research, 14(3), 206-221.

Klein, S. (2013, April 19). Adrenaline, Cortisol, Norepinephrine: The Three Major Stress Hormones, Explained. Retrieved from http://www.huffingtonpost.com/2013/04/19/adrenaline-cortisol-stress-hormones_n_3112800.html

Kreger, R. (2012, April 4). Why they can't feel joy: Narcissistic shallow emotions. Retrieved from https://www.psychologytoday.com/blog/stop-walking-eggshells/201204/why-they-cant-feel-joy-narcissistic-shallow-emotions.

Lazar, S. W., Kerr, C. E., Wasserman, R. H., Gray, J. R., Greve, D. N., Treadway, M. T., . . . Fischl, B. (2005). Meditation experience is associated with increased cortical thickness. NeuroReport, 16(17), 1893-1897. doi:10.1097/01.wnr.0000186598.66243.19

Lemonick, M. D. (2007, July 05). How We Get Addicted. Retrieved from http://content.time.com/time/magazine/article/0,9171,1640436-3,00.html

Louis De Canonville, Christine (2015). The Three Faces of Evil: Unmasking the Full Spectrum of Narcissistic Abuse, Black Card Books.

Marazziti, D., Akiskal, H. S., Rossi, A., & Cassano, G. B. (1999). Alteration of the platelet serotonin transporter in romantic love. Psychological Medicine Psychol. Med., 29(3), 741-745. doi:10.1017/s0033291798007946

Marks, L. (2012). Narcissism and the male heart wound. Of Spirit: Healing Body, Mind and Spirit. Retrieved from http://www.ofspirit.com/lindamarks21.htm

Mayer, F.S., Frantz, C. M. P., Bruehlman-Senecal, E., & Doliver, K. (2009). Why is nature beneficial? The role of connectedness in nature. *Environment and Behavior, 41*, 607-643.

McGowan, K. (2004, November 1). Addiction: Pay Attention. Retrieved from https://www.psychologytoday.com/articles/200411/addiction-pay-attention

Mental Health Daily. (2013). How To Overcome Adrenaline Addiction: Tips From A Former Addict. Retrieved March 4, 2016, from http://mentalhealthdaily.com/2013/03/02/how-to-overcome-adrenaline-addiction-tips-from-a-former-addict/

Odendaal, J., & Meintjes, R. (2003). Neurophysiological Correlates of Affiliative Behavior between Humans and Dogs. The Veterinary Journal, 165(3), 296-301. doi:10.1016/s1090-0233(02)00237-x

Palgi, S., Klein, E., & Shamay-Tsoory, S. G. (2016). Oxytocin improves compassion toward women among patients with PTSD.Psychoneuroendocrinology, 64, 143-149. doi:10.1016/j.psyneuen.2015.11.008

Perry, B.D. (2000). Traumatized children: How childhood trauma influences brain development. The Journal of the California Alliance for the Mentally Ill 11:1, 48-51.

Reece, G. (2013, February 25). The Trauma Bond/Abusive Relationships. Retrieved from http://garyreece.blogspot.com/2013/02/the-trauma-bondabusive-relationships.html

Reinert, D. F. (2005). Spirituality, Self-Representations, and Attachment to Parents: A Longitudinal Study of Roman Catholic College Seminarians. Counseling and Values, 49(3), 226-238. doi:10.1002/j.2161-007x.2005.tb01025.x

Sethi, A., Gregory, S., Dell'acqua, F., Thomas, E. P., Simmons, A., Murphy, D. G., Craig, M. C. (2015). Emotional detachment in psychopathy: Involvement of dorsal default-mode connections. *Cortex, 62*, 11-19. doi:10.1016/j.cortex.2014.07.018

Sieben, N. (2013, January 30). Stories of Healing Emotional Trauma in my Acupuncture Clinic. Retrieved from http://blog.nicholassieben.com/?p=379

Sherman, D. K., & Cohen, G. L. (2006). The psychology of self-defense: Self-affirmation theory. In M. P. Zanna (Ed.) *Advances in Experimental Social Psychology, 38,* 183-242. San Diego, CA: Academic Press.

Smithstein, S. (2010, April 19). Dopamine: Why It's So Hard to "Just Say No" Retrieved from https://www.psychologytoday.com/blog/what-the-wild-things-are/201008/dopamine-why-its-so-hard-just-say-no

Teicher, M. (2006). Sticks, Stones, and Hurtful Words: Relative Effects of Various Forms of Childhood Maltreatment. *American Journal of Psychiatry Am J Psychiatry, 163*(6), 993. doi:10.1176/appi.ajp.163.6.993

Twenge, Jean M., and W. Keith. Campbell. The Narcissism Epidemic: Living in the Age of Entitlement. New York: Free, 2010. Print.

Vaknin, S., & Rangelovska, L. (2007). *Malignant self-love: Narcissism revisited.* Prague: Narcissus Publications.

Vaknin, S. (2012, April 25). Psychopathic Narcissists: The Uncanny Valley of Cold Empathy. Retrieved April 11, 2016, from https://samvaknin.wordpress.com/2012/04/25/psychopathic-narcissists-the-uncanny-valley-of-cold-empathy/

Walker, P. (2013). Complex PTSD: From surviving to thriving: A guide and map for recovering from childhood trauma. Azure Coyote Publishing.

Wlassoff, V., Ph.D. (2015, January 24). How Does Post-Traumatic Stress Disorder Change the Brain? Retrieved from http://brainblogger.com/2015/01/24/how-does-post-traumatic-stress-disorder-change-the-brain/

Watson, R. (2014, October 14). Oxytocin: The Love and Trust Hormone Can Be Deceptive. Retrieved from https://www.psychologytoday.com/blog/love-and-gratitude/201310/oxytocin-the-love-and-trust-hormone-can-be-deceptive

Share the Gift of Self-Care and Freedom from Toxic Relationships!

Leave a Review

If you enjoyed this book and found it helpful, be sure to leave a review and share the book on social media so that other survivors can also check it out!

Follow Self-Care Haven on Social Media

Website ~ www.selfcarehaven.org

Facebook Page ~ www.facebook.com/selfcarehaven

Twitter ~ www.twitter.com/selfcarehaven

Blog ~ www.selfcarehaven.wordpress.com

Huffington Post ~ www.huffingtonpost.com/author/shahida-arabi

Thought Catalog Articles ~ www.thoughtcatalog.com/shahida-arabi

About the Author

Shahida Arabi is the #1 Amazon bestselling author of *The Smart Girl's Guide to Self-Care* and *Becoming the Narcissist's Nightmare: How to Devalue and Discard the Narcissist While Supplying Yourself*, which was featured as a #1 Amazon Bestseller in Personality Disorders for six consecutive months. She graduated summa cum laude with a Master's degree from Columbia University where she studied the effects of bullying across the life-course trajectory.

As an undergraduate student at NYU, Shahida studied English Literature and Psychology and was President of its National Organization for Women (NOW) chapter. She is the founder and editor of the blog, Self-Care Haven, which has over 2 million views and has been shared worldwide in all 196 countries. Her viral blog entry, "Five Powerful Ways Abusive Narcissists Get Inside Your Head" has also been shared worldwide and her work has been endorsed by numerous clinical psychologists, mental health practitioners, bestselling authors, and award-winning bloggers.

Shahida is passionate about using her knowledge base in psychology, sociology, gender studies and mental health advocacy, as well as her own personal experiences, to help survivors of emotional and psychological trauma stage their own recovery from abuse. Her writing has been featured on The Huffington Post, The National Domestic Violence Hotline, MOGUL, Yoganonymous, Elephant Journal, Dollhouse Magazine, Introvert Dear, The West 4th Street Review, Thought Catalog, the Feministing Community blog, author Lisa E. Scott's blog and Harvard-trained psychologist Dr. Monica O'Neal's website. She is currently working on her second book on narcissistic abuse and has a new online monthly coaching program for survivors. She also hosts a popular YouTube channel on narcissistic abuse called Self-Care Haven.